B A S I C

LEGAL WRITING

Pamela R. Tepper, Esq.
Southeastern Paralegal Institute
Dallas, Texas

Contributing Author
Herbert G. Feuerhake, Esq.
Norwalk, Connecticut

GLENCOE

Macmillan/McGraw-Hill

Lake Forest, Illinois
Columbus, Ohio
Mission Hills, California
Peoria, Illinois

Library of Congress Cataloging-in-Publication Data

Tepper, Pamela R., 1957–
    Basic legal writing / Pamela R. Tepper: contributing author,
Herbert G. Feuerhake.
       p. cm. — (Legal studies series)
    Includes index.
    ISBN 0-2-800011-0 : $31.25
    1. Legal composition.   I. Feuerhake, Herbert G., 1956–
II. Title. III. Series.
KF250.T467   1992
808' .06834—dc20   91–33716
                                         CIP

Send all inquiries to:
GLENCOE DIVISION
Macmillan/McGraw-Hill
936 Eastwind Drive
Westerville, OH 43081

ISBN 0-02-800011-0

Printed in the United States of America.

1 2 3 4 5 6 7 8 9 HESS 99 98 97 96 95 94 93 92 91

OTHER TITLES

IN THE

LEGAL STUDIES SERIES

Basic Law Office Management

Basic Legal Research

Basic Family Law

Introduction to Paralegal Practice

Basic Civil Litigation

Defining the Law: A Basic Legal Dictionary

ABOUT THE AUTHORS

Pamela R. Tepper currently teaches legal research and writing at the Southeastern Paralegal Institute and at Southern Methodist University in Dallas, Texas. She practices in the areas of corporate law, commercial litigation, probate, and juvenile law.

Herbert G. Feuerhake is a litigation specialist with a focus on general commercial litigation, but with substantial exposure to securities law, municipal law, and workers compensation defense. He is also a professional writer.

CONTENTS

PREFACE

Legal writing is a skill that can be mastered. By learning the basics of concise and effective legal writing, and appreciating the intangibles of style, the paralegal can develop an ability to render arguments in forceful and lucid prose. The paralegal can aid clients through the clear and unambiguous presentation of their positions, coming to write with an attribute that even many attorneys lack—*confidence*.

This book is designed specifically for the paralegal and the tasks performed by the paralegal. It is a comprehensive and accessible approach to basic legal writing. We have attempted to provide a foundation on which to build basic skills in legal writing. The range of communications covered in these pages is wide—from the complexity of an appellate brief to the simplicity of a cover letter. Regardless of the level of complexity, however, effective communication is always important and, for the unwary, often elusive. It has been the goal of this volume to provide the paralegal with the practical tools and, most important, the sense of clarity so necessary to the expression of ideas.

As noted throughout this book, different jurisdictions have specific procedural rules to follow when submitting legal documents. Those rules should always be consulted and should be used to accompany the general writing techniques presented in this book.

Organization of the Text

The text is composed of 13 chapters and begins where the paralegal with a writing assignment normally begins—with legal research. The remaining 12 chapters focus on the practical aspects of legal writing. The student learns that decisions written by judges are not always models to be emulated; that the centuries-old traditions of the law are both a valued bond and a constraining hindrance to clear writing; that there are audiences to be identified, purposes to be defined, language to be chosen, arguments to be made; that there is a time for the adversarial and a time for the objective; that there are many different types of legal documents, from letters to memoranda to pleadings to briefs to contracts to wills; and that legal writing is both fraught with pitfalls and brimming with possibilities.

Text Design

Each chapter begins with a topic outline, followed by a Commentary section that was created for the purpose of illustrating the application of legal writing concepts to the practice of law. Any reference to names and places existing in either the past or present is purely coincidental. Each chapter also begins by identifying objectives that set the goals to be achieved in the chapter. The objectives section is a guide to the chapter and provides a focus for understanding the concepts presented in that chapter. The chapters build on one another, therefore it is important to master the tasks and objectives in each chapter.

Although each chapter discusses the substantive points of legal writing, a unique section at the end of each chapter provides what are termed "Practical Considerations." Here helpful pointers and checklists are offered from the paralegal's perspective rather than the attorney's. The practical considerations section offers insights and suggests pitfalls that will guide the student when confronted with a legal writing assignment.

For convenience and review, each chapter ends with section summaries and review exercises. These summaries and review activities provide an overview of the general points discussed in the chapter and act as a study guide and quick reference.

This text was designed to be user-friendly. The lined margins provide ample space for both instructors and students to make notes within each chapter. Key terms are boldfaced and defined at first use, with a list of these terms appearing at the end of each chapter. Students are encouraged to write in these books, to complete the activities, and to keep this text at home or in the office as a handy reference guide.

Other Learning and Teaching Resources

The *Study Guide*, available as a supplement to this text, is designed as a student support in the study and practice of legal writing. Performing its numerous exercises will help the student achieve the objectives of this course. The *Study Guide* emphasizes skill building and application of that skill through exercises. These exercises are designed to assist the paralegal in drafting legal documents that will be required in a paralegal's daily routine.

To facilitate the teaching and learning process, an *Instructor's Manual* accompanies this text. Included are model course syllabi for classes that meet on the quarter system and for those on semester schedules. In addition, there are answer keys to all review and discussion questions contained in the text, along with tests and answers for each chapter.

Acknowledgments

The authors wish to gratefully acknowledge the contributions of the following reviewers, without whose considerable efforts, suggestions, ideas, and insights this text would not be the valuable tool it is.

William R. Buckley, Esq., Assistant Professor, Paralegal Studies, College of Great Falls, Great Falls, Montana

David A. Dye, Esq., Coordinator, Legal Assistant Program, Missouri Western State College, St. Joseph, Missouri

Anne E. Kastle, Esq., Faculty, Legal Assistant Program, Edmonds Community College, Lynnwood, Washington

Julia O. Tryk, Esq., Chair, Paralegal Program, Sawyer College of Business, Cleveland Heights, Ohio

Barbara J. Young, Esq., Academic Coordinator, Legal Assistant Studies, San Jose State University, San Jose, California

CHAPTER 1   Basics of Legal Research

OUTLINE

COMMENTARY

Six months ago your firm's client, Mr. Jones, subleased some excess warehouse space to Mr. Smith (a sublease is a lease between a tenant and a subtenant, as opposed to one between the owner-landlord and the original tenant). Under the terms of the sublease, subtenant Smith was to make his payments directly to the landlord. After only two months, however, Smith stopped making his payments, and the landlord has sued Jones for the back rent. Jones has come to your supervising attorney, who has requested from you a memorandum outlining the basic law that applies in this situation, namely: What is the liability of the original tenant when a subtenant fails to pay the landlord?

Welcome to the world of legal research! The field of law is complex, with the American legal system generating over 100,000 published opinions each year, volumes upon volumes of new and existing statutory materials, and thousands of treatises and articles analyzing the evolution and application of the law. No one individual can ever hope to master every element, angle, and detail without spending research time in the law library. Whenever a new situation arises requiring the application of legal principles, you will be faced once again with that question—What is the law? In this chapter, you'll learn how to find answers.

OBJECTIVES

Legal research is a complicated but logical system providing access to the many sources of law. After completing this chapter, you will be able to:

1. Understand a citation.
2. Describe the difference between official reporters and private reporters.
3. Explain the key-number system.
4. Use a digest.
5. Differentiate between slip laws, session laws, and codes.
6. Shepardize a case or a statute.
7. Find the text of an administrative regulation.
8. Use secondary sources such as legal encyclopedias and treatises.
9. Identify a computer query.
10. State some general principles about how to begin researching, and how to know when to stop.

1–1 Legal Research in General

Congress, the fifty state legislatures, and the thousands of local legislatures all generate legislation in the form of statutes and ordinances. The federal court system, the fifty state court systems, and the local court systems all churn out written opinions. The many executive agencies and departments release regulations and quasi-judicial decisions. Moreover, these activities have been going on for years, decades, centuries! As a result, an enormous quantity of law has been produced and, theoretically, must be sorted through when addressing a legal research problem.

A comprehensive law library, the storehouse for all these materials, is indeed an impressive sight. With rows and rows of uniform volumes, shelves of multi-volume treatises and statutory codes, looseleaf binders with up-to-the-minute pronouncements and, as of the last few years, computer terminals, the available resources are vast.

Although the volume of material that might apply to a given research problem is truly staggering, you should not throw up your hands and say, "Impossible!" before you even start. Fortunately, there is help. Over the years there has developed a logical, thorough, and even ingenious system of research aids that enables you to focus on the heart of your research problem.

There are a few basic concepts to keep in mind as you begin your study of this system. First, when faced with a specific research project, you need to understand your goal before you start. Are you interested in finding out what the current law is? Are you interested in tracing the development of the law? Do you need to determine precisely what the law was at some specific time when events critical to the resolution of your client's problem occurred? Or are you simply interested in a general understanding of a new area of the law? Your approach will differ depending upon your goal.

Second, you should consciously devise an approach that is both thorough and efficient. It would be unwise simply to plunge in. The complexity of the subject matter and the potential for getting lost and confused in a mass of materials requires that you think before you act.

Finally, if you do become stumped or confused, as you inevitably will, get help. Consult with your supervising attorney. Ask another paralegal. Talk to the librarian (law librarians are helpful and often extremely knowledgeable about both research in general and the peculiarities of their specific law library). Don't give up your solo efforts too quickly, but don't waste time floundering, either. Sometimes a brief tip from someone with experience can save you hours of frustration.

As your skills develop, you will begin to understand that mastering legal research is a continuing process in which new ideas and information enable you to refine and perfect your own personal approach. The following sections introduce you to some of the resources available to assist in the process. There are other resources—indeed, whole books have been written on the subject of legal research—but those described herein are the most important. The chapter concludes with a discussion of some practical legal research techniques.

1–2 Precedential Value: Primary Authority versus Secondary Authority

Before we discuss the many available resources, let's consider an important and basic principle that underlies all legal research.

Imagine for a moment an appellate judge sitting in her chambers, having just left the courtroom where opposing sides in an appeal have concluded oral argument. On her desk are the competing briefs, each filled with references to cases, statutes, treatises, and other sources, each presenting a compelling rationale. How does the judge weigh the relative merits of the differing points of view? How does she decide who wins and who loses?

Although every judge has a characteristic style and every case its own peculiar twist, there is in fact a pattern to the manner in which judicial decision making proceeds. As a general proposition, decisions are based upon the precedential value of the competing sources cited by the parties. Legal research thus becomes a search for those authorities with the most powerful precedential value.

Precedential value is the force that a cited authority exerts upon the judge's reasoning. In order to determine the degree of precedential value of a given authority, the judge determines whether it is primary or secondary; if primary, he or she must determine whether it is mandatory or merely persuasive.

Primary authority is composed of the original text of the sources of law— the language of court opinions, the provisions of constitutions, the requirements of statutes, the guidelines of agency regulations. Primary authority is, in effect, the law itself.

Primary authority can be either mandatory or persuasive. **Mandatory authority** is binding upon the court considering the issue—a statute or regulation from the relevant jurisdiction that applies directly; a case from a higher court in the same jurisdiction that is directly on point; or a constitutional provision that is applicable and controlling. It is best to rely upon mandatory authority in your research, because the court is compelled to follow it. If two primary authorities conflict (as where a statute has been passed to counteract a court opinion, or where principles embedded in the applicable constitution render a statute unconstitutional) the court is compelled to follow the mandatory authority.

All nonmandatory primary authority is **persuasive authority**. A case on point, but from a different jurisdiction, or from a lower or equivalent court in the same jurisdiction, would constitute persuasive authority, as would a statute on point but from a different state.

Secondary authority, on the other hand, is a step removed from the original text. It may consist of the comments of an expert expressed in a treatise. It may be found in the pages of a legal encyclopedia, or in articles in a law review, or in analysis set forth in a looseleaf service. It may include the unofficial provisions of a "restatement" of the law. Whatever the source, however, all forms of secondary authority have one thing in common—they are not the law itself, but rather analyses of the law.

Apply these concepts with a simple example. Assume you are writing a brief to be considered by an intermediate appellate court in California. A case on point decided by the California Supreme Court would constitute mandatory authority. If such a case existed and was the only applicable mandatory authority, you might not have to go further in your research. If no such case existed, and no other mandatory authority existed, then a case on point decided by the Nevada Supreme Court would constitute persuasive primary authority—which means that your California intermediate appellate court, although not bound by the Nevada decision, might at least be persuaded by its logic. Finally, in addition to citing primary authorities, you might also want to cite to the principles enunciated in a respected treatise in the applicable field. The treatise, though only a secondary authority, might be held in such esteem by the court that it, too, has substantial persuasive value. Indeed, a secondary authority might be given more persuasive weight by a court than a non-mandatory primary authority.

In the pages that follow, we will be considering numerous different authorities. As you read these pages, and later in your research, you should always keep in mind the concepts of primary and secondary authority. In the context of a specific research project, you should also consider whether a given primary authority is mandatory or merely persuasive.

1–3   Finding Case Law

Judicial opinions, which are often simply referred to as cases, are published in a continuing series of hardbound volumes called **reporters**. Reporters are organized not by topic but chronologically. This poses the problem of how to find those cases relevant to a given research topic without sifting through every case in every volume.

In this section we discuss methods of dealing with this obstacle. A logical starting point is the citation concept.

Citations

We will begin by mentioning a case decided by the United States Supreme

Court, *Marbury v. Madison*, 5 U.S. (1 Cranch) 137, 2 L.Ed. 60 (1803), and ask: Why all those numbers and letters after the name of the case? The letters and numbers, together with the name *Marbury v. Madison* (note that the name of a case is always underlined or in italics in legal briefs, memos, and letters), constitute the citation for the reported opinion. A **citation** (also called a cite) provides information that directs you to the exact page in the exact volume of each reporter in which the text of this case appears. We will analyze each component of the citation, but first a word about consistency in citation form.

As you can imagine, with the large number of courts in the American system, there are many different reporters that publish judicial opinions, each requiring a unique citation. There is also a need for citations associated with statutes, regulations, municipal codes, treatises, law review articles, and other legal publications and materials. In order to minimize inconsistency in practice, a standard system of citation, called the Uniform System of Citation (published in book format by the law reviews of several leading law schools) is almost universally accepted as the model of correct citation form. Because the book in which it appears has a bright blue cover, the system is known informally as the **bluebook** system, and to check a legal document to verify proper citation form is known as "bluebooking." Bluebooking is a task that paralegals are often called upon to perform, so you should obtain a copy of the bluebook and learn how to use it. Throughout this chapter we provide proper bluebook citation form for various research sources; when you see such a reference, consult your bluebook to see how we determined the correct form.

Now let's return to our consideration of the citation for *Marbury v. Madison*. First, let's take the name of the case. There are literally pages of rules on proper identification of parties in the name portion of a citation. You should check your bluebook to review some of the trickier aspects. For most cases, however, it is sufficient to remember that the name of a lawsuit (for citation purposes) will contain the name of one plaintiff and one defendant: last name only for individuals; generally the full name for a business entity (for example, "Widgets, Inc."). The parties in this particular case were William Marbury and James Madison; thus the name of this case becomes *Marbury v. Madison*.

Now we turn to the remaining components of the citation. We'll analyze each group of letters and numbers, one at a time.

First we'll consider (1 Cranch), which we can deal with quickly. In the early days of the U.S. Supreme Court, there were no government-published reporters, and William Cranch was one of several individuals who published private reporters of Supreme Court decisions. The federal government eventually sanctioned some of these reporters, and each of the first ninety volumes of official Supreme Court decisions bears the name of the individual private reporter who was sanctioned at the time. The case of *Marbury v. Madison* appears in the first volume of Cranch's reports, hence the designation "1 Cranch." Such private reporters disappeared before the end of the nineteenth century, thus you will only see citations to private reporters for very old cases.

The next group, "5 U.S. 137," is relevant to current practices. The federal government now prepares and publishes its own official set of decisions, called *United States Reports*. There are currently more than 490 volumes in *United States Reports*. Volumes 1–90 incorporate the exact pagination of the ninety volumes of the private reporters—the government simply adopted the private reporters as its own official reporter for that time period. The designation 5 U.S. 137 in the citation for *Marbury v. Madison* indicates that the case appears in the fifth volume of *United States Reports* at page 137. Because the fifth volume of *U.S. Reports* incorporates the pagination of 1 Cranch, the case also appears on page 137 of 1 Cranch.

Two basic rules can be drawn from the citation 5 U.S. 137. First, volume number always appears before the reporter's abbreviation. Second, the page number always appears after the abbreviation.

The next group of letters and numbers in our example is "2 L.Ed. 60." This group refers to another reporter, published by the Lawyers' Co-Operative Publishing Company, called *United States Supreme Court Reports, Lawyers' Edition*, which also publishes Supreme Court cases. It is often referred to simply as the Lawyers' Edition, abbreviated for citation purposes as "L.Ed." Thus the case of *Marbury v. Madison* also appears in volume 2 of the *Lawyers' Edition* reports, at page 60 (remember our rule: volume number before abbreviation, page number after). The *Lawyers' Edition* set is a private reporter. You will learn more about the need for, and great usefulness of, such reporters in succeeding sections of this chapter.

When a case text is found in two or more reporters, the citations for that case are known as **parallel citations** (see Figure 1–1). When parallel citations exist, the official reporter is always listed first. Thus for *Marbury v. Madison* the official citation "5 U.S. (l Cranch) 137" precedes the parallel citation, "2 L.Ed. 60." We discuss official and private reporters in more detail in later sections.

The final reference in the citation is (l803). This is, as you might have guessed, the year in which *Marbury v. Madison* was decided. The year of decision, in parentheses, is always included at the end of the citation. Sometimes the name of the court that decided the case will also appear within this final parenthesis. Since some reporters publish decisions from several courts and even several states, it is sometimes impossible to discern the court by simply identifying the reporters; hence proper citation for a case appearing in such a reporter must include identification of the specific court that decided the case.

Citations are the keys that unlock the information in a law library. Your understanding of the citation concept will improve as you work your way through the following sections, and especially as you do your own research. Several citation exercises appear at the end of this chapter.

Official Reporters

An **official reporter** is one sanctioned by the court generating the opinions contained within its pages. The *United States Reports*, for example, is the official reporter for Supreme Court decisions, and is published by the U.S. government. Most of the states have one or more official reporters for the decisions

Figure 1–1 Parallel Citations

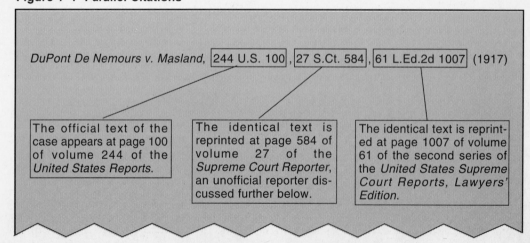

DuPont De Nemours v. Masland, 244 U.S. 100 , 27 S.Ct. 584 , 61 L.Ed.2d 1007 (1917)

| The official text of the case appears at page 100 of volume 244 of the *United States Reports*. | The identical text is reprinted at page 584 of volume 27 of the *Supreme Court Reporter*, an unofficial reporter discussed further below. | The identical text is reprinted at page 1007 of volume 61 of the second series of the *United States Supreme Court Reports, Lawyers' Edition*. |

of their various courts. Many of these are published by the respective state governments; for some states, however, the reporter designated as official is one of the private reporters from the National Reporter System (to be discussed further) or some other private reporter.

The citation of a case from a state that has an official reporter will list the official reporter first, generally followed by parallel citations to the National Reporter System. Check your bluebook and find the rule that establishes the appropriate order.

Official reporters are generally less useful than the private reporters. The volumes are often published only long after the opinions are released, and they are generally not indexed well, limiting their usefulness for research purposes.

National Reporter System

By the end of the 1880s, the West Publishing Company of St. Paul, Minnesota had developed a private reporter system covering the decisions of all the states. Called the National Reporter System, it contained seven **regional reporters** corresponding to geographic areas of the country. This system is still in use today. The seven regional reporters, with their abbreviations for citation purposes, are:

Northeastern Reporter	N.E.
Atlantic Reporter	A.
Southeastern Reporter	S.E.
Southern Reporter	S.
Northwestern Reporter	N.W.
Southwestern Reporter	S.W.
Pacific Reporter	P.

Each of these reporters contains the decisions of the courts of several states. Table 1–1 shows those states currently covered by each reporter. Each regional reporter contains all of the decisions of the highest court, and often many of the decisions of one or more lower courts of these states for the time period covered.

As the number of volumes in each of these regional reporters reached 200 or 300 volumes, a second series was initiated, with the numbering starting over again at Volume 1. The second series is designated in a citation by the indicia "2d" appearing after the abbreviation. Whereas a case in the first series of

Table 1–1 States Covered in Specific Regional Reporters

Regional Case Reporter	States Covered
Atlantic	Connecticut, Delaware, D.C., Maine, Maryland, New Hampshire, New Jersey, Pennsylvania, Rhode Island, Vermont
Northeastern	Illinois, Indiana, Massachusetts, New York, Ohio
Northwestern	Iowa, Michigan, Minnesota, Nebraska, North Dakota, South Dakota, Wisconsin
Pacific	Alaska, Arizona, California, Colorado, Hawaii, Idaho, Kansas, Montana, Nevada, New Mexico, Oklahoma, Oregon, Utah, Washington, Wyoming
Southeastern	Georgia, North Carolina, South Carolina, Virginia, West Virginia
Southwestern	Arkansas, Kentucky, Missouri, Tennessee, Texas
Southern	Alabama, Florida, Louisiana, Mississippi

Pacific Reporter, for example, might have the citation "197 P. 32" (meaning the text appears at page 32 of volume 197 of the first series), a later case in the second series might have the citation "5 P.2d 17" (meaning the text appears on page 17 of Volume 5 of the second series).

Because the number of cases generated by the courts of California and New York is extensive, the West Company established two separate reporters, the *California Reporter* and the *New York Supplement*, to handle the volume of opinions. Although the decisions of the highest courts of these states continue to be published in their respective regional reporters (California's in the *Pacific Reporter*, 2d Series; New York's in the *Northeastern Reporter*, 2d Series), the separate supplementary reporters publish the significant lower court decisions as well. The citation abbreviation for the *California Reporter* is Cal. Rptr.; for *New York Supplement* it is N.Y.S. or N.Y.S. 2d.

The National Reporter System remains current not only through the frequent publication of bound volumes, but also by issuance of **advance sheets**, which are softcover pamphlets containing the most recent cases (and paged exactly as they will later appear in the permanent bound volumes). Cases may appear in these advance sheets many months, and even more than a year before they appear in an official reporter, making the regional reporters significantly more current, hence more useful, than the official reporters of most states.

Each volume in the National Reporter System contains a table of cases in the front, listing alphabetically by state all those cases whose full text appears in that volume. Each volume also contains subject indexes in the rear of the volume (the subject indexes appear near the front of the advance sheets). The foundation for these indexes is the "key number system," which is perhaps the single most important element in American legal research.

Key Numbers and Digests

The **key number system** employed in the National Reporter System (and most other West publications, many of which are addressed later) is a detailed system of classification that currently divides the law into more than 400 separate categories or topics (see Figure 1–2 for a sample page listing some of these topics). More categories are added as the development of the law requires. Each category is divided into subcategories. There are often hundreds or even thousands of subcategories in a given topic. Each subcategory is assigned a key number.

Each and every case that is to be published in the National Reporter System is analyzed and assigned one or more key numbers based upon the legal principles addressed in the opinion. This analysis and assignment of key numbers has been taking place continuously since the 1880s.

Key numbers are listed near the beginning of an opinion, each followed by a brief paragraph setting forth the corresponding legal principle drawn from the case. A key-numbered paragraph is called a **headnote**. Headnotes are numbered consecutively, and corresponding reference numbers are inserted into the text of the case, indicating the precise location from which the legal principle in the headnote is drawn. Figure 1–3 (see pages 10 and 11) shows pages from a typical National Reporter System case, *Great Western Savings Bank v. George W. Easley Co.*, 778 P.2d 569 (Alaska, 1989), and identifies various elements of key numbering.

The key numbers form the basis of the **digest** system. A digest is a collection of all the headnotes from an associated series of volumes, arranged alphabetically by topic and by key number. For example, the most recent digest associated with the *Pacific Reporter* includes all the headnotes from all the cases beginning with those from volume 585 of the second series and continuing to

Figure 1–2 Digest Topics

UPDATING WITH WESTLAW ®

WESTLAW provides easy and quick access to those cases reported after the latest available digest supplementation.

The WESTLAW query is entered in any appropriate caselaw data base of interest. The query format used substitutes a numerical equivalent for the digest topic name and adds the key number through the use of "K" as illustrated in the search for later Contracts ⟜ 155 cases published after January 1, 1988.

ad(after 12-31-87) & 95K155.

1 Abandoned and Lost Property	31 Appearance	68 Canals
	33 Arbitration	69 Cancellation of Instruments
2 Abatement and Revival	34 Armed Services	
	35 Arrest	70 Carriers
3 Abduction	36 Arson	71 Cemeteries
4 Abortion and Birth Control	37 Assault and Battery	72 Census
	38 Assignments	73 Certiorari
5 Absentees	40 Assistance, Writ of	74 Champerty and Maintenance
6 Abstracts of Title	41 Associations	
7 Accession	42 Assumpsit, Action of	75 Charities
8 Accord and Satisfaction	43 Asylums	76 Chattel Mortgages
	44 Attachment	76A Chemical Dependents
9 Account	45 Attorney and Client	76H Children Out-of-Wedlock
10 Account, Action on	46 Attorney General	
11 Account Stated	47 Auctions and Auctioneers	77 Citizens
11A Accountants		78 Civil Rights
12 Acknowledgment	48 Audita Querela	79 Clerks of Courts

Reprinted with permission from *West's Digest*, copyright 1990 by West Publishing Co.

the present. (Important note: If you want to search through older cases as well, you have to check through other digests covering earlier periods; a thorough search is not complete until all time periods covering all cases have been checked.) Figure 1–4 (see page 12) shows a partial index page from the topic "Contracts," which includes the key number associated with headnote 5 from *Great Western Savings Bank*. Figure 1–5 (see page 12) shows the digest page on which the full text of this headnote appears.

Digests are an excellent place to begin many research projects. By identifying relevant topics and key numbers and then searching through the corresponding headnotes, you will be able to locate citations for cases that appear to be analogous to the issues posed by your research problem. You can then use the citation included with the headnote to review in detail the published opinion as it appears in the reporter. Since our previous example, using *Great Western Savings Bank*, started with a case and worked backward to show you how the case, key number, headnote, and digest topic all fit together, let's take one more example, based upon the landlord/tenant problem from the Commentary to this chapter, to see how a typical research session might proceed.

We begin by isolating an appropriate topic. Look through the list of topics found in Figure 1–6 on page 13. Do you see any topics that might prove useful to our research problem? You should have found the topic *Landlord and Tenant*. The next step is to locate that topic in the digest and look at the topic index, which appears at the beginning of the topic. Searching through the key numbers listed in the index, we find one, key number 80(2) (Figure 1–7 on page 13), that relates to our Commentary problem (which, as you recall, concerns the liability of the original tenant to the landlord).

Figure 1–3 Pages From a Typical National Reporter System Case

569 Alaska   **GREAT WESTERN SAV. v. GEORGE W. EASLEY**
Cite as 778 P.2d 569 (Alaska 1989)

GREAT WESTERN SAVINGS
BANK, Appellant,

v.

GEORGE W. EASLEY CO.,
J.V. Appellees.

SATORI GROUP, LTD., Michael
Emery, and Steve Matlin,
Cross-Appellants.

v.

GREAT WESTERN SAVINGS BANK,
Cross-Appellee.

Nos. S-2344, S-2345.

Supreme Court of Alaska.

July 28, 1989.

General contractor filed mechanics' lien foreclosure suit against construction lender, which was subsequently consolidated with other action, for breach of contract and negligent disbursement of loan proceeds, for declatory judgment subordinating lender's deed of trust on property to contractor's mechanics' lien, and for other tort and contract theories. Developer filed cross-claim against lender for breach of contract. Lender filed cross-claim against developer for foreclosure, indemnity, and contribution for rent collected. The Superior Court, Third Judicial District, Anchorage, J. Justin Ripley, J., granted default judgment for contractor against lender and granted equitable subordination. Lender and developer appealed. The Supreme Court, Matthews, J., held that: (1) statutory mechanics' lien scheme did not preempt action against developer for breach of contract and tortious conduct; (2) jury question existed as to whether contractor waived its right to direct payment; (3) jury question existed as to whether contractor reasonably relied on implied assertion that change orders had been approved by lender; (4) order of subordination could be viewed as order in aid of collection of judgment; and (5) entry of default judgment against developer on

lender's cross-claim foreclosed developer from claiming that lender breached its contract with developer.

Affirmed.

1. Mechanics' Liens ⟜ 216

Statutory mechanics' lien scheme does not preempt actions by construction contractors against construction lenders for breach of contract tortious conduct. AS 3435.045–34.35.120.

2. Contracts ⟜ 332(2), 334

General contractor's complaint against construction lender, which alleged that lender had contractual obligation to make direct payments to contractor, that lender breached contract, and that contractor suffered damages, sufficiently put lender on notice of claims against it and of grounds upon which they rested; complaint did not have to specifically allege consideration for contract. Rules Civ.Proc., Rule 8(a).

3. Mechanics' Liens ⟜ 246

Statutory mechanics' lien scheme did not preempt general contractor's action against construction lender for breach of contractual obligation to make direct payments to contractor. AS 34.35.045–34.35.120.

4. Appeal and Error ⟜ 863.866(3), 927(7), 934(1)

In reviewing denial of motions for directed verdict or judgment notwithstanding the verdict, Supreme Court does not weigh conflicting evidence or judge credibility of witnesses, but rather its role is to determine whether evidence, when viewed in light most favorable to nonmoving party, is such that reasonable persons could not differ in their judgment as to facts.

5. Contracts ⟜ 237

Construction lender's promise that it would make direct payments to general contractor was supported by consideration, as promise was given in satisfaction of a condition to modification of construction contract.

Headnote Number

Topic

Key Number

Headnote Paragraph

Figure 1–3, cont.

Western on notice of the claims against it and of the grounds upon which they rested. There was no need to allege consideration. The second amended complaint satisfied the requirements of Civil Rule 8(a).

[3]　Next, Great Western claims *Donnybrook* preempts Easley Company's contract theory. As previously discussed, assuming a valid contract exists, Great Western cannot use the mechanics' lien statutes to evade a duty imposed by contract.

Finally, Great Western argues that the trial court erred in failing to grant its motions for a directed verdict and judgment notwithstanding the verdict. According to Great Western, Easley Company's contract claim failed for lack of consideration because Easley Company had a pre-existing duty to build the project, and alternatively, if a contract existed, Easley company waived its rights under the contract.

[4]　In reviewing denial of motions for a directed verdict[8] or judgment notwithstanding the verdict, we do not weigh conflicting evidence or judge the credibility of witnesses. Rather, our role is to determine whether the evidence, when viewed in the light most favorable to the nonmoving party, is such that reasonable persons could differ in their judgment as to the facts. *Mullen v. Christiansen*, 642 P.2d 1345 (Alaska 1982). *See also Knight v. American Guard & Alert, Inc.*, 714 P.2d 788, 792 (Alaska 1986). There was sufficient evidence to create a reasonable difference of opinion here.

[5]　O'Brien's August 15, 1984, letter to Easley Company provides in pertinent part:
Dear Mr. Easley:
Pursuant to you [sic] contract with the Satori Group, Ltd. for the construction of the Liberty Center ... we agree to reserve construction funds in the amount of $1,035,000 which are committed for the sole purpose and use of the general contractor, George W. Easley Company, and will make all payments up to this amount directly to said general contractor upon appropriate approvals of pay estimates by the owner, architect, and Great Western Federal Savings Bank.

There was evidence that this letter was given in satisfaction of a condition to the modification of the construction contract, which was modified on August 14, 1984. Thus, there was consideration for the promise the letter contained.

[6]　Whether Easley Company waived its rights to direct payment is a more difficult question. During the construction of the Liberty Center, Great Western disbursed every pay request to Satori instead of Easley Company. Easley Company did not object to Great Western about this practice, but evidence suggests that George Easley protested to Satori. This conduct could amount to an implied waiver of Easley Company's right to direct payment. However, "[t]o prove an implied waiver of a legal right, there must be direct, *unequivocal* conduct indicating a purpose to abandon or waive the legal right, or acts amounting to an estoppel by the party whose conduct is to be construed as a waiver." *Milne v. Anderson*, 576 P.2d 109,112 (Alaska 1978) (emphasis added).

George Easley's testimony that he protested to Satori about the bank's disbursements allows, in our opinion, reasonable minds to differ on whether Easley Company waived its right to direct payment. Accordingly, we conclude that the trial court did not err in denying Great Western's motions for directed verdict and judgment notwithstanding the verdict.

3. *Equitable Estoppel*

The jury found that Great Western was estopped from denying that it had approved Change Orders Nos. 1 and 2 and awarded Easley Company $287,214.49. Great Western argues that the court erred in allowing the issue of equitable estoppel to go to the jury because the equitable estoppel theory was not pled, except in the

> Reference to headnote

> Passage that establishes legal principle addressed in headnote

Reprinted with permission from 778 P.2d 569, copyright 1989 by West Publishing Co.

Figure 1–4 A Partial Index Page

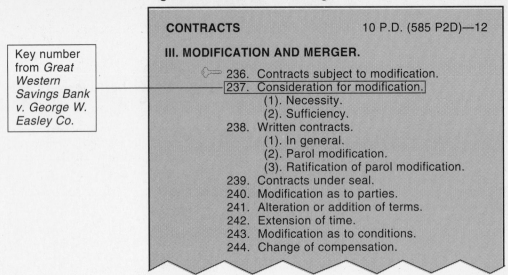

Key number from *Great Western Savings Bank v. George W. Easley Co.*

CONTRACTS   10 P.D. (585 P2D)—12

III. MODIFICATION AND MERGER.

   236. Contracts subject to modification.
   237. Consideration for modification.
        (1). Necessity.
        (2). Sufficiency.
   238. Written contracts.
        (1). In general.
        (2). Parol modification.
        (3). Ratification of parol modification.
   239. Contracts under seal.
   240. Modification as to parties.
   241. Alteration or addition of terms.
   242. Extension of time.
   243. Modification as to conditions.
   244. Change of compensation.

Reprinted with permission from 10 P.D. 12, copyright 1990 by West Publishing Co.

Figure 1–5 Digest Page

Headnote from *Great Western Sav. Bank v. George W. Easley Co.*

237   CONTRACTS   10 P.D.(585 P.2d)—264

For later cases see same Topic and Key Number in Pocket Part

Alaska 1989. Construction lender's promise that it would make direct payments to general contractor was supported by consideration, as promise was given in satisfaction of a condition to modification of construction contract.
   Great Western Sav. Bank v. George W. Easley Co., J.V., 778 P.2d 569.

Or.App. 1989. To be binding, modification of contract must be supported by consideration.
   Jole v. Bredbenner, 768 P.2d 433, 95 Or. App. 193.

237(1) Necessity.

Ariz.App. 1981. A written contract may be modified by subsequent oral changes that are supported by consideration.
   Coronado Co., Inc. v. Jacome's Dept. Store, Inc., 629 P.2d 553, 129 Ariz. 137.

lacks consideration and cannot serve as modification of existing contract.
   Ferrer v. Taft Structurals, Inc., 587 P.2d 177, 21 Wash.App. 832.

237(2). Sufficiency.

N.M. 1989. Forbearance may be consideration for a contract modification when either an express agreement to forbear exists or when the circumstances otherwise suggest that a contract ought to be enforced by implying such an agreement.
   Superior Concrete Pumping, Inc. v. David Montoya Const., Inc., 773 P.2d 346, 108 N.M. 401.

Wash.App. 1983. Without mutual change of obligations or rights, subsequent agreement lacks consideration and cannot serve as modification of existing contract.
   Ebling v. Gove's Cove, Inc., 663 P.2d 132, 34 Wash.App. 495, review denied.

Reprinted with permission from 10 P.D. 264, copyright 1990 by West Publishing Co.

The next step is to look under key 80(2) for headnotes. If we find a relevant headnote, we can use the citation provided with the headnote to locate and read the full text of the case as it appears in a reporter. See if you can use this method to locate some relevant cases in the digest of your own jurisdiction.

The topics, key numbers, and headnotes are the most important segment of a digest, but there are other useful sections as well. These include the descrip-

Figure 1–6 Digest Topics

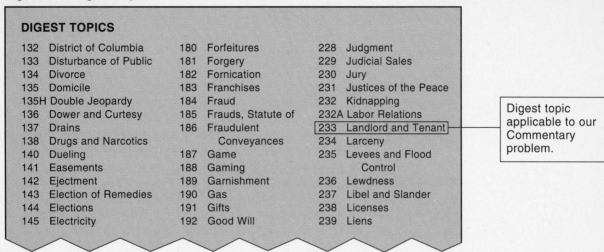

DIGEST TOPICS

132	District of Columbia	180	Forfeitures	228	Judgment
133	Disturbance of Public	181	Forgery	229	Judicial Sales
134	Divorce	182	Fornication	230	Jury
135	Domicile	183	Franchises	231	Justices of the Peace
135H	Double Jeopardy	184	Fraud	232	Kidnapping
136	Dower and Curtesy	185	Frauds, Statute of	232A	Labor Relations
137	Drains	186	Fraudulent	233	Landlord and Tenant
138	Drugs and Narcotics		Conveyances	234	Larceny
140	Dueling	187	Game	235	Levees and Flood
141	Easements	188	Gaming		Control
142	Ejectment	189	Garnishment	236	Lewdness
143	Election of Remedies	190	Gas	237	Libel and Slander
144	Elections	191	Gifts	238	Licenses
145	Electricity	192	Good Will	239	Liens

Digest topic applicable to our Commentary problem.

Reprinted with permission from *West's Digest*, copyright 1990, by West Publishing Co.

Figure 1–7 Key Number

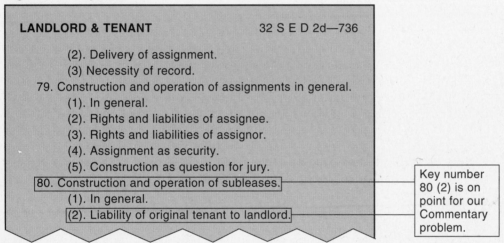

LANDLORD & TENANT   32 S E D 2d—736

(2). Delivery of assignment.
(3) Necessity of record.
79. Construction and operation of assignments in general.
    (1). In general.
    (2). Rights and liabilities of assignee.
    (3). Rights and liabilities of assignor.
    (4). Assignment as security.
    (5). Construction as question for jury.
80. Construction and operation of subleases.
    (1). In general.
    (2). Liability of original tenant to landlord.

Key number 80 (2) is on point for our Commentary problem.

Reprinted with permission from 32 S.E.D. 2d 736, copyright 1990 by West Publishing Co.

tive word index, the words and phrases section, the table of cases, and the plaintiff/defendant table. You should note that not every digest has all of these additional sections.

The **descriptive word index** is a subject index that provides a researcher with a quick survey of specific key numbers, often from several topics, which apply to a given subject area. To use the descriptive word index, we would first analyze our legal problem so as to identify terms that serve to define the issues presented. For our landlord/tenant problem, such terms would include *subletting*. Looking in our descriptive word index under "subletting" (see Figure 1–8), we not only find the same key number from the landlord and tenant topic that we found before (i.e., key number 80(2)), but also references to key numbers from entirely different topics (see, for example, the reference to key number 16(6) from the topic *Indians*, relating to the subletting of Indian lands). Although these other topics are not relevant to our current landlord/tenant problem, there will be times when the descriptive word index will help you find useful key numbers from less than obvious topics. The descriptive word index also enables you to avoid a line-by-line search through hundreds or even thousands of key number entries in the index of a more obvious topic (for example, rather than searching through the many key numbers in the "landlord and tenant" topic index, we were able to quickly find key number 80(2) by scanning Figure 1–8).

The descriptive word index might be thought of as a master index to all the key numbers contained in all the topics in the digest. Thus it is often an excellent place to start your research.

The **words and phrases** section of the digest is useful if your research issue turns upon the judicial construction ("construction" in this context is drawn from the verb "construe" and means "interpretation") of a specific word or phrase. The words and phrases are arranged alphabetically, with citations to those cases in which the word or phrase is construed.

Figure 1–8 Descriptive Word Index

SUBCONTRACTORS   2 Conn D—430

References are to Digest Topics and Key Numbers

SUBCONTRACTORS—Cont'd
MECHANICS' liens—Cont'd
  United States contracts. U S 741/2
  Waiver of right to lien by subcontractor under United States contract. U S 741/2
  Waiver of right to lien by taking contractor's note. Mech Liens 211(5)
NEGLIGENCE—
  Jury question, negligence in erection of structure. Neglig 136(22)
  Principal contractor's liability for sub-contractor negligence. Princ & A 159(1)
PAYMENT, failure to pay ground for rescission. Contracts 261(3)
PUBLIC contracts. Pub Contr 17
REFORMATION of instrument, unilateral mistake, failure to perform under rider. Ref of Inst 20
STATES, rights and remedies on contracts with States 1081/2
UNITED States, see this index Public Contracts
UNITED States contracts, action on bond of contractor. U S 67(3)
WORKERS' compensation to employees. Work Comp 334-361
  Action by injured laborer and employer's compensation insurer against subcontractor. Work Comp 2242
  Contruction projects, wrap-up pans. Work Comp 1063
  Effect of compensation acts as to other remedies. Work Comp 2166, 2167
  Number of employees. Work Comp 198
  Persons liable as third persons. Work Comp 2165-2167
  Public officers as employees. Work Comp 389
  Weight and sufficiency of evidence. Work Comp 1461
  Wrap-up plans, construction projects. Work Comp 1063

SUBDIVISIONS

SUBJACENT SUPPORT
MINERAL lands, injuries to surface soil. Mines 122

SUBJECT OF STATUTE
See this index Title of Laws

SUBJECTIVE SYMPTOMS
DISABILITY benefits, social security and public welfare. Social S 140.5(5)

SUBLETTING
CONSENT of lessor. Land & Ten 75(3)
CONSTRUCTION and operation of sublease. Land & Ten 80
CONTRACTS, generally, see this index Subcontractors
COOPERATIVE apartments. Land & Ten 360
COVENANTS affecting. Land & Ten 76 Breach. Land & Ten 104
EVICTION by sublessee's failure to pay taxes. Land & Ten 172(1)
EVICTION of subtenant. Land & Ten 1771/2
EVIDENCE. Land & Ten 801/2
INDIAN lands. Indians 16(6)
INJURIES to subtenant. Land & Ten. 164(5)
LEASED premises in general. Land & Ten 74-81
LIABILITIES and rights of subtenant. Land & Ten 80(3)
MANDATORY injunction to require renewal of lease as affected by subletting. Inj 57
MOBILE home parks. Land & Ten 373
MORTGAGE foreclosure action withdrawn with out sublessee's consent. Mtg 475
ORIGINAL tenant's liability to—
  Landlord. Land & Ten 80(2)
  Subtenant. Land & Ten 80(4)
PAROL agreements. Land & Ten 77
RAILROADS, see this index Railroads
RECOVERY of possession under law suspending remedy on ground of unauthorized subletting. Land & Ten 278.9(1)

Reference from a topic other than the obvious "Landlord & Tenant"

The same key number as found in the descriptive word index.

Reprinted with permission from 2 Conn D. 130, copyright 1990 by West Publishing Co.

Let's use a new example to demonstrate how the words and phrases section works. Suppose an important issue in a case you are handling in the United States District Court in California turns upon construction of the term *functional*. Turning to the words and phrases section of the *Federal Practice Digest 3d* (see Figure 1–9), you see a listing for the term *functional*. Going down the list of cases provided, you'll find that the case of *Vision Sports, Inc. v. Melville Corp.* was a California federal appeal decided by the ninth circuit (the abbreviation *C.A.9* is not proper bluebook form but is a format often seen). The citation reads "888 F.2d 609, 614." This tells you that the opinion begins on page 609, and at page 614 of that opinion there will be a judicial construction of the term *functional*. See Figure 1–10 on page 16, which reproduces page 614, and find the judicial construction.

In addition to the "words and phrases" digest section, the West Company also publishes a multivolume set called *Words and Phrases* that includes words and phrases from all jurisdictions for all time periods, and which provides not only citations but also headnotes for each word or phrase.

Figure 1–9 Words and Phrases Section

FRIVOLOUS   120 F P D 3d—96

FRIVOLOUS AND UNREASONABLE,
    Deretich v. City of St. Francis, D.Minn., 650 F.Supp. 645, 648.
FRIVOLOUS APPEAL
    U.S. v. One Parcel of Real Property With Bldgs., Appurtenances and Improvements, Known as the Rod and Reel Fish Camp, Located at Ocean Springs, Miss., C.A.5 (Miss.), 831 F.2d 566, 568.
    In re Lauricella, 9th Cir.BAP (Cal.), 105 B.R. 536, 541.
FRONT PAY,
    Hansard v. Pepsi-Cola Metropolitan Bottling Co., Inc., C.A.5 (Tex.), 865 F.2d 1461, 1469.
FROUDE NUMBER,
    In re Ohio River disaster Litigation, C.A.6 (Ohio), 862 F.2d 1237, 1243.
FRUIT OF THE POISONOUS TREE,
    Colorado v. Spring, U.S.Colo., 107 S.Ct. 851, 856.
FRUITS
    U.S. v. Pimental, C.A.2 (N.Y.), 810 F.2d 366, 368.
FRUSTRATION OF PURPOSE,
    Trustees of Colorado Statewide Iron Workers (ERECTOR) Joint Apprenticeship and Training Trust Fund v. A & P Steel, Inc., C.A.10 (Colo.), 812 F.2d 1518, 1523.
FUGITIVE FROM JUSTICE,
    U.S. v. Mittleider, C.A.10 (Wyo.), 835 F.2d 769, 772.
FULL AND FAIR OPPORTUNITY,
    Cullen v. Paine Webber Group, Inc., S.D.N.Y., 689 F.Supp. 269, 279.
FULL CREDIT BID,
    In re Mills, 9th Cir.BAP (Cal.), 73 B.R. 638, 642.
FULL DISCLOSURE,
    In re Kuykendahl Place Associates, Ltd., Bkrtcy.S.D.Tex., 112 B.R. 847, 849.
FULL OPPORTUNITY,
    In re Dominelli, C.A.9 (Cal.), 820 F.2d 313, 317.
FULL STRIP SEARCH,
    U.S. v. Talkington, C.D.Ill., 701 F. Supp. 809, 823.
FULLY FABRICATED,
    Carter Footwear, Inc. v. U.S., CIT, 669 F.Supp. 439, 443.
FULLY INTEGRATED,
    Calder v. Camp Grove State Bank, C.A.7 (Ill.), 892 F.2d 629, 632.
FUNCTIONAL, ————————————————— [Sample term]
    Fuddruckers, Inc. v. Doc's B.R. Others, Inc., C.A.9 (Ariz.), 826 F.2d 837, 842.
    Vision Sports, Inc. v. Melville Corp., C.A.9 (Cal.), 888 F.2d 609, 614. ——— [Case in which term "functional" is construed.]
    Schwinn Bicycle Co. v. Ross Bicycles, Inc. C.A.7 (Ill.), 870 F.2d 1176, 1188.
    Vaughan Mfg. Co. v. Brikam Intern., Inc., C.A.7 (Ill.), 814 F.2d 346, 349.
    Service Ideas, Inc. v. Traex Corp., C.A.7 (Wis.), 846 F.2d 1118, 1123.

Reprinted with permission from 120 F.P.D. 3d 96, copyright 1990 by West Publishing Co.

Figure 1–10 A Judicial Construction of *Functional*

888 FEDERAL REPORTER, 2d SERIES   614

which appears not only on Vision's clothing hangtags, but is featured prominently on Vision's clothing itself. The district court found that the VSW logo is not functional. Functionality is a question of fact, reviewed under the clearly erroneous standard.[6] *Clamp Mfg. Co. v. Enco Mfg. Co.*, 870 F.2d 512, 514 (9th Cir.1989); *Fuddruckers*, 826 F.2d at 842. A product feature or package design is functional if it is essential to the product's use or if it affects the cost or quality of the article. *Id.; First Brands*, 809 F.2d at 1381.

[10] Citing this court's decision in *First Brands*, Melville contends that the district court erred in determining that the VSW

Because of the nature of the district court's preliminary injunction, the rationale of *First Brands* does not apply here. As Vision points out, Melville is not enjoined from using the colors red, black, or white on its clothing labels or screen print. It is enjoined from using these colors in a particular graphic display which may be confusingly similar to the VSW logo format employed by Vision. This case is substantially different from *First Brands*, where the effect of the proposed injunction would have been to prevent competitors from using yellow as a background color on their antifreeze containers. *Cf. Chevron Chem. Co. v. Voluntary Purchasing Groups, Inc.*, 659 F.2d 695,

Passage that construes the term "functional."

Reprinted with permission from 888 F. 2d 614, copyright 1990 by West Publishing Co.

The **table of cases** section of a digest lists all the cases whose text appears in the associated volumes. The cases are listed alphabetically by name of the plaintiff. See Figure 1–11, which shows *Vision Sports, Inc. v. Melville Corp.* as it appears in the table of cases in *West's Federal Practice Digest, 3d.*

If you know the name of a case but not the citation, the table of cases will provide you with this information, enabling you to locate the text of the opinion. In addition to the National Reporter citation, you will find the official citation and the procedural history of the case (i.e., whether it has been affirmed or reversed on appeal), as well as a list of the key numbers assigned to that case. Locate these elements in Figure 1–11.

Sometimes you only know the name of the defendant in a case. Some digests (state and federal digests, but not regional reporters) have a **defendant/plaintiff table** listing the cases alphabetically by first defendant. The defendant/plaintiff table contains parallel citations, but not procedural history or key numbers; of course, if you want this information for a case you've found in this table, simply look it up in the table of cases (now that you've learned the plaintiff's name). Figure 1–12 on page 18 shows the listing for *Vision Sports, Inc. v. Melville Corp.* as it appears in the defendant/plaintiff table.

This discussion has focused on the digests in the West system, which are of preeminent importance in legal research. There are also digests for many official reporters, the *American Law Reports* (*A.L.R.*) system, and other private reporters. The *A.L.R.* system is discussed further. You should check your jurisdiction for other official or private digests.

Pocket Parts

The purpose of a multivolume digest—facilitating research—requires that it reference the most recent cases. Each volume, however, is manufactured to last for years. It would be prohibitively expensive to purchase new hardbound volumes every year, so how do these sets stay current?

The answer is through the use of **pocket parts**. Pocket parts are annual (or sometimes more frequent) supplements. Each pocket part corresponds to one volume of the digest set, and is fitted into a pocket inside the back cover of the book. The pocket part contains all the recent headnotes that would have appeared in the main volume had they been available when it went to press. These headnotes are organized in the pocket part as they would have been in the main volume—in the West system, for example, by topic and key number.

In addition to annual pocket parts, digests can be supplemented at more frequent intervals by individual paperbound volumes that collect all the material subsequent to the most recent set of pocket parts. In this manner, the content of the digest set is kept current.

Pocket parts are used in many legal publications besides digests, including the *American Law Reports* series, state and federal statutory sets, legal encyclopedias, and even some treatises. These other publications are discussed further.

When doing legal research, it is absolutely essential that you check for pocket parts! If you haven't assured yourself that you've checked all pocket parts and all paperbound volumes updating pocket parts, then you haven't finished your research. You may even have missed the most recent case on the subject! Get in the habit of checking each resource you use to verify that you've utilized its latest update—be it a pocket part, a paperbound volume, or some other form of update.

Figure 1–11 Table of Cases

VIVADO		116 F P D 3d—211
References are to Digest Topics and Key Numbers		

UW 1006, 100 LEd2d 195, den'g cert Kilgore v. McClelland, 637 FSupp 1253.

Virginia ex rel. State Bd. of Elections v. Kilgore, USVa, 108 SCt 1731, 486 US 1006, 100 LEd2d 195, den'g cert Kilgore v. McClelland, 637 FSupp 1241.

Virginia ex rel. State Bd. of Elections v. Kilgore, USVa, 108 SCt 1731, 486 US 1006, 100 LEd2d 195, den'g cert McConnel v. Adams, 829 F2d 1319.

Virginia Hill Partners 1, In re, Bkrtcy-NDGa, 110 BR 84.—Bankr 2397(2); Fed Cts 6.

Virginia Hosp. Ass'n v. Baliles, CA4 (Va), 868 F2d 653, reh den, cert gr in part 110 SCt 49, 107 LEd2d 18, aff Wilder v. Virginia Hosp Ass'n, 110 SCt 2510.— Admin Law 229; Assoc 20(1); Civil R 110, 209; Courts 90(1); Fed Cts 13.5, 47, 269; Lim of Act 58(1).

Virginia Hosp. Ass'n v. Baliles, CA4 (Va), 830 F2d 1308, appeal after remand 868 F2d 653, reh den, cert gr in part 110 SCt 49, 107 LEd2d 18, aff Wilder v. Virginia Hosp Ass'n, 110 SCt 2510—Judgm 668(1), 675(1), 707, 715(1), 720, 724.

Virginia Mansions Apartments, Inc., In re, WDPa, 108 BR 557.— Lim of Act 5896).

Virginia Mansions Apartments, Inc., In re, Bkrtcy WDPa, 102 BR 444.—Bankr 2923, 3352; Mun Corp 975, 978(7); Tax 57, 508, 589.

Virtual Network Services Corp., In re, NDIll, 98 BR 343, aff 902 F2d 1246.—Bankr 2967.5.

Virtual Network Services Corp., In re, BkrtcyNDIll, 97 BR 433.— Compromise 17(1).

Virtual Network Services Corp., In re, BkrtcyNDIll, 92 BR 784.— Bankr 2609.

Virtual Network Services Corp. v Affilliated Telephone. Bkrtcy NDIll, 92 BR 784. See Virtual Network Services Corp., In re.

Virtual Network Services Corp. v. Brook Furniture. BkrtcyNDIll, 97 BR 433. See Virtual Network Service Corp., In re.

Virtual Network Services Corp. v. U.S., NDIll, 98 BR 343. See Virtual Network Services Corp., In re.

Visco by Visco v. School Dist. of Pittsburgh. WDPa, 684 FSupp

1310.—Schools 148(2), 154(4).

Visidats Corp., In re BkrtcyNDCal, 84 BR 673.—Jury 11(1), 19(9).

Vision Sports, Inc. v. Melville Corp., CA9 (Cal), 888 F2d 609.— Fed Cts 815; Inj 138.6, 138.15, 138.18' Trade Reg 43 44, 407, 413, 414, 523, 587, 596, 626, 628, 704, 726.

Vision Sports, Inc. v. Melville Shoe Corp., CA9 (Cal). 888 F2d 609. See Vision Sports, Inc. v. Melville Corp.

Visiting Nurse Ass'n of Western Pennsylvania,In re. BkrtcyWDPa, 101 BR 462.—Trusts 102(1), 136 or 1361/2

Vita Food Products of Illinois, Inc. v. US, USWis, 95 SCt 1324, 420 US 945, 43 LEd2d 423, en'g cert U S v. Ewig Bros Co, Inc., 502 F2d 715

Vita Food Products of Illinois, Inc. v. U.S., USWis, 95 SCt 1324, 420 US 945, 43 LEd2d 423, den'g cert US v. Goodman, 353 FSupp 250.

Vital Breathing Products, Inc., In re, BkrtcyNDGa, 98 BR 97.— Bankr 2435, 2437; Sec Tran 92.

Vitale v. Aetna Cas. & Sur. Co., CA8(mo), 814 F2d 1242.—Fed

Case name, citation, topics, and key numbers

Reprinted with permission from 116 F.P.D. 211, copyright 1990 by West Publishing Co.

Figure 1–12 Defendant Plaintiff Table

118 F P D 3d—173 MENDEL

Consult Plaintiff Table for Key Number Digest Classification and Case History

MELINSON—Glenside, Inc, BkrtcyEDPa, 80 BR 687.

MELINSON—Humphrey's Pest Control, Inc, BkrtcyEDPa, 80 BR 687.

MEL JARVIS CONST. CO., INC.—ADM Mill. Co., NDNY, 685 FSupp 147.

MELLAS—Walsh, CA7 (Ill), 837 F2d 789.

MELLENGER—Kirby, CA11 (Fla), 830 F2d 176.

MELLENGER—Kirby, SDFla, 715 FSupp 349.

MELLIN —Muse, DCNY, 212 FSupp 315.

MELLON —Continental Can Co., Inc, CA11 (Fla), 825 F2d 308.

MELLON BANK (EAST) NAT. ASS'N—Doyle, EDPa, 75 BR 381.

MELLON BANK (EAST) NAT. ASS'N—Doyle, EDPa, 71 BR 323.

MELLON BANK (EAST) NAT. ASS'N—First Pennsylvania Bank, NA, CA3 (Pa). 859 F2d 295.

MELTON—U.S., CA5 (Miss), 883 F2d 386.

MELTON—Williams, DCGa, 568 FSupp 104.

MELTON—Zerman, CANY, 735 F2d 751.

MELUCCI —U.S., CA1 (RI), 888 F2d 200.

MELVAN —U.S., CDCal, 676 FSupp 997.

MELVILLE CORP.—Vision Sports, Inc, CA9 (Cal), 888 F2d 609.

MELVILLE SHOE CORP.—Vision Sports, Inc. CA9 (Cal), 888 F2d 609.

MELVIN—U.S., CMA, 26 MJ 145.

MEMBERS OF LOUISIANA STATE BD. OF PARDONS—Serio, CA5(La), 821 F2d 1112.

MEMBERS OF NEW YORK STATE CRIME VICTIMS BD.—Simon & Schuster, Inc. SDNY, 724 FSupp 170.

MEMBERS OF THE BD. OF EDUC. OF ST. VRAIN VALLEY SCHOOL DIST. RE-1J—Rowley by Rowley, CA10 (Colo), 863 F2d 39.

MEMPHIS POLICE DEPT. City of Memphis, Tenn.— Garner, CATenn, 600 F2d 52.

MEMPHIS PUB. CO.—Reid, CATenn, 521 F2d 512.

MEMPHIS, TENN., CITY OF—E.E.O.C., DCTenn, 581 FSupp 179.

MEMPHIS, TENN., CITY OF—Watson, CATenn, 303 F2d 863.

MEMPHIS TENN., MEMPHIS POLICE DEPT., CITY OF—Garner, CATenn, 600 F2d 52.

MENA—U.S., CA11(Fla), 863 F2d 1522.

MENARD—Bernstein by Bernstein, CAVa, 728 F2d 252.

MENARD—Bernstein by Bernstein, DCVa, 557 FSUpp 92.

MENARD FIBERGLASS PRODUCTS, INC.—Kobell For and on Behalf of N.L.R.B., WDPa, 678 FSupp 1155.

MENDEL—Marshall-Silver Const. Co., Inc, CA3(Pa), 894 F2d 593.

MENDEL—Marshall Silver Const. Co., Inc, CA3 (Pa), 835 F2d 63.

MENDEL—Mitchell-Huron Production Credit Ass'n, DSD,

The same case alphabetized by defendant.

United States Supreme Court Decisions

The regional reporters of the National Reporter System collect cases from the 50 state court systems. What about the federal courts? Where are federal decisions collected, and how do we go about finding the federal cases we need for our research? Let's start with the Supreme Court.

There are four principal sources of the decisions of the U.S. Supreme Court. Two you already know from our discussion of the *Marbury v. Madison* citation—*United States Reports* and *United States Supreme Court Reports, Lawyers' Edition*. These two sources comprise bound volumes and advance sheets. There is a third source composed of bound volumes and advance sheets—the *Supreme Court Reporter*, published by the West Publishing Company. There is also an important source published in looseleaf format—*The United States Law Week*.

The *United States Reports* series, as you recall, is the official series, and its publication (even the advance sheets) lags far behind the issuance of opinions, making it less useful than the other sources for research purposes. In addition, *U.S. Reports* also lacks research aids such as effective indexing by topic, available in the other sources. Perhaps the most useful contribution of *U.S. Reports* is its presentation of a syllabus (a relatively detailed summary) of each decision, prepared by the official court reporter. These syllabi, however, appear in the private sources as well.

The *Lawyers' Edition* series is a private source published by the Lawyers' Co-Operative Publishing Company. These volumes are now in their second series, abbreviated for citation purposes as *L.Ed.2d*. They are indexed according to a system that differs from the West key number system, but which also utilizes the headnote device. There are two features of the *Lawyers' Edition* volumes, in addition to their timely publication, that make them useful research tools. First, they often provide summaries of the briefs of the opposing attorneys, which are not found in *U.S. Reports* or the *Supreme Court Reporter*. Second, each volume contains annotations, which are in-depth articles that analyze selected issues raised in some of the more important cases appearing in that volume, and identify additional relevant cases. You will learn more about annotations in the section on the *American Law Reports* (*A.L.R.*) series.

The *Supreme Court Reporter* (citation abbreviation *S.Ct.*) is a publication of West Publishing Company. It utilizes the same key number/digest system seen in the National Reporter System, making it a useful resource for cross-referencing decisions in the state courts and the lower federal courts.

Although both the *Lawyers' Edition* and the *Supreme Court Reporter* issue advance sheets much sooner than does *U.S. Reports*, preparation of headnotes and annotations (and other production realities) still produces a lag time between issuance of the opinions and their appearance in print. To meet the immediate needs of the legal community, *The United States Law Week* publishes full texts of the decisions almost immediately upon their issuance by the Supreme Court. The *U.S. Law Week* publication is a **looseleaf service**, publishing pages with prepunched holes for insertion into looseleaf binders. In addition to the Supreme Court decisions, it contains sections on other recent legal developments. You should cite to *U.S. Law Week* only when the Supreme Court decision has not yet appeared in one of the other advance sheets (citation abbreviation *U.S.L.W.*). The *U.S. Law Week* is published weekly, with special editions when the Supreme Court is releasing substantial volumes of opinions.

There are other sources of Supreme Court decisions, as well. These include other looseleaf services (such as the *U.S. Supreme Court Bulletin*, published by Commerce Clearing House), newspapers (which are never cited as a source for the text of an opinion), and the various on-line computer services (which we will discuss further).

Federal Court Decisions

With the importance attached to decisions of the federal courts in the American legal system, it is odd to note that there is no official government reporter of federal decisions below the level of the Supreme Court. The reporters prepared by the West Publishing Company for federal decisions are the *Federal Supplement* (publishing decisions of the United States District Courts and certain other courts since 1932) and the *Federal Reporter*, (dating back to 1880 and currently publishing decisions of the appellate circuits; prior to 1932 the *Federal Reporter* published U.S. District Court cases as well). These are the standard sources for federal case law, cited respectively as *F. Supp.* and *F.* or *F.2d*. Federal cases prior to 1880 are collected in the West set *Federal Cases*.

There are also several reporters in the West system that print only those federal decisions relating to a specific topic. For example, *Federal Rules Decisions* is cited as *F.R.D.* and contains decisions relating to the Federal Rules of Civil Procedure and the Federal Rules of Criminal Procedure. *West's Bankruptcy Reporter* (cited *Bankr.*) contains decisions of the federal bankruptcy courts.

All these West reporters utilize the key number/digest system. There are other sources of federal cases as well, including sources related to specific topics and the *A.L.R., Federal* series.

American Law Reports (A.L.R.)

The Lawyers' Co-Operative Publishing Company produces several series of volumes in addition to the Lawyers' Edition of the *Supreme Court Reports*. In this section we discuss the *American Law Reports* series, referred to as *A.L.R.*

The *A.L.R.* series publishes full texts of only certain state and federal court decisions, which are selected for the level of interest generated by the issues that they address (see Figure 1–13). Each individual case selected is followed by an **annotation**, which provides an in-depth analysis of a specific and important legal issue raised in the accompanying decision, together with an extensive survey of the way the issue is treated in various jurisdictions. Many cases are cited and summarized in these annotations, making them excellent research sources. An example of the first page of such an annotation is found in Figure 1–14 and an interior page is found in Figure 1–15, page 22. The *A.L.R.* volumes are now in their fourth series, cited as *A.L.R.4th.*

A second set of *A.L.R.* volumes is called *A.L.R. Federal*. It is structured identically to the standard *A.L.R.* series, with selected cases (all federal) followed by annotations on the federal issues presented.

There is a digest collecting all the *A.L.R.*, *A.L.R. Federal*, and *Lawyers' Edition* headnotes arranged alphabetically by topic, called the *A.L.R. Digest*. A much

Figure 1–13 An Example of an *A.L.R.* Case

SUBJECT OF ANNOTATION

Beginning on page 531

Sufficiency of evidence of nonrevocation of lost will where codicil survives

In re ESTATE OF Clifford P. KUSZMAUL, Deceased

District Court of Appeal of Florida, Fourth District
June 25, 1986
491 So 2d 287, 11 FLW 1428, 84 ALR 4th 527

SUMMARY OF DECISION

A petition for the administration of a will was denied by a Florida trial court where the original of the will was not found after the testator's death, but instead, only a conformed copy of the original will and the original of an executed codicil thereto were found.

The District Court of Appeal of Florida, Fourth District, Letts, J., reversed and remanded. The court held that while there is a presumption that a will which was in the possession of the testator prior to death and which cannot be located subsequent to death was destroyed by the testator with the intention of revoking it, and this presumption may only be overcome by competent and substantial evidence, there was substantial and competent evidence to overcome the presumption in the present case where the original of the executed codicil found with the conformed copy of the original will among the testator's personal possessions stated in its concluding paragraph that the testator thereby ratified and confirmed his last will and testament except insofar as any part thereof was modified by the codicil. The court held that this was sufficient evidence that the original will has not been revoked, particularly in the light of two Florida statutes which provided that the execution of a codicil referring to a previous will has the effect of republishing the will as modified by the codicil, and that even if a will has

Reprinted with permission from 84 *A.L.R. 4th* 527, copyright 1990 by Lawyers' Co-Operative Publishing.

more useful research aid is the Index to Annotations, which indexes all the annotations in A.L.R. 3d, A.L.R. 4th, A.L.R. Federal, Lawyers' Edition, and other Lawyers' Co-Op volumes as well.

The volumes issued by Lawyers' Co-Op comprise what the company calls the **Total Client-Service Library**. All volumes in this library cross-reference related passages in the other volumes. (See Figure 1–14.)

Other Private Reporters

Although the West and *A.L.R.* systems are by far the most important private reporters, there are other private reporters which exist or have existed in the past in various jurisdictions. When doing research you must make sure that you have accounted for all potential sources of cases, including other private reporters. This can be accomplished by conferring with your local legal librarian or your supervising attorney, by referring to the bluebook, which lists reporters for each jurisdiction, or by conducting your own thorough library search for potential sources. The latter method, although more difficult, will provide you with useful exposure to the law library.

Looseleaf Services

Yet another source of case law is found in the looseleaf services, introduced in the discussion of *U.S. Law Week* in the section on Supreme Court cases. There

Figure 1–14 First Page of *A.L.R.* Annotation

ANNOTATION

SUFFICIENCY OF EVIDENCE OF NONREVOCATION OF LOST WILL WHERE CODICIL SURVIVES

by

Gavin L. Phillips, J.D.

TOTAL CLIENT-SERVICE LIBRARY® REFERENCES

79 Am Jur 2d, Wills §§ 628, 694, 696; 80 Am Jur 2d, Wills §§ 1071-1091

Annotations: See the related matters listed in the annotation.

25 Am Jr Pl & Pr Forms (Rev), Wills, Forms 11-15, 21-23, 241

39 Am Jur Proof of Facts 2d 177, Interference With Right to Share of Decedent's Estate

9 Am Jur Trials 601, Will Contests

US L Ed Digest, Wills §§ 28, 32

ALR Digest, Wills §§ 114, 116

Index to Annotations, Codicils; Wills

Auto-Cite®: Cases and annotations referred to herein can be further researched through the Auto-Cite® computer-assisted research service. Use Auto-Cite to check citations for form, parallel references, prior and later history, and annotation references

Reprinted with permission from 84 *A.L.R. 4th* 531, copyright 1990 by Lawyers' Co-Operative Publishing.

is a large number of looseleaf services covering a wide variety of topics. The major publishers are the Bureau of National Affairs (BNA), Commerce Clearing House (CCH), and Prentice-Hall. The specific format of each depends upon the publisher, the nature of the material covered, and the scope of the service.

A few generalizations apply to most looseleaf services. Each usually applies to only one topic; for example, the *Federal Securities Law Reporter* published by CCH relates only to laws regulating securities issuance and transactions. Weekly updates are usually provided in the form of prepunched supplement or replacement pages to be inserted into the binder in which the service is maintained. Coverage often extends to both state and federal cases relating to the topic, as well as applicable statutes and textual analysis. Looseleaf services

Figure 1–15 Interior Page of *A.L.R.* Annotation

§3 NONREVOCATION OF LOST WILL—CODICIL 84 ALR 4th

84 *ALR* 4th 531

republishing the will, it rejected the argument of the proponents of a missing will and an existing codicil that the presumption under the law as to the destruction or attempted revocation of a lost will does not operate with respect to the will unless the codicil is also destroyed or unless there is additional evidence to support the presumption that the claimed lost will was destroyed or revoked. The court pointed out that a will and a codicil are two different instruments, generally separately executed.

The court in Re Estate of Steel (1966) 8 **Ohio** Misc 133, 37 Ohio Ops 2d 70, 219 NE2d 236, stated in dictum that a codicil, however well preserved, is dependent upon a will for its force and effect and thus cannot be used to substitute for a will which has been lost or mutilated after the codicil was completed. The court cited Re Ayres' Will (1940, App, Franklin Co) 36 **Ohio** L Abs 267, 43 NE2d 918, this section, as support for its position that the codicil demonstrates only that there was a valid will in existence at the time the codicil was executed and not necessarily thereafter.

III. Effect of Particular Factors

§4. Codicil found together with copy of will

In the following cases, the courts determined that, where an executed codicil was found among the decedent's papers together with a copy of a missing will, the presumption that the missing will had been destroyed by the decedent with the intent to revoke the will was overcome.

The court in Re Estate of Kuszmaul (1986, **Fla** App D4) 491 So 2d 287, 11 FLW 1428, 84 ALR4th 527, reversed the trial court's decision and held that a conformed copy of a will, found together with an original executed codicil, was sufficient to uphold the provisions of that will and its codicil, despite the absence of the original executed will. The court distinguished the case of Re Estate of Baird (1977, **Fla** App D4) 343 So 2d 41, §7[c], because, unlike that case, here the discovered executed codicil was accompanied by a copy of the missing will. The court also pointed out two statutory provisions which provided that the execution of a codicil referring to a previous will has the effect of republishing the will as modified by the codicil, and that even if a will has been revoked it may be republished and made valid by the execution of a codicil republishing it with the formalities required by the law for the execution of wills.

Based upon statutory authority, the court in Re Estate of Smith (1985) 145 **Mich** App 634, 378 NW2d 555, held that the original of a codicil which incorporated by reference a prior will was a separate and independent testamentary instrument, the terms of which could be established by reference to the copy of the prior missing will found with the original executed copy of the codicil, and that both documents must be admitted to probate; the codicil as a valid testamentary instrument, and the copy of the prior will for the purpose of proving the dispositive provisions of the codicil. The court acknowledged the common-law presumption of revocation

Reprinted with permission from 84 *A.L.R. 4th* 538, copyright 1990 by Lawyers' Co-Operative Publishing.

are often organized in a complex but extremely effective manner, with numbered paragraphs and topical indexes. For a detailed explanation, refer to the explanatory materials that are included with each service. Often cases are summarized in the text but reprinted in full in companion looseleaf volumes; these companion volumes are organized in a manner similar to reporters, and some looseleaf services ultimately reissue them in permanent bound volumes.

Many of the cases in the looseleaf services are reprinted nowhere else, not even in the reporters of the West Company. For this reason, the looseleaf services can be a valuable resource. It is convenient to have textual materials and cases and statutes from many jurisdictions all in one location and with one common system of indexing. Finally, the weekly updates often make the loose leaf services the most current source of information available.

Slip Opinions

A **slip opinion** is the first format in which a judicial opinion appears. It is individually paginated (beginning with page one) and is often simply the typewritten text generated by the court's own clerical staff. In some states, slip opinions are gathered together informally in a binder or folder at the law library or the courthouse. In other states, slip opinions are published, but their high expense and delayed availability make them impractical research tools. The published slip opinion may even appear after the advance sheet version is available.

Shepardizing

Now that you have learned about the many sources of cases and the many ways of finding the cases that relate to your particular research subject, you may be wondering, How can I be sure a case I found hasn't been overruled? This is, in fact, a very important consideration. Just because a case appears as a published opinion in a reporter doesn't mean the principles established in the case are still "good law" (that is to say, still valid precedents). The opinion may have been reversed on appeal, or a later decision by a higher court in a different case may have resolved the same legal issue in a different way, overruling the earlier decision.

The solution to this concern is an amazing series of volumes known as *Shepard's Citations*. The *Shepard's* system is so useful that verifying the precedential value of a case is now referred to as "**shepardizing**."

The *Shepard's* system updates every case ever printed in every commonly used reporter. Think about that for a second. Let's say that you found a 1965 case from your jurisdiction that covers our landlord/tenant problem. Without *Shepard's*, you'd have to search through the text of every subsequent case to see if your 1965 case had been overturned. But with *Shepard's*, the task is greatly simplified. The *Shepard's* system lists every reference ever made to your case!

The easiest way to demonstrate the system is by example. Remember our Alaska contract case, *Great Western Savings Bank*? Let's shepardize it. We won't do a full search, because by the time this book gets to print the search will already be incomplete. But you'll understand the basic principles even through our partial search.

Figure 1–16 on page 24 is a page from *Shepard's Pacific Reporter Citations*. Highlighted are the notations for "778," "P.2d," and "569," which correspond to the citation for our case. We've located the correct *Shepard's* set, found the reference to volume 778 of the second series, and found the reference to page 569 of that volume. Turning to the entry under the 569 notation, we find a citation to a New York case, 557 N.Y.S.2d 255. Figure 1–17 on page 25 is page 255 from volume 557 of the second series of the *New York Supplement*. Sure enough, there is a reference to our case!

Figure 1–16 A Page From *Shepard's Pacific Reporter*

PACIFIC REPORTER, 2d SERIES | Vol. 778

778 P.2d 569 is cited at 557 N.Y.S.2d 255

The small superscript identifies the headnote cited.

–1306–	–42–	r792P2d299	–470–	s785P2d825	–721–	(238Mt511)
(238Mt414)	s784P2d531		792P2d^{8}1192	f790P2d^{4}649	Calif	785P2d191
	780P2d^{1}1339	–300–	792P2d^{9}1193	f790P2d^{6}649	j267CaR392	
–1313–	789P2d^{2}316	d795P2d^{1}275				–876–
(238Mt408)			–476–	–545–	–731–	(238Mt496)
	–51–	–307–	j780P2d1184	s788P2d1078	(116Ida609)	
–1326–	s784P2d532	s790P2d311	795P2d1057			–879–
788P2d386			Cir. 10	–549–	–737–	(239Mt1)
	–59–	–326–	905 F2d318	Case 4	(116Ida615)	f784P2d^{3}411
–1331–	j783P2d654	782P2d^{2}875		270CaR^{10}48		785P2d191
790P2d			–479–		–744–	f788P2d327
[^{14}1115	–108–	–332–	US cert den	–569–	(116Ida622)	
	j780P2d1359	(70Haw573)	in110SC3261	NY	j791P2d1282	–885–
–1352–	782P2d1128		Cir. 10	557NYS2d	Nj	(239Mt20)
785P2d^{4}322	784P2d226	–336–	911F2d^{4}418	[255	570A2d14	
	789P2d869	(116Ida586)				–888–
–1359–			–488–	–581–	–757–	(239Mt12)
1ExER109	–118–	–340–	793P2d870	US cert den	(116Ida635)	
	794P2d^{2}89	(116Ida590)		in110SC725	792P2d929	–892–
–1377–			–497–	11CoLR18	795P2d^{8}301	(239Mt42)
(308Ore191)	–129–	–359–	(308Ore254)			
	US cert den	NJ	786P2d^{1}746	–602–	–774–	–895–
–1379–	in110SC2576	570A2d450	j786P2d748	(161Az237)	(116Ida652)	(239Mt25)
(97OrA527)	j781P2d546		796P2d^{2}1244	US cert den		785P2d201
s784P2d441	j782P2d667	–370–	796P2d^{3}1244	in110SC1528	–778–	
	789P2d154	791P2d^{1}749	Wash	s110lZ264	(161Ida656)	–900–
–1385–	789P2d994	791P2d^{2}749	788P2d^{1}10	s110SC2583		(239Mt38)
(97OrA676)	789P2d			cc108LZ762	–797–	
11InL475	[^{21}1015	–377–	–499–	cc110SC152	(116Ida675)	–902–
	790P2d	cc737FS1153	(98OrA66)	j110SC3108		(239Mt70)
–1388–	[^{13}1312	792P2d979		j58USLW	–801–	789P2d1220
(98OrA1)	790P2d		–500–	[5032	(116Ida679)	
s784P2d1099	[^{19}1315	–390–	(98OrA69)			–906–
	j263CaR512	Cir. 10		–634–	–804–	(239Mt47)
–1392–	f263CaR^{2}631	727FS1389	–503–	(161Az269)	(116Ida682)	
Case 1	f263CaR^{5}631	d727FS^{3}130	(98OrA75)	Wyo	795P2d^{1}913	–912–
(98OrA57)	f263CaR^{6}631		r7902d1137	j792P2d231		11MeLR276
s784P2d1100	f264CaR426	–395–	s784P2d1100	NC	–809–	14PcL295
	268CaR426	(238Mt393)	781P2d1273	389SZ46	(116Ida687)	
Vol. 778	268CaR813		781P2d^{2}1274	12MeLR7		–920–
	268CaR^{21}83	–402–			–811–	785P2d^{5}323
–1–	Wyo	(238Mt470)	–504–	–643–	(116Ida689)	f788P2d^{1}410
787P2d^{3}536	787P2d^{9}87		(98OrA83)	(161Az278)		f788P2d^{5}411
796P2d^{3}696		–406–	s784P2d1101		–815–	
	–174–	(238Mt478)		–667–	(116Ida693)	–932–
–11–	s272CaR195		–506–	US cert den		f795P2d^{1}106
s783P2d53	f265CaR906	–410–	(98OrA93)	in 110SC519	–818–	795P2d107
	f267CaR740	(238Mt485)	s784P2d1100		(116Ida696)	
–16–	267CaR^{5}746	1ExER161		–685–	795P2d913	–933–
14PcL308	268CaR485		–508–	d788P2d^{1}1277		10CoLR341
	j268CaR906	–416–	(98OrA97)	Ariz	–821–	
–20–	e272Car651	(239Mt23)		791P2d1047	(116Ida699)	–945–
790P2d50			–509–			f790P2d^{1}541
	–241–	–419–	(98OrA100)	–704–	–823–	
–21–	(161Az206)	(239Mt58)		796P2d83	791P2d^{7}1333	–953–
782P2d968		785P2d^{1}720	–510–	796P2d^{16}86	f791P2d^{4}1335	(308Ore199)
	–259–		(98OrA161)	Mont	12MeLR28	
–26–	(161Az224)	–421–		j793P2d809	12MeLR126	–958–
782P2d^{6}201		(239Mt54)	–512–	1ExER133		(308Ore290)
	–266–		(98OrA165)		–859–	
–32–	(161Az231)	–460–	s784P2d1100	–716–	(238Mt398)	–962–
795P2d^{1}1181		792P2d		(70Haw597)		(98OrA58)
	–269–	[^{17}1197	–531–	784P2d^{1}863	–862–	
–40–	(161Az234)	793P2d877	786P2d281	784P2d^{2}863	(238Mt451)	–963–
s781P2d1322		1ExER137		787P2d687		(98OrA62)
	–285–		–538–		–874–	s784P2d1099

Reprinted with permission by Shepard's McGraw-Hill.

Figure 1–17 A Citation to a New York Case

FRATTO v. WESTERN REG. OFF-TRACK BETTING   255
Cite as 557 N.Y.S.2d 255 (Sup. 1990)

The Legislature provided discretion to the court to authorize such relief as "such other relief as to the court may seem necessary and proper." This broad grant of judicial discretion is deemed sufficiently comprehensive to include granting leave to plead claims for punitive damages. This conclusion is reinforced by the Legislature's making diversion a felony and by the decisional authorities in other jurisdictions. *Great Western Savings Bank v. George N. Easley Co., 778 P.2d 569; Zerman v. Lufthansa German Airlines,* 699 P.2d 1274. In both of the cited authorities, the Supreme Court of Alaska affirmed judgments for punitive damages where the evidence allowed the jury to find tortious conduct entailing outrageous behavior in misapplying funds entrusted for the payment of construction costs.

report with copies to counsel for all parties with the Court on or before July 5, 1990 at 9:30.

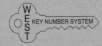

Mario FRATTO, Plaintiff,

v.

WESTERN REGIONAL OFF-TRACK BETTING CORPORATION, Defendant.

Supreme Court, Seneca County.

June 22, 1990.

> Cite to 778 P.2d 569

Reprinted with permission from *537 N.Y.S.2d* 255, copyright 1991 by West Publishing Co.

This reference didn't overturn our case; a court from one state, New York in this example, cannot overturn the decisions of another state, Alaska in this example. However, suppose an Alaskan court had overturned our case? What then?

The *Shepard's* system would place a small *o* in the margin by the entry, which stands for *overruled*. The *Shepard's* system employs a whole series of marginal abbreviations (listed in Figure 1–18 on page 26), which summarize the direct procedural history and subsequent treatment of the case. The absence of a marginal abbreviation next to the reference to 557 N.Y.S.2d 255 for our case is an indication that, although the case was cited, it was not cited for any of the significant reasons requiring marginal notation. Scan the page reprinted in Figure 1–16 and find as many marginal notations as you can, then use Figure 1–18 to find out what each one means.

You might be saying to yourself, Why bother with the marginal notations? Why not just look up every case in which your case is cited? After all, for *Great Western Savings Bank* there was only one case to look up. For the answer to this question, we suggest you try shepardizing *Marbury v. Madison.*

The level of specificity provided in the entries goes even further. For cases with several headnotes, the entry will often identify by the use of a small numeral (see the entries for pages 685 and 823 in Figure 1–16) the headnote to which the referenced citation refers.

The *Shepard's* system has other uses in addition to verifying precedential value. It can help you find parallel citations, for example, and other cases that are similar in content to the case being shepardized.

There are *Shepard's* sets for most reporters, as well as for statutes, law review articles, and other publications. Although the basic system is easy to master, you should spend some time looking over the actual sets in your law library. The high volume of opinions generated by the court system has required many *Shepard's* sets to adopt a multivolume format that can be somewhat confusing. You must be sure you have shepardized your case in all necessary volumes. All the information you need to assure yourself of this is printed right on the covers or bindings of the applicable Shepard's volumes, so mistakes can only be the result of sloppiness. Take your time and be thorough—shepardizing is an important task, often performed by paralegals.

1–4 Finding Statutes and Constitutions

In addition to finding cases, you will need to locate the text of applicable statutes and constitutions. These sources of law are also organized in a logical fashion.

Figure 1–18 Marginal Abbreviations

ABBREVIATIONS—ANALYSIS

History of Case

a	(affirmed)	Same case affirmed on appeal.
cc	(connected case)	Different case from case cited but arising out of same subject matter or intimately connected therewith.
D	(dismissed)	Appeal from same case dismissed.
De	(denied)	Review or rehearing denied.
GP	(granted and citable)	Review granted and ordered published.
Gr	(granted)	Review or rehearing granted.
m	(modified)	Same case modified on appeal.
Np	(not published)	Reporter of Decisions directed not to publish this opinion.
Op	(original opinion)	Citation of original opinion.
r	(reversed)	Same case reversed on appeal.
Re	(republished)	Reporter of Decisions directed to publish opinion previously ordered not published.
s	(same case)	Same case as case cited.
S	(superseded)	Substitution for former opinion.
v	(vacated)	Same case vacated.
US	cert den	Certiorari denied by U.S. Supreme Court.
US	cert dis	Certiorari dismissed by U.S. Supreme Court.
US	reh den	Rehearing denied by U.S. Supreme Court.
US	reh dis	Rehearing dismissed by U.S. Supreme Court.
US	app pndg	Appeal pending before the U.S. Supreme Court.

Treatment of Case

c	(criticised)	Soundness of decision or reasoning in cited case criticised for reasons given.
d	(distinguished)	Case at bar different either in law or fact from case cited for reasons given.
e	(explained)	Statement of import of decision in cited case. Not merely a restatement of the facts.
f	(followed)	Cited as controlling.
h	(harmonized)	Apparent inconsistency explained and shown not to exist.
j	(dissenting opinion)	Citation in dissenting opinion.
l	(limited)	Refusal to extend decision of cited case beyond precise issues involved.
o	(overruled)	Ruling in cited case expressly overruled.
p	(parallel)	Citing case substantially alike or on all fours with cited case in its law or facts.
q	(questioned)	Soundness of decision or reasoning in cited case questioned.

Reprinted with permission by Shepard's/McGraw-Hill.

Slip Laws and Session Laws

The U.S. Congress and the 50 state legislatures pass many bills each year. These bills become statutes with the signature of the President or governor.

The first format in which a newly signed statute appears is called a **slip law**. A slip law is an official publication of a single statute or *act* (a group of related statutes). A slip law usually identifies a public act number or other official designation associated with this single statute or act. The federal government and most states issue slip laws, but they are rarely used for research purposes because there are other, more comprehensive formats in which the new statute will shortly appear.

The second format in which new statutes appear is a compilation called the **session laws**. Session laws are permanent collections of the statutes of one jurisdiction, printed periodically in chronological order of issuance, and with each new edition including only those laws passed since the previous edition. The federal session laws are printed in a series called the *Statutes at Large*. Each of the states has its own version of session laws.

Statutes concerning diverse subjects are generated in each legislative session, with no particular order to their issuance. Session laws are useful for checking recent legislation, but they are often inadequately indexed and difficult to use for comprehensive research.

Codes

The solution to the problem of research in statutes is provided by the code. A **code** is a set of volumes, issued by order of the legislature, that groups statutes by subject matter and is well indexed, in order to make the statutes more accessible for research purposes. Federal statutes are contained in the *United States Code* (cited as *U.S.C.*); check your library to find the government edition of your state's statutory code.

A code is sometimes deemed the official text of some or all of the statutes it contains. It is important to consider, for a moment, this concept of "official" as it applies to statutes. As a practical matter, if one assumes that each version of a text accurately reproduces the true text, it doesn't matter which is official. On occasion, however, the text of one version may contain an error, creating a situation where different versions of the same statute exist. Under such circumstances it becomes important to know which version—slip or session or code—is deemed by the legislature to be the official version. For the federal government, portions of the *United States Code* have been officially adopted, making the code version official for those portions; for other federal statutes, the official version is found in the *Statutes at Large*. You should check your own jurisdiction to verify which version of its statutes is the official one.

Annotated Codes

An **annotated code** is one that provides, in addition to the text of the codified statutes, such information as: those cases which have construed the statute; those law review articles which have discussed it; the procedural history of the statute (amendments or antecedents); cross-references to superceded codifications; cross-references to related statutes; and other information. The availability of this information makes the annotated codes valuable reference tools. All states have at least one annotated code, and in some large states publishers issue competing versions. The principal annotated codes for the federal statutes are the *United States Code Annotated* (*U.S.C.A.*) published by the West Company and the *United States Code Service* (*U.S.C.S.*) published by the Lawyers' Co-Operative Publishing Company. A passage from *West's Annotated California Codes* appears in Figure 1–19. You should check your law library to learn more about the annotated code in your state.

Figure 1–19 A Passage From *West's Annotated California Codes*

ORGANIZATION AND BYLAWS   **§211**
Div. 1

§ 211.   Bylaws; adoption, amendment or repeal

   Bylaws may be adopted, amended or repealed either by approval of the outstanding shares (Section 152) or by the approval of the board, except as provided in Section 212. Subject to subdivision (a)(5) of Section 204, the articles or bylaws may restrict or eliminate the power of the board to adopt, amend or repeal any or all bylaws.
(Added by Stats.1975, c. 682, § 7, eff. Jan. 1, 1977.)

Historical and Statutory Notes

Derivation: Former § 500, added by Stats. 1947, c. 1038, p. 2316, § 500, amended by Stats. 1953, c. 967, p. 2344, § 2.
   Civ.C § 301, amended by Code Am.1873-74, c. 612, p. 200, § 63; Stats.1901, c. 157, p. 344, § 65; Stats.1929, c. 711, p. 1264, § 9. Superseded by Civ.C. § 301, added by Stats.1931, c. 862, p. 1773, § 2, amended by Stats.1933, c. 533, p. 1365, § 10.

   Civ.C. § 304, amended by Code Am.1873-74, c. 612, p. 201, § 65; Stats.1885, c. 141, p. 130, § 1; Stats.1901, c. 157, p. 345, § 68; Stats.1905, c. 416, p. 555, § 3. Superseded by Civ.C. § 301, added by Stats.1931, c. 862, p. 1773, § 2, amended by Stats.1933, c. 533, p: 1365, § 10.

Cross References

Bylaws,
   Generally, see § 9910 et seq.
   Nonprofit cooperative marketing associations, see Food & Agricultural Code § 54111 et seq.
   power of corporations to make, see § 207.
   Reorganization under federal laws, amendment or repeal of, see § 1400.
Cooperative corporations, see § 12450 et seq.
   Nonprofit corporations, see § 5037.
   Nonprofit mutual benefit corporations, see § 7150 et seq.
   Nonprofit public benefit corporations, see § 5150 et seq.
   Nonprofit religious corporations, see § 9150 et seq.

Law Review Commentaries

   Corporations and the intertemporal conflicts. John K. McNulty (1967) 55 C.L.R. 12.
   Number of corporate directors. (1953) 27 So.Cal.L.R. 78.
   Repeated violation of by-laws by corporate officers may result in their waiver or repeal. (1942) 30 C.L.R. 195.
   Restriction of close corporate share-

holder's right to transfer shares. (1965) 53 C.L.R. 692.
   Stock transfer restrictions and the close corporation. (1966) 17 Hast.L.J. 583.
   Tender offer defensive tactics: A proposal for reform. Mary Siegal (1985) 36 Hast.L.J. 377.
   Waiver of provisions of by-laws by acquisescence in continuous violation of by-laws by officers. (1942) 30 C.L.R. 195.

107

Reprinted with permission from *West's Annotated California Codes*, copyright 1990 by West Publishing Co.

Most state annotated codes are published in hardbound volumes updated with advance sheets and pocket parts. Some are published in looseleaf format. Provision is generally made for publication of some version of the session laws (usually without annotation, but including an index and possibly a table of codified statutes affected), which may appear even before the government's version of the session laws.

Local Ordinances

There are far too many local systems in use to make anything but the broadest generalizations about practices regarding the publishing and availability of local ordinances. Many municipalities have a code of ordinances analogous to a statutory code. Municipal codes rarely have case citations, although there is some coverage in the individual state editions of Shepard's. Check your local library for more information about the system in your community.

Legislative History

Sometimes the language of a statute may not be entirely clear, and a dispute may arise over its meaning. In such a case the **legislative history** can be consulted. A legislative history is composed of the transcripts of the legislative debates leading up to the passage of the bill that became the statute. For some bills the legislative history can be extensive. Legislative histories for federal statutes are generally on file at the more comprehensive law libraries; for those pertaining to state statutes, you may have to dig a little deeper. Go to the state library at your state's capital or the legislative archives; check the location of these records for your own state. To obtain the legislative history of an out-of-state statute, you will almost certainly have to contact a library in that state.

Constitutions

The Constitution of the U.S. is reprinted and annotated in both the *U.S.C.A.* and *U.S.C.S.* It is also printed by the federal government in a separate pamphlet, and can be found as an appendix in a wide variety of sources. The *U.S.C.A.* set is cross-referenced to the West key number system, and the *U.S.C.S.* system to the Total Client-Service Library system, so that these sets can be utilized to initiate broad multiresource research. The availability of annotation information is as important (perhaps even more important) when researching the Constitution as when researching statutes, in that the impact and accepted meaning of the broad provisions of the Constitution can only be gauged through an analysis of court interpretations.

The text of state constitutions is likewise found in annotated state codes (and unannotated versions as well). State constitutions vary widely in terms of length and depth of coverage, with some going into great detail about the workings of state government. Access to the cases and cross-references found in the annotations remains important.

There are many other resources relating to the Constitution and state constitutions. However, for most of your purposes as a paralegal, the constitutional texts found in the annotated codes will adequately fulfill your requirements.

Figure 1–20 *Federal Register*

22821

Rules and Regulations

Federal Register

Vol. 56, No. 96

Friday, May 17, 1991

This section of the FEDERAL REGISTER contains regulatory documents having general applicability and legal effect, most of which are keyed to and codified in the Code of Federal Regulations, which is published under 50 titles pursuant to 44 U.S.C. 1510.

The Code of Federal Regulations is sold by the Superintendent of Documents. Prices of new books are listed in the first FEDERAL REGISTER issue of each week.

DEPARTMENT OF JUSTICE

Immigration and Naturalization Service

8 CFR Parts 103, 299, 392, and 499

[INS No. 1292-91]

RNS No. 1115-AC06

Posthumous United States Citizenship for Certain Aliens; Immigration and Nationality Forms; Display of Control Numbers; Fees

AGENCY: Immigration and Naturalization Service, Justice.

ACTION: Interim rule with request for comments.

SUMMARY: This rule implements the Posthumous Citizenship for Active Duty Service Act of 1990,

Immigration and Naturalization Service, Room 5304, 425 1 Street, NW., Washington, DC 20536. Please include INS Number 1292-91 on the mailing envelope to ensure proper and timely handling.

FOR FURTHER INFORMATION CONTACT: Stella Jarina, Senior Immigration Examiner, Immigration and Naturalization Service, Room 7228, 425 1 Street NW., Washington, DC 20536, Telephone: (202) 514-3946.

SUPPLEMENTARY INFORMA-TION: Section 329A of the Immigration and Nationality Act, as added by the Posthumous Citizenship for Active Duty Service Act of 1990, Public Law 101-249, provides for the granting of posthumous citizenship to an alien or noncitizen national of the United States who dies as a result of injury or disease incurred in or aggravated by service in an active-duty status in the United States Armed Forces during World War I, World War II, the Korean Hostilities, the Vietnam Hostilities, or in other periods of military hostilities. In addition, to be eligible for a grant of posthumous citizenship, the person's induction, enlistment, or reenlistment in the Armed Forces must qualify under the provisions of section 329 (a)(1) or (a)(2) of the Act.

This interim rule sets forth the eligibility criteria, identifies who may request posthumous citizenship on

Forces and gave their lives in the protection and defense of this nation. By virtue of their military service, and consequent loss of life, these persons have clearly demonstrated a commitment to support and defend the Constitution and laws of the United States. This new law acknowledges their commitment and helps ensure that their sacrifices were not made in vain. As this is a symbolic measure, the granting of posthumous citizenship does not confer any benefit nor make applicable any provision of the Immigration and Nationality Act, as amended, to the surviving spouse, parent, son, daughter, or other relative of the decedent.

The Service's definition of the term "next-of-kin" for purposes of seeking a deceased person's posthumous naturalization includes the immediate family members listed under sections 201(b)(2)(A)(i) and 203(a) of the Act. These family members are the surviving spouse, son or daughter, parent, and brother or sister of the decedent. The definition clearly provides that it is the decedent's nearest relative who will be permitted to seek this benefit, to the exclusion of more remote relatives.

The term "another representative" is limited to the properly appointed representative of the decedent's next-of-kin. A Service Organization recognized by the Department of

---

1–5 Finding Administrative Regulations and Decisions

There is a wide variety of federal, state, and municipal agencies that issue regulations. The ability to find these regulations and the administrative decisions construing them is an important element of your skills as a paralegal.

Federal

Federal regulations have been printed for over 50 years in the *Federal Register*, a daily journal of all regulations (as well as proclamations, orders, and notices) issued by federal agencies. The *Federal Register* (cited as *Fed. Reg.*) is analogous to the *Statutes at Large* in that it publishes regulations chronologically, rather than by subject, and thus is unwieldy for comprehensive research. There is an annual compilation of all effective regulations arranged by subject, however, called the *Code of Federal Regulations* (cited and often abbreviated as *C.F.R.*). By checking the current *C.F.R.* and all subsequent issues of the *Federal Register*, you can identify those regulations effective in a given area. Figure 1–20 shows a passage from the *Federal Register*; Figure 1–21 from the *C.F.R.*

Administrative agencies also render quasi-judicial decisions. There is no single federal publication that gathers all administrative decisions in one place, as the *C.F.R.* does for federal regulations. Rather, every agency publishes its own decisions. For example, the Nuclear Regulatory Commission publishes its decisions in a series called the *Nuclear Regulatory Commission Issuances*. For more

Figure 1–21 *Code of Federal Regulations*

Food and Drug Administration, HHS § 600.3

SUBCHAPTER F—BIOLOGICS

PART 600—BIOLOGICAL PRODUCTS: GENERAL

Subpart A—General Provisions

Sec.
600.3 Definitions.

Subpart B—Establishment Standards

600.10 Personnel.
600.11 Physical establishment, equipment, animals, and care.
600.12 Records.
600.13 Retention samples.
600.14 Reporting of errors.
600.15 Temperatures during shipment.

Subpart C—Establishment Inspection

600.20 Inspectors.
600.21 Time of inspection.
600.22 Duties of inspector.

AUTHORITY: Secs. 201, 501, 502, 503, 505, 510, 519, 701, 704 of the Federal Food, Drug, and Cosmetic Act (21 U.S.C. 321, 351, 352, 353, 355, 360, 360i, 371, 374); secs. 215, 351, 352, 353, 361 of the Public Health Service Act (42 U.S.C. 216, 262, 263, 263a, 264).

SOURCE: 38 FR 32048, Nov. 20, 1973, unless otherwise noted.

CROSS REFERENCES: For U.S. Customs Service regulations relating to viruses, serums, and toxins, see 19 CFR 12.21—12.23. For U.S. Postal Service regulations

logics Evaluation and Research of the Food and Drug Administration.

(e) "State" means a State or the District of Columbia, Puerto Rico, or the Virgin Islands.

(f) "Possession" includes among other possessions, Puerto Rico and the Virgin Islands.

(g) "Products" includes biological products and trivalent organic arsenicals.

(h) "Biological product" means any virus, therapeutic serum, toxin, antitoxin, or analogous product applicable to the prevention, treatment or cure of diseases or injuries of man:

(1) A virus is interpreted to be a product containing the minute living cause of an infectious disease and includes but is not limited to filterable viruses, bacteria, rickettsia, fungi, and protozoa.

(2) A therapeutic serum is a product obtained from blood by removing the clot or clot components and the blood cells.

(3) A toxin is a product containing a soluble substance poisonous to laboratory animals or to man in doses of 1 milliliter or less (or equivalent in weight) of the product, and having the property, following the injection of non-fatal doses into an animal, of causing to be produced therein another soluble substance which specifically neutralizes the poisonous substance and which

specific information, you can contact the relevant agency directly or check the looseleaf services devoted to the relevant topic (these services include regulations and administrative decisions in their coverage).

State and Local

The systems employed by the states and municipalities to compile administrative regulations and decisions vary widely, although many are based loosely on the federal format already described. Some jurisdictions update their publication of regulations fairly frequently, others only occasionally. In many instances you must contact the relevant agency directly in order to identify the current effective regulations. You should learn the system that applies in your state and in any local jurisdiction in which you will be working.

1–6 Secondary Sources

All the materials we've discussed in this chapter have been primary sources. There are a variety of secondary sources as well—sources a step removed from the primary authority, but valuable for their analytic insights and useful explanations.

Legal Encyclopedias

A **legal encyclopedia** is a multivolume compilation that provides in-depth coverage of every area of the law. Such a purpose is difficult to achieve in practice: legal encyclopedias tend to overgeneralize and are thus rarely cited as authority for a point of law. They should not be disregarded in conducting research, however, since they provide useful general information about a broad range of topics, and can thus be used to obtain background information about an unfamiliar area. They also provide citations to cases, a useful starting point for research.

There are two well-known legal encyclopedias. The first, published by the West Company, is called *Corpus Juris Secundum* (cited as *C.J.S.*). The *C.J.S.* set references the West key number system, so that researchers can often go directly from the encyclopedia review to the appropriate digest volume to find relevant case law quickly.

The second set, *American Jurisprudence, 2d* (cited as *Am. Jur. 2d*), is published by the Lawyers' Co-Operative and, as part of the Total Client-Service Library, includes references to *A.L.R.* annotations and other Lawyers' Co-Operative publications as well as cases from all reporters. Like *C.J.S.*, *Am. Jur. 2d* is very useful for learning and as a starting place for research but is not looked upon as authoritative. A page from an *Am. Jur. 2d* reference relevant to our landlord/tenant problem appears in Figure 1–22.

Encyclopedias have also been published summarizing the law of some of the larger states, including Texas (*Texas Jurisprudence 2d*, published by Lawyers' Co-Operative), New York (*New York Jurisprudence 2d*, also published by Lawyers' Co-Operative), Illinois (*Illinois Law and Practice*, published by the West Company), and several others. These encyclopedias have strengths and limitations similar to those of *C.J.S.* and *Am. Jur. 2d*.

Figure 1–22 Landlord and Tenant Reference

C. Rights and Liabilities

1. In General

§ 500. Generally; lessee's liability for rent.

It is well settled that when a lessee sublets the leased property, his estate and leasehold interest are extinguished to that extent.[18] Nevertheless, a subletting does not in any manner affect the liability of the lessee to his lessor for the payment of rent or the performance of the convenants of the lease.[19] This is particularly true where the lease provides that the lessee shall remain responsible, and where the lessor has no control over the selection of the sublessee.[20] Thus, the original lessee is liable for any violation of the covenants of the lease by the sublessee, whether he knew of such violation or not.[1]

The mere collection or receipt of rents by a lessor from subtenants, and the crediting of them to the account of his lessee, does not operate to release the lessee from continued liability to the lessor.[2] In order to release the lessee from his liability for the rent of the subtenant on the theory of substitution, an agreement, express or implied, on the part of the landlord to accept the subtenant as his tenant, must be shown.[8]

16. Cedarhurst Park Apartments, Inc. v Milgrim, 55 Misc 2d 118, 284 NYS2d 330; Sarner v Kantor, 123 Misc 469, 205 NYS 760.

Sear v House Property & Invest. Soc. (Eng) LR 16 Ch Div 387.

Annotation: 31 ALR 2d 831, 835, § 4.

17. Edelman v F. W. Woolworth Co. 252 Ill App 142; Broad & Branford Place Corp. v J. J. Hockenjos Co. 132 NJL 229, 39 A2d 80.

Annotation: 31 ALR 2d 831, 837, § 4.

18. Byrd v Peterson, 66 Ariz 253, 186 P2d 955.

19. Brosnan v Kramer, 135 Cal 36, 66 P 979; Bless v Jenkins, 129 Mo 647, 31 SW 938 (in which part of the premises was sublet and the lessee was held liable for the subtenant's rent after the expiration of the term of the original lease, the subtenant having held over); Kenyon v Young, 48 Neb 890, 67 NW 885; Dixie Fire & Casualty Co. v Esso Standard Oil Co. 265 NC 121, 143 SE2d 279; Ernst v Conditt, 54 Tenn App 328, 390 SW 2d 703; Bishop v Associated Transport, Inc. 46 Tenn App 644, 332 SW2d 696; Pressler v Barreda (Tex Civ App) 157 SW 435 (holding that a lessee is not released from his liability to pay rent to the lessor by the fact that he sublet, notwithstanding that

his lease contained a covenant permitting him to sublet and providing that in such case the subtenants are to pay rent directly to the lessor); Agen v Nelson, 51 Wash 431, 98 P 1115.

20. Bishop v Associated Transport, Inc. 46 Tenn App 644, 332 SW2d 696.

Practice Aids.—Lease provision for continuing liability of lessee. 7 AM JUR LEGAL FORMS, LANDLORD AND TENANT, Forms 7: 1355, 7:1356.

1. Dixie Fire & Casualty Co. v Esso Standard Oil Co. 265 NC 121, 143 SE 2d 279.

2. Beall v White, 94 US 382, 24 L Ed 173; Brosnan v Kramer, 135 Cal 36, 66 P 979 (holding that a lessee is not released from his liability by the fact that the lessor had collected rent from the sublessee); Texas Loan Agency v Fleming, 92 Tex 458, 49 SW 1039.

Annotation: 36 ALR 316, 319.

3. Schachter v Tuggle Co. 8 Ga App 561, 70 SE 93; Cuesta v Goldsmith, 1 Ga App 48, 57 SE 989 (holding that mere knowledge of the fact that the lessee had sold out his business to the subtenant, and that the latter has possession, is not sufficient to work a substitution).

[49 Am Jur 2d]

Reprinted with permission from *49 Am. Jur. 2d* 482, copyright 1990 by Lawyers' Co-Operative Publishing.

Restatements

The uniform laws were drafted with the hope of standardizing state statutes in selected areas of law. The *Restatements* were conceived to perform a similar purpose for the common law. In the 1920s a group of distinguished legal experts formed the American Law Institute for the purpose of drafting organized and detailed studies of the common law in certain areas. They feared that the growing complexity and inconsistency of common law would undermine our legal system; their solution was to create a body of law approved by an independent committee of distinguished legal scholars and available to all who wished to cite to it. *Restatements* have been issued in several areas of the law (including contracts, property law, torts, and conflict of laws, among others). Subsequent developments have resulted in the issuance of second editions in several areas, for example the *Restatement of the Law of Torts, 2d*.

The courts have been receptive to the law as expressed in the *Restatements*, which now carry more authoritative weight than the legal encyclopedias. However, you should keep in mind that the *Restatements*, as a secondary authority, do not overrule existing case precedent in a jurisdiction. They might persuade a court, but they can never mandate a particular result.

The text of the *Restatements* may provide useful support if you are attempting to overturn a precedent in your jurisdiction that goes against generally accepted *Restatement* doctrine. In addition to the text, you may also find useful the cross-references to cases. Some Shepard's volumes are devoted to identifying all cases citing *Restatement* provisions.

Treatises and Texts

A **treatise** is a scholarly study of one area of the law. Treatises differ from *Restatements* in that they are usually the work of one author or group of authors, rather than the result of a collective effort such as that expended to make the *Restatements* so broadly accepted.

Treatises vary with regard to the force of their persuasiveness. Some, like William Prosser's classic text on tort law, currently published by West Company as *Prosser and Keeton on the Law of Torts*, 5th Ed. (West, 1984), is widely recognized as authoritative and often cited by the courts. Others are less widely accepted.

Treatises also vary with regard to depth of treatment. Some are multivolume, some a single volume. A one-volume treatise is commonly referred to as a *text*. The West Company publishes a series of one-volume scholarly **texts** known collectively as **hornbooks** (the Prosser work is part of this series), as well as much less thorough paperback treatments known collectively as the **nutshell** series. Nutshells generally provide good introductions to areas with which you are not familiar, whereas hornbooks fill in many more of the gaps. Neither hornbooks nor nutshells are often cited in legal briefs on disputed points (Prosser being a notable exception), although generally accepted legal principles are sometimes informally categorized as "hornbook law." The Foundation Press publishes a series of textbooks as well.

Some treatises are multivolume works covering a subject area in extraordinary detail, and some of these have had wide acceptance by the courts over the years (*Wigmore on Evidence* is a good example). Whether or not persuasive when cited to the court, such comprehensive treatises are usually useful for the purpose of learning about an area of law or finding cases on point.

When using a treatise or text, there is one important consideration to keep in mind. You must determine whether the scholarly purpose of the author(s) was to state the law as it *is* or as it *should be*. If presenting the law as it is, it will be valuable as a tool to find primary sources. If presenting the law as it should be, the persuasive value of the conclusions will be affected by their relationships to existing precedent, in conjunction with the logic of the argument presented and the prestige of the author(s).

Law Reviews and Periodicals

In addition to multivolume or book-length treatises, there are also legal publications that print articles of interest. **Law reviews** are periodicals edited by the top students at each law school, featuring scholarly articles by leading authorities and notes on various topics written by the law students themselves. A law review usually carries the name of its law school as part of its title (for example, the *Harvard Law Review* or the *University of Pennsylvania Law Review*). Like many other secondary sources, these articles are most valuable as learning tools or sources of citations to relevant primary authorities, and are not often cited in briefs. Nevertheless, an article in a leading law review by a top scholar can have a substantial impact on the profession.

There are also numerous legal periodicals published by bar associations or private publishers. These periodicals vary in quality from scholarly journals to newletters. Some are useful as research tools for the profession as a whole; others provide limited information to defined segments of the bar.

Figure 1–23 A Page From a Looseleaf Service

Federal
Securities Law Reporter

Federal Regulation of Securities

Laws, Regulations, Forms, Rulings and Decisions
Currently Supplemented and Indexed

IN SEVEN VOLUMES

VOL. 1—Securities Act of 1933 (Securities Issues); Topical Index; General Guide

VOL. 2—Securities Act; Securities Act Forms; Securities Exchange Act of 1934 (Securities Trading); Stock Exchanges

VOL. 3—Exchange Act; Over-the-Counter Markets; Proxies; Municipal Trading

VOL. 4—Exchange Act; Insider Trading; Recordkeeping; Exchange Act Forms; Public Utility Holding Companies

VOL. 5—Holding Companies; Trust Indenture Act and Forms; Investment Company Act and Forms; Investment Advisers

VOL. 6—Rules of Practice; Accounting Rules; Regulation S-K; Financial Reporting Releases and Codification; Accounting and Auditing Enforcement Releases; Staff Accounting Bulletins; Finding Lists; Release Lists; Case Table

CURRENT VOLUME—No-Action and Interpretative Letters; New SEC Rulings; New Court Decisions; Cumulative Index; Case Table for New Developments; Topical Index to New Developments

CCH Editorial Staff Publication

Commerce Clearing House, Inc.
PUBLISHERS of TOPICAL LAW REPORTS
4025 W. PETERSON AVENUE, CHICAGO, ILLINOIS 60646

For many years the primary finding tool for periodicals was the *Index to Legal Periodicals*, published by H.W. Wilson Company. *The Current Law Index* and *Legal Resource Index*, published by the Information Access Company, have appeared in recent years as competitors. All these volumes are indexed to subjects and authors, and are available from the on-line computer services as well as in the CD/ROM format (these advanced technologies are discussed further).

Looseleaf Services and Annotations

The textual treatment that looseleaf services and annotations provide is a valuable resource. Annotations provide broad analysis and extensive case summaries. The looseleaf services bring together in one topical reporter applicable case texts, statutes, regulations, and independent analysis. A page from a looseleaf service is reproduced in Figure 1–23 on page 35.

1–7 Computerized Research and Alternative Media

The technological explosion that has made this the information age has made available significant new tools for legal research. These tools—computers, on-line data services, microtext, and CD/ROM technology—have not replaced the traditional primary and secondary sources, but rather have broadened their accessibility and deepened their usefulness.

LEXIS and WESTLAW

The two foremost computer-based legal research systems are **LEXIS** and **WESTLAW**. Each contains the full text of an enormous number of documents, from case opinions to statutes to law review articles. Cases on WESTLAW also have the West Company's key numbers and headnotes. Like other on-line data systems, WESTLAW and LEXIS require that you have a computer, a modem, and the applicable software package. By linking into these systems you obtain the ability to research in four ways:

- First, by allowing a researcher to obtain the text of a specific known document. For example, suppose you need to look at a specific statute from another state, or a case from a reporter not contained in your firm's library. Enter the appropriate information into LEXIS or WESTLAW, and in a short time the full text will appear on your screen.

- Second, performing research in the normal sense (on-line digests or indexes can be reviewed to find applicable materials).

- Third, by searching selected **databases** for key terms or phrases. For example, you could search all the cases from California that use the phrase "strict liability." In addition, because some legal concepts are too complicated to compress to a single word or term, these systems allow you to search for groups of words or terms based upon their proximity—for example, a search for the terms "strict liability" and "ultrahazardous substance" when they appear in the same sentence. Stringing together key terms and words to form a **query** is a skill that takes time and practice to refine.

- Fourth, by some combination of these first three methods. For example, using WESTLAW you might want to obtain headnotes under a specific key number (the traditional research method) that contain a specified query term (the third method listed).

LEXIS and WESTLAW have simplified such tasks as cite-checking and shepardizing, provided instant access to enormous volumes of legal source material, and in only a few years, established an important role in legal research. By learning these systems and practicing the art of querying, you will add to your marketability as a paralegal.

Other On-Line Data Services

In addition to LEXIS and WESTLAW, there are other services specifically devoted to legal issues, such as VERALEX (keyed to the *A.L.R.* system), *Juris* (available only to Justice Department employees) and FLITE (available only to federal employees). In addition, many of the thousands of on-line data services are useful to lawyers, carrying such information as stock quotations, legislative activity, or corporate performance.

Microfilm and Microfiche

Many legal publications have been photographed and miniaturized into the available microtext formats. **Microfiche** reproduces the publications on filmlike sheets; **microfilm** on filmlike rolls. These microtext formats, requiring the use of a mechanical enlarger or viewer, are tremendous space-savers. The National Reporter System, statutes, legislative histories, and selected legal periodicals are all available in microfilm or microfiche.

CD/ROM

One of the more amazing advances in information technology is the **CD/ROM** format (compact disk/read-only memory). Up to 200,000 pages of text can be stored on a single disk and reproduced on a computer screen. These texts cannot be searched for terms in the way WESTLAW or LEXIS can (this is the significance of the "read-only" designation), but nevertheless provide an enormous volume of text in an extremely small space, and can often be integrated with an on-line legal database. The scope of publications available on CD/ROM is expanding all the time.

1–8 Practical Considerations – How to Begin and When to Stop

To a great extent one learns how to do legal research by doing it. There is no easy substitute for the benefits of hours of trial and error, nor is there a painless path to satisfying revelation. There are, however, two areas that are fundamental—how to begin your research and when to stop. We'll leave the middle to you.

As we said at the outset of this chapter, you must isolate your goal and prepare a plan, or risk being overwhelmed by literally millions of pages of materials in the sources we have identified. A legal encyclopedia is a good place to start; it provides a broad overview of the subject area, and might cite to a useful annotation or a case from your jurisdiction. The next stop is probably the index to the relevant annotated statutory code, to see whether a statute governs or affects the issues at hand. If there is a relevant statute, both the text of the statute and the supplemental information provided (case citations, legislative history, references to periodicals) may prove helpful. Next, go to the digest. Using the descriptive word index, the "words and phrases" section, and the topic indexes, search for relevant case law. Finally, look for secondary sources. There may be law review articles, restatement provisions, or treatises that can contribute breadth and depth to your analysis.

Now assume that you've been researching for some time. You've checked a wide variety of sources, read and photocopied a number of cases, statutes, and secondary sources, taken pages of notes, and found that there is so much material available that you could "go on forever." How do you know when to stop?

There is no easy answer to this question. A definitive reference in a mandatory authority, once adequately shepardized, may supply all the information you need. A less tidy research session may be finished when newly explored avenues yield references to the same cases, statutes, and secondary sources. If you have looked in several competing sources (for example, a West digest and an *A.L.R.* annotation) and turned up the same references, your research is probably adequate.

Finding the same references over and over does not guarantee that you are finished; with legal research, like most things in life, absolute certainty is elusive. A thorough search of the most useful references that maximizes your coverage within the constraints of the client's problem (you cannot spend $5000 of research time on a $1000 case), however, is reasonable cause to believe that you've found the essential sources.

SUMMARY

1–1

Before starting a legal research problem, isolate your goal and formulate a plan or approach. Then, if you get lost or confused, get help.

1–2

Precedential value is the force that a cited authority exerts upon a judge's reasoning. Primary authority consists of the original text of court opinions, constitutions, statutes, and agency regulations. Mandatory authority is primary authority that a court must follow; persuasive authority need not be followed, although its logic may be persuasive. Secondary authority is a step removed from the original text—not the law itself, but an analysis of the law.

1–3

Reporters are series of volumes containing judicial opinions. Opinions can be located by searching for the volume and page number identified in a citation. Proper citation form is established by the bluebook. The key number system was established by the West Company to index cases appearing in its private reporters, including the regional reporters of the National Reporter System. Digests collect headnotes, which are points of law drawn from a case and categorized under one or more applicable key numbers, and organize them consecutively by topic and key number. Pocket parts are used to update bound volumes. Annotations are found in the *American Law Reports* volumes; they summarize and provide citations for judicial opinions. Looseleaf services are books with binders in which pages can be easily inserted or replaced, and which often publish case texts. Slip opinions are individually paginated texts of judicial opinions, almost always typewritten, and are usually the first format in which opinions are published. Shepardizing is a unique method by which researchers can determine whether a case has been overruled or cited by other courts.

1–4

Slip laws are publications of a single statute or act. Session laws are publications of the statutes of a jurisdiction, printed chronologically as they are enacted, and with each new edition including only those laws passed since the last edition. A code groups statutes by subject matter, and is generally well indexed. Annotated codes provide, in addition to the statutory text, information associated with each statute, including citations to judicial opinions that have construed that statute. A legislative history comprises legislative debates leading up to the enactment or defeat of a proposed statute. The text of constitutions is usually printed as part of a corresponding code or annotated code.

1–5

Federal regulations appear in the *Federal Register* or the *Code of Federal Regulations*. Federal administrative decisions are available from the agencies rendering the decision or from looseleaf services covering the applicable subject area. The availability and format of state and local regulations and administrative decisions varies widely from state to state and locality to locality.

1–6

A legal encyclopedia is a multivolume compilation purporting to provide in-depth coverage of every area of the law. Restatements are drafted by distinguished panels of legal experts for the purpose of developing and encouraging a uniform approach to various areas of common law. A treatise is a scholarly study of one area of the law, differing from a restatement in that it is usually the work of one author or group of authors, rather than a panel of experts.

Texts are one-volume treatises. Law reviews are periodicals edited by law students. Looseleaf services and annotations include secondary discussions of legal topics, as well as texts of cases and statutes.

1–7

LEXIS and WESTLAW are computer-based legal research systems. A query is a string of key terms or words used in a computer search. Microfiche, microfilm, and CD/ROM are alternative research media with significant use and applications.

1–8

A good place to begin legal research is with a legal encyclopedia, followed by a search in the relevant statutory codes, digests, reporters, and secondary sources. When different research techniques and sources begin to turn up references to the same cases and statutes, that may be an indication that your research is complete.

REVIEW

Key Terms

Before proceeding, review the key terms listed below to be sure you understand each one. If necessary, read over the corresponding section of the chapter. When you are ready to test your understanding, answer the Review Questions.

precedential value
primary authority
mandatory authority
persuasive authority
secondary authority
reporters
citations
bluebook
parallel citations
official reporter
regional reporter
advance sheet
key number system
headnote
digest
descriptive word index
words & phrases
table of cases
defendant/plaintiff table
pocket parts
looseleaf service
annotations
Total Client-Service Library
slip opinion
shepardizing
slip laws
session laws
code
annotated code
legislative history
legal encyclopedia
Restatements
treatises
texts
hornbooks
nutshells
law reviews
LEXIS
WESTLAW
database
query
microfiche
microfilm
CD/ROM

Questions for Review and Discussion

1. What is a citation?
2. How do official reporters and private reporters differ?
3. What is the key number system?
4. What is a digest?
5. Describe the difference between slip laws, session laws, and codes.
6. What does "shepardizing" mean?
7. Where can the text of administrative regulations be found?
8. What is a legal encyclopedia? What is a treatise?
9. What is a query?
10. How should you begin a research project, and once you've begun, how do you know when to stop?

Activities

1. Find the case for 104 S.Ct. 615, 78 L. Ed. 2d 443 and answer the following questions:
   a) What is the name of the case?
   b) What date was the case decided?
   c) Which reporter contains headnotes with topics and keys?
2. Find the case of *Parker v. Twentieth Century-Fox Film Corp.* All you know is that the case originated in California.
   a) What is the citation of the case?
   b) What year was the case decided?
3. Determine whether your state law libraries have the following legal sources and identify the name of each book.
   a) State Case Reporter
   b) Regional Reporter
   c) State Digest
   d) State Encyclopedia
   e) State Statute
4. Locate the cases below and identify the name of the case and the year the case was decided.
   a) 398 N.E. 2d 148
   b) 164 A.2d 451
   c) 375 P.2d 246
   d) 97 S.Ct. 2549
   e) 676 F.2d 385
   f) 252 U.S. 416
   g) 597 S.W.2d 134
   h) 298 So.2d 97
   i) 281 N.W.2d 804
   j) 214 Cal. Rptr. 177

CHAPTER 2   The Case Brief

OUTLINE

COMMENTARY

Your supervising attorney has an upcoming court hearing. One of her part-ners has brought to her attention a relevant case, *Davis v. Gomez*, 207 Cal.App.3d 1401, 255 Cal.Rptr. 743 (Cal. Ct. App., 1989). You have been provided with a copy of the case (see Figure 2–2) and asked by your supervising attorney to highlight the important points for her review. She wants the complicated opin-ion crystallized into a straightforward summary.

Accomplishing this task requires the preparation of a "case brief." In the last chapter, you learned how to find the law. In this chapter, you will learn how to analyze it.

OBJECTIVES

In the pages that follow, you will learn how to summarize a single case into the concise format know as a case brief. After completing this chapter, you will be able to:

1. Distinguish between a case brief and a trial or appellate brief.
2. Describe the components of a printed opinion.
3. Explain the usefulness of star-paging.

4. Differentiate between a majority opinion and a dissent.
5. Describe the components of a case brief.
6. Identify the relevant facts in an opinion.
7. State the issues presented by a written opinion.
8. Trace the procedural history of a case as set forth in the opinion.
9. Identify the holding of the court and the disposition of the case.
10. Analyze and summarize the reasoning behind an opinion.

2–1 The Case Brief Distinguished

The word *brief* has two separate and distinct connotations in legal practice. First, it can refer to a document filed with a court to present the legal argument of one party in a lawsuit, citing as many cases, statutes, and other sources of law as are deemed necessary to support the argument. Such a brief is usually further identified by including the level of the court in which the brief is filed: if in the trial court, it is a *trial brief*; if an appellate court, it is an *appellate brief*. These briefs do not provide an objective discussion of the law, but rather a one-sided argument intended to persuade the court of the validity of the party's position. We discuss such briefs in some detail in later chapters.

The word *brief* also appears in the term *case brief*. A **case brief** is an objective summary of the important points of a single case. If properly prepared, it will provide the reader with a concise abstract of the reasoning of the opinion, as well as important collateral information such as case name, citation, and identity of the parties. The key word is *objective*—the case brief should accurately reflect the meaning of the case, whether that meaning is helpful to your client or harmful.

As you might have guessed, the case brief is not a document prepared for the eyes of the court, nor is it shared with opposing parties. It is an internal document, designed to help attorneys develop an objective understanding of the impact of existing case law on the viability of their client's position. Only when such an understanding is reached can persuasive strategies be developed.

In this chapter we address the components of a printed opinion, the components of a case brief, and some general comments on the meaning and use of a case brief.

2–2 The Components of a Printed Opinion

As you have learned, reporters are collections of printed opinions, or cases. A case brief is a summary of one of these cases. In order to understand the method of briefing a case, then, it is necessary to learn about the components of a printed opinion. You are already familiar with some of these components from the previous chapter.

Figure 2–1 on page 44 reprints a full page from volume 255 of the *California Reporter* (which, as you recall, is the West publication for additional California decisions beyond those already appearing in the *Pacific Reporter*). The page shown (page 743) is the first page of our subject case, *Davis v. Gomez*, and it contains a wealth of information.

Figure 2–1 From the *California Reporter*

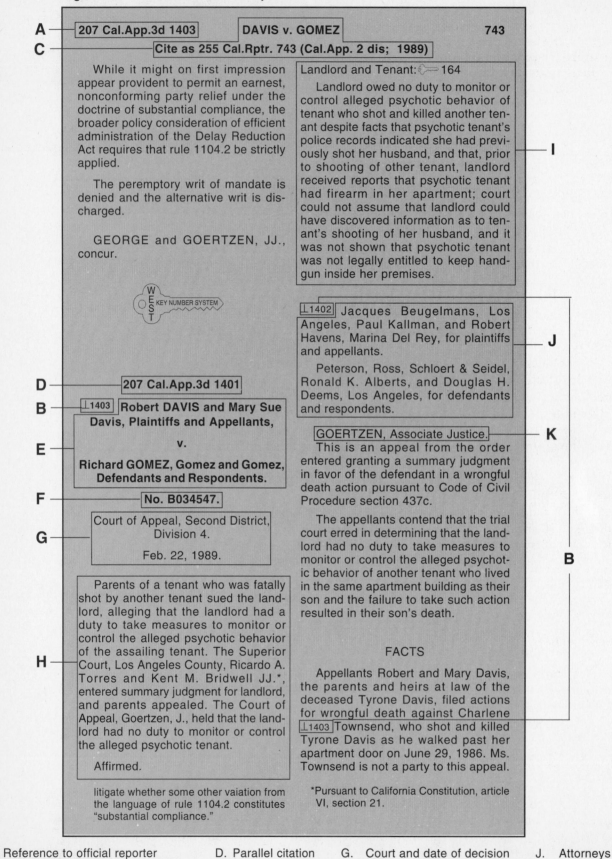

A. Reference to official reporter   D. Parallel citation   G. Court and date of decision   J. Attorneys
B. Star-paging notations   E. Full case name   H. Case synopsis   K. Judge
C. Short-form case name with citation   F. Docket number   I. Headnote

Let's start with the left side of the top line, identified as *A* in Figure 2–1. The notation "207 Cal. App. 3d 1403" is a reference to a page from the official reporter, the *California Appellate Reports*, where *Davis v. Gomez* also appears. Page 1403 is the last page from that reporter, which is reproduced here on page 743 of the *California Reporter*. Private reporters often provide information as to the pagination in the official reporter.

Star-Paging

Pagination as it appears in the official reporter is reflected in a private reporter through the use of **star-paging**. Star-paging is a practice that enables us to identify the page breaks in one reporter by reviewing the decision as reprinted in another reporter. The three star-paging notations identified as *B* in Figure 2–1 identify the page breaks for pages 1401, 1402, and 1403 as they appear in the *California Appellate Reports*. By utilizing these star-paging notations when writing a brief, the drafter can reference the page and volume of important language as it appears in both West's *California Reporter* and the official *California Appellate Reports*, even though she only has the *California Reporter* at hand. Star-paging is often (but not always) found in private reporters; it is never found in official reporters, and thus constitutes an additional reason why private reporters can be superior to official reporters as research tools.

Shorthand Case Name

We next turn to the section we have labeled *C* in Figure 2–1. This is the **shorthand** form of the case name, with an instruction as to the appropriate citation. These instructions do not always conform to the rules set down in the bluebook; where there is a discrepancy, you should follow the bluebook (for example, the reference to "2 Dist." goes beyond the bluebook requirements). In any event, this citation will appear on alternate pages.

Parallel Citation

The *D* label shows the correct **parallel citation** for the case in *California Appellate Reports*, "207 Cal.App.3d 1401." Just as a reminder, this means that the case begins on page 1401 of volume 207 of the third series of that reporter.

Full Name of Case

E is the full name of the case, identifying all the parties and their roles (i.e., plaintiff or defendant; appellant or respondent). The full name, together with the docket number, court, and date of the decision, is called the **caption** (labels *E*, *F*, and *G* combined).

Docket Number, Court, and Date

The *F* identifies the docket number of the case. A **docket number** is assigned by the court to the case for its own administrative purposes. If you visited the appropriate courthouse and asked to see the file for this case, you would need to provide the docket number so that they could locate it in their files.

The *G* label provides the full name of the court that rendered the opinion, and the date of rendering. In this case the Court of Appeal, Second District, Division 4 handed down its decision on February 22, 1989.

Synopsis

Item *H* is called the **synopsis** of the case. It is an extremely short summary, prepared not by the court but by the publisher. It identifies the issue, the procedural history, and the ruling of the court in the instant case ("instant" is used in legal documents to mean *present* or *current*; this instant case is *Davis v. Gomez*). The synopsis is in a sense a preview; since it is an unofficial editorial addition, it should never be formally cited, but only informally reviewed.

Sometimes a synopsis is prepared by the official reporter of decisions. Such an "official" synopsis is called a **syllabus**, as you learned in Chapter 1's discussion of *United States Reports* (where each U.S. Supreme Court case is given a syllabus). Although "official," a syllabus is not part of the court's opinion and, like the synopsis, should never be formally relied upon or cited.

West Key Number and Headnote

I identifies the West key number and headnote. Since this case has only one headnote, there is no need to number it or reference it elsewhere in the opinion; if there were more than one headnote, each would be numbered and referenced as in the example of *Great Western v. Easley* in Figure 1–3 from the last chapter.

Attorneys and Judge

J identifies the attorney for the parties; *K* identifies the judge who wrote the opinion of the court, Associate Justice Goertzen.

Text and Disposition

The name of the judge who wrote the opinion is followed by the text of his or her opinion. The text or body of the decision contains the detailed reasoning by which the court reached its result. That result, which appears at the end of the opinion and is often simply a word or two telling the reader who won the lawsuit, is called the court's **disposition**. (For full text and disposition, see Figure 2–2.)

The text of an opinion generally sets forth the facts of the case and the procedural history. It then analyzes the issues presented and, citing precedent and drawing upon applicable legal principles and logic, reaches a conclusion. The text is the heart of a case; it is from the text that analogies can be drawn to pending controversies.

In *Davis v. Gomez* the court quotes at considerable length from the trial court's original opinion on the summary judgment motion at issue. Indeed, the quotation from that opinion is longer than the appellate court's first contribution. Although references to an underlying opinion are often seen in the text of an appellate opinion, such extended quoting is not a common practice.

Figure 2–2 The Court's Disposition

207 Cal.App.3d 1403   DAVIS v. GOMEZ   **743**
Cite as 255 Cal.Rptr. 743 (Cal.App. 2 dist., 1989)

While it might on first impression appear provident to permit an earnest, nonconforming party relief under the doctrine of substantial compliance, the broader policy consideration of efficient administration of the Delay Reduction Act requires that rule 1104.2 be strictly applied.

The peremptory writ of mandate is denied and the alternative writ is discharged.

GEORGE and GOERTZEN, JJ., concur.

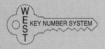

207 Cal.App.3d 1401

⊥1403 **Robert DAVIS and Mary Sue Davis, Plaintiffs and Appellants,**

v.

Richard GOMEZ, Gomez and Gomez, Defendants and Respondents.

No. B034547.

Court of Appeal, Second District, Division 4.

Feb. 22, 1989.

Parents of a tenant who was fatally shot by another tenant sued the landlord, alleging that the landlord had a duty to take measures to monitor or control the alleged psychotic behavior of the assailing tenant. The Superior Court, Los Angeles County, Ricardo A. Torres and Kent M. Bridwell JJ.*, entered summary judgment for landlord, and parents appealed. The Court of Appeal, Goertzen, J., held that the landlord had no duty to monitor or control the alleged psychotic tenant.

Affirmed.

litigate whether some other variation from the language of rule 1104.2 constitutes "substantial compliance."

Landlord and Tenant ⟜ 164

Landlord owed no duty to monitor or control alleged psychotic behavior of tenant who shot and killed another tenant despite facts that psychotic tenant's police records indicated she had previously shot her husband, and that, prior to shooting of other tenant, landlord received reports that psychotic tenant had firearm in her apartment; court could not assume that landlord could have discovered information as to tenant's shooting of her husband, and it was not shown that psychotic tenant was not legally entitled to keep handgun inside her premises.

———

⊥1402 Jacques Beugelmans, Los Angeles, Paul Kallman, and Robert Havens, Marina Del Rey, for plaintiffs and appellants.

Peterson, Ross, Schloert & Seidel, Ronald K. Alberts, and Douglas H. Deems, Los Angeles, for defendants and respondents.

GOERTZEN, Associate Justice.

This is an appeal from the order entered granting a summary judgment in favor of the defendant in a wrongful death action pursuant to Code of Civil Procedure section 437c.

The appellants contend that the trial court erred in determining that the landlord had no duty to take measures to monitor or control the alleged psychotic behavior of another tenant who lived in the same apartment building as their son and the failure to take such action resulted in their son's death.

FACTS

Appellants Robert and Mary Davis, the parents and heirs at law of the deceased Tyrone Davis, filed actions for wrongful death against Charlene ⊥1403 Townsend, who shot and killed Tyrone Davis as he walked past her apartment door on June 29, 1986. Ms. Townsend is not a party to this appeal.

*Pursuant to California Consitution, article VI, section 21.

Figure 2–2 Cont.

Appellants also named as defendants in the actions the partnership which owned the apartment building where the shooting took place, respondents Richard Gomez, Rudy Gomez and Maria Gomez.

Carl McGill was the manager of the respondent's apartment building and a City of Los Angeles Police Officer. He claimed that in early April, 1986, Ms. Townsend's mental condition began to "deteriorate." By May 1986, it was apparent that Ms. Townsend was "losing her mind."

Ms. Townsend never threatened him or anyone in Mr. McGill's presence. But Mr. McGill heard Ms. Townsend "grumbling off as if she was talking to somebody" in a loud voice while she was alone in her apartment.

Other tenants complained to Mr. McGill that they felt threatened by her actions. The other tenants began avoiding the area in front of her apartment. Gerald Lewis told Mr. McGill that he had seen a gun in Ms. Townsend's living room. Bernadette Gillette came to him several times and told him Ms. Townsend was talking to herself out loud and was in the front window of her apartment moving her hands as if she was casting spells on those who walked by.

Jim Ross, another policeman who resided in the building, told Mr. McGill about the spell-casting behavior and said he was "worried about everybody's safety . . . because of her behavior." He also had seen the gun in her living room.

Mr. McGill stated that about a month before the shooting he telephoned Robert Gomez and told him that Ms. Townsend was "acting very peculiar and a lot of people are scared to go past her window to get downstairs." Mr. McGill also repeated the reports of the presence of the gun. Mr. Gomez replied that he "would check into it."

Richard Gomez did not take any action on the complaint before Tyrone was shot. There was also other evidence that the Gomez defendants did not investigate Ms. Townsend's background or references before renting the apartment to her and after the above complaints were reported to them by Mr. McGill.

The trial court's memorandum of ruling on the motion for summary judgment stated in pertinent part:

"It is well-established that the landlord of residential property owes certain duties not only to tenants, but also ⊥1404 third-party guests and visitors. (*See Uccello v. Laudenslayer* (1975) 44 Cal.App.3d 504, 118 Cal.Rptr. 741.) Under certain circumstances, that duty may be absolute, imposing 'strict liability' on the landlord for dangerous conditions of the rented premises. (*See Becker v. IRM Corp.* (1985) 38 Cal.3d 454, 213 Cal.Rptr. 213, 698 P.2d 116.)

"Still, it is not enough to surmise that the landlord should have done 'something' in response to a given situation. Instead, it is essential to define that 'something' in fairly precise terms. Otherwise, the law would be requiring adherence to an unknown standard of conduct, recognized only with 20-20 hindsight.

"Preliminarily, this Court does not believe that any landlord should be expected to check the references or background of a prospective tenant for reasons other than to protect the landlord's *own* interest. Nor was it within the reasonable province of either Mr. McGill or his employers to diagnose Ms. Townsend as 'psychotic.' What, then, should these defendants have done, and in what way was their failure to so act a proximate cause of plaintiff's loss? (Emphasis in original.)

"Plaintiffs argue that the Gomez defendants had both the power and the opportunity to evict Ms. Townsend on the basis of her reported behavior. (*See Uccello v. Laudenslayer, supra*, 44 Cal.App.3d at pp. 512-513, 118 Cal.Rptr. 741.) Certainly, a landlord owes a duty to preserve the quiet enjoyment of all tenants. In extreme cases, eviction of a troublesome tenant may provide the only practical means to abate a nuisance which affects other tenants. Notably, those other tenants would not share the power of eviction, and would otherwise be limited to remedies of a less certain nature.

"Still, the evicted tenant also has rights, and a landlord had better be

Fig. 2–2 cont.

extremely careful and sure of his/her grounds before instituting eviction proceedings. Under circumstances of the present variety, the landlord is often caught in the middle of competing tenant interests, and stands at risk no matter what course of action is decided upon. It is usually a classic 'no win' situation. Yet, if it were reasonably foreseeable that an innocent tenant might be killed, the possibility of legal laction by the evicted tenant obviously becomes of subordinate concern.

"Although the reported conduct of Ms. Townsend was perhaps disquieting, and while 'casting spells' may be considered aggressive behavior of sorts, none of it involved any physical violence or real threat to cause bodily harm (depending, perhaps, on whether one believes in the occult virulence of 'spells'). Nor did her open possession of a firearm necessarily invite ⊥1405 speculation that she was actually disposed to use it indiscriminately against another tenant.

"Consequently, while her conduct might have represented a common nuisance, it does not follow that anyone should have foreseen the escalation of that behavior into a fatal shooting. The reality is that persons exhibiting similarly 'bizarre' behavior are to be seen on the streets of every metropolitan community. Fortunately, few are ever actually dangerous.

"Although the issue of foreseeability is usually for the trier-of-fact to determine, the facts presented here simply do not support a finding that the shooting of plaintiff's decedent was reasonably foreseeable from the unusual and bothersome, but otherwise innocuous behavior reported.

"Certainly, the failure of these defendants to eliminate a mere nuisance is not the same as their failing to prevent a serious criminal act. This case is therefore distinguishable from the situation where a landlord neglects to provide adequate lighting or security in a *known* high-crime area. The mere failure to evict a 'nuisance' tenant, while representing a breach of duty to other tenants, would not be the proximate cause of a fatal shooting. A separate duty, touching upon different interests,

would have to appear. (Emphasis in original.)

"Plaintiff Mary Sue Davis further suggests that the Gomez defendants should have requested a 72-hour psychiatric hold and observation. (See Welf. & Inst. Code, § 5000, et seq.) aside from the obvious legal repercussions of inducing the commencement of civil commitment proceedings (Welf. & Inst. Code, § 5150), the Court can discern no reason to impose this as the special duty of a landlord. Tenants are not so helpless that they must rely upon their landlord to pursue every alternative which is equally available (and equally risky) to all.

"Plaintiffs' most persuasive argument is that the Gomez defendants should at least have investigated further to determine whether Ms. Townsend posed a serious threat to the other tenants. They were certainly in a position to approach her and discuss the problem. Ostensibly, it might *then* have become reasonably foreseeable that Ms. Townsend was inclined toward actual violence. Yet, to assume that this failure to investigate was a proximate cause of the shooting represents a quantum leap in plaintiffs' logic. Clearly, investigation alone would at most have revealed the danger, although even that amounts to little more than speculation. It would not have alleviated the potential risk of harm. Something more would then have been required. Again, that 'something' is not easily defined. (Emphasis in original.)

⊥1406 "Based upon the facts presented, and resolving every conflict in favor of plaintiffs, this Court concludes as a matter-of-law that the Gomez defendants breached no legal duty that was a proximate cause of the tragic events which ultimately transpired. In reaching this decision, the Court draws upon much of the reasoning expressed in *Alva v. Cook* (1975) 49 Cal.App.3d 899, 123 Cal.Rptr. 166. Although that case involved somewhat different facts, and arose in a different procedural setting, the issues are remarkably similar."

DISCUSSION

Appellants' contention is dependent upon the assumption that Ms. Townsend was "brandishing and

Fig. 2–2 cont.

exhibiting a firearm for more than two months before Tyrone Davis' murder." We have reviewed the record and find no evidence whatsoever of the "brandishing and exhibiting" to which appellants refer.

As the trial court stated: "Plaintiff's most persuasive argument is that the Gomez defendants should at least have investigated further to determine whether Ms. Townsend posed a serious threat to the other tenants." We cannot assume, however, that the landlord could have discovered the information Mr. McGill belatedly obtained from another police officer after the fatal shooting, that Ms. Townsend's criminal records showed that she had shot her husband.

As was stated in *Leakes v. Shamoun* (1986) 187 Cal.App.3d 772, 776, 232 Cal.Rptr. 171, "an injured person must also show that the landlord had the right and ability to cure the condition. [Citations.]" The trial judge focused on this critical factor in granting the motion for summary judgment. We conclude that the trial court's decision was proper as a matter of law since appellants have also failed to establish what action the landlord could have taken, even with a reasonable investigation, with respect to Ms. Townsend's deteriorating mental condition. Nor have appellants shown that Ms. Townsend was not legally entitled to keep a handgun inside her premises. Other than the handgun's possession, Ms. Townsend had shown no dangerous tendencies. (See *Id.*, at p. 788, 232 Cal.Rptr. 171.)

The trial court carefully analyzed all the factors properly considered under *Rowland v. Christian* (1968) 69 Cal.2d 108, 113, 70 Cal.Rptr. 97, 443 P.2d 561. It determined, as a matter of law, that there was no duty owed by the landlord to the tenant. There is no error.

⊥1407 THE JUDGMENT IS AFFIRMED.

ARLEIGH M. WOODS, P.J., and GEORGE, J., concur.

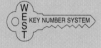

Turning to the end of the opinion, you will see the disposition. The decision of the lower court was **affirmed**, meaning that the appellate court agreed with the trial court. If the appellate court had disagreed, the decision of the lower court would have been **reversed**. Sometimes an appellate court agrees with some parts of an appealed decision but disagrees with other parts, resulting in a disposition in which the decision is "affirmed in part and reversed in part." Sometimes the disposition requires that the case be sent back to the lower court for further consideration, as would have been the case if the appellate court had reversed the trial court in *Davis v. Gomez*. Such decision has been reversed and **remanded**.

Sometimes an appellate court simply voids the decision of the lower court. The disposition under these circumstances uses the term **vacated**.

Most appellate cases are decided by a panel of several judges. If all the judges agree on the correct disposition of the case, the decision is rendered *per curiam*. Occasionally the judges on the panel disagree about the proper disposition. In such a case the majority rules, hence the majority judges issue the binding decision of the court, written as a **majority opinion**. A judge who agrees with the majority opinion is said to **concur**. A judge who agrees with the ultimate result but wishes to apply different reasoning from that in the majority opinion can file a **concurring opinion**, which sets forth the alternative reasoning (in *Davis v. Gomez*, Justice Woods and Justice George concurred; since they wrote no separate opinion, they presumably agreed with the reasoning of Justice Goertzen's opinion).

If a judge disagrees with the result reached by the majority, he or she is said to **dissent**. An opinion outlining the reasons for the dissent often critiques the majority and concurring opinions, and is known as a **dissenting opinion**.

It is possible that an individual judge agrees with part of the majority decision and disagrees with part. He or she is then said to "concur in part and dissent in part," and this judge, too, can set forth his or her reasoning in a separate opinion.

Some decisions, particularly those of the U.S. Supreme Court, may have several written opinions with various coalitions of judges concurring and dissenting on different points. It sometimes requires a fair amount of analysis to unravel the meaning of the court's disposition in such a case. In any event, a written opinion always identifies which judges concurred and which dissented.

Although most of this analysis relates to appellate opinions, trial court opinion can also be published in reporters. If a trial court opinion relates to a decision on a pending motion, the disposition will either **grant** or **deny** the motion. If the opinion is a final decision after trial, the disposition will indicate that judgment was entered for either plaintiff or defendant.

In analyzing the disposition and the text, you should keep in mind the concepts of **holding** and *dictum* (plural *dicta*). The court's holding is that aspect of the decision which directly affects the outcome of the case; it is composed of the reasoning necessary and sufficient to reach the disposition. *Dicta*, on the other hand, are statements made by the court that are beyond what is necessary to reach the disposition. For example, if a court suggests that a different result might have been reached if certain facts had been different, such a statement is *dictum* (as you read *Davis v. Gomez*, you will see an example of *dictum*). The difference between holding and *dictum* is important: a holding carries the precedential force of *stare decisis*, whereas *dictum* serves as a nonbinding guidance to future courts.

2–3 The Components of a Case Brief

Rather than simply recite and define the components of a case brief, in this section we take you step-by-step through the preparation of a comprehensive case brief for *Davis v. Gomez* (the finished product appears as Figure 2–3 at the end of this section).

Reading the Case

You cannot brief a case until you understand it, and you cannot understand it until you read it. Furthermore, when you read it, you should read the entire case, from start to finish. This might seem obvious, and indeed it should be, but it is a basic rule too often honored in the breach. Resist the temptation to skim, to rely on the editor's synopsis, to rely on the headnotes, or to search for the disposition without reading the court's underlying reasoning. There are problems ahead for those who think that they don't have the time to read the whole case or can get everything they need from the first and last page. Indeed, as we discuss, in *Davis v. Gomez* you will see excellent examples of the sorts of peculiarities a close reading can reveal.

Remember also that one reading is rarely enough for anyone, and certainly not enough for a beginning paralegal. At a minimum, you should read the case once to develop a general understanding of the obvious points and a second time to pick out the more subtle points. You should probably read it a third time to verify the points you found in the first two readings, then constantly refer back for specifics as you prepare your case brief. Before proceeding with this chapter, read *Davis v. Gomez* with care.

Identification of the Case

The first component of a case brief is, of course, to identify the case. This is done in our case brief both at the top of the page and in the citation section:

Case Brief — Davis v. Gomez

Citation:
Davis v. Gomez, 207 Cal.App.3d 1401, 255 Cal.Rptr. 743
(Cal.Ct.App., 1989)

Parties

The parties section of our case brief will reveal the peculiarities we referred to earlier. It is not entirely clear from this decision just who the parties are:

Parties:
Robert Davis (plaintiff/appellant); Mary Sue Davis (plaintiff/appellant); Charlene Townsend (defendant); Robert Gomez (defendant/respondent); Gomez and Gomez (defendant/respondent). [Note: The identity of the respondents is not entirely clear. The caption of the case identifies only the two defendants listed here, Richard Gomez individually, and some entity named "Gomez and Gomez." The opinion refers to a "partnership," presumably "Gomez and Gomez," but identifies three individuals (Richard Gomez, Rudy Gomez, and Maria Gomez) as "respondents." There is also a reference to a "Robert" Gomez at page 744. It will be assumed herein that the "Gomez defendants," regardless of their individual identity, and regardless of the nature of their partnership, were all co-owners. The confusion does not appear to have an impact on the decision of the court.]

The identities of the plaintiffs are clear. Both in the caption of the case and in the text, the plaintiffs are identified as the parents of the decedent (*decedent* is a legal term referring to a deceased person, in this case Tyrone Davis, the tenant who was killed), Robert Davis and Mary Sue Davis. It is also clear that these two plaintiffs are also the appellants.

It is not clear, however, exactly who are defendants. First look at the caption of the case. It would seem from the caption that there are two defendants—Richard Gomez and some entity called "Gomez and Gomez." Then, in the first paragraph on page 744 of the decision, the court refers to the defendant "partnership," which one might assume to be "Gomez and Gomez." But in the same sentence the court seems to equate the concept of "partnership" with individual "respondents" Richard Gomez, Rudy Gomez, and Maria Gomez. Suing a partnership is procedurally different from suing the partners themselves as individuals, but the court seems to skirt and confuse this distinction. Finally, to make matters even more confusing, further down in the same column on page 744 the court makes a reference to a "Robert" Gomez, although from the context it appears it should read "Richard" Gomez, since the very next paragraph indicates that "Richard Gomez did not take any action on the complaint before Tyrone was shot."

As it turns out, these discrepancies do not have any impact on the court's decision. Nevertheless, two lessons should be taken. First, as we emphasize at great length in later chapters, it is extremely important to express yourself clearly in every legal document you draft. The ambiguity in this decision could have been eliminated had the court used more care in draftsmanship. Second, you have to read with great attention to detail. A discrepancy like this can give you an opening to distinguish a case cited by your opponent; conversely, it could be used by your opponent to discredit a case cited by you. You must analyze opinions with great care.

In any event, since the discrepancies did not affect the court's decision, the case brief deals with the problem by identifying the "Gomez defendants" as a group. Incidentally, the "Gomez defendants" are also the respondents; that is to say, they are responding to the appeal brought by the plaintiff-appellants.

As to defendant Charlene Townsend, there is no indication of the lower court's action with regard to the claims brought by plaintiffs against her, nor is she a party to the appeal. This information is duly noted in the case brief.

Issues

The **issues** in the appeal are those points on which the appeal was based. Our case brief identifies them as follows:

> *Issues:*
> 1. Under California law, does the landlord of a multiple-unit dwelling owe a duty to the tenants therein to monitor or control the alleged psychotic behavior of a fellow tenant in the same building, or to warn the other tenants of dangers associated with such alleged psychotic behavior?
> 2. To the extent such duty exists, was it breached in this case?

The derivation of these issues is straightforward. The plaintiffs assert that the trial court was wrong in finding, as a matter of law, that the Gomez defendants had breached no duty by failing to protect their son from the attack of the allegedly psychotic Charlene Townsend. The court must address and decide this issue. The concept of making a finding "as a matter of law" will be discussed further in our analysis of the case brief's section on prior proceedings.

One quick and easy method of drafting the issues section is to determine the holding, then turn the holding into a question. This method is not recommended, however, because it requires working backwards.

Facts

The **facts** that should be included in a case brief are those which are necessary to gain a full and accurate understanding of the impact of the court's decision. Our case brief reads as follows:

> *Facts:*
> On June 29, 1986, Tyrone Davis, a tenant in a building owned by the Gomez defendants, was shot and killed by a fellow tenant in the same building, Charlene Townsend.
>
> Prior to the shooting, Townsend had been exhibiting symptoms of allegedly psychotic behavior, of which the Gomez defendants were aware. In addition, Townsend possessed a gun, of which the Gomez defendants were also aware.
>
> The Gomez defendants took no action with regard to the Townsend situation prior to the incident in which she shot and killed Davis.
>
> Plaintiff Robert Davis and plaintiff Mary Sue Davis are the parents of the deceased Tyrone Davis.

The key facts in this decision are the awareness on the part of the Gomez defendants of Townsend's condition, their failure to investigate further, and their failure to take any action. The failure to investigate ultimately becomes significant because the decision seems to hint that, if investigation had been made and other facts (such as Townsend's criminal record, revealing that she had shot her husband) had come to the knowledge of the Gomez defendants, a duty to intervene might have arisen based on their expanded knowledge of potential dangers.

Other facts are less important. It is not necessary, for example, that the reader know that the name of the manager of the apartment building was Carl McGill, nor that at least two residents of the building were police officers. Thus these facts are absent from our case brief.

Important facts affecting the decision of the court are considered to be **relevant** and **material**. If a fact is unimportant, it is considered immaterial; if unnecessary to understand the court's decision, it is considered irrelevant. The concepts of relevancy and materiality are not entirely distinct; there is a certain amount of overlap in meaning and usage.

Prior Proceedings

In order to understand the meaning of an opinion, the reader must first understand the procedural history of the case. Often the procedural setting is a crucial consideration in evaluating the extent to which the opinion can be applied to your client's case. The **prior proceedings** section of our case brief for Davis v. Gomez reads as follows:

> *Prior proceedings:*
> Plaintiffs filed an action for wrongful death against Charlene Townsend, and also against the Gomez defendants as owners of the building. Summary judgment was granted in favor of the Gomez defendants in the Superior Court, Los Angeles County. Plaintiffs appealed the granting of summary judgment. There is no indication in this decision as to the disposition with regard to defendant Charlene Townsend; she is not a party to this appeal.

Thus the plaintiffs originally brought suit against both Charlene Townsend and the Gomez defendants. The Gomez defendant filed a motion for summary judgment, which is a document seeking to demonstrate that there are not material factual disputes to be decided, and that based on the facts as they are known they are entitled to judgment "as a matter of law" (the phrase *as a matter of law* is used in the context of summary judgment motions or other situations in which facts are not in dispute, indicating that there is no need to make further inquiry into the facts, and that since the facts have been established, one side is entitled to prevail under existing law). The trial court agreed and granted the motion. The plaintiffs appealed.

As for Charlene Townsend, there is no indication regarding disposition of the claims against her. It is possible that they were still pending in the trial court at the time this opinion was rendered, but there is no way to tell from the text of this opinion.

Holding

The holding of a case is, of course, the most important element. The holding establishes the precedent—the rule of law in the case. The holding section of our case brief reads as follows:

> *Holding:*
> Under the circumstances present in this case, the failure of the landlord to take action with regard to tenant Townsend's allegedly psychotic behavior was NOT a proximate cause of the shooting death of tenant Davis.

The wording of this section must be precise. You must carefully read the case and extract the meaning of the court's ruling, being careful neither to overextend nor underestimate the scope.

Let's look more closely at the language we've chosen, so that you can get a sense of the necessary precision. The first phrase, "Under the circumstances present in this case," should set off an alarm in the reader. By drawing attention to the specific circumstances present, the drafter of the case brief has tipped off the reader that the court has rendered a decision in which the facts were taken into consideration in reaching its result. In other words, given a different factual setting, the application of the same general legal principle might nevertheless result in a different holding. For example, in *Davis v. Gomez*, if the Gomez defendants had begun an investigation and discovered that Townsend had shot her husband in the past, a duty to take action to protect the other tenants might have arisen.

What does it mean when a court qualifies its decision by limiting it to the specific facts of the case before it? It means that future parties who seek to use the case to support their argument must show how the facts of their case are analogous. It also presents an opportunity for a party seeking to discredit the precedential value of the case to distinguish it based upon the facts.

The wording of the next portion of our holding section is important as well. It indicates that the "failure to take action" was "NOT the proximate cause" of the shooting (*proximate cause* means one that foreseeably resulted in the ultimate effect; it is a concept used in tort law to determine liability).

Again, you must be careful. Look back at the issues section. The question we asked was whether the landlord "owe[d] a duty to the tenants" to control the psychotic tenant, or to warn the tenants of the danger. The landlord won the case; why then can't we simply say that the court held that landlords have no duty to take action or warn?

We can't, because that's not the holding. The court held that given the facts present *here*, the landlord had no duty. So we know that under at least one set of circumstances (namely, those present in this case) no duty was found. But it is entirely possible that under another set of circumstances a duty to take action or warn could arise. The court clearly left open that possibility. So if our case brief read, "The court held that a landlord has no duty to take action against, or warn tenants about, a psychotic tenant," it would be inaccurate. The court simply held that, under the circumstances present in *Davis v. Gomez*, no such duty had arisen.

Reasoning

In the **reasoning** section of our case brief, we analyze the rationale behind the court's holding:

> *Reasoning:*
> The trial court found that, though a landlord has a "duty to preserve the quiet enjoyment of all tenants," and though the behavior of tenant Townsend might have represented a "common nuisance" which the landlord has some duty to abate, "it does not follow that anyone should have foreseen the escalation of that behavior into a fatal shooting." Therefore, as a matter of law, the court held that the landlord's failure to take action was NOT the proximate cause of the decedent's death.
>
> The appellate court adopted the reasoning of the trial court. It also pointed out that there was no evidence to support the contention that Townsend had been "brandishing and exhibiting" the gun, nor did plaintiffs establish what action the landlord allegedly "could have taken, even with a reasonable investigation, with respect to Ms. Townsend's deteriorating mental condition."
>
> There is *dictum* which indicates that if an investigation had been conducted by the Gomez defendants and had revealed reason to believe that tenant Townsend was dangerous, a duty to warn or take other action might have arisen.

The first paragraph clarifies the scope of the trial court's holding, which found that although the landlord does have certain duties with regard to a tenant's "quiet enjoyment" of the premises, including a duty to abate (lessen or do away with) a "common nuisance," the landlord's failure to take action under the circumstances present in this case was not a violation of any alleged duty to protect the safety of the decedent, and hence not the proximate cause of the accident "as a matter of law." This passage, then, explains why the trial court, in its holding, did not simply assert the absence of a duty as the reason the landlord won the case. There are duties owed by a landlord to a tenant, but there is no violation of such a duty that can be pointed to by plaintiffs as the proximate cause of the death of Tyrone Davis.

The second paragraph of the reasoning section analyzes the appellate court's rationale. It first points out that the appellate court adopted the trial court's reasoning. It then notes that the appellate court also relied, in reaching its conclusion, upon plaintiffs' lack of evidentiary support for one of their key contentions (that Townsend had been "brandishing and exhibiting the gun") as well as the inability of plaintiffs to identify steps that the landlord could or should have taken to avoid the shooting.

The final paragraph further clarifies the circumstances that the appellate court suggests might have caused a duty to arise on the part of the Gomez defendants. The court concluded that, had the Gomez defendants investigated the situation and found reason to believe that tenant Townsend was dangerous, a duty to warn other tenants might have arisen. However, since such an investigation did not take place, this conclusion is not part of the court's holding but merely *dictum*.

Disposition

The purpose of the disposition section of the case brief is to alert the reader to the outcome of the case. The key to drafting it is to be concise. In *Davis v. Gomez*, where the appellate court found that the trial court was correct in granting summary judgment in favor of the Gomez defendants, the disposition can be relayed in one word: "Affirmed." For a more complex disposition, it might be necessary to expand this section.

2–4 Practical Considerations

There you have it—a complete and concise case brief for *Davis v. Gomez*. Having followed the step-by-step logic behind that case brief, you have now gained the raw skills necessary to unravel the law that lurks within the thousands, indeed millions, of opinions that fill every law library.

Of course, you will need much practice to refine those skills, and you will learn much about the law along the way. Some things that you learn will surprise you—such as the fact that not all judges write with clarity. You will also learn that opinions are written assuming that readers are trained to understand legal concepts and decipher legalese. You must be prepared to overcome these obstacles. Keep your legal dictionary at hand, learn as much as you can about the substantive law, learn where to find the answers to questions that arise, persevere until you understand the problem at hand, and don't be afraid to ask for help.

As you gain experience in case briefing, you will develop your own techniques, or learn techniques preferred by your supervising attorney. For example, in order to conserve space, some firms prefer case briefs that identify the litigants (parties to a lawsuit) as *P* and *D* rather than as plaintiff and defendant, or sometimes by the Greek letters π (pi) for plaintiff and Δ (delta) for defendant. Another shorthand notation is the letter *K* for contract. No one technique is preferable; but whatever format or style you choose, remember that your brief must be thorough, accurate, and understandable to those who need to read and rely upon it.

Finally, in preparing a case brief you should always keep in mind the goal of the attorney for whom you are working. For some cases an extensive and detailed analysis will be necessary; for other cases, little more will be needed than a brief statement of the facts and holding. Some case briefs are thus long and formalized; others short. You and your supervising attorney are a team, and to function well as a team you must coordinate your goals.

These first two chapters have provided you with an introduction to the American legal system, the challenge of legal research, and basic case analysis. Now it's time to turn to the task of legal writing.

Figure 2–3 Case Brief

Case Brief – Davis v. Gomez

Citation:
Davis v. Gomez, 207 Cal.App.3d 1401, 255 Cal.Rptr. 743 (Cal.Ct.App., 1989)

Parties:
Robert Davis (plaintiff/appellant); Mary Sue Davis (plaintiff/appellant); Charlene Townsend (defendant); Robert Gomez (defendant/respondent); Gomez and Gomez (defendant/respondent). [Note: The identity of the respondents is not entirely clear. The caption of the case identifies only the two defendants listed here, Richard Gomez individually, and some entity named "Gomez and Gomez." The opinion refers to a "partnership," presumably "Gomez and Gomez," but identifies three individuals (Richard Gomez, Rudy Gomez, and Maria Gomez) as "respondents." There is also a reference to a "Robert" Gomez at page 744. It will be assumed herein that the "Gomez defendants," regardless of their individual identity, and regardless of the nature of their partnership, were all co-owners. The confusion does not appear to have an impact on the decision of the court.]

Issues:
1. Under California law, does the landlord of a multiple-unit dwelling owe a duty to the tenants therein to monitor or control the alleged psychotic behavior of a fellow tenant in the same building, or to warn the other tenants of dangers associated with such alleged psychotic behavior?
2. To the extent such duty exists, was it breached in this case?

Facts:
On June 29, 1986, Tyrone Davis, a tenant in a building owned by the Gomez defendants, was shot and killed by a fellow tenant in the same building, Charlene Townsend.
   Prior to the shooting, Townsend had been exhibiting symptoms of allegedly psychotic behavior, of which the Gomez defendants were aware. In addition, Townsend possessed a gun, of which the Gomez defendants were also aware.
   The Gomez defendants took no action with regard to the Townsend situation prior to the incident in which she shot and killed Davis.
   Plaintiff Robert Davis and plaintiff Mary Sue Davis are the parents of the deceased Tyrone Davis.

Prior Proceedings:
Plaintiffs filed an action for wrongful death against Charlene Townsend, and also against the Gomez defendants as owners of the building. Summary judgment was granted in favor of the Gomez defendants in the Superior Court, Los Angeles County. Plaintiffs appealed the granting of summary judgment. There is no indication in this decision as to the disposition with regard to defendant Charlene Townsend; she is not a a party to this appeal.

Holding:
Under the circumstances present in this case, the failure of the landlord to take action with regard to tenant Townsend's allegedly psychotic behavior was NOT a proximate cause of the shooting death of tenant Davis.

Reasoning:
The trial court found that, though a landlord has a "duty to preserve the quiet enjoyment of all tenants," and though the behavior of tenant Townsend might have represented a "common nuisance" which the landlord had some duty to abate, "it does not follow that anyone should have foreseen the escalation of that behavior into a fatal shooting." Therefore, as a matter of law, the court held that the landlord's failure to take action was NOT the proximate cause of the decedent's death.
   The appellate court adopted the reasoning of the trial court. It also pointed out that there was no evidence to support the contention that Townsend had been "brandishing and exhibiting" the gun, nor did plaintiffs establish what action the landlord allegedly "could have taken, even with a reasonable investigation, with respect to Ms. Townsend's deteriorating mental condition."
   There is *dictum* which indicates that if an investigation had been conducted by the Gomez defendants and had revealed reason to believe that tenant Townsend was dangerous, a duty to warn or take other action might have arisen.

Disposition:
Affirmed.

SUMMARY

2–1

A case brief is an objective summary of the important points of a case. This is different from a trial brief or appellate brief, each of which is drafted not to be objective, but rather to persuade.

2–2

The typical printed opinion appearing in a reporter contains several characteristic components. Star-paging enables the reader to identify page references from other reporters. The shorthand case name identifies the case at the top of the page. The parallel citation provides references to other reporters in which the case text appears. The full name of the case identifies all the parties and their position in the litigation (for example, plaintiff or defendant). The docket number is assigned to the case by the court for administrative purposes, and is usually included along with the date the decision was rendered and the full name of the court. The synopsis is an extremely short summary of the case prepared not by the court, but by the publisher of the reporter. A syllabus is a summary prepared by the court. Key numbers and headnotes are included, as well as the attorneys and judges involved in the matter and, of course, the text and disposition of the case. Decisions can be affirmed or reversed or subject to some other disposition. There can be majority opinions, dissenting opinions, and concurring opinions. The holding of a court is that aspect of the decision which directly affects the outcome of the case; *dictum* is a statement made by the court that goes beyond what is necessary to reach the disposition.

2–3

When preparing a case brief, you must first read the relevant case, then follow several steps to produce a document with several components. First, identify the case. Second, describe the parties. Third, identify the issues that were before the court for decision. Fourth, set out the relevant facts. Fifth, trace the procedural history of the case. Sixth, identify the holding of the court, taking great care to reflect accurately the precise parameters of the court's decision. Seventh, analyze the court's reasoning, again taking great care to restate and summarize the court's rationale. Eighth, alert the reader to the outcome of the case with a concise, shorthand statement of the court's disposition.

2–4

In drafting case briefs, you must overcome obstacles such as poorly drafted or highly technical judicial opinions. Over time you will develop your own style or learn the characteristic style preferred by your firm. Alway keep in mind the goal that you and your supervising attorney are attempting to accomplish with the drafting of the case brief. This goal will influence length, formality, and general content.

REVIEW

Key Terms

Before proceeding, review the key terms listed below to be sure you understand each one. If necessary, read over the corresponding section of the chapter. When you are ready to test your understanding, answer the Review Questions.

case brief
star-paging
shorthand case name
parallel citation
caption
docket number
synopsis
syllabus
disposition
affirmed
reversed
remanded

vacated
per curiam
majority opinion
concur
concurring opinion
dissent
dissenting opinion
grant
deny
holding
dictum
issues
facts
relevant
material
prior proceedings
reasoning

Questions for Review and Discussion

1. What is the difference between a case brief and a brief written for a trial or appellate court?
2. What are the components of a printed opinion?
3. Why is star-paging useful?
4. What is the difference between a majority opinion and a dissent?
5. What are the components of a case brief?
6. How do you identify the relevant facts in an opinion?
7. How do you identify the issues presented by a written opinion?
8. How do you locate the procedural history of a case as set forth in the opinion?
9. What is a holding? What is a disposition?
10. What is the reasoning of an opinion?

Activities

1. Read *Tarasoff v. Regents of the University of California*, 551 P.2d 334 (California 1976) and *Thompson v. County of Alameda*, 614 P.2d 728 (California 1980) and answer the following questions:
   a) What is the holding in Tarasoff? In Thompson?
   b) Are the results different? If so, list the reasoning of each court for reaching its decision.
   c) Can these cases be reconciled?
2. In your law library, find *Trump v. Chicago Tribune*, 616 F.Supp. 1434 (S.D. N.Y. 1985) and answer the following questions:
   a) Name the parties to the case.
   b) Identify the court and the case reporter.
   c) List the West topics and keys in the case.
   d) Identify the objectives of the parties.
   e) List the prior proceedings.

CHAPTER 3   Introduction to Legal Writing

OUTLINE

COMMENTARY

On Monday morning you receive a telephone call from a friend who is buying a new car. The language of the contracts, credit agreements, warranties, and disclaimers has left him in a panic—it's too complicated to understand! He wants to make an appointment to have you review and explain the various provisions.

Your supervising attorney suggests you obtain copies of the contracts, then draft a letter to your friend explaining them in everyday language. Simplifying complicated legal documents is a task you will perform as a paralegal.

OBJECTIVES

Up to this point, you've been learning background information and valuable research skills. Now you're ready for an introduction to legal writing. After completing this chapter, you will be able to:

1. Define "legalese."
2. Describe a "term of art."
3. List basic techniques for good legal writing.
4. Identify the audience for a legal document.

5. Describe the difference between an "objective" purpose and an "adversarial" purpose.
6. Apply the "IRAC" method for defining and researching a legal issue.
7. Balance time constraints.
8. Organize a legal document.
9. List several different types of legal documents.
10. Identify two different types of pleadings.

3–1 Tradition and Trend in Legal Writing

Most people have the same reaction as the friend in our Commentary to legal documents—panic. They consider legal writing to be complicated, cumbersome, and incomprehensible. Although some legal writers do, in fact, allow their writing to deteriorate, most are reasonably competent. Why, then, is the image of legal writing so negative?

One answer, oddly enough, is the importance of precision. As with all writing, good legal writing requires **clarity**, *conciseness*, *accuracy*, and *simplicity*—but above all else, it must be **precise**. It is essential that every person interpreting a document take the same meaning from the words chosen. This leads to an unwritten rule of law—namely, that once a given usage is agreed to have a given meaning, it should ever after be the accepted method of conveying that meaning. Any change from that usage necessarily implies that an alteration of that meaning is intended.

This unwritten rule has led to a reliance on archaic legal language. Terms that originated hundreds of years ago and which sound odd in the context of our modern language are still used in legal documents because their meaning is accepted. Legal **jargon**, often referred to as **legalese**, is characterized by the frequent use of Latin, French, and Old English terms unfamiliar to most present-day vocabularies. You have already seen such Latin terms as *in re* and *ex parte* as they are used in case names (*ex parte* also has another meaning, as we will note). Other terms commonly used include *res ipsa loquitor* (a Latin term from tort law meaning "the thing speaks for itself"), *voir dire* (a French term for the questioning of a potential juror for evidence of prejudice or unfitness), and *writ* (an Old English term for an order of a court, or the first written notice of a lawsuit). These are just a sampling. Other examples of legalese are listed in Table 3–1, but a complete list would be enormous.

Legalese is also characterized by usages rarely seen elsewhere. Such phrases as, "Hereof fail not but by these presents make due and proper return," or "Comes now James Jones, Plaintiff in the above-styled and numbered cause, who does by these presents make due complaint," are examples of archaic sentence structure seen in legal documents. Such words as *aforementioned* or *hereinafter*, seldom used in everyday language, clutter legal sentences. These practices are often a holdover from centuries of Anglo-Saxon jurisprudence.

Wordiness is another characteristic of legalese. Lawyers often use a phrase with a combination of synonymous, hence redundant, words. Such phrases as *cease and desist*, *null and void*, and *give, devise and bequeath* date back to a time when two or three similar words were used to ensure clarity. Documents had to interpreted correctly by people of different nationalities, in an era when language lacked the consistency of modern times. Although historically there may have been distinctions between the words used, current legal practice has for the most part erased them and rendered such phrases redundant.

Tradition has been a powerful force in the law, as you might expect from a system in which the concepts of precedent and *stare decisis* play so important

Table 3–1 Examples of Legalese

The following table provides examples of legal jargon with the corresponding definitions in plain English. One of the challenges of legal writing is to exercise good judgment in deciding whether to employ legal terminology (which may have value for its precision or its standing as a term of art) or plain English.

Legalese	Translation
a fortiori	for a stronger reason
certiorari	discretionary request to the U.S. Supreme Court or other appellate court for review of a case
demurrer	request by defendant for a dismissal of a cause of action
duces tecum	to bring with you; a form of writ or request
ex parte	1. concerning the application of; 2. independent contact with an official, usually the judge, without the presence of the opposing side
inter alia	among other things
laches	principle of equity in which the passage of time prohibits pursuit of a cause of action
remittitur	judicial review and revision of an excessive judgment
res ipsa loquitor	the thing speaks for itself; in tort law, a doctrine that allows a finding of negligence without proof thereof
sua sponte	by the judge's own motion
tort	civil wrongdoing to another person
voir dire	to speak the truth; in practice refers to the examination of prospective jurors
writ	an order of the court, or the first pleading filed in a lawsuit

a role. Things are done a certain way because that is how they have always been done; certain language is used because it has always been used. Thus, not only for the reason of precision, but also because of institutional custom and perhaps even out of sentiment, the legal profession has clung to traditional language at the expense of broader understanding. Therefore language that is clear to a trained lawyer or paralegal is unclear to the average citizen, leading to the negative image of "legalese."

More often than not, legalese is used from habit rather than necessity. The objective of precision can be better achieved by rigorous and exacting use of modern language than by reliance on anachronistic formulas. As Richard Wydick observes in his book *Plain English for Lawyers* (Durham, NC: Carolina Academic Press, 1985):

> [W]e use eight words to say what could be said in two. We use arcane phrases to express commonplace ideas. Seeking to be precise, we become redundant. Seeking to explain, we become verbose. Our sentences twist on, phrase within clause within clause, glazing the eyes and numbing the minds of our readers.

The modern trend in legal writing is to emphasize broader comprehensibility. Whenever possible, **plain English** should be used. Long, complicated sentences should be the exception, not the rule. Archaic terms and phrases should be replaced by equivalent modern language. When one word is sufficient, avoid redundant combinations.

Of course, the survival of some legalese is inevitable, and even justifiable. Just as it is easier for doctors to use certain medical terminology, so it is easier for lawyers to use certain shorthand **terms of art** despite their obscurity to the general public. For example, the concise term *voir dire* mentioned previously requires a lengthy explanation in plain English, as does the alternate meaning of *ex parte* (contact with an official of the court in the absence of the opposing party). You must, however, use good judgment when evaluating the desirability of using legalese, and more often than not, there is a better alternative in plain English.

Legal writing needs to be demystified. Many people are under the impression that legal documents must be complicated, and that quality is related to complexity. This is simply not so. Indeed, the best expression of an idea is often the simplest composition that accurately conveys the intended meaning. The use of archaic legal terms and phrases should be minimized and plain English used instead. In the next few chapters we focus on techniques that:

- employ short, succinct sentences;
- minimize legalese;
- avoid redundancy;
- emphasize simple language in simple form (subject-verb-object) using accepted rules of grammar; and
- remind us that writing is reading—and good writing will only develop when we reread what we have written.

3–2 Prewriting Considerations

Now you know why legal language often causes people to panic. You know that eliminating excess legalese can help to reduce that panic. You have learned that some legalese remains useful. You have also learned that certain rules which apply to all forms of writing, such as the superiority of short sentences and simple words, apply to legal writing as well. Before you refine your knowledge of legal writing techniques, however, you must address four preliminary considerations: identifying your **audience**; identifying your purpose; defining and researching the issues presented; and evaluating time constraints.

Identifying the Audience

Lawyers prepare a wide range of writings for a diverse group of recipients. Some will be read by highly trained judges; others by less sophisticated clients. Before beginning a writing task, a lawyer or paralegal must determine:

- to whom the document is directed;
- the level of legal expertise of that person or persons; and
- the degree of that person or persons' familiarity with the subject.

There may be particular problems in a given situation, for example, language barriers or physical or mental disability. As a paralegal, you have to learn how to overcome potential obstacles.

Don't make assumptions when determining the audience. For example, you might think that the audience for a demand letter is easy to identify: the person upon whom your client is making demand, or in other words, the person to whom the letter is addressed. Such an assumption could lead to a critical error if your demand letter must meet statutory requirements in order to be effective. Consider a demand letter to be sent to a physician accused of malpractice. There may be a statute that outlines specific requirements for you to put the physician "on notice" of the claim. In such a case, the demand letter is drafted for two audiences—the physician who is being notified, of course, and, equally important, the court that may eventually have to determine whether the requirements have been met. The court will not appear in the salutation, nor even, quite possibly, in the letter itself—yet the judge who may someday evaluate the letter is a crucial segment of the audience who must be considered.

Identifying the Purpose

In order to draft any effective writing, you must identify your purpose. Do you want to update a client on the status of a lawsuit? Do you want to convince a court that your client's position should prevail in a pending motion? Are you summarizing a deposition transcript? Depending on your purpose, your approach to the task will differ markedly. It is therefore critical that you identify this purpose before you begin drafting.

The purpose of most legal documents falls into one of two broad categories—**objective** or **adversarial**. Objective documents accurately convey information and avoid bias. A letter to your client estimating his chances for success would be an objective document, as would an interoffice memo summarizing the current state of the law that applies to a given set of facts. Adversarial documents, on the other hand, are argumentative, drafted to emphasize the strong points of your client's position and the weaknesses of the opposing party's. They are *not* objective; they are *not* designed to balance both sides. A demand letter written to press your client's opponent or a brief submitted to persuade an appellate court are examples of adversarial documents.

Some documents have both objective and adversarial elements. For example, when drafting a contract proposal you will be seeking to reflect accurately the agreement of the parties (an objective purpose), while at the same time construing all ambiguous aspects of the agreement in your client's favor (an adversarial purpose).

By determining your purpose, you establish a focus that will enable you to accomplish your objective in every document you draft. In Table 3–2 we identify some strategies for accomplishing different purposes.

Table 3–2   Strategies for Different Writing Purposes

Purpose	Strategy
To Inform	1. Identify audience 2. Determine extent of audience's knowledge 3. Research relevant information 4. Determine what you desire to communicate
To Persuade	1. Identify audience 2. Determine relevant information 3. Research relevant information 4. Emphasize positive information and present in most favorable light 5. Convince audience that your position is the better position
To Discover Information	1. Identify audience 2. Determine information you need 3. Research relevant sources 4. Determine information that audience may possess 5. Elicit information that is important without revealing your position
To Prepare Legal Documents	1. Identify audience 2. Determine legal requirements 3. Elicit client's needs

Defining and Researching the Issues

Once you've identified your audience and determined your purpose, are you ready to begin writing? The answer is "No." Before you begin writing, you must define the issues presented and conduct the research necessary to address these issues.

For some documents, this last prewriting consideration may be easy. If, for example, you are simply updating a client on recent developments in a case, the issue is identical to the purpose (informing the client) and the research may be as simple as reviewing the file or even relating from memory.

In much legal writing, however, you will have to analyze the issues implied by your purpose and address them so as to accomplish your objective. A commonly used technique is the **IRAC method**:

- Identify the *issue* involved;
- Determine the *rule of law*;
- *Apply* the rule of law to the facts of your matter; and
- Reach a *conclusion*.

Taking the first letter of the four key items yields the mnemonic (memorizing) device *IRAC*. Let's take a closer look at each of these items.

The Issue The **issue** is the legal problem presented. For example, the issue in our Commentary problem is the meaning of the documents involved in the purchase of a new car. You have to inform your friend of several things—what the documents mean, whether they meet all legal requirements, and whether he has any option to negotiate their content.

The Rule of Law Having determined the issue, you must research the law to identify relevant statutes, regulations, cases, and constitutional provisions. Those sources that apply constitute the **rule of law** controlling the issue. For example, taking our Commentary situation, a statute might require certain portions of the contract to be written in plain English or in oversized typeface, or a case might have held that certain financing disclosures are required.

Applying the Law to the Facts The rule of law is an abstract concept that must be analyzed in the context of the particular facts of your client's matter. Applying the law to the facts enables you to address the issue in a manner meaningful to your client. Suppose, for example, that your research on our Commentary problem has shown that a car dealership must orally inform a purchaser of the repossession provisions in a sales contract. After you apply this rule of law to the facts of your specific matter, the letter to your friend might read in part as follows:

> The dealership is required to inform all prospective purchasers of their rights in the event of nonpayment, and to have the prospective buyer initial the relevant provisions of the contract. Your initials, however, do not appear next to those provisions.

The letter thus takes the rule (which requires initialing) and applies it to the facts (your friend did not initial his contract).

The Conclusion The result of your analysis is your **conclusion**. Carrying forward the Commentary example to this final step, your letter to your friend might conclude:

The dealership has failed to comply with the requirement that you initial provisions that explain your rights upon nonpayment. This is an important requirement of state law, and the contract is therefore rendered voidable at your discretion.

The conclusion is the summation of your analysis. It answers the questions raised by the issues.

Time Constraints

Deadlines are a fact of life in legal practice. Virtually every document filed with a court is governed by a time requirement. In addition, practical considerations often create unofficial deadlines (a client may need certain legal questions answered immediately to gain an edge on his competitors). Finally, as a paralegal you will be expected to complete tasks within the time assigned by your supervising attorney.

An important prewriting consideration is thus to evaluate the time available and allocate your efforts accordingly. A brief due in 48 hours will be prepared in a fashion and on a schedule quite different from one due in four weeks. You must learn to budget your time without affecting the quality of your writing—which can be accomplished by organizing efficiently and taking advantage of all available resources (for example, if an old case involved similar issues, you might use the research from that file as a starting point).

3–3 Organizing the Legal Document

Organizing the document might be considered your final prewriting consideration, but it is better to think of it as the first consideration in the writing stage itself. Your plan of organization provides the blueprint by which your document will be crafted.

Outlining

The best method of organizing a legal document is by outlining. An **outline** is the skeleton of a legal argument, advancing from the general to the specific. You have no doubt prepared outlines in other contexts in the past. A legal outline differs from these other outlines in content but not concept. It is intended to help you to critically examine your approach, leading to a document that flows logically to a conclusion which accomplishes your purpose. An outline will assist you in:

- focusing on logical development;
- preventing critical omissions; and
- evaluating how well you accomplish your purpose.

An outline may use a sentence format or a shorthand topic format. When using a topic format, be sure you include enough information to enable you to remember why you included each topic. Unless you are comfortable or familiar with a particular subject area, the fuller sentence format is preferable. An accepted format for an outline is illustrated in Figure 3–1, page 68.

Figure 3–1   Example of an Outline

```
    I.  [General Topic]

        A.  [Issue]

            1.  [Rule of law]
            2.  [Application of law to the facts]
            3.  [Conclusion]

        B.

            1.
            2.
            3.

   II.  Requirements of Financing Documents

        A.  Disclosure of repossession procedure in event of nonpayment

            1.  Purchaser must initial the relevant sections.
            2.  Our client did not initial the documents.
            3.  Conclusion: the contract is voidable at our client's discretion.

        B.

            1.
            2.
            3.

  III.  Conclusion
```

Outlining is an effective method to focus and strengthen your document. It provides a guide that, carefully followed, leads to an organized and effective document.

An Alternative to Outlining

An alternative to a written outline is to separate your raw research into categories. This can be accomplished by using file cards or by grouping photocopies of related cases and statutes (for cases and statutes that overlap issues, place a separate copy in each group, or remind yourself with a post-it note). By ordering the cards or groups of photocopies in a logical sequence, you create in effect an unwritten outline—you have made decisions about organization and development. This method is somewhat unorthodox, but as you gain experience it may be a practical timesaver.

3–4   Types of Documents

There are many different types of legal documents, which we discuss in later chapters. Let's consider a few right now.

Letters

Correspondence is essential in virtually every legal matter. **Letters** to the client, to opposing counsel, to the court, to witnesses, to government agencies—the list is endless. Demand letters, opinion letters, retainer letters, settlement letters, update letters advising of case status or court date—some are objective, some adversarial, all important.

Internal Memoranda

An interoffice memorandum explains the law so as to inform and educate the attorneys. As mentioned, this memo is an objective writing that relates both good news and bad about the law as it applies to the client's case, and it can be used as a basis for strategy, as basic research for a brief, or as background when drafting pleadings or other documents.

Operative Documents

Many documents have, as a result of their language and content, legal effects beyond the mere transmission of information. Executed contracts, leases, wills, and deeds are examples of **operative documents** that lawyers and paralegals draft. Such documents serve to define property rights and performance obligations, and slight alterations in meaning can have great impact on the parties involved. Without minimizing the importance of precision in every document drafted, it is safe to say that you should be doubly attentive to accuracy in operative documents.

A Few Words About Forms

Many types of legal documents, particularly operative documents, incorporate **forms**. Forms are documents that set forth standard language which is the accepted format for accomplishing a given purpose. Recourse to a form is a decision to be made by your supervising attorney, although he or she may delegate some discretion to you.

The language in forms may be cumbersome and confusing, with excessive use of legalese and archaic construction. Forms are valuable, however, based upon their widespread acceptance. This is the paradox of precision—that a document confusing on its face due to peculiar language is actually precise as a result of years, even centuries, of accepted meaning.

There are forms for deeds, for wills, and for leases: indeed, there are multi-volume sets of forms covering an enormous range of legal transactions. Most forms provide standard language with blank spaces where specific information from your case can be inserted; others provide the standard language with examples of information from other transactions, which must then be modified to fit your specific situations. The standard language in these forms, often referred to as **boilerplate**, should not be changed unless you are instructed to do so by your supervising attorney.

An example of a legal form is the promissory note found in Figure 3–2 on page 70.

Pleadings

Pleadings are documents filed with the court in a pending lawsuit that define the issues to be decided by the court at trial. The claims, counterclaims, defenses, and special defenses of the parties constitute the pleadings. The document that initiates a lawsuit is the **complaint**, filed by the plaintiff. The defendant

Figure 3–2 Sample of a Promissory Note Form

PROMISSORY NOTE

$ _____   _____ , Texas A.D. 19____

   For value received _____ promises to
pay to _____ on order, the sum of _____ dollars, with
interest from date at the rate of _____ per cent per annum, both principal
and interest payable at _____

_____.

   This note payable in _____ installments of

_____

_____

   All past due principal and interest on this note shall bear interest at the rate of ten
per cent per annum.

   It is understood and agreed that the failure to pay this note, or any installment as
above promised, or any interest hereon, when due, shall at the option of the holder of
said note, mature the full amount of said note, and it shall at once become due and
payable.

   And it is hereby especially agreed that if this note is placed in the hands of an
attorney for collection, or collected by suit, or in probate or bankruptcy proceedings
_____ agree to pay a reasonable amount additional on the principal and
interest then due thereon as attorneys' fees.

Address: _____   _____

Phone: _____   _____

---

responds to the complaint with an **answer**, replying to the claims of the plaintiff. There can be other pleadings as well. Pleadings are adversarial documents, drafted to place your client's position in the best light, and they must be prepared in the format prescribed by the court's rules of procedure.

Motions

A **motion** requests that the court take an action. It can be filed by either the plaintiff or the defendant in a lawsuit. A defendant might file a "motion to strike," asking the court to rule out part of the plaintiff's claim on the grounds that it fails to state a claim supported by the applicable rules of law. Either party might file a "motion *in limine*," seeking a preliminary ruling on an issue of evidence. Or either party might file a "motion for summary judgment," arguing that there are no disputed questions of fact and that the matter can be decided based on an application of the law to the undisputed facts. Indeed, the number of different motions is high, limited only by the imaginations of counsel. Motions are always adversarial documents, drafted to favor your client's position.

Briefs

A **brief** is a formal written argument presented to the court, usually countered by a brief written by the opposing party. Note the important difference between a case brief, which you studied in detail in Chapter 2 (an objective document) and the formal brief presented to a court, which is adversarial. A brief filed with the trial court is called a *trial brief*; if filed with an appellate court it is called an *appellate brief*. A close relative of the brief is the *memorandum of law to the court*, which performs exactly the same function as a brief, but is usually filed in support of a less significant motion. The difference between a formal brief and a memorandum of law to the court is more semantic than real.

Discovery Documents

The procedural rules governing lawsuits have liberal provisions that allow for **discovery**, when the opposing parties obtain information in the hands of the other party. Requests for documents or for responses to written questions (called **interrogatories**) are important adversarial documents that enable litigants to learn as much as possible about their opponent's case before trial. Although response to discovery requests must be honestly provided (hence they are objective), in fact an adversarial element often creeps into these responses, which can lead to time-consuming disputes in court.

3–5   Practical Considerations

Legal writing is an extremely varied subject area, with documents ranging from an informal client letter to a full-scale Supreme Court brief. There is room for both great eloquence and extreme brevity. There is a time for objectivity and a time for partisanship. There is a role for legalese and a role for plain English. Perhaps most important of all, there is a need for precision—a need to communicate ideas in a concise and unambiguous fashion.

A few practical considerations are universal. First, do all necessary background research. This includes the prewriting considerations outlined, as well as checking for technical requirements such as court rules on format. See Figure 3–3, which discusses some of the requirements of an appellate brief in Federal Court.

Second, always make your purpose clear by the use of a straightforward introduction. Readers do not enjoy guessing. Assuming too much about the expectations or knowledge of your audience can result in a document that confuses rather than enlightens.

Third, fully explain your position. Satisfy yourself that your points progress logically. Guide the reader through the subject matter. Avoid arriving at conclusions before exhausting your analysis.

Figure 3–3   Example of Federal Appellate Brief Requirements

Rule 28. Briefs
  (a) Brief of the Appellant. The brief of the appellant shall contain under appropriate headings and in the order here indicated:
  (1) A table of contents, with page references, and a table of cases (alphabetically arranged), statutes and other authorities cited, with references to the pages of the brief where they are cited.
  (2) A statement of the issues presented for review.
  (3) A statement of the case. The statement shall first indicate briefly the nature of the case, the course of proceedings, and its disposition in the court below. There shall follow a statement of the facts relevant to the issues presented for review, with appropriate references to the record (see subdivision (e)) . . .
  (b) Length of Briefs. Except by permission of the court, or as specified by local rule of the court of appeals, principal briefs shall not exceed 50 pages, and reply briefs shall not exceed 25 pages, exclusive of pages containing the table of contents, tables of citations, and any addendum containing statutes, rules, regulations, etc.

Fourth, prepare a conclusion that concisely ties together the entire document. Again, be straightforward. As the introduction made your intent clear, so your conclusion should make the achievement of that purpose clear.

Finally, reread! Writing is nothing more than creating documents to be read. It is impossible to gauge how another person will read a document unless you yourself read it. By rereading you can see where your document succeeds and fails, then revise it into a precise, flowing finished product.

SUMMARY

3-1

Because of the long-standing and wide acceptance of the meaning of the words of which they are composed, legalese and anachronistic usages persist in legal writing. Although some terms of art remain useful, good legal writing is generally characterized by short, succinct sentences, a minimum of legalese, avoidance of redundancy, emphasis on simple language in simple form, and a recognition of the importance of rereading what you've written.

3-2

Prewriting considerations include identifying the audience and recognition that the sophistication of the audience will affect the nature of the language used; identification of the purpose, which will generally be either objective or adversarial; and a commitment to properly defining and researching the issues presented. A good method of analyzing the issues is the IRAC method, in which you identify the issue involved, determine the relevant rule of law, apply the rule of law to the facts of your matter, and reach a conclusion. The final prewriting step is to take into account the time constraints associated with your writing project.

3-3

Legal documents are often organized with the help of an outline, which is the framework of the proposed content, advancing from the general to the specific. An alternative to outlining is to group your raw research into categories, either by using file cards or by physically gathering related materials.

3-4

There are many different types of legal documents, including letters, internal memoranda, operative documents, forms, pleadings, motions, briefs, and discovery documents.

3-5

Writing is an extremely varied subject area. Keep in mind the following considerations: do all necessary background research; make your purpose clear with a straightforward introduction; fully explain your position; prepare a concise conclusion that ties your argument together; and finally, reread what you've written to ensure that you've accomplished your purpose.

REVIEW

Key Terms

Before proceeding, review the key terms listed below to be sure you understand each one. If necessary, read over the corresponding section of the chapter. When you are ready to test your understanding, answer the Review Questions.

clarity
precision
jargon
legalese
plain English
terms of art
audience
objective purpose
adversarial purpose
IRAC method
issue
rule of law
conclusion
outline
letters
internal memoranda
operative documents
forms
boilerplate
pleadings
complaint
answer

motion
brief
discovery
interrogatories

Questions for Review and Discussion

1. What is legalese?
2. What is a term of art?
3. What are some of the basic techniques associated with good legal writing?
4. What is the audience of a legal document?
5. What is the difference between an objective purpose and an adversarial purpose?
6. What is the IRAC method?
7. How can a paralegal effectively balance time constraints?
8. How does a writer go about organizing a legal document?
9. Name several different types of legal documents.
10. What are the two types of pleadings?

Activities

1. Review the promissory note in Figure 3–2.
   (a) Determine the purpose of the document and the audience.
   (b) Edit out all the legalese and unnecessary words.
2. Obtain a copy of your state's appellate brief requirements and identify all the constraints and legal requirements for filing a brief with your state.

CHAPTER 4   The Mechanics of Construction

OUTLINE

COMMENTARY

You have attended a deposition with your supervising attorney, taking notes on the questions posed and testimony given. Your notes reflect the rapid-fire context—scribbled sentence fragments, abbreviations, and jottings to jog your memory.

Afterward your supervising attorney informs you that, since that transcript is not expected for three weeks, she would like a summary of the deposition. She asks that you translate your notes into a written memorandum.

As you sit at your desk with your notes, you begin to ponder the basic principles of writing—words as the bricks of which a sentence is built, rules the mortar by which it is held together. Words and rules—language and grammar—provide the foundation from which good writing ascends.

OBJECTIVES

In this chapter we discuss some key elements of grammar—the rules of proper English—as they relate both to legal writing and to all writing. We analyze the basics: punctuation, sentence construction, and paragraphing. Then, in

Chapter 5, we turn to an examination of words—the pitfalls and possibilities of language.

After completing this chapter, you will be able to:

1. Set apart a parenthetical phrase.
2. Employ commas to provide clarity.
3. Identify two methods of combining the clauses of a compound sentence.
4. Inject certainty into a series with semicolons.
5. Format a block quotation.
6. Group passages with brackets and parentheses.
7. Separate sentence segments with a dash.
8. Distinguish simple, complex, and compound sentences.
9. Avoid sentence fragments and run-ons.
10. Draft a paragraph with a topic sentence, a body, and transitional language.

4–1 Punctuation

We affect the meaning of spoken language all the time—with the tone of our voice, by hesitating or speeding up, with facial expressions, hand movements, and the subtleties of body language. All these techniques are physical—and thus unavailable to writers. The writer must learn to recreate in the mind of the reader the impressions left by these embellishments. One way to accomplish this is by the artful use of punctuation. Let's consider some of its more significant aspects.

The Comma

Commas recreate verbal pauses. They separate distinct concepts and eliminate confusion, enabling the writer to establish a rhythm and maintain clarity. Commas often travel in pairs. They surround and set off phrases, as with the parenthetical phrase in Figure 4–1:

Figure 4–1   Use of Commas

> The plaintiff, who performed every act required of her by the terms of the contract, is seeking damages from the defendant.

The phrase set apart between commas could have been placed within parentheses, hence the term **parenthetical phrase**. Parenthetical phrases are often placed between commas, although it is not mandatory, as Figure 4–2 shows.

Figure 4–2   Use of Commas in Parenthetical Phrase

> **Between commas:**
>
> The plaintiff, James Jones, is assisting in the investigation of his case.
>
> **Without commas:**
>
> The plaintiff James Jones is assisting in the investigation of his case.

Where the parenthetical is short, as with "James Jones," the choice is largely a matter of personal style. You seek a document that "flows" (more about flow in the next chapter) and must decide whether the commas advance fluidity or impede it. If the parenthetical is long, as in Figure 4–1, it should be set off by commas. Remember that you may use two commas to set off a parenthetical, or none, but never use just one. Figure 4–3 shows two incorrect uses of commas.

Figure 4–3 Incorrect Use of Commas in Parenthetical Phrase

> <u>**Incorrect:**</u>
>
> The plaintiff, who performed every act required of her by the terms of the contract is seeking damages from the defendant.
>
> The plaintiff who performed every act required of her by the terms of the contract, is seeking damages from the defendant.

How can you tell if a phrase is a parenthetical? One way is by reading the sentence without the phrase. If the sentence remains logical and grammatically correct, the phrase is likely a parenthetical. Parenthetical phrases supplement, or add information to, a thought that is already complete. Try reading the sentence in Figure 4–1 without the parenthetical phrase—it is less informative, but grammatical and logically complete.

If a phrase is **restrictive** (specifying or restricting the application of something), it is *not* parenthetical, and should not be set apart by commas, as Figure 4–4 shows.

Figure 4–4 Use of Commas in Restrictive Phrase

> <u>**Correct:**</u>
>
> Bankers who violate these statutes should go to jail.
>
> <u>**Incorrect:**</u>
>
> Bankers, who violate these statutes, should go to jail.

In the correct example, the phrase "who violate these statutes" specifies *which* bankers; it cannot be removed without changing the fundamental meaning of the sentence. The incorrect sentence creates the impression that *all* bankers violate the statutes (try reading it without the phrase).

We have noted that commas often travel in pairs. There are, of course, entirely proper sentences in which you will find only a single comma. A parenthetical, for example, may appear at the beginning of a sentence, as in Figure 4–5:

Figure 4–5 Parenthetical Phrase at Beginning of Sentence

> Having performed every act required of him by the terms of the contract, the plaintiff is seeking damages from the defendant.

A single comma is also seen where a conjunction such as *but* or *and* joins two complete thoughts, as in Figure 4–6:

Figure 4–6   Use of Commas With Conjunction

The deposition transcript is lengthy, and its contents are fascinating.

or

Her eyesight is failing, but she heard the impact.

A common error in comma usage occurs when dealing with a series. There should be a comma after all but the last item in the series, as shown in Figure 4–7:

Figure 4–7   Use of Commas in Series

Correct:

The judge, jury, and prosecutor listened intently as defense counsel examined the witness.

Incorrect:

The judge, jury and prosecutor listened intently as defense counsel examined the witness.

This rule, however, does not necessarily apply to law firm names, something which, as a paralegal, you will be dealing with regularly, as in Figure 4–8:

Figure 4–8   Use of Commas in Law Firm Names

Correct:

Able, Baker & Charlie

Incorrect:

Able, Baker, & Charlie

There are many other specific rules governing the use of commas, some of the more important of which are set forth in Table 4–1. Once you have determined the message you intend, the comma can be a powerful means of avoiding confusion. As a paralegal drafting documents, you should be using commas to maximize clarity first, fluidity second.

The Semicolon

The **semicolon** is a close cousin of the comma. It is used to indicate a break in thought, though of a different sort than that indicated by a comma. Rather

Table 4–1 Some Examples of Comma Usage

Use Comma To:	Example:
set apart transitional language	Indeed, the statute is applicable and controlling.
set apart quotes	The defendant stated, "I'm innocent."
indicate an omission	The defendant went to Florida; his brother, to New Jersey; and his wife, to Florida.
clarify a date or number	1,000,000 January 1, 1992
set apart "yes" and "no"	Is the statute controlling? No, it is not.

than merely separating two thoughts, a semicolon also suggests a relationship between the two—making it a useful tool for an attorney or paralegal trying to make a point.

Semicolons are often used to join the components of a **compound sentence**. A compound sentence is one in which the clauses could stand separately, each ending with a period. In addition to using a semicolon or a period, a third method of expressing such a compound is with a comma and a conjunction, as we saw in Figure 4–6. In Figure 4–9 we express the first sentence from Figure 4–6 in these three different ways.

Figure 4–9 Expressions of Compound Sentences

> **With semicolon:**
>
> The deposition transcript is lengthy; its contents are fascinating.
>
> **As two sentences:**
>
> The deposition transcript is lengthy. Its contents are fascinating.
>
> **With conjunction and comma:**
>
> The deposition transcript is lengthy, and its contents are fascinating.

In this instance the original choice, with comma and conjunction, is probably the best choice, because the writer probably intended to imply no relationship between the two clauses (i.e., the length of the deposition is not what made it fascinating). Consider, however, the sentence in Figure 4–10:

Figure 4–10 Strategic Use of Semicolon

> The defendant's blood alcohol level was twice the legal limit; his driving was erratic and led to the accident.

The use of the semicolon in this sentence implies the close relationship between the defendant's blood alcohol level and the erratic driving and subsequent accident. Although the two-sentence or comma-conjunction methods would convey the same information, the semicolon method conveys it with more force and is preferable.

A semicolon can also be useful in distinguishing separate elements in a series, particularly when commas are used in describing each individual element, as in Figure 4–11:

Figure 4–11   Use of Semicolon to Distinguish

> **Correct:**
>
> The witness identified defendant Jones, the butler; defendant Smith, the cook; and defendant Brown, the gardener.
>
> **Incorrect:**
>
> The witness identified defendant Jones, the butler, defendant Smith, the cook, and defendant Brown, the gardener.

The incorrect example would be correct if the witness had identified five separate people: (1) defendant Jones, (2) the butler, (3) defendant Smith, (4) the cook, and (5) defendant Brown (who was the gardener). However, if three witnesses were identified, the first sentence is clear and the second is confusing and misleading. Indeed, even if the second example were intended because there were five witnesses, it would still be preferable to separate all five by semicolons, so that confusion created by the lack of parallelism among the elements—some identified by name, some by occupation—would be eliminated.

Quotations

The use of quoted materials adds support to memoranda, briefs, letters, and any other legal writing in which the writer is trying to build an argument. Failing to follow the rules with regard to quotation marks, however, may distract the reader and detract from the force of your position.

When using a quote, should you include it in the body of the document or set it aside as a **block quote**? Although the context, and your ear for rhythm, will often dictate the better choice, a good rule of thumb is that any quote longer than 50 words (generally about three to five lines) should be set apart. This 50-word rule is incorporated into *A Uniform System of Citation* (the bluebook) for briefs and other court documents.

If the block quote format is chosen, the quoted passage is indented and single-spaced. Quotation marks are omitted at the beginning and end, but interior quotation marks should be kept. The citation appears on the line immediately following, at the original left margin. An example is shown in Figure 4–12.

Figure 4–12   Block Quote

> It has been said that the case of *Swift v. Tyson* is based upon a fallacy:
>
> > The fallacy underlying the rule declared in Swift v. Tyson is made clear by Mr. Justice Holmes. The doctrine rests upon the assumption that there is "a transcendental body of law outside of any particular state but obligatory within it . . .," [and] that federal courts have the power to use their judgment as to what the rules of common law are . . .
>
> *Erie Railroad v. Tompkins*, 304 U.S. 64, 58 S.Ct. 817, 82 L.Ed. 1188 (1938), quoting from Holmes's dissent in *Black and White Taxicab and Transfer Co. v. Brown and Yellow Taxicab and Transfer Co.*, 276 U.S. 518, 533, 48 S.Ct. 404, 72 L.Ed. 681 (1928).

Note the use of brackets and ellipses (which we discuss further), as well as the use of a period to conclude the citation. Also note that the quote within the quote uses standard double quotation marks, since the outside quotation marks are omitted. If outside quotation marks are included, as when a quoted passage appears in the body of the text rather than in a separate block, the interior quotation marks would be single:

Figure 4–13   Interior Quotation

> The witness stated, "I heard the defendant shout, 'I didn't mean to kill her!'"

In addition to the standard purpose of attributing words to a specific source, quotation marks can also be used to indicate irony or sarcasm, or to identify or set apart a word or passage:

Figure 4–14   Use of Quotation Marks to Indicate Purpose

Irony:

Defendant argues that plaintiff benefited from defendant's partial performance of the obligations of the contract, but this "benefit" is hardly what was intended by the contract or anticipated by the plaintiff.

Sarcasm:

The alleged "witness" was not even present at the scene of the accident.

To identify:

In this contract the word "deliver" means to place in the plaintiff's hands, not send to him in the mail.

Using quotation marks to identify a word or phrase is common and acceptable. Using them for an ironic or sarcastic purpose is generally inappropriate in documents filed with a court, and under any circumstances should be done only after careful reflection.

A common source of confusion with regard to quotation marks is whether concluding punctuation goes inside the final quotation mark, or outside. Table 4–2 lists the rules for different punctuation marks.

Table 4–2   Concluding Punctuation

<u>Placement of Quotation Marks</u>

1. The period: A quotation mark appears *after* a period.

2. The comma: A quotation mark appears *after* a comma.

3. The question mark: A quotation mark appears *after* a question mark.

4. The semicolon: A quotation mark appears *before* a semicolon.

5. The colon: A quotation mark appears *before* a colon.

Parentheses, Brackets, and the Ellipsis

Clarity often demands grouping or special identification of text. This can be accomplished with punctuation: **parentheses** ( ) and brackets unite cohesive passages, **brackets** [ ] indicate changes or additions, and an **ellipsis** (...) indicates the elimination of text from an extended quote.

Parentheses are an alternative to the commas we used in Figure 4–1, as shown in Figure 4–15:

Figure 4–15 Use of Parentheses

> The plaintiff (who performed every act required of her by the terms of the contract) is seeking damages from the defendant.

The two figures, 4–1 and 4–15, are identical except that in 4–15 we've replaced the commas with parentheses. Since both are grammatically correct, how do you choose between parentheses and commas? In general, the closer the relationship between the parenthetical clause and the main sentence, the stronger the tendency to favor the commas. If the relationship is slight, parentheses are the better choice. The relationship in Figure 4–1 and 4–15 probably justifies commas (it is the plaintiff's performance that entitles her to damages), whereas the sentence in Figure 4–16 is better expressed with parentheses:

Figure 4–16 Use of Parentheses

> The plaintiff (who is eighty-five years old) is seeking damages from the defendant.

The choice is, in these instances, simply a matter of degree. When choosing a particular sentence construction, it is often wise to consider balance and variety in your document as a whole. The need for balance and variety or for parallel construction (discussed further in Chapter 5), will often dictate your choice where it would otherwise be a toss-up.

Some confusion may arise over using parentheses with other punctuation marks. As a general rule, you should leave out ending punctuation *within* the parentheses unless it is a question mark or an exclamation point; with regard to the remainder of the sentence, punctuate it exactly as you would if the material contained within the parentheses were missing (this means the final punctuation mark should be outside the final parentheses, as you see at the end of this sentence).

In Figure 4–12 we saw the word *and* in brackets. What do brackets signify? Generally speaking, brackets appearing in a quote identify some departure from the original text—in Figure 4–12 the addition of "and" to the original text makes the quote grammatical without changing the meaning. Brackets are also often used to change capitalization in a quoted passage to conform to the sentence in which it appears, as in Figure 4–17:

Figure 4–17 Use of Brackets to Identify Departure From Text

> The court noted that "[t]he fallacy underlying the rule in *Swift v. Tyson* is made clear by Mr. Justice Holmes."

Compare this to the block quote in Figure 4–12, and note how the bracketed lower-case *t* here incorporates the quote into the flow of the sentence.

Brackets have other uses as well. They may be used as parentheses within parentheses, and are used to enclose the word *sic*, a Latin term used to signify an error of spelling or usage in a quoted passage. In addition, brackets can be used to insert editorial comments or explanations into quoted materials, as in Figure 4–18:

Figure 4–18   Use of Brackets to Insert Editorial Comment

The language of the will states, "Any member of the Jones family [there are four surviving members] alive at the time of my death shall be entitled to $1000 from my estate."

Another mark used to specially identify text is the ellipsis. Unlike brackets and parentheses, however, an ellipsis indicates the *omission* of text. It is formed by three dots (periods), as we saw in Figure 4–12. Punctuation that precedes or follows the omitted text may be included or excluded, depending on the needs of the sentence (the comma, for example, was retained after the ellipsis in Figure 4–12). A few simple rules govern the use of the ellipsis. First, there should be a space before the first dot, between each dot, and after the last dot. Second, when the words omitted follow a complete sentence, the sentence should end with the actual period, followed by the three spaced ellipsis points. Finally, when omitting a paragraph or more, the use of a line of dots is sometimes suggested (each spaced several spaces apart), although the three-dot device at the end of the last passage before the omission is also acceptable.

The ellipsis can be a valuable writing tool. Quotes are not always perfectly attuned to the context of your document. By judicious use of the ellipsis, you can eliminate extraneous passages and take your reader right to the heart of the matter.

Hyphens and Dashes

Hyphens are used to draw together groups of words to form a single idea—"up-to-date" is an example. As language evolves, accepted usage for such combinations often changes, and there is not always a consensus on proper form (for example: closeup/close-up; byproduct/by-product). In addition, although there are some standard rules (for example: hyphenate fractions such as one-half), they often have exceptions (don't hyphenate fractions when used as nouns, as in, "She wrote one half of the brief"). Perhaps it is best to forget the general rules about hyphens and, when in doubt, look it up in a dictionary. Hyphens are also used to divide words at the end of a line. The division must come between syllables, and it is wise to use a dictionary if the division is not obvious.

Dashes are longer than hyphens and are used for limited purposes. They can substitute for parentheses or parenthetical commas—as in this sentence—and can also be used to separate the segments of a two-part sentence, as in Figure 4–19:

Figure 4–19   Use of Dashes to Separate Two-Part Sentence

His testimony was useless—biased, inconsistent, and obviously false.

Dashes are often used to indicate the word *to* when used with page numbers, dates, or other numerical references ("Earl Warren was Chief Justice from 1953–1969").

The Colon

Colons have several purposes. They follow the salutation in a letter, are used in expressions of time (for example: 10:48 p.m.), and can lead into a specified list:

Figure 4–20 Colons Preceding a List

> The statutory protection has three prerequisites: adequate notice, sufficient documentation, and a completed application.

Colons can also perform a function similar to a semicolon or period: joining together related phrases, as in this sentence. In general, a colon signifies a closer relationship than does a semicolon or a comma. Explanatory clauses are often preceded by a colon (for example, in Figure 4–19, a colon could substitute for the dash), as are quotations (see Figure 4–12).

Question Marks and Exclamation Points

Question marks are used in the ordinary manner in legal writing, with one caveat (warning): since the purpose of advocacy is to persuade, there is little place for rhetorical questions, hence little use for question marks in briefs or other documents filed with a court, other than formally stating the questions to be addressed.

Likewise, the **exclamation point** carries with it an air of informality that has little, if any, place in formal legal writing. Even if you find a certain fact extraordinary, it is better simply to state the fact than to emphasize it with an exclamation point.

The Apostrophe

Apostrophes arise primarily in two situations—contractions and possessives. As a general rule, contractions should be avoided in legal writing. "Cannot" is better than "can't"; "would not" than "wouldn't"; "it is" than "it's." Incidentally, it is unforgivable to confuse "it's" with "its"—the former is always a contraction of "it is," the latter always a possessive, as in "Its deadline is next week.")

Possessives are, of course, unavoidable. The general rule is to form a possessive for a singular noun by adding an apostrophe and an *s*. For a plural noun, you can usually simply add an apostrophe. The rule is the same for proper names. Although there are exceptions (e.g., men's, children's), in general you should follow this rule even when the result might seem odd:

Figure 4–21 Use of Apostrophe in Possessives

> Justice Stevens' opinion was lengthy.

4–2   Sentence Construction

A sentence uses words, punctuation, and rules of grammar to convey an idea. It is in the sentence that your writing begins to take form. Sentences should carry the reader through your document with a minimum of confusion. Let's turn now to the basics of sentence construction, then focus on a few things to watch out for.

The Simple Sentence: Subject/Verb/Object

Every sentence has a subject and a verb (also called a predicate). On occasion the subject is physically absent but implicit from the context; such usages, although acceptable in literature, have no place in legal writing. The simplest sentence structure is subject/verb:

Figure 4–22   Subject/Verb Sentence Structure

> The plaintiff won.

The subject in the sentence in Figure 4–22 is *The plaintiff* and the verb is *won*. Most sentences also contain an object that identifies the "receiver" of the subject's action:

Figure 4–23   Simple Sentence

> The plaintiff won the trial.

The object in this sentence—which tells what the plaintiff won—is *the trial*. This sentence format—subject/verb/object—is the most effective means of conveying ideas, and is known as the **simple sentence**. The further your writing departs from this level of simplicity, the weaker it may become.

Modifiers: Adjectives and Adverbs

The simple sentence may leave the reader asking questions. What kind of trial was it? How did the plaintiff win? To answer these questions, a writer can use **modifiers**—adjectives and adverbs—to add information. Adjectives modify nouns, adverbs modify verbs, as in Figure 4–24:

Figure 4–24   Use of Modifiers

> The plaintiff easily won the lengthy trial.

In Figure 4–24, "easily" is an adverb describing how the trial was won, and "lengthy" is an adjective describing the trial itself.

Beginning writers often make the mistake of equating lengthy descriptions with good writing. They may think that the more adverbs and adjectives they use, the better their writing will be. This is a false assumption. It is possible to create clear images in the mind of the reader and evoke powerful responses using nothing more than subjects and verbs. Indeed, more often than not, modifiers confuse rather than clarify. The sentence in Figure 4–24 may lead the reader to wonder—"lengthy" compared to what? "easily" as opposed to what? Although it is unfair to evaluate a sentence out of context (perhaps "length" and "ease" are essential to the writer's point), in general you should minimize the use of modifiers.

The Complex Sentence: Clauses

Although the simple subject/verb/object format is generally best, there are often circumstances that justify a departure. The addition of clauses creates a **complex sentence:**

Figure 4–25   Complex Sentence

> The plaintiff, who had spent a fortune in legal fees, won the trial.

In this sentence the phrase "who had spent a fortune in legal fees" is a **subordinate** (dependent) **clause** describing the subject of the sentence, and the rest of the sentence forms an **independent clause** that could stand on its own (i.e., without the subordinate clause) as a complete sentence.

Variety in sentence structure tends to create a more readable document, and the use of clauses to combine ideas contained in a succession of simple sentences can improve your writing. Your goal is to make your point in the simplest manner possible without becoming boring. Complex sentences give readers variety and interest.

The Compound Sentence

Compound sentences have two or more clauses, each of which is independent and could stand alone as a complete sentence. The clauses of a compound sentence are joined by either semicolons or conjunctions and commas to form a new sentence containing closely related ideas:

Figure 4–26   Compound Sentences

> **Comma and conjunction:**
>
> The plaintiff won the trial, and her triumph was the result of hard work by her attorney.
>
> **Semicolon:**
>
> The plaintiff won the trial; her triumph was the result of hard work by her attorney.

In a compound sentence, the semicolon is never followed by a coordinate conjunction such as and or but, but can be followed by certain subordinate conjunctions such as *however* or *although*. A comma, on the other hand, can never be used to separate compound clauses without a conjunction:

Figure 4–27   Separating Compound Clauses

<u>Correct:</u>

The defendant lost the trial; however, since he was thorough in his preparation and argued with eloquence, he should have no regrets.

The defendant lost the trial, but since he was thorough in his preparation and argued with eloquence, he should have no regrets.

<u>Incorrect:</u>

The defendant lost the trial; but since he was thorough in his preparation and argued with eloquence, he should have no regrets.

The defendant lost the trial, since he was thorough in his preparation and argued with eloquence, he should have no regrets.

Compound sentences, together with simple and complex sentences, lend welcome variety to your writing.

The Run-on Sentence and the Sentence Fragment

Run-on sentences have too many clauses for one grammatical sentence, **sentence fragments** too few. This is not the same as saying that run-ons are too long and fragments too short. A sentence can be too long or short stylistically, but grammatically correct. Run-ons and fragments are grammatically incorrect:

Figure 4–28   Run-ons and Fragments

<u>Run-on Sentence (incorrect):</u>

The plaintiff won the trial was long.

<u>Correct:</u>

The plaintiff won. The trial was long.

The plaintiff won the long trial.

<u>Sentence Fragment (incorrect):</u>

Testifying in great detail about the contract.

<u>Correct:</u>

The defendant is testifying in great detail about the contract.

The defendant was on the stand for two hours, testifying in great detail about the contract.

The run-on was eliminated by separating it into two sentences, or, alternatively, one grammatical sentence restructured to include two ideas. The fragment was corrected by identifying the subject who performed the action of "testifying." The second correct version is slightly more informative than the first. When choosing among alternative corrections, make sure the result is either a simple, complex, or compound sentence that expresses what the original, incorrect version intended.

Run-ons and fragments are indefensible in legal writing, where clarity is critically important. There is no excuse for allowing errors of sentence construction to muddle your point and confuse the reader.

4–3   Paragraphing

A paragraph is more than just a group of sentences—it is a group of related sentences. A paragraph uses sentences to convey an idea, which is introduced in the **topic sentence**, usually the first sentence of the paragraph. Having introduced the idea, the paragraph develops it in the **body**. Then, having developed the idea, the paragraph performs a **transitional function** that facilitates orderly progression through the entire document. Let's look at each of these individual areas—topic sentence, body, and transition.

The Topic Sentence

The topic sentence of a paragraph is necessary because, quite simply, a paragraph must have a topic. Each sentence in a paragraph must be tied to that topic and must advance it in some way. Sentences must avoid digressions, and even "essential" digressions should be tied somehow to the purpose of the paragraph. Otherwise, the digression belongs in a paragraph of its own.

That being said, let us consider the topic sentence. It generally appears at the beginning of a paragraph and, particularly in legal writing, typically states a proposition, which is then supported in the remainder of the paragraph.

Figure 4–29   Topic Sentence at Beginning of Paragraph

The defendant's conduct with regard to the accident constituted negligence, and possibly recklessness. She was driving at a speed far beyond the speed limit. She was wearing neither glasses nor contact lenses, though her driver's license requires that she do so. She was weaving from lane to lane as a result of intoxication. Each of these offenses was a violation of her duty to drive with care, and therefore constitutes negligence. Taken together, they represent a blatant disregard for the rights of others that rises to the level of recklessness. In short, she was a threat to any driver unfortunate enough—as was plaintiff—to be on the same road.

The topic sentence in Figure 4–29 is underlined, and summarizes the argument to come. The sentences that follow support the point established by the topic sentence, culminating in the final two sentences which repeat the point dramatically.

Topic sentences do not always appear as the first sentence in a paragraph. Sometimes they don't even appear at all—they may be implicit. But the writer who omits the topic sentence is asking a favor of the reader—to store the information provided, sentence by sentence, until the purpose is revealed and the information can be logically fitted into the overall argument. This requires patience on the part of the reader, which constitutes a risk on the part of the writer—a risk that the reader will lose interest before the purpose has been made plain. It may be a risk worth taking—the drama or tension created may add to the overall impact—but it remains a risk nonetheless. In Figure 4–30 we see a paragraph with topic sentence at the end:

Figure 4–30   Topic Sentence at End of Paragraph

> The defendant was driving at a speed far beyond the speed limit. He was wearing neither glasses nor contact lenses, though his driver's license requires that he do so. He was weaving from lane to lane as a result of intoxication. <u>In short, his conduct at the time of the accident constituted negligence and possibly recklessness: he was a threat to any driver unfortunate enough, as was plaintiff, to be on the same road.</u>

The patience required of the reader, and the problems this might pose, should be immediately apparent. In general then, place your topic sentences at the beginning of each paragraph—and when you depart from this structure, do so with care.

The Body

The body of the paragraph contains the material that you claim supports the contention raised in the topic sentence. In Figure 4–29, for example, the sentences describing the defendant's excessive speed, failure to wear corrective lenses, and lane-weaving as a result of intoxication all support the assertion of the topic sentence that defendant was negligent and possibly reckless.

Paragraph development in legal writing often uses basic principles of argumentation. Having stated a proposition in the topic sentence, the writer endeavors to defend or support it in the succeeding sentences using one of several techniques. The proposition can be compared to similar situations; it can be contrasted with, or distinguished from, different situations; it can be explained or illustrated by a straightforward definition or example; it can be demonstrated logically, reasoning from basic principles; or it can be arrived at by some combination of these techniques, or related variants. Whatever technique is used, remember to tie your argument to the topic sentence. In Figure 4–31 on page 90, we show a topic sentence with various alternative follow-ups.

That there is relationship and overlap between and among these techniques is evident. The last two alternatives (explaining and reasoning), for example, are obviously closely related.

You should note that it is possible to use more than one technique in the same paragraph. For example, it is easy to imagine a paragraph that both compares analogous cases and distinguishes dissimilar cases, combining the methods of the first two alternatives.

Figure 4–31 Topic Sentence With Follow-Up

Topic sentence:

The defendant is not legally responsible for the injuries suffered by the plaintiff, who fell in defendant's store.

Compare and analogize:

Like the storekeeper in the case of *Jones v. Smith* (who was found to have used due care), she had placed large warning signs in prominent positions.

Contrast and distinguish:

Unlike the negligent storekeeper in *Brown v. Blue*, who allowed his employees to leave a freshly washed floor unattended and unidentified, the defendant stationed a clerk by the wet floor to warn customers, and provided a large sign that read, "Caution: Wet Floor!"

Explain or illustrate:

Legal responsibility requires a showing of negligence, and negligence requires the existence of a duty owed to the injured party. Because plaintiff was a burglar trespassing on the premises after hours, no duty was owed.

Reason or demonstrate through logic:

Only the owner of the premises can be held liable under the facts as proven by plaintiff. Defendant herself was not the owner of the premises in question; the building was owned by a corporation. Therefore defendant cannot be held responsible for the injuries suffered by the plaintiff.

Transitional Language

Transitional language provides signals to readers about the material they are reading. It reassures readers that there is a relationship between the writer's various points, and it serves to clarify that relationship. It is important, particularly in legal writing, that the reader follow, step-by-step, the progression of the argument. You can accomplish this by, quite simply, telling the reader what the argument is, as we discuss further in Chapter 5. It is this "telling" function that transitional language performs.

Figure 4–32 Transitional Language

Next, we will consider the cases that are distinguishable.

Since the cases all support the plaintiff's position, the conclusion is inevitable.

For example, the plaintiff in *Jones v. Smith* was held liable on facts similar to those in the instant matter.

Table 4–3 Transitional Words and Phrases

Passing of Time	Contrast or Opinion	Introduction	Summary/ Conclusion	Addition
Meanwhile	However	Initially	Therefore	Furthermore
Still	Notwithstanding	To begin	Accordingly	Moreover
Since	On the contrary	In order that (to)	Hence	Similarly
Ultimately	In contrast	Primarily	Consequently	Additionally
Presently	Although	First	In conclusion	In addition to
	Nevertheless		Finally	

The transitional language used—*next, since*, and *for example*—ties each sentence to other sentences in the writing, signalling the reader that there is a connection. See Table 4–3 for other examples of transitional language.

The transitional function can also be performed by using parallel construction or repetition, as in Figure 4–33:

Figure 4–33   Parallel Construction or Repetition

> The corporate statutes do not apply because *the business is not a corporation*; the partnership statutes do not apply because it is not a partnership; and the public utility statutes do not apply because it is not a public utility.
>
> *The business is not a corporation* because stock has never been sold nor corporate filings completed.

In the first paragraph, the parallel construction using the phrase *do not apply* ties the paragraph together; in the second paragraph, the phrase *The business is not a corporation* repeats a phrase taken from the first paragraph, providing the reader with an implicit indication that the sentences to come will explain the proposition first stated in the first paragraph. Repetition and parallel construction are in many instances (as here) virtually identical concepts. We consider them further in the next chapter.

4–4   Practical Considerations

The use of proper punctuation, sentence structure, and paragraphing techniques enables you to communicate ideas clearly. After mastering these basics you can begin to apply more subtle and complicated techniques.

A first draft often contains inconsistencies that will distract the reader and undercut your arguments. The first step in eliminating these problems is to review your draft for errors in the basics. A slight revision to a basic element often leads to dramatic improvement. By eliminating misleading punctuation, or adding punctuation to clarify, you ensure that your sentences accurately convey your ideas. When you vary sentence structure and eliminate run-ons and fragments, your paragraphs combine these ideas into a coherent argument. Finally, by structuring your paragraphs into logical units with clearly defined transitions, you carry the reader along the path to your conclusion.

SUMMARY

4–1

Punctuation embellishes writing and removes ambiguity. Commas can be used to set apart parenthetical phrases; semicolons can join the components of a compound sentence or clarify the elements in a list or series. Quotations add support to memoranda and briefs; parentheses, brackets, and ellipses group or identify special passages of text or omitted text. Hyphens draw words together, whereas dashes separate parenthetical clauses or disparate elements of a two-clause sentence. Colons can introduce quotes or lead into specified lists. Question marks and exclamation points are informal usages, and should be used sparingly in formal or legal writing (although question marks are acceptable for use in "questions presented" sections of memoranda or briefs). Apostrophes indicate contractions (although contractions are generally considered informal and should be avoided in legal writing) and possessives.

4–2

Simple sentences contain a subject and verb, and may contain an object and modifiers. Complex sentences contain a subordinate clause, and compound sentences contain at least two clauses that could stand alone as complete grammatical sentences. Simple sentences are preferable, although the need for variety (which prevents writing from becoming monotonous) suggests that complex and compound sentences be used as well. Excessive use of modifiers (adjectives and adverbs) undercuts your writing. A run-on sentence fails to join its component clauses grammatically; a sentence fragment lacks a subject or verb.

4–3

A paragraph needs a topic sentence to introduce its subject matter to the reader. The topic sentence is usually at the beginning of the paragraph. The body of the paragraph develops the subject matter introduced by the topic sentence. Transitional language helps guide the reader through the various paragraphs and sections of the document, carrying the reader smoothly from the beginning of the document to the end.

4–4

The first step in eliminating inconsistencies in a first draft is to review the draft for errors in the basics—punctuation, sentence structure, and paragraphing.

REVIEW

Key Terms

Before proceeding, review the key terms listed below to be sure you understand each one. If necessary, read over the corresponding section of the chapter. When you are ready to test your understanding, answer the Review Questions.

commas
parenthetical phrase
restrictive phrase
series
semicolon

compound sentence
block quote
parentheses
brackets
ellipsis
hyphen
dash
colon
question mark
exclamation point
apostrophe
simple sentence
modifiers

complex sentence
subordinate clause
independent clause
run-on sentence
sentence fragment
topic sentence
body
transitional function

Questions for Review and Discussion

1. What is a parenthetical phrase, and how can it be set apart?
2. Describe one way in which commas can bring clarity into a sentence.
3. How can compound clauses be combined?
4. How do semicolons inject clarity into a series?
5. Briefly describe the format for a block quotation.
6. How are parentheses and brackets used to group passages in a sentence?
7. When should a dash be used to separate segments of a sentence?
8. Describe: a simple sentence; a complex sentence; and a compound sentence.
9. What is a sentence fragment? What is a run-on sentence?
10. Describe the function of a topic sentence; define *body* in the context of paragraph structure; and explain what is meant by *transitional language*.

Activities

1. Rewrite the following passage:
   The Supreme Court, held that a "subject to legal documentation" provision in a hand-written document executed by parties after they had agreed on material terms of sale did not establish, as a matter of law, that no sales agreement had been reached.
2. Proofread and edit the following paragraph:
   I direct that my ~~just and and~~ legal debts and funneral expenses ~~and all~~ federal ~~and~~ state estate and inheratance taxes imposed upon my estate or any beneficiary therof including the portion of any such tax attributable to the proceeds of policies of insurance on my life or other property not constituting a part of my probate estate, be paid in full out of my residuary estate as soon as convenient. This direction s not obligatory upon my Executrix and he is specifically given the right or renew and extend, in any form that she deems beast, any debt ~~or~~ charge existing at the time of my death, ~~including~~ any morgage on my home and similarly my Executrix shall have the right and power to incur indebtedness and to borrow money for the purpose of paying any or all of the aforesaid debts, expenses and taxes.

CHAPTER 5   Effective and Persuasive Legal Writing

OUTLINE

COMMENTARY

Your supervising attorney has asked that you prepare a draft memorandum in support of a motion he will be filing with the trial court. You perform the necessary research and return to your office, with pages of notes and a small pile of photocopied cases and statutes. You're now confident in your knowledge of punctuation, sentence structure, and paragraphing, but you want to bring more than just grammatical correctness to this memorandum—you want to prepare a document that will persuade the court. Now that you know the rules, you want to learn to evaluate words—to use language effectively to accomplish your purpose.

OBJECTIVES

Now that you've learned basic rules of grammar, sentence construction, and paragraphing, it's time to address some of the finer elements of writing. After completing this chapter, you will be able to:

1. Inject clarity and precision into your writing.
2. Define rhythm, flow, and voice.
3. Use similes and metaphors to make a colorful point.
4. Avoid ambiguity and redundancy.
5. Make subjects and verbs agree.
6. Use a simple method to eliminate obscurity in your writing.
7. Compare and contrast periodic sentences and cumulative sentences.
8. Differentiate active voice from passive voice, and know when to use each.
9. Use structured enumeration to identify the items in a list.
10. Logically develop your arguments.

5–1 Writing Is Reading

A writer strings together words to be read. The audience may be merely the writer him- or herself, as with a diary; one other person, as with a letter; or many thousands, as with a newspaper article or book, but in all cases the words written are intended, ultimately, to be read.

Writing, then, as we noted in Chapter 3, is *reading*.

This might seem simplistic. Of course writing is reading, you're saying to yourself. Everybody knows that—what's the big deal?

The big deal is simply that, although most people understand the connection, they fail to make use of it to improve their writing.

The point might be clearer if stated this way: "Writing is *re*reading." Too many novice writers fail to understand that to create "good writing," they must reread what they've written—placing themselves in the position of the reader—and improve it through revision. Not even the best writers are above the constant need to refine and perfect their drafts.

This person we've referred to before—"the reader"—is the key to the whole writing process. Good writers get inside the reader's head. They analyze the quality of the words they've chosen by analyzing their impact upon the reader. Only after such analysis can they be sure that their point has been successfully conveyed.

The process of writing is perhaps best illustrated by a comparison. A sculptor starts with a block of granite, which he then chips and shapes until it matches his vision. A writer must *create* her block of granite, called a first draft. Only then can she go about the business of "chipping and shaping" her writing by **rereading, editing,** and revising to match her vision. Let's investigate this process.

5–2 The Possibilities of Language

In Chapter 4 we identified words as the bricks of good writing and rules as the mortar, but we confined our discussion to rules. In this section we turn to words to explore the possibilities of language.

Brevity, Clarity, and Precision

Brevity leads to strong, tight writing. To be brief is to be forceful. A writer must be stingy with words; he must be efficient and focused.

Brevity, of course, requires work. An old story is illustrative: when asked why she had composed such a long piece, a writer responded, "I didn't have time to make it shorter." Editing takes time; expressing complex concepts in concise packages requires perseverance.

Brevity does not imply the elimination of detail. The writer need not reduce the argument's scope. Rather, the argument must be stated succinctly. This is demonstrated in Figure 5–1:

Figure 5–1 Being Brief

<u>Incorrect:</u>

The defendant's conduct was clearly wrong, in that the careless manner in which he maintained the subject premises, combined with the fact that he failed to issue a warning of any kind, certainly violated the duty that he owed to the plaintiff, and hence this court should find that the defendant was negligent.

<u>Correct:</u>

The defendant's negligence is established by his failure to maintain the subject premises and his failure to warn the plaintiff.

The two examples convey the same message; the correct version, however, does so with force and brevity.

Clarity is likewise key. Good writing accurately conveys its intended message—no more, no less. Every passage less than clear is a passage over which the reader stumbles, hesitates, or worse, loses interest. The writer must make her message plain:

Figure 5–2 Being Clear

<u>Incorrect:</u>

The witness testified about the accident only on the second day of the trial.

<u>Correct:</u>

Only on the second day of the trial did the witness testify about the accident.

On the second day of the trial, the witness testified only about the accident.

The first version is incorrect because it can be interpreted as having either of the meanings of the two correct versions.

Closely related to clarity is **precision**. Clarity requires that your writing be open to no more than one interpretation; precision requires that this one interpretation represent the point you seek to convey:

Figure 5–3 Being Precise

> <u>Incorrect:</u>
>
> The testimony establishes that the defendant had the unique habit of walking around his block at 3:00 a.m.
>
> <u>Correct:</u>
>
> The testimony establishes that the defendant had the unusual habit of walking around his block at 3:00 a.m.

It is unlikely that defendant is the only person ever to demonstrate such a habit (the most common meaning of the word *unique*), and even more unlikely that such a meaning was intended by the writer. Choose your words with care.

Brevity, clarity, and precision are essential characteristics of good writing. By analyzing and editing your writing to assure that it is succinct, clear, and precise, you gain an added benefit—a deeper, clearer understanding of your own argument.

Voice

Writing **voice**, in general, is a concept that is easy to define but difficult to analyze. It can be defined as the sound heard in the mind of the reader, or the impression created by virtue of the words chosen. Analyzing this sound, the "voice," is challenging because a writer can only "hear" her own mind, not that of the reader.

Defined more loosely, voice is the poetic aspect of prose writing—the flow and rhythm, the tone, the lyrical quality of the words. Such considerations might seem out of place in legal writing, but not if viewed as means rather than ends. The point is not to create a document that reads like a poem; the point is first to determine the tone you seek, then use voice to help achieve such a tone.

In the last chapter, we touched upon **flow**. A document flows when the reader moves easily through the text from point to point and from argument to argument. The reader's expectations are fulfilled because the writer has provided the elements that the reader needs to understand the content. Establishing flow is the first element of voice.

How is flow established? By using effective transitions (which we've touched on before and will discuss further) and by employing logical development (which we also discuss further), a writer creates a document that carries the reader along. Rereading is once again the key, followed by editing. Improving flow often requires "cutting and pasting": moving paragraphs around. Having placed raw information in a first draft, the writer sets about the task of logical ordering. It also helps to set aside your writing for a time, *then* reread it—the flaws are often readily apparent, since you are not so immersed in the details of your argument.

Rhythm is an important element of voice as well. A sentence has, so to speak, peaks and valleys and plateaus. A good writer manipulates the terrain, so that major points sit atop the peaks. Suppose you want to emphasize the believable nature of the testimony of an anxious witness. Consider Figure 5–4:

Figure 5–4 Rhythm in Voice

<u>Incorrect:</u>

The witness was credible, though nervous.

<u>Correct:</u>

The witness, though nervous, was credible.

The high points in a sentence often come at the beginning and at the end, as in this simple example. In the incorrect version the reader is left with the lingering impression that the nervousness undercut the credibility. In the correct version, the impression left is that, despite the nervousness, the witness was credible.

Analysis of rhythm is not so easy as simply making your strongest points first and last in a sentence or paragraph, however. It requires an analysis of style in general, and style in writing is a concept difficult to pin down. Consider the following two examples, both grammatically correct, but one more effective than the other:

Figure 5–5 Rhythm to Increase Impact

<u>Ineffective:</u>

The defendant's car had nonfunctional headlights, as well as barely audible horn and insufficient brakes.

<u>Effective:</u>

The defendant's car had neither functional headlights, nor an audible horn, nor sufficient brakes.

The effective example conveys the same information, but does so with impact.

Several techniques can be used to increase impact. In Figure 5–5, the power of a series that lists three items is apparent. The rhythm inherent in a list of three is more effective than a series of two or four or any other number:

Figure 5–6 Rhythm Inherent in Lists

<u>Two-item series:</u>

The defendant's car had neither functional headlights nor an audible horn.

<u>Four-item series:</u>

The defendant's car had neither functional headlights, nor an audible horn, nor sufficient brakes, nor adequate steering.

The list of two is acceptable, although its abrupt ending is a less powerful construction than a list of three. (Note that this analysis is in terms of *rhythm*, not the fact that the sheer evidentiary weight of three items is superior to two.) The list of four simply goes on too long. If it is essential to pass along all the information, the list of four might have been better stated as in Figure 5–7:

Figure 5–7 Four-Item List

> Defendant's car had neither functional headlights, nor an audible horn, nor sufficient brakes. Indeed, it even lacked adequate steering.

The four-item sentence has been broken into two sentences, the first of which uses the rhythmic power of three.

The effective example from Figure 5–5 also works well because it uses **parallel construction**. Parallel construction means repeating usages to make a point, to suggest either a connection or a contrast. Certain word combinations naturally fall into parallel structures—the "neither/nor" combination, for example, or the "former/latter" combination:

Figure 5–8 Parallel Construction

> The judge addressed the accused juvenile in her chambers, then, separately, the juvenile's parents. To the former, she urged the need for maturity; to the latter, the need for discipline.

Parallel construction in Figure 5–8 and in the effective sentence from Figure 5–5 requires that grammatical usage be consistent. Compare the two examples in Figure 5–9:

Figure 5–9 Agreement in Parallel Construction

> <u>Incorrect:</u>
>
> Legal writers should communicate in a clear manner, concisely, and be effective.
>
> <u>Correct:</u>
>
> Legal writers should communicate clearly, concisely, and effectively.

In the correct example, all three modifiers are adverbs relating back to and agreeing with the verb *communicate*. In the incorrect example, the relationship and agreement are muddled. Novice writers often shy away from parallel construction, believing that variety is always better than parallelism. Don't make this mistake—parallel construction has impact.

Under other circumstances, however, variety is an important element of good writing. To give just one such example, consider the following: although simple sentences (subject/verb/object) are often the most powerful, used exclusively they can lead to a monotonous, droning voice that actually drains the power from your words. A mixture of simple, complex, and compound sentences adds texture to the presentation of your thoughts. Thus, whereas variety should be avoided in parallel comparisons, it is desirable in other contexts.

We have noted that the point of establishing voice is not to make your document read like a poem, but rather to achieve the desired tone. But what *is* the desired tone? In legal writing, you generally seek to evoke a formal, assertive tone. To achieve such a tone, avoid light, familiar language; be straightforward without being ponderous. Your writing should be neither stuffy nor conversational. Stay away from the flip comment; keep your analysis sharp and your language focused.

Similes and Metaphors

Similes and metaphors are figures of speech useful to legal writers. A **simile** is a direct comparison of dissimilar objects, for the purpose of emphasizing a common characteristic. A **metaphor** also links dissimilar objects, but it is more powerful than a simile in that it equates, rather than compares, the objects:

Figure 5–10 Simile and Metaphor

<u>Simile:</u>

A good simile is like a good after-dinner speech: short and to the point.

<u>Metaphor:</u>

Metaphors are valuable weapons in the legal writer's arsenal.

When using metaphors, be careful of that entertaining but ineffective species, the mixed metaphor:

Figure 5–11 Mixed Metaphor

Metaphors are valuable tools in the legal writer's arsenal.

Until soldiers shower their enemies with hammers and screwdrivers, tools are not to be found in an arsenal!

Used selectively, metaphors and similes make a vivid impression in the mind of the reader. Be wary, however, of overuse, which can erode an otherwise effective argument.

5–3 Pitfalls in Language

Language presents potential problems, as well as possibilities. When drafting legal documents, there are several pitfalls to avoid.

Ambiguity

Ambiguity exists when a writer has failed in the obligation to provide precision and clarity. In the law, as in perhaps no other subject area, ambiguity can have devastating consequences. At best, ambiguity creates hardships and confusion for the reader; at worst, it can adversely affect your client's essential rights. The legal writer's words must convey her intended message—no more, no less. Consider the following example:

Figure 5–12 Pronoun Ambiguity

Neither plaintiff nor defendant knew he had executed the contract without authority.

The sentence in Figure 5–12 is ambiguous because the reader is left wondering: who is "he?" Was it the plaintiff who had executed the contract without authority? Was it the defendant? Did *both* plaintiff and defendant unknowingly execute the contract without authority? Were both plaintiff and defendant unaware that some third party had executed the contract without authority? Because she is left wondering, the reader's inquiry is interrupted and perhaps inhibited. She loses the point of the argument, and she may abandon it altogether. Although the broader context from which this sentence was drawn may clear up some of the confusion, it might have been better stated in one of the following ways:

Figure 5–13 Unambiguous Alternative

<u>Example 1:</u>

Neither plaintiff not defendant knew that plaintiff had executed the contract without authority.

<u>Example 2:</u>

Neither plaintiff nor defendant knew that plaintiff's agent had executed the contract without authority.

<u>Example 3:</u>

Both plaintiff and defendant were unaware that each had executed the contract without authority.

Figure 5–12 provides an example of **pronoun ambiguity**. Pronoun ambiguity results from an unclear indication about the noun to which the pronoun refers back—in Figure 5–12, the pronoun "he."

Another form of ambiguity arises when the placement of a modifying clause obscures the object of the modification:

Figure 5–14 Object Ambiguity

The testimony of the accounting expert led to the vindication of the corporation's accounting process as a result of its accuracy.

Was it the testimony that was accurate, or the accounting process? Both, we hope, but you see the problem. The placement of the clause obscures the reference of the pronoun "its." Two alternatives appear in Figure 5–15:

Figure 5–15 Unambiguous Alternative

The accurate testimony of the accounting expert vindicated the corporation's accounting process.

or

The accounting expert vindicated the corporation's accounting process by testifying to its accuracy.

Sexism

Sexist references and gender-based differentiation, which reinforce sexual stereotypes, have no place in legal writing. Consider the question of sexism when choosing pronouns that relate back to occupational nouns. For example, you should not always use the pronoun *he* when referring to a judge, or *she* when referring to a paralegal. One solution to this problem is to use "he or she," although this can be awkward, particularly when used repeatedly. Another alternative is to make a conscious effort to vary or alternate the pronouns used. This latter alternative has been employed in this book.

Another option is to make your original noun plural, enabling you to use a plural (hence gender-neutral) pronoun:

Figure 5–16 Relating Back to Occupational Nouns

<u>Gender-specific:</u>

When a judge considers a brief, she reviews form as well as substance.

<u>Gender-neutral:</u>

When judges consider briefs, they review form as well as substance.

The use of plurals eliminates the gender differentiation, but, like the "he or she" construction, can also create an awkward feel to the sentence. You will have to use your judgment abut the best means of eliminating sexist references.

Clichés and Slang

Clichés are, by definition, overused figures of speech. Legal writing should be crisp and fresh, with points made in clear, logical language that avoids vague references and shopworn phrases. In Figure 5–17, we identify a few of the many clichés to be avoided:

Figure 5–17 Clichés

> Slow as molasses
>
> Kill two birds with one stone
>
> Birds of a feather
>
> The blind leading the blind

If a seasoned writer were to use a cliché to make a point, she would generally set off the cliché with quotation marks. However, after careful reflection, most such usages, although perhaps seeming clever at first, will be seen to be stylistically weak:

Figure 5–18 Setting Off the Cliché

> To say that defendants are "birds of a feather" is to commit an injustice to birds.

Similarly, slang should be avoided. Defendant did not "rip off" the plaintiff; damages are not "30,000 bucks." Legal documents can be undermined by sloppy, colloquial usages.

Note that avoiding clichés and slang should not dampen your enthusiasm for the occasional simile or metaphor. But remember that tired, overused similes or metaphors such as "clear as mud" or "beating around the bush" don't inspire anyone.

Failure of Subject and Verb to Agree

Nothing confuses the reader or undermines a sentence more quickly than failure to use the proper verb form. The verb must always agree with its subject. Consider, for example, the compound subject:

Figure 5–19 Subject/Verb Agreement

> <u>Incorrect:</u>
>
> The traffic and weather was terrible on the day of the accident.
>
> <u>Correct:</u>
>
> The traffic and weather were terrible on the day of the accident.

Although both traffic and weather are singular, the subject of the sentence is "traffic *and* weather," which has two elements and hence requires a plural verb (were).

Certain phrases introduced by subordinate conjunctions are not considered part of the subject, despite their obvious relation to the subject, and thus are not taken into consideration when determining verb form:

Figure 5-20 Phrases Introduced by Subordinate Conjunctions

> Correct:
>
> The judge, as well as plaintiff's counsel, was stunned by the verdict.
>
> Incorrect:
>
> The judge, as well as plaintiff's counsel, were stunned by the verdict.

The subject is "judge" and the verb is "was"; "plaintiff's counsel" is not considered to be part of the subject.

A descriptive prepositional phrase that itself contains a noun can be misleading. Be sure that the verb form agrees with the subject, not the descriptive phrase's noun:

Figure 5-21 Prepositional Phrases With Nouns

> Incorrect:
>
> The lineup of defendants were a sorry sight.
>
> Correct:
>
> The lineup of defendants was a sorry sight.

The first example is incorrect because the verb was made to agree with the noun "defendants," although that noun is not the subject of the sentence. In the correct example, the verb agrees with the true subject, "lineup." The noun "defendants" is part of the prepositional phrase "of defendants," which merely describes the lineup.

A question often arises with regard to verb usage when the subject is "jury." Is a jury a group of individuals, requiring a plural verb, or a single entity, requiring a singular verb? The answers is, it depends: when a jury is acting in unison, use the singular; when acting individually, use the plural:

Figure 5-22 Verb Usage With "Jury"

> Correct use of singular:
>
> The jury was unanimous in its verdict of acquittal.
>
> Correct use of plural:
>
> The jury were hopelessly divided on the issue of defendant's negligence.

The second example is accepted usage, despite the strange sound. It might be better to use the following clearer version:

Figure 5-23 Correct Use of Plural

The jurors were hopelessly divided on the issue of defendant's negligence.

Jargon

Legal **jargon** or "**legalese**" is useful if used in moderation, and if the audience understands it. We discussed some of the problems and benefits of legalese in Chapter 3. To summarize, if you can say it in plain English, say it that way; if your audience is sophisticated legal professionals (as with, for example, an appellate brief), use language that the audience expects and understands, including "terms of art"; and if you feel compelled to use legalese in a document intended for a layman to read (for example, in a letter explaining a technical legal problem to a client), be sure to explain carefully any terms that the average person might not understand.

Redundancy and Verbosity

Just as ambiguity is the result when clarity and precision are disregarded, so redundancy and verbosity are the result when brevity is lost. That is a slightly verbose way of saying: "Get to the point! And don't repeat yourself!"

Redundancy exists when the writer has made the same point over and over. Say it *once*. Say it *forcefully*, but say it *once*. (Is this paragraph now redundant?) Don't underestimate the intelligence of the reader. You have to use your own judgment in particular instances, but generally speaking, repeated hammering on the same point can offend or bore the reader, and actually weaken an otherwise powerful argument.

Verbosity is simply the use of an excessive number of words, or excessively complicated words, to make a point. Some novice writers mistake verbosity for impressive analysis; in fact, it seems pompous and often indicates a lack of command of the subject matter. Keep your sentences as short as possible (given the need for variety) and use the simplest words you can: the defendant was "insensitive," not "obtuse"; the departure was "hasty," not "precipitate"; the road was "slippery," not "lubricious."

5-4 Tell Them!

A writer begins with an advantage: he knows what he wants to say. But this knowledge can turn into a disadvantage. Why? The reason is simple—because the reader doesn't share the same foreknowledge. The reader doesn't know what the writer wants to say until he says it. And if a writer gets so caught up in the particulars of his argument that he loses touch with this fact, the quality of his writing begins to plummet. He will fail to provide the hints and signals that the reader needs and wants. His message will become obscure.

How do you do away with the obscurity? Often you can cure it by simply telling the reader what you're talking about. Even an excellent writer can become so wrapped up in the details of her argument that she fails to put them in proper perspective. The solution is to step back and review the overall argument for the reader's benefit.

Topic Sentences and Transitions

By rereading an obscure passage, summarizing its importance in your mind, then reintroducing it with the summary, you provide the introduction that the reader needs. In Figure 5–24, note the improvement from the addition of a simple sentence that merely states, up front, the intended message:

Figure 5–24 Providing an Introduction

Without a lead-in:

In *Jones v. Smith*, the plaintiff claimed that the will was invalid because one of the alleged witnesses had been blind at the time of the will's execution. The court found, however, that the witness had been blind in one eye only. In the present case before the court, the witness in question was blind in both eyes at the time of execution, was partially deaf as well, and hence could not have properly witnessed the testator's signature.

With an informative lead-in:

The case of *Jones v. Smith* is distinguishable, and does not support the plaintiff's contention that the will was properly witnessed. In *Jones v. Smith*, the plaintiff claimed that the will was invalid because one of the alleged witnesses had been blind at the time of the will's execution. The court found, however, that the witness had been blind in one eye only. In the present case before the court, the witness in question was blind in both eyes at the time of execution, was partially deaf as well, and hence could not have properly witnessed the testator's signature.

Simply by telling the reader, at the outset, what will be addressed, the whole passage becomes easier to understand.

This concept of telling the reader what to expect is directly related to the concept of the **topic sentence**, which we discussed in Chapter 4. Indeed, what we've done in Figure 5–24 is nothing more than add a topic sentence. Our approach in this subsection is different from our previous discussion of topic sentences and **transitions**, however. In the last chapter, we were building a paragraph from the ground up, that is, **drafting**. In this subsection, think about it from a different perspective—think about it as **troubleshooting**. You've written a document, and you've reread it, and you know something's wrong. You've corrected all the punctuation and grammatical errors, you've removed the clichés, you've been succinct—and still something's missing. What can it be?

Think back for a moment to our discussion, near Figure 4–29, of a paragraph that holds back the topic sentence until the end. We noted that such paragraph structure requires patience on the part of the reader, and creates the risk that the reader will lose interest. Now imagine an entire *document* requiring such patience—it's *inevitable* that the reader will lose interest in such a document. A little of this technique might create useful tension, but a reader should not be kept waiting from beginning to end to find out the writer's point in a brief. Provide topic sentences and transitions to eliminate obscurity—in short, *tell them*!

The problem can exist even within an individual sentence. Some sentences, called **periodic sentences**, force the reader to store information until the end (analogous to the paragraph with topic sentence at the end). Contrast such a periodic sentence with the **cumulative** (also called "loose") **sentences** in Figure 5–25:

Figure 5–25 Periodic and Cumulative Sentences

> **Periodic sentence:**
>
> The treasurer of the corporation, who was elected by unanimous consent of the board of directors, who had been publicly acclaimed by both the corporation's chief executive officer and the local business media, and who in fifteen years of service had never missed a single day of work, has been missing for three weeks, was last seen at the Los Angeles airport, and is believed to have flown to South America with a substantial amount of embezzled funds.
>
> **Cumulative sentences:**
>
> The treasurer of the corporation is believed to have flown to South America with a substantial amount of embezzled funds. Missing for three weeks, and last seen at the Los Angeles airport, he had never missed a day of work in fifteen years of service. He had been elected by the unanimous consent of the board of directors, and had been publicly acclaimed by both the corporation's chief executive officer and the local business media.

The point is obvious. The periodic example makes the reader work, whereas the cumulative example requires the writer to work harder so that the reader need not.

When "something's missing," improving topic sentences and transitions so as to minimize the work the reader must do will often help cure the problem. But remember, even periodic sentences can have dramatic impact, used sparingly:

Figure 5–26 Dramatic Impact of Periodic Sentence

> The witness, unruffled in demeanor, untroubled by conscience, and unaffected by the presence of the victim's relatives, testified about her role in the murder.

Like so many other aspects of writing, the final decision on sentence structure is a judgment call. But now you have a foundation on which to base your judgment.

Active Voice versus Passive Voice

We've discussed "voice" as a stylistic aspect of writing. One important element of voice is the active/passive split. In **active voice**, the subject of the sentence performs the action; in **passive voice**, the subject of the sentence is the object of the action:

Figure 5–27 Active vs Passive

> **Active:**
>
> The defendant violated the law.
>
> **Passive:**
>
> The law was violated by the defendant.

In the first example, the subject ("defendant") performed the action ("violated"), and the grammatical object ("the law") is also the object of the action. In the second example, "the law" remains the object of the action that the sentence describes, but grammatically it has taken the role of the subject.

Active voice is generally preferable to passive voice. Novice legal writers sometimes adopt a passive voice, since it sounds formal, but this usually weakens the power of their words. Again, *tell them*. It is generally better to describe the action than the result. Dull writing can often be enlivened by rewriting passive passages in the active voice.

Passive construction should not be entirely abandoned, however. If the point of the sentence focuses on the object, passive construction may be preferred. In Figure 5–28, the passive example would be preferable if the writer were discussing the difficulty of enforcing certain laws, whereas the active example would be preferable if the writer were discussing the habits of pedestrians:

Figure 5–28 Active/Passive Preference

> **Active voice:**
>
> Pedestrians have repeatedly violated the jaywalking law, with no enforcement action taken.
>
> **Passive voice:**
>
> The jaywalking law has been repeatedly violated by pedestrians, with no enforcement action taken.

Structured Enumeration

Sequential points are often difficult to follow if not clearly labeled. **Structured enumeration**, which specifically identifies each point, can eliminate the difficulty. Again, the purpose is to tell the reader precisely what is meant:

Figure 5–29 Structured Enumeration

> **Without structured enumeration:**
>
> The elements of negligence are all present here. The defendant owed a duty to the plaintiff, and the duty was breached. This breach was the proximate cause of the plaintiff's injury. The plaintiff suffered damage as a result.
>
> **With structured enumeration:**
>
> The elements of negligence are all present here. First, the defendant owed a duty to the plaintiff. Second, the duty was breached. Third, this breach was the proximate cause of the plaintiff's injury. Fourth, the plaintiff suffered damage as a result.

The structured enumeration makes the paragraph easier to follow and understand. Legal analysis often requires lists of complex factors; structured enumeration helps the reader to comprehend such lists.

Take a Positive and Definitive Approach

Positive statements are almost always more forceful than negative ones.

Figure 5–30 Negative/Positive Statements

> <u>Negative:</u>
>
> The club did not accept his application.
>
> <u>Positive:</u>
>
> The club rejected his application.

If you are trying to make a point, use the positive approach. If you are trying to deemphasize a point, use the negative approach. For example, suppose the person whose application was rejected in the preceding example sued the club alleging racial discrimination. The club's counsel might use the following sentence in her statement of facts:

Figure 5–31 Muting the Negative

> Although plaintiff was not accepted for membership in the club, the club was unbiased in reaching its decision.

This sentence mutes the impact of the rejection, which is the goal of the club's counsel.

You should also be **definitive** when taking a position. There are few words more useless, for example, than "clearly":

Figure 5–32 Being Definitive

> <u>Incorrect:</u>
>
> The defendant was clearly negligent.
>
> <u>Correct:</u>
>
> The defendant was negligent.

An assumption is built into the incorrect example—an assumption that there are factors to be weighed, and that, based upon these factors, a "clear" conclusion can be reached. Using the word "clearly" in this way actually invites the reader to challenge the main proposition, to weigh the evidence and determine for himself just how "clear" it is that defendant was negligent.

The correct example simply states a proposition: "defendant was negligent." Period. It assumes no analysis, it simply provides the conclusion. This is the best way to present your points—forthrightly, with confidence, and without qualification. Vague, qualifying words such as "quite," "very," and "rather" have no place in legal writing. The road was not "very slippery," it was "slippery"; the defendant is not "unquestionably guilty," she is "guilty."

This is not to say that you should not support your conclusions with analysis. Such analysis is, of course, essential. By all means, point out the testimony that the road was slippery; by all means, point out that the fingerprints left on the gun were the defendant's. Nor is it to say that no one will challenge your conclusions if you state them forthrightly—they surely will. But in stating the propositions upon which your argument rests, don't undercut them by your own word usage. State them conclusively. You want your audience to know something—so *tell them*!

5–5   Logical Development

It takes more than bricks and mortar to build a house; there must be an architect as well. So it is with good writing: there must be central organizing principles within a document, so that the individual components work together to accomplish the overall objective. There must be structure and a plan.

The key to organization is logical development. Logical development is present in a writing when each point follows naturally from its predecessor. You have learned that you can use topic sentences, transitions, and structured enumeration to ensure that the reader has a reasonable understanding of where the argument is going. In addition to these techniques, you should also analyze your document on a larger scale, as an organic whole.

Several methods can be used to achieve logical development.

IRAC Method

We discussed the **IRAC method** in Chapter 3. It involves: (1) identifying the issue; (2) determining the rule of law; (3) applying the rule of law to the facts of your case; and (4) reaching a conclusion. This structure can be applied to a paragraph or to a series of paragraphs constituting a single argument. By using the IRAC format, the development of each individual argument will be logical. If your documents involve multiple arguments, you have to order them according to one of the overriding principles that follow.

Strongest Argument First

Writers often place their strongest argument first. By opening with their strength, they can then build on this foundation. Weaker points may be buttressed by association.

Chronological Development

Sometimes arguments are best ordered chronologically, particularly when they fit in a complex factual context, or when the order of events is crucial to the analysis. For example, in a business dispute over the performance of an electronic component built by defendant and purchased by plaintiff, there may be many letters, test reports, and field results that touch upon the knowledge of the parties and the positions taken and the risks assumed by the parties. The legal arguments may build upon the chronological development. In such a case, chronological assessment is essential, particularly with regard to your statement of facts.

When ordering your arguments chronologically, you must take special care that your strongest argument not get lost. One possible solution is a preliminary summary that emphasizes your important points, followed by the detailed chronological analysis.

Outlining and Subheading

Outlining has already been identified as a preliminary step in writing. By starting with an outline, the writer has a framework within which to work. The outline also provides a shorthand format in which the larger argument can be grasped, and against which the logic of its development can be measured.

Subheadings are useful both as transition tools (more will be said about this in future chapters) and as a form of outline. By reviewing your subheadings, you can analyze how the elements of your argument fit into the organic whole. If the progression, as seen through the subheads, does not seem logical, then the body of the argument is probably not logically developed.

5–6 Practical Considerations

A novice writes a paragraph. He rereads it. It isn't good. It fails to make the point he wanted to make. The logic doesn't follow from beginning to end. Is he a bad writer?

He might think he is—but he isn't.

He isn't, at least, if he recognized the cardinal rule of writing: that almost no one gets it right on the first try.

He isn't a bad writer if he recognizes the weaknesses in his paragraph and then takes out the tools of an editor—a pencil, eraser, scissors, and tape (or their word-processing equivalents)—to begin the task of improving it. Rereading, editing, revising, reworking, shifting paragraphs, substituting words, inserting explanations, deleting redundant elements, eliminating grammatical errors, crossing out, inserting, rereading, rereading, *rereading*—these are the elements that go into good writing.

Nothing you've learned about rules, style, design, and persuasiveness will be of any use if you fail to understand that writing is reading.

Nor is the process easy. "A writer is someone for whom writing is more difficult than it is for other people," said Thomas Mann. Writing is hard work, designed, ironically, to create the appearance of effortlessness—and, in the case of legal writing, to persuade.

SUMMARY

5–1

A good writer recognizes that writing is reading, and that she must reread what she has written, placing herself in the position of the reader, and improve it through revision.

5–2

Good writing requires brevity, clarity, and precision. Include necessary details, but be succinct. Accurately convey your intended message, no more and no less, and make sure the words you have chosen are open to no more than one interpretation. Writing voice is the "sound" that the reader hears in his mind; defined more loosely, it is the poetical or lyrical aspect of writing. Flow is established by combining logical development with a commitment to rereading and editing, so that the reader moves easily from point to point in the finished product. Rhythm in a sentence refers to the varying levels of emphasis of the words—the high points and the low points. Good sentence rhythm can be obtained by employing such techniques as placing the points you wish to emphasize at the beginning or end of a sentence, not hidden in the middle; recognizing the rhythmic power inherent in a series or list of three points; and using parallel construction to emphasize and clarify your points. Similes compare dissimilar objects, metaphors equate them. Both are useful figures of speech that a writer can employ to make a colorful point.

5–3

Legal writers must avoid ambiguity. Two things to look out for are pronoun ambiguity and unclear placement of modifying clauses. Sexist references have no place in legal writing, and can be eliminated by using plural forms, by using "he or she," or by alternating male and female pronouns. Clichés and slang are overused or excessively informal usages, which are out of place in legal writing. A good writer makes sure her verbs agree with her subjects, which requires a careful evaluation of which nouns constitute the subject and which perform some other function in the sentence. Never be redundant, since repetition can undercut, rather than emphasize, your strong points. Don't mistake verbosity for persuasive analysis; it is almost always better to keep your sentences short, your analysis brief, and your words simple.

5–4

Obscurity can often be cured simply by telling the reader what you are talking about. Use topic sentences and transitions to make your writing flow easily for the reader. Emphasize the active voice (in which the subject performs the action), but don't eliminate the passive voice entirely. It can be useful where the object of the action is the important point. Structured enumeration enables the reader to follow sequential points easily. Emphasize the strengths of your argument with positive language; deemphasize the weaknesses by stating them in a negative manner. Always be definitive.

5–5

Use the IRAC method as a foundation for logical development. State your strongest arguments first, and use chronological development, preliminary outlining, and explanatory subheadings as devices to improve the manner in which your document develops, so that the reader more easily grasps your arguments.

5–6

Almost no one gets writing right on the first try. Reread, edit, and revise until you are satisfied that your points have been presented in the best manner possible.

REVIEW

Key Terms

Before proceeding, review the key terms listed below to be sure you understand each one. If necessary, read over the corresponding section of the chapter. When you are ready to test your understanding, answer the Review Questions.

rereading
editing
brevity
clarity
precision
voice
flow
rhythm
parallel construction
similes
metaphors
ambiguity
pronoun ambiguity
verb agreement
jargon
legalese
redundancy
verbosity
topic sentence
transition
drafting
troubleshooting
periodic sentence
cumulative sentence
active voice
passive voice
structured enumeration
definitive
IRAC method
chronological development
outlining
subheadings

Questions for Review and Discussion

1. How can writing be made clear and precise?
2. What do rhythm, flow, and voice mean in the writing context?
3. How are similes and metaphors used?
4. How are ambiguity and redundancy avoided?
5. How are subjects and verbs made to agree?
6. Describe a simple method to eliminate obscurity in your writing.
7. Describe the difference between a periodic sentence and a cumulative sentence.
8. What is the difference between active voice and passive voice, and when should each be used?
9. What is structured enumeration?
10. How can arguments be logically developed?

Activities

1. Rewrite the following passage from *Cooley v. Board of Wardens* (1851) using proper punctuation and plain English.

   That the power to regulate commerce includes the regulation of navigation, we consider settled. And when we look to the nature of the service performed by pilots, to the relations which that service and its compensations bear to navigation between the several States, and between the ports of the United States and foreign countries, we are brought to the conclusion, that the regulation of the qualifications of pilots, of the modes and times of offering and rendering their services, of the responsibilities which shall rest upon them, of the powers they shall possess, of the compensation they may demand, and of the penalties by which their rights and duties may be enforced, do constitute regulations of navigation, and consequently of commerce, within the just meaning of this clause of the Constitution.

2. Identify the trouble spots in sentence structure in the following passage from *Ranta v. McCarney*, (Supreme Court–North Dakota, 1986).

   We believe a fair reading of Section 27-1101 and *Christianson* indicate a preference by both the Legislature and our Court of furthering the strong policy consideration underlying the prohibition against the unauthorized practice of law that occurs in this State by barring compensation for any such activities.

3. Rewrite the following passage from *United States v. Nixon* (1974) by simplifying the sentences and word choice.

[In this case] the traditional contempt avenue to immediate appeal is peculiarly inappropriate due to the unique setting in which the question arises. To require a President of the United States to place himself in the posture of disobeying an order of a court merely to trigger the procedural mechanism for review of the ruling would be unseemly, and would present an unnecessary occasion for constitutional confrontation between two branches of the Government. Similarly, a federal judge should not be placed in the posture of issuing a citation to a President simply in order to invoke the review. The issue whether a President can be cited for contempt could itself engender protracted litigation, and would further delay both review on the merits of his claim of privilege and the ultimate termination of the underlying criminal action for which his evidence is sought. These considerations lead us to conclude that the order of the District Court was an appealable order. The appeal from that order was therefore properly "in" the Court of Appeals, and the case is now properly before this Court on the writ of certiorari before judgment.

CHAPTER 6   The Initial Client Interview and the Internal Memorandum of Law

OUTLINE

COMMENTARY

Your supervising attorney calls you into her office to tell you about a telephone call she just received from the friend of a client. The friend, whose name is Mr. Giles, has briefly described a problem he is experiencing with regard to a power of attorney document. The problem appears to be urgent, but your supervising attorney could not discuss the details with Mr. Giles because she is in a rush to get to court for a trial.

Your assignment: Call Mr. Giles, schedule an appointment today for an initial client interview, conduct the interview yourself, then prepare an internal memorandum summarizing the facts of, and law relating to, Mr. Giles's problem.

OBJECTIVES

The first five chapters introduced you to writing and research in the American legal system. In Chapter 6, you begin to put your knowledge to use. After completing this chapter, you will be able to:

1. Identify preliminary considerations in a client interview.
2. Accomplish the practical and technical objectives of a client interview.
3. Prepare a postinterview memorandum.
4. Describe the objective nature of an internal memorandum of law.
5. List several purposes of an internal memorandum of law.
6. Identify the information that should be included in the heading section of a memorandum of law.

7. Explain the importance of the "issues presented" section.
8. Identify the purpose of the "short summary of the conclusion" section.
9. Prepare an appropriate statement of facts.
10. Identify key elements in the "discussion" section.

6–1 The Initial Client Interview

The **initial client interview** if the first stage of any writing project. This does not mean that, after receiving a writing assignment, the first thing you should do is schedule an interview. You shouldn't—this would often be wastefully duplicative.

It does mean, however, that the initial client interview affects every subsequent writing assignment. The information you obtain, with updates and supplementation, provides the foundation upon which the matter proceeds.

Preliminary Considerations

Although our focus in this section is on the interview's impact on the writing process, a few preliminaries must be considered.

First, before beginning your investigation into the facts of the matter, be sure to identify yourself as a paralegal. You are not someone who is authorized to practice law, and the interviewee should understand this. You are, however, someone whose knowledge of the case is protected under the **attorney/client privilege** (assuming the interviewee is a client or prospective client; if a nonclient, such as an eyewitness, the privilege does not apply). Privilege is important because it enables the interviewee to speak freely and honestly, without fear of self-incrimination of fear that you could be compelled by subpoena to reveal the information provided. You should also make the client aware that you are trained as a paraprofessional; this should be emphasized to cultivate the client's confidence.

Second, the matter off fees may also arise, particularly if the interviewee is a new or potential client, as in the Commentary to this chapter. You should consult your supervising attorney about how to field questions on fee structure. The client is entitled to a precise understanding of this structure, but the responsibility to inform him is ultimately the attorney's.

Finally, you should prepare all documents that will be required during the interview, including retainer letters, authorization to obtain medical or employment records, and other documents. You should also review any materials already in your firm's file on the matter. If you are aware of any of the details of the client's problem, you should perform some background research to familiarize yourself with the substantive areas of law that seem to be applicable.

The Interview

The interview itself has a practical purpose and a technical purpose. The practical purpose is to establish a positive relationship with the client. You want to impress upon the client the firm's professional approach and commitment to her matter.

The technical aspect relates to the primary purpose of the interview—fact gathering—and brings into focus the relationship between the interview and the writing process.

It is in the initial interview that you begin to develop an understanding of the factual context of the client's problem. This investigation sets the stage for future writing projects, whether related to litigation, drafting of operative documents to construct a deal, or some other purpose.

The investigation conducted in an initial interview should be thought of as proceeding in distinct segments. First, you need to get a broad overview of the situation. An interviewer who does not know the "big picture" will initially be unable to fit the facts he learns into a coherent framework, adrift, like a reader analyzing a paragraph with no topic sentence. The overview is also important because the client may not convey the details in a logical manner, resulting in confusion if the interviewer (that is, you) lacks a framework. Thus you should start by asking for (1) the client's basic problem, in broad terms, and (2) the result the client seeks.

Once you have obtained this information, you have the framework needed to collect and correlate the details. In the second segment of the interview, then, you allow the client to recite the specifics of the problem. You may need to prod the client, or you may need to ask focused questions to obtain facts that are legally significant, but which the client may not realize are important. In this segment of the interview you should ask the client open-ended questions. In essence, you are saying to the client: "Tell me what happened."

After the client has told her story you should begin to ask detailed questions. By using your knowledge of the area of law involved, you can obtain the specific information you and your supervising attorney need.

Finally, at the end of the fact-gathering segment, review the entire matter with the client. By going over the same ground a second time (more quickly, of course, than before), you will catch any inconsistencies between your interpretation of the client's statements and the client's intended meaning.

There is a substantial literature on interviewing techniques, and an in-depth review is beyond the scope of this book. If you keep in mind your goal, however—to get the client's story—and avoid putting words in the client's mouth (for example, don't use leading questions, which suggest a response), you will have a head start on perfecting your own style.

Note Taking and the Postinterview Memorandum

During the interview you should be taking comprehensive notes. Don't let your note taking interfere with the progression of the interview, but make sure you keep an accurate record of the client's statements. You will be referring to these notes in the final segment of the interview, when you review the entire account with the client.

After the interview, you should prepare a memorandum relating the client's statement in detail. This is not the internal memorandum of law that we discuss in the remainder of this chapter; it is simply a review of the content of the client interview, for the case file. This memorandum should be prepared immediately after the interview, when the details remain fresh in your mind and the references in your notes (including abbreviations and summaries) are still familiar to you. If you wait too long, your own notes may become incomprehensible.

6–2 The Internal Memorandum of Law

Once a client interview is completed, the resources of a law office are brought to bear on attending to the client's needs. The first step in this process is often the preparation of an internal memorandum of law.

An **internal memorandum of law** is a document that provides an objective analysis of the issues presented by the client's matter. Although memoranda differ in completeness, complexity, and the stage of the matter at which they are prepared, the purpose is always the same: to *inform*, to *explain*, and to *evaluate*. Internal memoranda analyze the law as it relates to the client's matter for such purposes as

- deciding whether to take the case;
- determining how to proceed on the case;
- providing a summary of the facts and the law;
- preparing for a hearing; and
- drafting appropriate operative documents.

The key to understanding the internal memorandum of law is in understanding its point of view—objective. The internal memorandum is not intended to advocate the client's position; it is intended to provide an objective assessment of the client's position. It is thus prepared only for review by the members of your law firm, and perhaps the client's inner circle. This differentiates the internal memorandum from a brief filed with a court, which is written from an advocate's perspective.

The format of the internal memorandum may vary from project to project, from firm to firm, and even from lawyer to lawyer (or department to department) within the same firm, depending on personal style preferences. When preparing a memorandum, you should make sure that you understand the format preferred by your supervising attorney. In general, however, most internal memoranda have the following components:

- heading;
- statement of issues presented;
- short summary of the conclusion;
- statement of facts;
- discussion and analysis of the law and facts, with citations to applicable authorities; and
- conclusion.

In the next several subsections we discuss each of these components in turn. As we do so we make reference to figures drawn from an internal memorandum.

The Heading

The **heading** identifies the party for whom the memorandum was prepared; by whom it was prepared; the date of preparation; and the subject matter. The heading for our memorandum appears in Figure 6–1.

The person for whom the memorandum is prepared is usually the attorney who gave you the assignment, and the person actually preparing the memorandum is usually you. This standard scenario may differ in an individual case, however. For example, an associate attorney may ask you to prepare a draft of a memorandum that he will ultimately submit to a partner under his own name (or with both your names). Make sure you understand this circumstance from the outset.

Figure 6-1 Example of Heading

```
                      MEMORANDUM

  TO:        J. Mark, Senior Partner

  FROM:      R. Lang, Paralegal

  DATE:      June 1, 1992

  RE:        Giles v. Harris
             The validity of a transfer of a joint venture
             interest with a blank power of attorney.
```

The next element of a heading is the date. If it takes more than one day to prepare a memorandum, do not identify the date when you started the memorandum, nor all the dates on which you worked on it, but rather the date on which you submit it. You should take care that shepardizing (or other updating) has been completed through that date.

Finally, the heading must identify the subject matter of the memorandum. This usually involves a brief capsule description of the legal issues presented, and possibly identification of the client as well. Although this information may be well known at the time of preparation both to you and the memorandum's recipient, it helps, for future reference, to label it. Such labeling also greatly assists in indexing when the memorandum is placed in the firm's permanent research files, which many firms maintain to avoid duplicating research.

The Statement of Issues Presented

The statement of issues presented identifies the legal and factual issues to be discussed in your memorandum. In framing these issues, be concise and direct, and number each issue (unless there is only one).

Figure 6-2 shows an example of appropriate form for a statement of issues presented. Each issue should be no longer than one or two sentences, and should generally be drafted to be answerable with a "yes" or "no" response.

Although the statement of issues presented is short, the time needed to prepare it may not be. In order to frame the issues properly, you must understand the facts and the relevant substantive law. Often your research will be well underway before you have adequate understanding even to draft a proper statement of issues presented. This may be true even if the ultimate statement amounts to a single short sentence summarizing a single simple issue. Take care in your analysis.

Often your supervising attorney will provide you with a preliminary statement of the issues that she wants investigated, or which she believes are relevant. If that is the case, then your memorandum should be limited to these points. If, however, your research indicates that other areas are more relevant, or at least worthy of consideration, you should consult with your supervising attorney and determine whether further research is warranted. Be careful not to go far afield from the original assignment without authorization; you may

Figure 6-2 Statement of Issue Presented

```
  Under Texas law, is the transfer of a joint venture inter-
  est with a blank power of attorney valid?
```

waste valuable time and money. Your supervising attorney should provide you with an understanding of the limits of your research; often, as your working relationship is established, you will develop an intuitive understanding of the requirements of a given project. When in doubt, however, ask.

Short Summary of the Conclusion

The purpose of the **short summary of the conclusion** is to provide the reader with a quick answer to the "yes or no" questions raised by the issues. It is always short, but rarely quite as simple in actuality as a mere "yes" or "no." There are generally qualifiers needed to provide a response representative of the analysis and conclusion to follow.

The short summary of the conclusion is useful for two purposes. First, to the attorney too busy to review the memorandum completely, it provides a capsule summary; second, to those who will study the memorandum in detail, it provides a preview of the end result, helping to place the analysis in perspective. An example is found in Figure 6–3.

Figure 6–3 Short Summary of the Conclusion

```
Yes. Since the power of attorney presented was devoid of any
terms, it did not contain the necessary elements to be a
valid power of attorney. The acts of the agent exercised
under such an invalid power of attorney are not binding on
the principal. However the cases hold that, if the princi-
pal received any personal benefits from the transaction, the
issue of ratification might be sufficient to validate the
acts of the agent.
```

Statement of Facts

The **statement of facts** sets forth the significant facts obtained in the client interview or provided to you by your supervising attorney, or otherwise present in the client's file. Individual facts are deemed legally significant if they are necessary for an understanding of or have an impact upon the conclusion drawn, with regard to the issues addressed in the memorandum. Although the intended scope and depth of the memorandum is a factor to consider in deciding whether to include specific facts, as a general rule you should lean toward inclusiveness.

Facts should be neither embellished nor downplayed, nor interpreted in the "best light." Rather, they should be objectively and accurately portrayed so that the reader can assess the situation presented. After your review of available materials, you may determine that further investigation is needed for a fair presentation; if so, discuss it with your supervising attorney and proceed if authorized.

A simple, logical, and understandable presentation of the facts is crucial, so that the reader has a clear understanding of the context in which the issues are analyzed and the conclusion reached. Chronological development is often best; sometimes it may be useful to emphasize crucial facts first, then demonstrate how they fit into the chronological whole. Figure 6–4 illustrates a clear, concise statement of facts.

Figure 6–4 Statement of Facts Section

```
Statement of Facts:

   Mr. Giles went to a pre-Thanksgiving party at the home of
Mr. Swan. Swan had been his friend and attorney for approx-
imately two years.
   At the party, Giles and Swan discussed Giles's desire to
purchase a piece of real estate before the end of the year.
Giles indicated that he was going out of town for
Thanksgiving, and would not be back until on or about January
1. Swan stated that he could close the real estate transac-
tion if Giles would execute a power of attorney. Giles then
signed a document entitled "Power of Attorney," which Swan
kept. Giles then left the party, and departed on his trip.
   While Giles was away, Swan was contacted by Giles's part-
ner, Mr. Harris, regarding a joint venture transaction com-
pletely unrelated to the real estate transaction. Harris
told Swan that Giles was supposed to assume all of Harris's
interest in the joint venture before January 1. Swan told
Harris he had a power of attorney to close a real estate
transaction, but did not know how he could help Harris out.
Harris suggested to Swan that he could use the power of
attorney to facilitate the transfer of the joint venture
interest. Swan hesitated, but Harris indicated that Giles
would not receive the tax benefits attendant to the trans-
fer if he did not close the deal before December 31. Swan
finally agreed to execute the transfer of the joint venture
interest using the power of attorney, and shortly thereafter
the deal was completed.
   When Giles came back to town, he was furious, and told Swan
that he did not want to assume the entire joint venture
interest, and wanted the transaction voided.
```

Discussion and Analysis

The **discussion and analysis** section is the heart of the memorandum. In this section you will be:

- identifying points of law and supporting them with citations;
- quoting from relevant cases, statutes, and other sources; and
- relating your research to the facts of your matter.

Always remember that your purpose is to discuss objectively the strengths and the weaknesses of your case. You must view the issues not only from your client's perspective, but also from that of your opponent. The negative side of your client's position will surface eventually; the internal memorandum prepares your firm to deal with such weaknesses. Discuss both those points that operate to your client's advantage, and those likely to be cited against him; identify counterpoints to your own strong arguments and counterpoints to the opponent's. The reader should get a sense of how an objective observer might look at the matter.

As with the statement of facts, and indeed the other components of a memorandum as well, the scope and depth of your discussion will vary with the intended use. In some cases, your assignment will be to prepare an exhaustive survey of the law in a given area, citing all possibly relevant cases and statutes, and perhaps even providing separate copies or abstracts of these primary sources. In other cases, the assignment will be to obtain a quick answer, citing only the most relevant cases. Know your assignment, and hence your goal, from the outset.

Quotations from cases can be as useful in a memorandum as they are in other projects (and they are often incorporated into later briefs), and references to secondary sources can give added support to your arguments. All these possibilities should be discussed with your supervising attorney, and you should be sure that you understand her expectations before you begin.

Discuss the cases, statutes, and other material *favoring* your client first. Describe how they support your argument, and how they may be attacked. Then discuss the materials that go *against* your client's position, stating how they are harmful, and whether and how they can be distinguished.

Emphasize primary sources over secondary, and mandatory precedents over merely persuasive precedents. If the issues involved are state law issues, emphasize research in state law sources; if federal issues, emphasize federal sources.

You should constantly integrate the law and the facts. Don't do this at the expense of an extended discussion of a complicated legal concept, however; by all means, make the status and meaning of the law clear. But make sure the reader understands throughout the discussion, and particularly at the end, how the law affects the specific facts of the client's matter.

An example of a proper discussion section appears in Figure 6–5. Note how bluebook citation form is used. You should not deviate from proper citation form just because the memorandum is to be used internally, rather than filed with a court. Your text may someday to incorporated into a brief; the more accurate its form and substance, the more valuable the memorandum will be.

Figure 6–5 Discussion Section

<u>Discussion:</u>

A power of attorney creates an agency relationship whereby one person, the principal, appoints another person, the agent, to act on the principal's behalf. *Lawler v. Federal Deposit Insurance Corp.*, 538 S.W. 2d 245 (Tex. Civ. App., Dallas 1976, writ refd n.r.e.). The relationship is consensual. *Texas Processed Plastics, Inc. v. Gray Enterprises, Inc.*, 592 S.W. 2d 412 (Tex. Civ. App., Tyler 1979, no writ); *Green v. Hanon*, 367 S.W. 2d 853 (Tex. Civ. App., Texarkana 1963, no writ). The law specifically defines a power of attorney as "(A)n instrument by which the authority of one person to act in the place and stead of another as attorney in fact is set forth." *Olive-Sternberg Lumber Co. v. Gordon*, 143 S.W. 2d 694 (Tex. Civ. App., Beaumont 1940, no writ). The document in this case identified neither the principal, nor the agent, nor the extent of the authority of the agent. The document's validity is thus questionable.

However, before one can determine the validity of the document, it must be interpreted. Under Texas law, certain rules of construction and interpretation must be followed. The rules of construing a document date back as far as 1889, to the leading case of *Gouldy v. Metcalf*, 75 Tex. 455, 12 S.W. 830 (1889). In *Gouldy*, the Texas Supreme Court set out the rules of construction for a power of attorney:

[W]hen an authority is conferred upon an agent by a formal instrument, as by a power of attorney, there are two rules of construction to be carefully adhered to:

1. The meaning of general words in the instrument will be restricted by the context, and construed accordingly.

2. The authority will be construed strictly, so as to exclude the exercise of any power which is not warranted, either by the actual terms used or as a necessary means of executing the authority with effect. *Id*. at 245.

Figure 6–5 cont.

Expanding the guidelines set forth in *Gouldy*, case law establishes that "all powers conferred upon an agent by a formal instrument are to receive a strict interpretation, and the authority is never extended by intendment or construction beyond that which is given in terms, or is necessary for carrying the authority into effect, and the authority must be strictly pursued." See *Bean v. Bean*, 79 S.W. 2d 652 (Tex. Civ. App., Texarkana 1935, writ refused); *Dockstader v. Brown*, 204 S.W. 2d 352 (Tex. Civ. App., Fort Worth 1947, writ refd n.r.e.).

In applying the rules of construction, for a power of attorney to be valid certain elements must be contained within the document. The necessary elements are the name of the principal, the name of the agent, and the nature and extent of the authority granted. *Sun Appliance and Electric, Inc. v. Klein*, 363 S.W. 2d 293 (Tex. Civ. App., Eastland 1962, no writ).

The power of attorney in the present matter contained only the signature of the principal and nothing else. In analyzing the power of attorney under the strict considerations, the essential terms of the power of attorney were missing. As such, it appears that the document does not comply with the legal definition of a power of attorney.

The facts further indicate that the power of attorney was executed for a specific purpose, although not stated. Giles had orally instructed Swan to use the power of attorney to consummate a real estate transaction only. As stated in *Giddings, Neiman-Marcus v. Estes*, 440 S.W. 2d 90 (Tex. Civ. App., Eastland 1969, no writ):

> The authority will be construed strictly, so as to exclude the exercise of any power which is not warranted either by the actual terms used or as a necessary means of effecting the authority with effect.

Since no authority was conferred to Swan by the document, he could not have acted on Giles's behalf. Consequently, any acts performed by Swan for Giles under the power of attorney are invalid.

However, the facts reveal that Swan had acted as Giles's attorney on a number of occasions. This may give rise to an implication that Swan was acting with apparent authority. This is defined as "such authority as a reasonably prudent man, using diligence and discretion in view of the principal's conduct, would naturally and reasonably suppose the agent to possess." *Great American Casualty Company v. Eichelberger*, 37 S.W. 2d 1050 (Tex. Civ. App., Waco 1931, writ refd). Thus, as the Houston Court of Civil Appeals stated in its dicta:

> (A)n agency may arise with respect to third persons if acts or appearances reasonably lead third persons to believe that an agency in fact has been created. And . . . apparent authority of an agent to bind a principal, by want of ordinary care, clothes the agent with such indicia of authority as to lead a reasonably prudent person to believe that he actually has such authority. *Hall v. Hallamicek*, 669 S.W. 2d 368 (Tex. App., Houston 14th Dist. 1984, no writ).

Harris may try to use apparent authority as a means to validate the transfer, as Giles has the burden of proof that Swan did not have the authority to act on Giles's behalf: *Dockstader v. Brown*, 204 S.W. 2d 352 (Tex. Civ. App., Fort Worth 1947, writ refd n.r.e.).

There is a problem with the apparent authority argument, however. Harris knew that the power of attorney was for a specific purpose: to close the real estate transaction. The law is very

Figure 6–5 cont.

clear in that a third party has a duty to inquire into the scope and fact of the agency, and the burden is on the third party to "ascertain at his peril the nature and scope of the authority of such agent." *Lawrie v. Miller*, 2 S.W. 2d 561 (Tex. Civ. App., Texarkana 1928, no writ); *Eliot Valve Repair v. Valve*, 675 S.W. 2d 555 (Tex. App. Houston 1st Dist. 1984, no writ; *Boucher v. City Paint & Supply*, 398 S.W. 2d 352 (Tex. Civ. App., Tyler 1966, no writ).

Mr. Harris neither investigated nor examined the extent of Swan's authority. As such, Giles cannot be held responsible for the acts of Swan and their effect.

In analyzing the facts and the law, it is apparent that the document that purports to be a power of attorney is not a valid one and that Swan did not have the authority to act on Giles's behalf under any circumstance. Consequently, the power of attorney is valueless and any action resulting from the use of the document is void.

Although the case law appears to be in our client's favor, there is an issue that may be raised by the defense which weakens our case substantially. The issue is the principal's ratification of the transaction. Ratification requires that the principal have full and complete knowledge of all material facts pertaining to the transaction prior to any affirmation of the act. *Leonard v. Hare*, 161 Tex. 28, 336 S.W. 2d 619 (1960). For ratification to occur, the principal must retain the benefits and "the critical factor in determining whether a principal has ratified an unauthorized act by his agent is the principal's knowledge of the transaction and his actions in light of such knowledge." *Land Title Company of Dallas, Inc. v. Stigler*, 609 S.W. 2d 754, 756 (Tex., 1980); *First National Bank in Dallas v. Kinnabrew*, 589 S.W. 2d 137 (Tex. Civ. App., Tyler 1979, writ refd n.r.e.). In the event that it is determined that Giles took benefits from Swan's actions, specifically tax benefits, the transaction may be valid, regardless of whether the initial power of attorney was legally sufficient.

Conclusion

Although the discussion section forms the heart of your memorandum, the **conclusion** is the culmination. In a few sentences you summarize what your research has shown about the law relating to your client's problem. You may even recommend a course of action, if that was part of your assignment.

Though coming to a conclusion generally means stating your opinion about how the legal issues will be resolved, it does not imply that you should become an advocate when drafting your conclusion. If you have strong reservations about your conclusion, or believe that a court could easily justify a different ruling, say so. Once again, you must keep in mind the most important rule of the internal memorandum of law—*objectivity*!

An example of a good conclusion is found in Figure 6–6 on page 126.

Figure 6–6 Conclusion Section

> **Conclusion:**
>
> Since the power of attorney did not grant specific authority to the agent, the power of attorney is void. Based upon the strict construction doctrine, one cannot construe a grant of authority which is nonexistent. The power of attorney contained neither the name of the agent, nor the purpose of the agency, nor the grant of authority to the agent, and therefore could not confer any powers upon the agent. The acts of the agent were improper, and the principal is not legally responsible for the effects of those acts. However, as noted, if the principal received any benefits from the transaction, the acts of the agent may be ratified, which would validate any acts of the agent. This would make the transaction valid.

6–3 Practical Considerations

An internal memorandum will inevitably involve at least some of your own opinions, since you must reach a conclusion based upon your research. It is important, however, that you let neither your opinions nor your conclusion color your analysis—which is to say, you must also include in your memorandum those portions of your research that go against your conclusion. The memorandum is designed to *inform* your supervising attorney, so that he is prepared to advocate on behalf of your client; it should not itself advocate a position.

In drafting your memorandum, remember the many basic rules you've learned in previous chapters. Use punctuation, sentence structure, and paragraphing to make your points clear; write with precision and forcefulness; avoid ambiguity, use logical development, and be sure your writing tells the reader what you want her to know.

Appendix   Sample Memorandum of Law

MEMORANDUM

TO: J. Mark, Senior Partner
FROM: R. Lang, Paralegal

DATE: June 1, 1992

RE: <u>Giles</u> v. <u>Harris</u>
            The validity of a transfer of a joint venture interest with
            a blank power of attorney.

<u>Issue Presented:</u>
Under Texas law, is the transfer of a joint venture interest with a blank
power of attorney valid?

<u>Answer to the Issue:</u>
Yes. Since the power of attorney presented was devoid of any terms, it did
not contain the necessary elements to be a valid power of attorney. The acts
of the agent exercised under such a limited power of attorney are not binding on the principal. However the cases hold that, if the principal received
any personal benefits from the transaction, the issue of ratification might
be sufficient to validate the acts of the agent.

<u>Statement of Facts:</u>
    Mr. Giles went to a pre-Thanksgiving party at the home of Mr. Swan. Swan
had been his friend and attorney for approximately two years.
    At the party, Giles and Swan discussed Giles's desire to purchase a piece
of real estate before the end of the year. Giles indicated that he was going
out of town for Thanksgiving, and would not be back until on or about
January 1. Swan stated that he could close the real estate transaction if
Giles would execute a power of attorney. Giles then signed a document entitled "Power of Attorney," which Swan kept. Giles then left the party, and
departed on his trip.
    While Giles was away, Swan was contacted by Giles's partner, Mr. Harris,
regarding a joint venture transaction completely unrelated to the real estate
transaction. Harris told Swan that Giles was supposed to assume all of
Harris's interest in the joint venture before January 1. Swan told Harris
he had a power of attorney to close a real estate transaction, but did not
know how he could help Harris out. Harris suggested to Swan that he could
use the power of attorney to facilitate the transfer of the joint venture
interest. Swan hesitated, but Harris indicated that Giles would not receive
the tax benefits attendant to the transfer if he did not close the deal
before December 31. Swan finally agreed to execute the transfer of the joint
venture interest using the power of attorney, and shortly thereafter the
deal was completed.
    When Giles came back to town he was furious, and told Swan that he did
not want to assume the entire joint venture interest, and wanted the transaction voided.

<u>Discussion:</u>
A power of attorney creates an agency relationship whereby one person, the
principal, appoints another person, the agent, to act on the principal's
behalf. <u>Lawler v. Federal Deposit Insurance Corp.</u>, 538 S.W. 2d 245 (Tex. Civ.
App., Dallas 1976, writ refd n.r.e.). The relationship is consensual. <u>Texas
Processed Plastics, Inc. v. Gray Enterprises, Inc.</u>, 592 S.W. 2d 412 (Tex.
Civ. App., Tyler 1979, no writ); <u>Green v. Hanon</u>, 367 S.W. 2d 853 (Tex.

Civ. App., Texarkana 1963, no writ). The law specifically defines a power of attorney as "[A]n instrument by which the authority of one person to act in the place and stead of another as attorney in fact is set forth." Olive-Sternberg Lumber Co. v. Gordon, 143 S.W. 2d 694 (Tex. Civ. App., Beaumont 1940, no writ). The document in this case identified neither the principal, nor the agent, nor the extent of the authority of the agent. The document's validity is thus questionable.

However, before one can determine the validity of the document, it must be interpreted. Under Texas law, certain rules of construction and interpretation must be followed. The rules of construing a document date back as far as 1889, to the leading case of Gouldy v. Metcalf, 75 Tex. 455, 12 S.W. 830 (1889). In Gouldy, the Texas Supreme Court set out the rules of construction for a power of attorney:

> [W]hen an authority is conferred upon an agent by a formal instrument, as by a power of attorney, there are two rules of construction to be carefully adhered to:
>
> 1. The meaning of general words in the instrument will be restricted by the context, and construed accordingly.
>
> 2. The authority will be construed strictly, so as to exclude the exercise of any power which is not warranted, either by the actual terms used or as a necessary means of executing the authority with effect. Id. at 245.

Expanding the guidelines set forth in Gouldy, case law establishes that "all powers conferred upon an agent by a formal instrument are to receive a strict interpretation, and the authority is never extended by intendment or construction beyond that which is given in terms, or is necessary for carrying the authority into effect, and the authority must be strictly pursued." See Bean v. Bean, 79 S.W. 2d 652 (Tex. Civ. App., Texarkana 1935, writ refused); Dockstader v. Brown, 204 S.W. 2d 352 (Tex. Civ. App., Fort Worth 1947, writ refd n.r.e.).

In applying the rules of construction, for a power of attorney to be valid certain elements must be contained within the document. The necessary elements are the name of the principal, the name of the agent, and the nature and extent of the authority granted. Sun Appliance and Electric, Inc. v. Klein, 363 S.W. 2d 293 (Tex. Civ. App., Eastland 1962, no writ).

The power of attorney in the present matter contained only the signature of the principal, and nothing else. In analyzing the power of attorney under the strict considerations, the essential terms of the power of attorney were missing. As such, it appears that the document does not comply with the legal definition of a power of attorney.

The facts further indicate that the power of attorney was executed for a specific purpose, although not stated. Giles had orally instructed Swan to use the power of attorney to consummate a real estate transaction only. As stated in Giddings, Neiman-Marcus v. Estes, 440 S.W. 2d .90 (Tex. Civ. App., Eastland 1969, no writ):

> The authority will be construed strictly, so as to exclude the exercise of any power which is not warranted either by the actual terms used or as a necessary means of effecting the authority with effect.

Since no authority was conferred to Swan by the document, he could not have acted on Giles's behalf. Consequently, any acts performed by Swan for Giles under the power of attorney are invalid.

However, the facts reveal that Swan had acted as Giles's attorney on a number of occasions. This may give rise to an implication that Swan was acting with apparent authority. This is defined as "such authority as a reasonably prudent man, using diligence and discretion in view of the principal's conduct, would naturally and reasonably suppose the agent to possess." Great American Casualty Company v. Eichelberger, 37 S.W. 2d 1050 (Tex. Civ. App., Waco 1931, writ refd). Thus, as the Houston Court of Civil Appeals stated in its dicta:

> [A]n agency may arise with respect to third persons if acts or appearances reasonably lead third persons to believe that an agency in fact has been created. And . . . apparent authority of an agent to bind a principal, by want of ordinary care, clothes the agent with such indicia of authority as to lead a reasonably prudent person to believe that he actually has such authority. Hall v. Hallamicek, 669 S.W. 2d 368 (Tex. App., Houston 14th Dist. 1984, no writ).

Harris may try to use apparent authority as a means to validate the transfer, as Giles has the burden of proof that Swan did not have the authority to act on Giles's behalf: Dockstader v. Brown, 204 S.W. 2d 352 (Tex. Civ. App., Fort Worth 1947, writ refd n.r.e.).

There is a problem with the apparent authority argument, however. Harris knew that the power of attorney was for a specific purpose: to close the real estate transaction. The law is very clear in that a third party has a duty to inquire into the scope and fact of the agency, and the burden is on the third party to "ascertain at his peril the nature and scope of the authority of such agent." Lawrie v. Miller, 2 S.W. 2d 561 (Tex. Civ. App., Texarkana 1928, no writ); Eliot Valve Repair v. Valve, 675 S.W. 2d 555 (Tex. App. Houston 1st Dist. 1984, no writ; Boucher v. City Paint & Supply, 398 S.W. 2d 352 (Tex. Civ. App., Tyler 1966, no writ).

Mr. Harris neither investigated nor examined the extent of Swan's authority. As such, Giles cannot be held responsible for the acts of Swan and their effect.

In analyzing the facts and the law, it is apparent that the document that purports to be a power of attorney is not a valid one and that Swan did not have the authority to act on Giles's behalf under any circumstance. Consequently, the power of attorney is valueless and any action resulting from the use of the document is void.

Although the case law appears to be in our client's favor, there is an issue that may be raised by the defense which weakens our case substantially. The issue is the principal's ratification of the transaction. Ratification requires that the principal have full and complete knowledge of all material facts pertaining to the transaction prior to any affirmation of the act. Leonard v. Hare, 161 Tex. 28, 336 S.W. 2d 619 (1960). For ratification to occur, the principal must retain the benefits and "the critical factor in determining whether a principal has ratified an unauthorized act by his agent is the principal's knowledge of the transaction and his actions in light of such knowledge." Land Title Company of Dallas, Inc. v. Stigler, 609 S.W.

2d 754, 756 (Tex., 1980); <u>First National Bank in Dallas v. Kinnabrew</u>, 589 S.W. 2d 137 (Tex. Civ. App., Tyler 1979, writ refd n.r.e.). In the event that it is determined that Giles took benefits from Swan's actions, specifically tax benefits, the transaction may be valid, regardless of whether the initial power of attorney was legally sufficient.

<u>Conclusion:</u>
Since the power of attorney did not grant specific authority to the agent, the power of attorney is void. Based upon the strict construction doctrine, one cannot construe a grant of authority which is nonexistent. The power of attorney contained neither the name of the agent, nor the purpose of the agency, nor the grant of authority to the agent and therefore could not confer any powers upon the agent. The acts of the agent were improper, and the principal is not legally responsible for the effects of those acts. However, as noted, if the principal received any benefits from the transaction, the acts of the agent may be ratified, which would validate any acts of the agent. This would make the transaction valid.

SUMMARY

6–1

Prepare all necessary documents ahead of time, and do preliminary background research. Before commencing the initial client interview, be sure to identify yourself as a paralegal. Be prepared to discuss fees. In the interview itself, establish a positive relationship with the client, and proceed in stages to gather the facts. Ask focused questions after the client has told his story, and review the entire fact pattern before he leaves. Then immediately prepare a postinterview memorandum.

6–2

The internal memorandum of law is designed to inform, to explain, and to evaluate. It is intended to assist with such things as deciding whether to take a case or determining how to proceed on a case. Its purpose is objective. The heading identifies the parties preparing and receiving the memorandum, the date of submission, and the subject matter covered. The statement of issues presented identifies the legal and factual issues to be discussed. The short summary of the conclusion provides a quick answer to the questions raised by the statement of issues presented. The statement of facts presents an accurate picture of the facts. The discussion and analysis section identifies applicable points of law and supports them with citations to, and quotes from, relevant cases, statutes, and other sources, always relating the research to the facts of the specific matter. The conclusion is the culmination of the research, summarizing the implications of your analysis and possibly including a recommended course of action.

6–3

Although an internal memorandum of law necessarily involves some of the writer's own opinions (since she must reach a conclusion), these opinions should not be allowed to color the analysis. The writer must remain objective, including in the text both those references that support her conclusions and those which go against it.

REVIEW

Key Terms

Before proceeding, review the key terms listed below to be sure you understand each one. If necessary, read over the corresponding section of the chapter. When you are ready to test your understanding, answer the Review Questions.

initial client interview
attorney/client privilege
postinterview memorandum
internal memorandum of law
heading
statement of issues presented
short summary of conclusion
statement of facts
discussion and analysis
conclusion

Questions for Review and Discussion

1. What are some factors that should be considered prior to conducting a client interview?
2. What are the practical and technical objectives of a client interview?
3. What is the importance of a postinterview memorandum?
4. What does it mean when we describe an internal memorandum of law as "objective?"
5. What are some of the purposes of an internal memorandum of law?
6. List the information that should be included in the heading section of an internal memorandum of law.
7. What is the importance of the "issues presented" section?

8. What is the purpose of the "short summary of the conclusion" section?
9. What factors should be considered in preparing an appropriate "statement of facts?"
10. What are the key elements of the "discussion" section?

Activities

1. Read *American Heritage Life Insurance Company v. Koch*, 721 S.W. 2d 611 (Tex. App., Tyler 1986, no writ) and draft the issue presented.
2. Draft the statement of facts as you would present it to your attorney in a memorandum of law by reading *First Texas Savings Association v. Jergins*, 705 S.W. 2d 390 (Tex. App., Fort Worth 1986, no writ).
3. Prepare a memorandum of law on the status of law in your state regarding the comparative negligence statute.

CHAPTER 7   The Basics of
Legal Correspondence

COMMENTARY

For over three months your client, Management Company Inc., has been attempting to collect overdue rent from a difficult tenant. Phone calls to the tenant and several meetings have accomplished nothing. A week ago, an officer of the client firm sought your firm's advice. His initial consultation with your supervising attorney was completed shortly thereafter.

As a result of the consultation, a decision was made to take immediate action. You have just been assigned to draft a letter to the tenant on behalf of the client, demanding payment of an overdue rent.

Preparing basic correspondence, including demand letters, is a task often performed by paralegals.

OBJECTIVES

In Chapter 7 we discuss different types of legal correspondence and the strategies behind them. After completing this chapter, you will be able to:

1. Identify three functions of legal correspondence.
2. Prepare appropriate letters for clients, opposing counsel, and the court.
3. State the purpose of using letterhead.
4. Identify the importance of an accurate date.
5. Prepare a reference line.
6. Prepare a blind carbon copy.
7. Prepare a demand letter.
8. Prepare a client opinion letter.
9. Prepare a third party opinion letter.
10. Use a letter to request information.

7–1 The Function of Legal Correspondence

inform, advise Confirm.

Although letter writing is something of a lost art in social communication, having been replaced by the telephone call, in business and legal matters it remains important. Letters form a permanent written record that can be relied upon later to reconstruct events. Used and drafted correctly, they help to prevent misunderstandings, broken agreements, and missed deadlines.

The legal profession relies on letters for three main purposes—to inform, to advise, and to confirm.

The Informative Letter

Letters that transmit information are known as **informative letters**, also called "for your information" or "FYI" letters. Such a letter might be sent to a client to inform him of the progress of a case, the status of billing and payment, or the need for information to prepare a deposition. An informative letter might also be sent to opposing counsel (for example, to provide dates of availability to schedule a deposition or trial), or to anyone to whom the attorney or paralegal need provide information.

The Advisory Letter

Advisory letters are more formal than informative letters. They offer legal opinions. This might be in the form of an objective analysis of the case at issue, as a detailed letter to a client. Or it might be written in a persuasive style from an advocate's perspective, as when an attorney writes to opposing counsel proposing settlement. Whatever form it takes, an advisory letter is detailed and formal. Research may be involved, and it must be done with the same care as any other research project. There may be statutory requirements to follow or questions of law that must be resolved. If the letter is incomplete or otherwise flawed, the result may harm your client.

Although the advisory letter is certainly informative, its content goes beyond that of an informative letter. The content and style often resemble more sophisticated legal writing, such as an internal memorandum or a brief.

The Confirmation Letter

In the course of a legal matter, information is often shared orally, by telephone or in person. In order to create a permanent record of the passing of such information, a **confirmation letter** is often sent, restating the content of the original oral communication. For example, when an attorney orally advises a client of a court date, a follow-up confirmation letter should immediately be sent. That way, there is no excuse for confusion.

A confirmation letter not only restates orally transmitted information, it also protects the attorney (and the paralegal) from future problems or repercussions. By establishing in writing the date of a court appearance, for example, or the terms of an orally agreed-upon settlement, there is a permanent record which can be referred to in the event of a disagreement.

7–2   Evaluating the Audience

The tone and style of a letter vary not only with the purpose, but also with the audience. Correspondence with your client, for example, may be less formal than a letter to the court, and less technical than a letter to opposing counsel. A different audience requires a different focus, attention, and style.

The Client

Regular contact with your clients is important, both to keep them informed and to minimize the anxiety they may feel because of their unfamiliarity with the legal system. In corresponding with clients, you should keep in mind several considerations.

First, provide concrete answers. Clients dislike lawyers and paralegals who hedge with vague language. This does not mean that you should misrepresent the state of affairs if it really is indefinite, but rather that you explain the indefinite state with concrete, clear language. If the law in your case is subject to several interpretations, say so clearly and identify the possible interpretations.

Second, write to the client's level of understanding. Avoid legalese or, if you must use it, *explain* it. Don't try to impress the client with your technical vocabulary; write in plain English. To do this is not to patronize or condescend—if a client, even an intelligent and educated client, has no legal training, there is no reason to subject her to difficult jargon.

Third, always be respectful and courteous to your clients. They have hired you because they have a legal problem, and it is probably a difficult time for them. Your compassion and understanding in your legal correspondence and face-to-face contacts can help them cope, whereas a harsh or pompous tone would cause more anxiety and ill will.

Finally, choose your words carefully. In litigation, a result is never certain; in a business deal or real estate transaction, the outcome is often unpredictable;

in negotiations, the other party is always an uncontrollable factor. Yet clients are always looking for certainties. They want to be told that everything will be all right. You must make it clear that your opinions are not *guarantees*. Avoid the temptation to act like an all-knowing legal forecaster; be accurate and honest, and communicate the uncertainties.

Opposing Counsel

Opposing counsel is not your friend in the case at hand, even if he is your friend in other contexts. Always remember that information shared with opposing counsel will be available to the opposing client (or might even be brought to the court's attention), and can be used against your client. Thus you must choose carefully what you communicate to opposing counsel. Be courteous in your correspondence with opposing counsel, but be cautious as well.

The Court

Correspondence directed to the court usually comes in one of three forms: either a cover letter accompanying documents to be filed; or a letter requesting a hearing date or other procedural assistance; or a formal letter to a judge stating a legal position.

Cover letters accompanying documents are usually standard form letters. They simply identify the documents and the date of filing. Such letters fulfill the confirmation function of correspondence—they provide a written record establishing that the documents were filed, and when. Copies generally need not be sent to opposing counsel.

A letter requesting a hearing date or other procedural assistance is similarly straightforward in its text—it simply makes a direct request. If such a letter is addressed to a judge, however, opposing counsel should receive a copy. If addressed to a clerk, the copy is optional.

A letter to a judge stating a legal position is less commonly seen, usually outside the standard course of a lawsuit, and it involves risks. If such a letter is sent, needless to say a copy should be sent to opposing counsel, and it should be prepared in a formal manner, as if it were a brief. Be concise, direct, and respectful to judges. Such a communication between one party in a lawsuit and the judge is called an *ex parte* communication (recall this term from our discussion of legalese in Chapter 3). Only under limited circumstances is such communication acceptable. The problem with *ex parte* communications is that the other side's opportunity to respond is limited. In any event, no such communication should ever be attempted by you without express authorization from your supervising attorney.

7–3 The Components of a Letter

The format of different types of letters varies, and different firms or attorneys may have different preferences, but the following are generally accepted as the standard components of most letters:

- letterhead;
- date;
- addressee;
- reference line;
- salutation;
- body;
- headers;
- closing; and
- carbon copy and blind carbon copy.

We consider each of these in turn in the following subsections.

The Letterhead

Most law firms and businesses have standard stationery, called **letterhead**, with the firm or company name, address, telephone number, and other relevant information. Law firm letterhead often lists, just below the firm name, all the attorneys in the firm.

When writing on behalf of your firm, use letterhead. It shows that you are associated with the firm, making the significance of the letter clear. It may even be relevant for professional liability insurance coverage.

Letterhead is used for the first page of a multiple-page letter. The other pages should be on matching paper, but without the letterhead.

The Date

The date appears below the letterhead. It is important for establishing an accurate chronology in a legal matter. Letters often go through several drafts over a period of several days; make sure the date on the letter matches the date of mailing.

The Addressee

The name of the person to whom the letter is written appears at the top left margin, just below the letterhead. If the letter is sent by other than U.S. mail (for example, by FAX or overnight delivery), the method of delivery should be indicated above the address block. Use titles, if applicable (for example, "Chairman William Jones"), and note that all attorneys should be addressed with the suffix "Esquire" or its abbreviation, "Esq." (as in "William Jones, Esq."). A typical address block is found in Figure 7–1.

Figure 7–1 Address Block

HAND DELIVERED

Ms. Susan Windsor, President
AACME SERVICE COMPANY, INC.
465 Commerce Blvd.
Lincoln, Nebraska 54321

The Reference Line

The **reference line** appears below the address block, and identifies the subject matter of the letter. It provides a quick (*very* quick) introduction for the reader, and helps your secretary to determine where to file the copy without reading the whole letter.

The detail in the reference line sometimes depends on the stage of the matter. The parties involved are always identified, along with a brief description of the matter. Some firms also include their internal file number and, if a lawsuit has been filed, the docket number is often included as well. If the parties are involved in several matters, or if only one aspect of a complex matter is addressed in the letter, there may be even more detailed identification. Figure 7–2 shows two examples of reference lines, one prior to litigation and the other afterward.

Figure 7–2   Reference Lines

<u>Prelitigation:</u>

Re: Our Client: Anytime Builders
       Our File #91-325
       Sale of Aacme Service Company, Inc.

<u>Litigation pending:</u>

Re: Anytime Builders, Inc. v. Aacme Service Company, Inc.
       Cause No. 91-00576-X
       Our File #91-325

The Salutation

The **salutation** appears below the reference line. It usually begins with the word ``Dear,'' even in formal correspondence. Use "Mr.," "Ms.," "Mrs.," or "Miss," unless you know the person to whom you are writing, and follow the name with a colon, which is more formal than a comma.

The Body

The **body** of a letter contains the information you wish to communicate. It may be as short as one or two sentences (if the purpose, for example, is simply to indicate that you have enclosed documents), or as long as several pages (for an in-depth legal analysis, such as an opinion letter).

As in most effective legal writing, the opening sentence and paragraph of your letters should summarize what you want to say and why. You should make it clear that you are representing the client, unless you have done this already in prior letters. You should use all the writing techniques you've learned—correct sentence structure, parallelism, conciseness, and so on.

Be sure to be complete. Cover all the material you need to communicate, both positive and negative. Avoid a pompous or arrogant tone. In fact, in letters to clients or other friendly parties, you may use a relatively informal tone, although you should be careful that the message is not distorted nor its importance undermined.

When you write an advisory letter, the tone should be formal and authoritative, just as you would write a brief or internal memorandum.

Figure 7–3 shows the body of a letter concerning the resolution of a dispute. In subsequent sections, we discuss the content of other types of letters.

Figure 7-3 Body of Confirmation Letter

> This letter will confirm our agreement regarding the sale of the Aacme Service Company, Inc. to Anytime Builders, Inc. As a result of our meeting of May 5, 1992, we agreed that Mr. Allen will provide my clients with books and records of the business. Once we have had an opportunity to review the books and records, we will be able to determine whether the sale of the business will be completed.
>
> I have received the weekly installment payment to Mr. Allen in the amount of $1,203.54. As I indicated to you at the meeting, I will be holding all future checks in trust until we can resolve the question of the purchase and sale of the business.
>
> It is my further understanding that some time next week we will meet again to determine whether the business will be sold to my clients, or whether Mr. Allen will reimburse all monies tendered for the purchase of the business to my clients.
>
> I hope we will be able to resolve this matter quickly.

The Header

As we stated, letterhead is used only for the first page of multipage letters. However, subsequent pages have identifying information as well, in the form of a **header**. A header appears at the top left margin of all subsequent pages, and identifies three elements: the person to whom the letter is addressed; the date of the letter; and the page number. A practical note: we indicated earlier that the date on the front of the letterhead page should be the date of mailing; this is obviously also true for the date appearing in headers. If the date on your letterhead and headers fails to match the postmark, you will seem disorganized; if different dates appear on the letterhead and headers in the same letter, you will look sloppy and careless. The amount of time it takes to check these details is minor; the impact of an error on your reputation can be great.

The Closing

A letter is generally concluded by one or two sentences at the end. A concluding message often contains such courteous statements as, "Please do not hesitate to call if you have any questions." Following the concluding message is the **closing**. In legal correspondence, the typical closing is "Very truly yours," followed by a comma. Note that the *V* in *Very* is capitalized, but the other words are not.

Examples of correct and incorrect concluding messages and closings are seen in Figure 7-4. Note that the correct concluding message ends with a peri-

Figure 7-4 Correct and Incorrect Closings of Letters

<u>**Correct closing of letter:**</u>

Thank you for your attention and courtesies.

Very truly yours,

P. R. Lang

<u>**Incorrect closing of letter:**</u>

Thanking you for your attention and courtesies, I remain,

Very truly yours,

P. R. Lang

od. It is outdated to end the concluding message with a comma leading into the closing, as in the incorrect example.

Most of the letters you prepare will be for the signature of your supervising attorney. Remember that it is improper, and indeed illegal, for a paralegal to give legal advice. If you do sign a letter, identify yourself as a paralegal or legal assistant (see Figure 7–5).

Figure 7–5 Appropriate Closing by a Paralegal

Very truly yours,

Mary Doe
Legal Assistant

Carbon Copy and Blind Carbon Copy

Copies of correspondence are often sent to parties other than the addressee. The client, for example, is often sent copies of letters to opposing counsel or the court. This fact is denoted at the end of the original letter by the notation *cc*, which stands for *carbon copy*. Although carbons have largely been replaced by photocopies, the reference has survived and can indicate either carbon copies or photocopies. After the *cc* come the names of any persons to whom the copy is sent. Thus the original addressee also knows who else has received copies.

Under certain circumstances the author of the letter may want to conceal from the original addressee who else has received a copy. The original letter, then, contains no notation about copies (i.e., no *cc*), but your file copy will contain the notation *bcc* (**blind carbon copy**), followed by the name of the blind copy recipient. The blind copy recipient's copy will also have the *bcc* designation, so that she will know it was a blind copy. Proper use of the *cc* and *bcc* designations requires good communication among the attorney, paralegal, and secretary; it is often wise, for example, to clip a note to the original with an instruction such as "bcc John Doe."

7–4 The Demand Letter

Many disputes are resolved through discussion and negotiation, but some are not. As negotiations stall, a client may need to make demands upon the opposing party. Sometimes clients want to make demands even before negotiations have begun. In your role as a paralegal, you will be drafting **demand letters** on behalf of your clients.

The purpose of a demand letter is to motivate a desired response—often, though not exclusively, the payment of a debt. In the following subsections we discuss several categories of demand letter, as well as some guidelines for preparing a response.

The Collection Letter

A **collection letter** demands payment of an amount claimed to be owed to your client. It is not, however, as simple as a "pay up or else" letter—in practice, the concept is more subtle than that. To prepare an effective collection letter, several considerations should be kept in mind.

First, understand your purpose. Again, this is not as simple as it may seem. Are you seeking immediate payment in full? Are you seeking partial payment? Are you seeking to create a written record of the amount claimed due? Are you trying to satisfy statutory notice requirements? Are you trying to accomplish some combination of these? Are you following up earlier client demands, or is your letter the first demand made upon the opposing party? As you can see, there are many factors to consider.

Second, determine if there are statutory rules or common law principles that affect your demand letter. If you fail to satisfy any applicable requirements, not only will your letter be faulty, but you may actually undermine your client's ability to collect.

Third, your letter should set forth your client's version of disputed events, and possibly undisputed events as well. State your claim in a concise, authoritative manner, setting forth the amount of the original debt, the date it was incurred, amounts already paid, interest due, the present amount due, and any other relevant terms. In addition, you should probably include supporting evidence, such as invoices, leases, promissory notes, or relevant correspondence.

Fourth, you should make your demand clear. Do not just demand payment, for example; demand payment by a certain date, called the **deadline date**. Tell the recipient what she can expect if she does not comply by that date, and be prepared to follow through—if your threats are exposed as empty, your credibility is damaged and your future ability to negotiate is undercut.

Fifth, if the opposing party is represented by counsel, be sure that you write to the attorney and not the party himself. It is a violation of codes of professional responsibility to write directly to a party who you know is represented by a lawyer.

The Fair Debt Collection Statutory Letter

The federal Fair Debt Collection Practices Act, 15 U.S.C. Sec. 1692–1692(o), regulates collection of debts owed by consumers. When preparing a collection letter that must comply with this statute's requirements, you should include the following information:

- the amount of the debt;
- the name of the creditor to whom the debt is owed;
- a statement that you assume the debt to be valid, unless the validity is disputed within 30 days;
- a statement that, if the consumer notifies the attorney in writing within the 30-day period that the debt or any part of it is disputed, verification of the debt will be obtained and sent to the consumer;
- a statement that, upon written request within the 30-day period, the attorney will provide the consumer with the name and address of the original creditor, if different from the current creditor; and
- a statement that the attorney is attempting to collect the debt, and that any information received will be used for that purpose.

Unless the federal statute is complied with, your collection letter may be faulty, and your attempt to collect for your client may fail. You should be familiar with this statute, and any similar legislation that is applicable in your state or region.

Figure 7–6   Example of a Minimally Aggressive Collection Letter

```
                              May 24, 1992

Mr. Travis Rande
CD'S UNLIMITED
1617 Concord Street
San Diego, CA 90404

     Re: Our Client: MOULDE PRODUCTIONS, INC.
         Balance Due and Owing: $5,325.87

Dear Mr. Rande:

   The law firm of Helman & Jones represents Moulde
Productions, Inc. in the above-referenced matter. On or about
January 4, 1992, Moulde Productions, Inc. provided you with
production services and air time for a commercial advertise-
ment on the "Music Review" television program. For these ser-
vices and air time, you agreed to pay Moulde Productions, Inc.
the total amount of $5,325.87. Presently, there is a balance
due and owing of $5,325.87.

   In order to alleviate any additional costs and expens-
es, your prompt attention to this matter is advisable. It
is expected that the entire amount will be paid within 30
days. Please contact me to discuss the matter immediately.
If we have not received a satisfactory response from you
within the time specified above, we will have no alterna-
tive but to pursue further remedies.

                         Very truly yours,



                         Jeanne J. Carr
```

Figure 7–6 shows a collection letter with a slightly aggressive tone. Figure 7–7 shows a more formal collection letter, written to collect a consumer debt in compliance with the federal Fair Debt Collection Practices Act.

The Consumer Protection Letter

Many states have created a statutory method for a consumer to file suit against a business that conducts its affairs in a deceptive or unfair manner. When drafting a demand letter setting forth a claim under such a statute, it is important to mention the statute in your letter, and to comply with all its requirements. As with other demand letters, the facts of your claim should be stated, as well as the amount of the demand; indeed, these things may be prerequisites to making a claim for punitive or other damages under the statute.

The basic requirements for a demand letter under the Texas statute appear in Figure 7–8, and a letter drafted to meet these requirements appears in Figure 7–9. If a statute has been passed in your state you should obtain a copy and review it.

Figure 7–7   Collection Letter Prepared in Compliance with the Federal Fair Debt Collection Practices Act

```
                        April 28, 1992

Ms. Linda Starr        CERTIFIED MAIL #P117784262
Burgers, Etc.          RETURN RECEIPT REQUESTED
645 Elm Street
Houston, Texas 77204

    Re: Our Client: AAA Equipment
        Amounts Due on Account: $8,847.58

Dear Ms. Starr:

    This law firm has been retained to represent AAA Equipment
in the above-referenced matter to effect collection of the
amount owed by your company, Burgers, Etc. On or about
February 4, 1992, our client provided Burgers, Etc. with
restaurant equipment for use in its hamburger business. The
cost of the equipment was $9,747.58, for which you paid $1,700
as a down payment, leaving a balance of $8,047.58. As per the
contract, the balance was due on or before March 15, 1992. The
balance is now past due. If $8,847.58 (constituting the orig-
inal $8,047.58 plus an additional sum of $800.00 as attorneys'
fees) is not received in this office within thirty (30) days
from the date of this letter, we will have no alternative but
to pursue whatever legal remedies are available to protect our
client's interests, including the filing of a lawsuit.

    Pursuant to the Fair Debt Collection Practices Act, 15
U.S.C. §§1692-1692(o), any such action could subject you to
additional liability for attorneys' fees and costs of suit.

    If the above amount is not disputed by you within thirty
(30) days from the date hereof, it will be presumed valid.
If the debt is disputed, verification of the debt will be pro-
vided by my client. Further, any information that you provide
the undersigned will be used in the collection of the debt.

    Please be assured this is not the beginning of a series
of collection letters. If we have not received a satisfac-
tory response from you within the time specified above, we
will have no alternative than to proceed to litigation. In
order to alleviate any additional costs and expenses, your
prompt attention to this matter is advised.

                    Sincerely,


                    Joseph Johnson
```

Figure 7–8   Texas Deceptive Trade Practices Act Basic Requirements for Demand Letter

§17.505 Notice: Offer of Settlement

(a) As a prerequisite to filing a suit seeking damages under Subdivision (1) of Subsection (b) of Section 17.50 of this subchapter against any person, a consumer shall give written notice to the person at least 60 days before filing the suit advising the person in reasonable detail of the consumer's specific complaint and the amount of actual damages and expenses, including attorneys' fees, if any, reasonably incurred by the consumer in asserting the claim against the Defendant. During the 60-day period a written request to inspect, in a reasonable manner and at a reasonable time and place, the goods that are the subject of the consumer's action or claim may be presented to the consumer. If the consumer unreasonably refuses to permit the inspection, the court shall not award the two times actual damages not exceeding $1,000, as provided in Subsection (b) of Section 17.50 of this subchapter.

Figure 7–9   Consumer Demand Letter

```
                                   April 25, 1992

Mr. Bryan Henley
Office Manager
SMITHTON CHIROPRACTIC CENTER
1487 Orange Grove Blvd.
Galveston, TX 77553

    Re: Your letter to Deborah Lee Jones dated March 20, 1992

Dear Mr. Henley:

    The undersigned law firm has been retained to represent
Ms. Deborah Lee Jones in the matter of her account with
Smithton Center. Ms. Jones purchased services from and made
use of therapeutic equipment in Smithton Center during the
summer of 1991.

    This letter is being sent pursuant to Section 17.505 of
the Texas Business and Commerce Code, hereinafter referred
to as the Deceptive Trade Practices Act ("DTPA"), which
requires that such a letter be sent sixty (60) days prior to
the initiating of litigation. The DTPA specifically provides
that you may tender a written offer of settlement within this
sixty (60) day period of time, and further provides that your
offer of settlement must include an agreement to reimburse
Ms. Jones for her attorneys' fees incurred to date. To date,
Ms. Jones has incurred $1,000 in attorneys' fees.

    After receiving medical treatment rendered by your clin-
ic on August 26, 1991, Ms. Jones experienced severely painful
muscle spasms as a direct result of that treatment.

    Ms. Jones attempted on several occasions to contact your
office without success.

    At no time was Ms. Jones informed by your clinic that
charges continued to mount even though she no longer sub-
scribed to therapy. Ms. Jones was told that aside from an
initial $150.00 charge, she would incur no further cost as
a result of her treatment.

    Ms. Jones' specific complaints are as follows:
(i)    you represented that goods and services had sponsor-
       ship, approval, characteristics, ingredients, uses,
       benefits, or qualities which they did not have;

(ii)   you advertised goods and services with no intent to
       sell them as advertised;

(iii)  you failed to disclose information that you knew at
       the time of the transaction, and such failure to dis-
       close was intended to induce Ms. Jones into a trans-
       action that she would not otherwise have entered into,
       in that you represented to Ms. Jones that the services
       would be rendered at no cost to her after payment of
       an initial $150.00;

(iv)   you engaged in an unconscionable action or course of
       action, by taking advantage of the lack of knowledge,
       ability, experience, or capacity of Ms. Jones to a
       grossly unfair degree; and

(v)    you charged Ms. Jones for services never rendered.

    As a result of your false, misleading, and deceptive acts
and practices and unconscionable conduct, Ms. Jones was
deceived into executing a purported agreement you now claim
obligates her to pay medical fees of $2,000.00. Not only does
she not owe this amount, but she has suffered damages in the
amount of at least $325.00 and has incurred attorneys' fees
```

in the amount of $1,000.00, as a result of your wrongful
acts. We urge you to make a written offer of settlement pursuant to Section 17.505 of the Texas Deceptive Trade
Practices Act. If settlement cannot be reached within
sixty(60) days, please take note that my client has authorized me to initiate a lawsuit on her behalf, to seek
(1) rescission of any agreements procured by your fraud, and
(2) the full measure of allowable damages, which can be
three times actual damages, plus attorneys' fees and court
costs.

As an additional cause of action, Ms. Jones has instructed me to initiate a lawsuit based upon your breach of contract, common law fraud, negligent entrustment, and medical
malpractice for misdiagnosing her condition and causing her
personal injury. Ms. Jones has instructed me to request
rescission of any agreements procured by your fraud, and to
seek punitive damages based upon the aforementioned fraudu-
lent representations made knowingly by Smithton Center and
its agents.

If I may be of any service to you or answer any of your
questions, please contact me either personally or through
your attorney.

Very truly yours,

Peter R. Moore

The Letter Notifying of Intention to Litigate

A special type of demand letter is the letter that places an opposing party or
counsel on notice that your client intends to initiate a lawsuit. This may be
combined with an ordinary letter demanding payment of an unpaid bill, or
may relate to a claim where the amount of damage is not immediately quan-
tifiable, as in a personal injury action or an action seeking an injunction.

Most parties, including insurance companies, like to avoid litigation where
possible; your intention to go to court, if perceived as realistic, may spur settlement talks. It may also backfire, however, creating a hostile reaction that
actually scuttles settlement talks. The risk involved is a matter of concern and
interest to you, but the decision on how to proceed will be made by your supervising attorney and the client.

When preparing a letter notifying of intention to litigate, you should:

- accurately state the facts;
- state the specific damages you claim, even if the amount is only an esti-
mate (as with a personal injury suit);
- state, if the claim is for other than money damages (as, for example, where
the proposed lawsuit seeks an injunction to remove toxic waste), the specific relief sought;
- emphasize your good faith and desire to work out the disagreement, if possible; and
- keep the tone courteous, not belligerent; this is more likely to lead to settlement.

These factors are general considerations; in a specific case, they may or may not apply. Consult with your supervising attorney for your strategy, but keep these things in mind. Figure 7–10 is an example of a letter notifying of intention to take a lawsuit to court.

As with other demand letters, an important concern is whether it should be sent under the attorney's name or the client's. If under the attorney's, the recipient may believe that it is too late to settle because the decision to start a lawsuit has already been made. Depending on the circumstances, you may want to send it under the client's name. Consult with your attorney on the proper procedure; and, even if you decide to send it under the client's name, you and your firm should still review (and probably actually draft) the letter.

Figure 7–10   Letter Notifying of Intention to Litigate

April 28, 1992

Ms. Carly Ford   CERTIFIED MAIL #P117784262
AAA Equipment   RETURN RECEIPT REQUESTED
645 Elm Street
Houston, Texas 77204

    Re: Gourmet Services, Inc.

Dear Ms. Ford;

    Please be advised that the undersigned has been retained by Gourmet Services, Inc. to represent them concerning their dispute with you on the equipment auctioned out of the New Orleans Restaurant. Please direct any future correspondence or communication to the undersigned.

    It is our understanding that you sold equipment owned by Gourmet Services, Inc. without their knowledge or permission. As previously communicated to you in a letter of December 12, 1991 from Gourmet Services, Inc., our client is prepared to settle this matter for the sum of $5,000.12. Demand is hereby made for payment in full of that amount in the form of a cashier's check or money order payable to Gourmet Services, Inc. and sent to the undersigned on or before ten (10) days from the date of this letter. Your failure to do so may result in litigation based upon wrongful conversion of the equipment, and possible other causes of action, which may result in the imposition of court costs, attorneys' fees, and interest. Our client does not desire to pursue this remedy, but is ready to do so if it is made necessary through your failure to comply with this demand.

    Unless you dispute the validity of this debt, or any portion thereof within thirty (30) days after receipt of this letter, the debt will be assumed to be valid. Should you dispute the validity of the debt within thirty (30) days from the date of receipt of this communication, a verification of the debt will be obtained and mailed to you.

    If you have any questions concerning our client's intention or wish to discuss this matter, please contact me.

        Sincerely,

        Lois J. Jackson

Responding to Demand Letters

When responding to a demand letter, the first step is to review the demand carefully with the client, pointing out the meaning and implications of the offer, and discussing what you believe to be the options for a response. When you begin to draft the response, be careful about reciting details. You should identify your position early, and counter any inaccurate factual claims made by the opposing side. You may want to avoid appearing aggressive, since this may do further harm to what may be a deteriorating situation; again, this is a judgment call.

One option almost always available is to request further information. This may "buy time" while the opposing party decides how to handle your request.

If you deny the claim, identify the reasons for your denial. If there are relevant cases or statutes that favor you, you may want to cite them. If there are documents that aid your cause, you may want to enclose copies. There may be strategic reasons to avoid such disclosure, however — so check with your supervising attorney first.

The best type of response to a demand letter, in general, is one that makes your position clear, but keeps the door open for negotiation. Be firm, though courteous in your denial, and try to provide a reason for keeping the dialogue open (for example, the request for further documentation). Remember that sometimes a forceful, aggressive approach may be necessary—for example, to threaten a counterclaim.

Figure 7–11 is a letter designed to maintain channels of communication. In Figure 7–12 appear a series of letters which ultimately resulted in the filing of a lawsuit.

Figure 7–11 Response to Notice of Litigation

```
                         May 4, 1992


Ms. Lois J. Jackson       CERTIFIED MAIL #P117784263
Attorney at Law           RETURN RECEIPT REQUESTED
2350 Alliance Street
Houston, Texas 77204


Re: Our Client: AAA Equipment
Your Client: Gourmet Services, Inc.

Dear Ms. Jackson:

   The undersigned represents AAA Equipment in the above-ref-
erenced matter. The matter that you have addressed in your
letter dated April 28, 1992 is disputed. I do not know the
basis of your claims, nor the substance of the claims.
Consequently, pursuant to the Fair Debt Collection Statute,
we are hereby placing you on notice that we do dispute the
validity of any claims that you are alleging in your letter
and request further investigation into this alleged debt.

   Thank you for your attention and courtesies.

                    Very truly yours,




                    Sue R. Miller
```

Figure 7–12   Series of Letters in Medical Malpractice Case

(a) Notice of Claim

February 21, 1992

Dr. Ned Radcliffe   CERTIFIED MAIL 3P117784223
18015 15th Street, Suite 310   RETURN RECEIPT REQUESTED
Goodnight, Texas 75020

Re: Lynn Murray
<u>Health Care Liability Claim</u>

Dear Dr. Radcliffe:

The undersigned represents Lynn Murray in the above-referenced matter. NOTICE IS HEREBY GIVEN that my client, Lynn Murray, has a "health care liability claim" against you, as the quoted term is defined in Article 4590i, §1.03, Subdivision (a), Paragraph (4) of the Revised Civil Statutes of Texas. This claim is based on the fact that you negligently administered and cared for Ms. Murray upon giving anesthesia on November 12, 1991, in the course of treating her to fill two abscessed teeth. As a result of your negligence, Ms. Murray suffered a sensitivity reaction to the anesthesia, including violent shaking of arms and legs, chattering of teeth, and convulsions.

Due to your negligence, Ms. Murray also contracted a severe skin reaction, triggered by the anesthesia. This condition has caused substantial rashes on her arms and upper body, and could in the future affect her entire body.

As a result of her reaction, Ms. Murray has had to engage the services of medical specialists and undergo and incur expenses for examination and diagnosis of the condition, for psychological consultation and for medication to help her condition, and she will have to continue various treatments, consultations, and medications in the future, and incur expenses therefor.

Prior to your negligence hereinabove referred to, Ms. Murray was twenty-eight (28) years old, in good health, and employed as a representative with MBI Corporation. As a result of your negligence, she has had to miss work at her job and has, therefore, lost wages and will be required in the future to lose further time from her job for an as-yet-undetermined period. As a further result of your negligence, she has suffered severe mental and physical pain and anguish, and in all probability will continue to suffer such mental and physical pain and anguish for the rest of her life, all to her further damage. To date, the amount of damages is $12,587.37, and continues to grow.

YOU ARE FURTHER NOTIFIED that this claim is given pursuant to the provisions of Article 4590i, Section 4.01, Subdivision (a) of the Revised Civil Statutes of Texas, and that, if it is not settled within sixty (60) days from the date this notice is given, the undersigned will commence an appropriate legal action against you to recover her damages.

Your prompt attention to this matter is advised.

Very truly yours,

Emma M. Costello

Figure 7–12 cont.

(b) Reply from Insurance Carrier

March 10, 1992

Ms. Emma M. Costello
Attorney at Law
6301 Marley Avenue
Anyplace, TX 75311

　　Re: Lynn Murray vs. Dr. Ned Radcliffe

Dear Ms. Costello:

Your notice letter addressed to Dr. Radcliffe has been referred
to us as the professional carrier for the doctor. It is my understanding that Dr. Radcliffe has previously forwarded your
client's medical records to you, along with a release executed
by your client on December 7, 1991. Thus, not only is there no
liability on the part of Dr. Radcliffe, your client has signed
a release.

I personally <u>guarantee</u> that if you file a lawsuit with regard
to this matter, it will be countered with a lawsuit against your
client for breach of contract and a Motion for Sanctions, since
the matter is a frivolous claim.

Please address any further correspondence or inquiries to my attention. Do not call or write the doctor with regard to this matter.

Sincerely,

Edward Z. Plant
MEDICAL INSURANCE COVERAGE COMPANY

(c) Response to Insurance Company's Letter

March 18, 1992

Mr. Edward Z. Plant
MEDICAL INSURANCE COVERAGE COMPANY
1601 Ohio Avenue, 5th Floor
Sandy, Illinois 42930

　　Re: Lynn Murray vs. Dr. Ned Radcliffe

Dear Mr. Plant:

　　This is in response to your letter dated March 10, 1992. I
do not appreciate the statement in your letter regarding the
filing of frivolous lawsuits. Perhaps you should investigate
the facts of this matter, as well as the law in Texas.

　　If you are trying to make threats to me regarding any claims
Ms. Murray has against Dr. Radcliffe, those threats are so noted.
However, let me assure you that I am well aware of the Texas
Rules of Procedure. I can further assure you that I intend to
pursue this matter, and will shortly be filing a lawsuit.

　　Let me encourage you, in the future, to investigate and
examine the facts of your cases before you begin threats of
Motions for Sanction.

　　If you choose to discuss this matter in a civil and professional manner, I would be happy to do so. Otherwise, you can
expect to be hearing from me with a lawsuit.

　　Your prompt attention to this matter is advised.

　　　　Very truly yours,

　　　　Emma M. Costello

7–5 The Opinion Letter

An **opinion letter** renders legal advice. Based upon specific facts, and applying information gained through research, it analyzes a legal problem and reaches a conclusion about the resolution of the problem. In the subsections that follow, we first discuss an opinion letter directed to your client, then address some separate considerations when the opinion letter is directed to a third party.

The Client Opinion Letter

A comprehensive client opinion letter should contain several distinct elements. Let's consider these elements.

Date   The date listed at the top of the letter is important. Your research must be accurate through that date. You cannot be held responsible for changes in the law, or new cases or statutes, that arise *after* that date, but you are responsible for all changes in the law *up to* that date.

Introductory Paragraph   An introductory paragraph should identify the issue or problem that the letter will address. Included in this paragraph should be a **disclaimer** (limiting claim or denial) indicating that the analysis that follows is based upon the facts as they are set forth in the letter. If a different version of the facts develops, the analysis may change as well. It is important that you emphasize this to protect yourself and your firm from liability—and it is important to emphasize to the client the need to provide accurate and complete factual information.

Facts and Background   The next section should set forth the facts and background that have been developed through client conferences and independent investigation. It should again be emphasized that the analysis is based upon these facts. You should take great care in gathering and presenting these facts. Remember that clients may have selective memories, concentrating on their strong points and forgetting their weak points. Thus, as with other writing projects, a good client interview is the foundation for a good opinion letter.

Conclusion   A brief statement of your conclusion may precede the analysis. This will help the client, or other reader, to follow the arguments to come. The scope of the conclusion should be indicated here, including any limitations or qualifications.

Analysis   This section is like the discussion section of the internal memorandum. In it you analyze the applicable case law, statutes, and other sources. Both strengths and weaknesses of your client's position should be discussed. Remember that you are balancing two goals here—informing the client, and accurately stating the law. This balance requires that you both (1) accurately present complicated legal concepts, and (2) present them in language the client can understand. Don't misrepresent by oversimplifying; take the time and effort necessary to make the document both accurate and understandable. This may, on occasion, require explaining things twice—once using terms of art or other complicated language, and a second time, describing what these terms and language mean in plain and practical language.

Be sure, again, to identify the limitations upon, and qualifications of, the analysis. Define all terms that might create confusion; identify the extent of your investigation; and indicate any and all assumptions on which the analysis is based.

Recommendation   In reaching her conclusion, an attorney rendering an opinion generally makes a recommendation to the client about the best approach to resolving the problem presented. This is perhaps the most important section of the opinion letter—where the attorney takes a position based upon his research. Again, emphasize that the opinion is based upon the facts as they are known to the attorney. If the attorney needs to qualify her position, or indicate problems, she should do so here as well as in earlier sections. Do not use qualifiers to make your position ambiguous, however—use them to describe precisely what you have concluded to be an ambiguous situation.

Directive   Your last paragraph should be an instruction or directive to the client to contact the attorney after reviewing the letter. This contact is important, because it will enable you, your supervising attorney, and the client to discuss and clarify any questions that the client has regarding the facts, the conclusion, and the recommendations.

Remember that, as a paralegal, you can *never* sign an opinion letter—only an attorney can render legal advice. However, you may be drafting these letters for an attorney to review. Figure 7–13 shows an example of a client opinion letter.

The Third Party Opinion Letter

There are occasions when a third party will require that your client provide a legal opinion, so that he can complete a transaction. For example, a client seeking a mortgage may need to provide the bank with a legal opinion regarding a title question. If you are called upon to draft such a letter, there are several points to remember. First, be sure to identify in the letter your relationship with the client. Second, indicate that, despite this relationship, your opinion is based upon honest and unbiased analysis. Third, use language that restricts the applicability of the opinion, for liability purposes—for example, stating, "This opinion has been prepared for the benefit of First National Bank only, and no other party may rely on the representations contained herein." Fourth, identify the reason for the opinion—for example, "This opinion has been requested by First National Bank in connection with a mortgage sought by my client, William Doe." Fifth, be sure that you clearly identify your opinion or conclusion. This can be done with plain, unequivocal language: "Based on the above, it is our opinion that . . ."; or "We hereby render the following opinions based upon the preceding analysis: . . . ." Finally, clearly identify who is rendering the opinion. For example, on the signature line, the signer (who, as we have noted, will always be an attorney) should probably sign not on his own behalf, but on behalf of his firm.

Figure 7–13 Client Opinion Letter

July 21, 1992

Mr. Neil Crosby
9250 Kingsley Road
Aurora, Colorado 80011

Re: <u>Evaluation of Insurance Claims</u>

Dear Mr. Crosby:

You have retained me to review the law regarding the responsibility of insurance companies to provide coverage for preexisting medical conditions.

I have reviewed the documentation that you have supplied to me. Based on the medical response from Dr. Stills, it appears that you did not have a preexisting condition at the time you applied for medical insurance. The problem is convincing the insurance company of that fact.

The most logical first step would be to send a letter to the insurance company detailing our position, namely that you did not have a preexisting condition at the time you applied for insurance. However, before a letter is sent, it would be appropriate for us to meet so that I may discuss with you the result of my research on the legal meaning of preexisting condition.

Briefly, the case law on this issue is unsettled. The courts generally look to the definition of "preexisting condition" in your insurance policy, then apply this to your medical history. There is no generally accepted definition of preexisting condition; it is determined by a judge or jury as a question of fact.

This means that estimating our chances for success will be difficult. Unfortunately, unless the insurance company willingly agrees with our position, the most logical next step would be to file a lawsuit against the insurance company for failing to pay your claims.

As we had discussed in our first meeting, this may be quite costly, with the results uncertain. Please call me in the next ten days so we can decide how to pursue this matter: whether to send the letter to the insurance company based on your medicals and my research, or not pursue the matter at all. I look forward to hearing from you.

Thank you for your attention and courtesies.

Very truly yours,

Steven N. Young

Most of these points are designed to define clearly the areas, and the limits, of your firm's liability for the opinion rendered, since in the third party situation, they may not be immediately clear. Figure 7–14 shows an example of a third party opinion letter.

Figure 7-14   Third Party Opinion Letter

                                          September 18, 1992

Ms. Roberta McMillan, Examiner
Individual Benefit Department
UNITED INSURANCE AGENCY
716 Milton Drive
Richmond, VA 32187

        Re: Our Client: Mr. Neil Crosby
            Health Coverage Due and Owing Under
            Policy number 718465023GB8A dated December 2, 1990

Dear Ms. McMillan:

    The undersigned represents Mr. Neil Crosby in the above-referenced matter. You have
requested a legal opinion of the law in the state of Texas on preexisting conditions as
it relates to my client. A brief synopsis of the facts is necessary.

    On December 2, 1990, Mr. Crosby became insured with United Insurance Agency for health
insurance with a quarterly premium of $187.60. A copy of the policy is attached hereto as
Exhibit A. The policy contained certain contractual obligations, one of which was to pay medical expenses, over and above the noted deductible, for the insured in the event of the occur-
rence of any health problems. In January, 1992, your company failed and refused to pay Mr.
Crosby for his health care costs, stating that he had a preexisting condition before the policy was issued and therefore was not covered under your company's policy. A representative
contended that Mr. Crosby did not properly and accurately inform your company of his medical history in answers supplied by him on your company's application for insurance. This
application, with the responses, is attached hereto as Exhibit B. As noted on the application, Mr. Crosby had not been diagnosed as having any type of disease condition within the
five (5) years prior to applying for insurance with United Insurance Agency.

    His policy was conditioned upon the information contained within the application being
"to the best of my [Mr. Crosby's] knowledge and belief . . . complete and true." Mr.
Crosby's information was in fact a truthful representation of his condition.

    United Insurance Agency never followed up his application with any type of medical exam-
ination by its own physicians. This was a condition that your company would have had to
so follow up as a condition precedent to justify any denial of coverage.

    The Texas Administrative Code, Section 3.3018 defines preexisting illness as:
        The existence of symptoms which could cause an ordinarily prudent person to seek
        diagnosis, care, or treatment within a five-year period preceding the effective
        date of the coverage of the insured person or a condition for which medical advice
        or treatment was recommended by a physician or received from a physician within
        a five-year period preceding the effective date of the coverage of the insured
        person.

    My client had no knowledge of any preexisting illness that would preclude coverage as
defined in the Texas statute. Further, the law requires knowledge of a preexisting condition, or that the insurer make independent investigation. My client did not have any latent
symptoms that were intentionally ignored. Your company had an affirmative duty to investigate independently my client's representation of "good health." Due to your company's
failure to investigate my client's health history, my client is not precluded from coverage. Mr. Crosby does fall within the protected class covered under your health insurance
application.

    United Insurance Agency knew of all medical records pertaining to the medical histo-
ry of Mr. Crosby, based upon the completed information and history. As a result, you are
contractually bound and responsible to pay his health expenses.

    Based on my evaluation of the law, it is my opinion that there should be complete reim-
bursement of all medical expenses of my client from the inception of the policy to the
present, as well as the payment of any future medical expenses.

    This opinion is based on the present state of the law, as well as the documentation
that has been supplied by my client, which included the insurance policy and application.
Please contact me at your earliest convenience so that we may discuss this matter.

    Thank you for your attention to this matter.

                                    Very truly yours,

                                    Steven N. Young

7–6 General Legal Correspondence

Legal correspondence comes in many forms. You've just learned about the demand letter and the opinion letter, but there are other categories as well. Earlier we touched briefly on the **transmittal letter**, a type of confirmation letter that accompanies information sent to a designated party. Sometimes documents sent with a transmittal letter must be signed or filed and returned; if that is the case, a return envelope with proper address and postage should be included, and the transmittal letter should contain instructions about what the receiver should do. Two examples of proper transmittal letters are found in Figure 7–15.

Figure 7–15 Transmittal Letters

(a) Transmittal Letter Forwarding Document to Opposing Counsel

```
                              May 15, 1992

Mr. Jeffrey Smith
Attorney at Law
701 Lawnview Avenue
Tulsa, OK 78910

     Re: No. 91-432-A
         O.K. Binding, Inc. vs. Southern Paper Co.

Dear Mr. Smith:

     Enclosed is a copy of Plaintiff's First Amended Original
Petition in the above-referenced matter, which has been
filed with the Court this date.

     Thank you for your attention and courtesies.
                         Very truly yours,



                         P.R. Lang
PRL/sst
```

(b) Transmittal Letter Forwarding Document to Court and Requesting Return of Document

```
                              May 15, 1992

Clerk of the Court
201st District Court
Tulsa, Oklahoma 78910

     Re: No. 91-432-A
         O.K. Binding, Inc. vs. Southern Paper Co.

Dear Clerk:

     I enclose the original and two copies of Plaintiff's
First Amended Original Petition. Please file the original
with the court's records and return a file-stamped copy to
this office in the enclosed self-addressed, stamped enve-
lope.

     Thank you for your attention and courtesies.

                         Very truly yours,



                         P. R. Lang
PRL/sst
```

Another type of correspondence is a letter requesting information. Such requests must be specific. By sending such a letter, you not only obtain information, but also create a record that the request was made. Typically the letter will request medical records, employment records, or other investigative materials. Figure 7–16 shows an example of a letter requesting medical information, and Figure 7–17 shows a letter requesting an administrative transcript.

Figure 7–16   Letter Requesting Medical Records

```
                                           October 23, 1992

CERTIFIED MAIL #P117824932
RETURN RECEIPT REQUESTED

Dr. Martin Banks
603 East 21st Street
Houston, TX 77015

    Re: Mrs. Beth Windsor

Dear Dr. Banks:

    Enclosed is an authorization for release of medical records signed by my client.
At this time, I would request that you forward to my office copies of all medical
records in your possession regarding Mrs. Windsor. Please have this information for-
warded to me by November 3, 1992.

    Thank you for your cooperation in this matter.

                              Very truly yours,


                              Colleen O. Hayward


COH/bng
```

Figure 7–17   Letter Requesting Administrative Transcript

```
                                           February 1, 1992

HAND DELIVERED

Office of the City Secretary
City Hall
Minneapolis, MN 75201

    Re: Certified Copy of Transcript of Hearings Held on April 1, 1991 and June 3,
        1991 before the Urban Rehabilitation Standards Board
        Property located at 7042 Rocky Road

Board Members:

    I hereby request that a certified transcript of the Urban Rehabilitation
Standards Board hearings on April 1, 1991 and June 3, 1991 on the property locat-
ed at 7042 Rocky Road, Minneapolis, Minnesota, be prepared by the City Secretary
of the City of Minneapolis. This transcript is now requested for the purpose of an
appeal to the District Court of Minneapolis County, Minnesota. Please advise when
the certified copies of the record will be ready for transmission to the court,
and I will have a courier transport them.

    Thank you for your prompt attention and courtesies.

                              Very truly yours,


                              Mark O. Walker
```

A **retainer letter** is a form of correspondence important in the practice of law, for it sets forth the agreement and relationship between the attorney and the client. Such things as fees and a description of the matter are included.

In an **authorization letter**, the client provides the attorney with official permission to contact her employers, doctors, or other individuals who have records that relate in some way to the matter at hand. The attorney drafts the authorization letter for the client's signature; the client reviews and signs it.

The list could go on and on. When preparing general legal correspondence, you should keep the following factors in mind:

- determine the purpose of your letter;
- identify to whom your letter is directed;
- communicate in plain English;
- if you use legalese or terms of art, explain your meaning unless the audience is trained in legal matters;
- be specific when requesting information;
- follow the guidelines we've discussed for demand and opinion letters;
- be polite and courteous; and
- send copies to the appropriate parties.

7–7   Practical Considerations

We end this chapter with one practical consideration: When framing correspondence, keep the ball in *your* court!

What does this mean? It's quite simple, and the best way to demonstrate is by example. Assume that your client has a dispute with a customer to whom he has supplied building materials, but from whom he has received no payment. You take the trouble to write a comprehensive demand letter, setting forth the terms on which you would be willing to settle the matter. The following are two possible closings to your letter (Figure 7–18); or consider the following comments from letters trying to schedule a deposition (Figure 7–19).

Figure 7–18 Closings to Your Letter

> **Closing 1: Ball in *opponent's* court:**
>
> Please advise as soon as possible if the enclosed terms are acceptable to you.
>
> **Closing 2: Ball in *your* court:**
>
> If we have not heard from you by September 1, 1992, we will assume the terms are unacceptable and immediately institute suit.

Figure 7–19 Closings to Your Letter

> **Comment 1: Ball in *opponent's* court:**
>
> Please advise whether September 1, 1992 is an acceptable date for the deposition of John Doe.
>
> **Comment 2: Ball in *your* court:**
>
> The deposition will be held on September 1, 1992, unless you advise that this date is unacceptable.

The point is this: when you leave the ball in your court, you have control over the situation, and inaction on the part of the other party will not impede your ability to take action. When you pass the ball to the other side's court, you place yourself in the position of having to wait for acceptance of an offer, or some other matter. Thus, you needlessly handicap your ability to respond to events as you see fit.

So, in drafting correspondence, use language that keeps your side in control of events. Keep the ball in your court!

SUMMARY

7–1

The legal profession uses correspondence to inform, to advise, and to confirm. Informative letters transmit information; advisory letters are more formal than informative letters and offer legal opinions; and confirmation letters create a permanent record of the oral sharing of information.

7–2

The tone of a letter varies with the audience as well as the purpose. Letters to clients should contain concrete answers and be written to the client's level of understanding. They should be drafted so as to avoid unreasonable expectations in the mind of the client. Letters to opposing counsel should be written with caution, since they may be used against your client. Letters to the court should be written with respect. You should generally send copies to opposing counsel, and be aware of the pitfalls of *ex parte* communications.

7–3

A letter generally contains the following components: a letterhead; the date on which the letter is sent; identification of the addressee; a brief, descriptive reference line; a salutation opening with "Dear" and followed by a colon; a body containing the message of the letter, which may be short or long, but which should always be written clearly; headers, which identify subsequent pages; a closing, often "Very truly yours" followed by the signer's name and position. Note that paralegals can *never* sign letters rendering legal advice. Finally, letters show the parties to whom copies have been sent; only your file copy should show those parties to whom blind carbon copies have been sent.

7–4

The demand letter is designed to motivate a desired response—often (though not exclusively) the payment of a debt.

Demand letters can be in the form of a standard collection letter; a "Fair Debt Collection" letter designed to comply with statutory requirements; a consumer protection letter; or a notice of intention to sue. In drafting a demand letter, you should state your purpose, clarify the action you expect the recipient to take, establish a deadline date, and, under most circumstances, maintain a tone that will keep channels of communication open. In responding to a demand letter, you should review and discuss the situation with your client and identify reasons why you deny the claim. The letter should deny inaccurate factual statements made by the opposition, make your position clear, and, as with a demand letter, keep the channels of communication open.

7–5

An opinion letter renders legal advice. In a client opinion letter, work to balance two competing considerations: (1) accurately presenting legal concepts; and (2) presenting them in language the client can understand. Make it clear that your analysis is based upon the facts as you understand them, and make your recommendations clear as well. A third party opinion letter must indicate your relationship with the client; the purpose of the letter; any limitations for liability purposes; and a clear statement of the bounds of the opinion.

7–6

Transmittal letters accompany information, confirming its nature and the fact that it was sent. Letters requesting information should be specific, and serve two purposes: to obtain information, and to create a record that the request was made. A retainer letter sets forth the agreement between attorney and client on fees and services to be rendered. An authorization letter enables the attorney to pursue an investigation for the client's benefit into records maintained by third parties.

7–7

An important practical point in drafting legal correspondence is to keep the ball in your court, which means that whenever possible, you should maintain control over subsequent events.

REVIEW

Terms

Before proceeding, review the key terms listed below to be sure you understand each one. If necessary, read over the corresponding section of the chapter. When you are ready to test your understanding, answer the Review Questions.

informative letter
advisory letter
confirmation letter
cover letter
ex parte
letterhead
reference line
salutation
body
header
closing
cc
bcc
blind carbon copy
demand letter
collection letter
deadline date
opinion letter
disclaimer
transmittal letter
retainer letter
authorization letter

Questions for Review and Discussion

1. Name three functions of legal correspondence.
2. List some characteristics of letters addressed to: clients; opposing counsel; and the court.
3. What is the purpose of using letterhead?
4. What is the importance of an accurate date?
5. How is a reference line prepared?
6. What is a blind carbon copy?
7. What is the purpose of a demand letter?
8. What is the purpose of a client opinion letter?
9. How does a third party opinion letter differ from a client opinion letter?
10. List two possible purposes of a letter that requests information, and describe its most important characteristic.

Activities

1. Your law firm has just been retained to represent a woman who has been injured in an industrial accident. Your attorney has instructed you to request the client's medical history. Draft the letter requesting the information.
2. A client has a claim against an insurance company for nonpayment of medical bills. Draft the representation letter to the insurance company.
3. Prepare a transmittal letter to the court sending the Defendant's Original Answer. (Remember to state that the opposing counsel has been notified of this transmittal.)

CHAPTER 8 The Basics of Pleadings

OUTLINE

COMMENTARY

Your firm's client, Mary Mackey, is 51 years old. After 30 years of continuous employment with XYZ Corporation, and despite a personnel file that contains exceptional performance reviews and no hint of misconduct, she was recently fired with no explanation and for no apparent reason. Based on conversations she has since had with former coworkers, she believes that she was replaced by a 23-year-old woman who came in at a higher salary despite minimal qualifications.

Your supervising attorney believes that Mrs. Mackey's termination constitutes age discrimination. He has written to XYZ Corporation, demanding that Mrs. Mackey be reinstated and that she be reimbursed for the weeks of salary missed since the firing. The corporation has rejected this demand, and refuses to discuss the situation further.

Your supervising attorney has decided that litigation can no longer be avoided. You have been assigned to draft a complaint on behalf of Mrs. Mackey.

OBJECTIVES

Drafting pleadings is a basic litigation skill important to master, both as a means of defining the issues in a lawsuit and as a means to develop a deeper understanding of the litigation process. After completing this chapter, you will be able to:

1. Differentiate fact pleading from notice pleading.
2. Prepare a caption.
3. Identify a certificate of service.
4. Explain why preliminary research is important to the proper drafting of a complaint.
5. Describe a count.
6. Identify a benefit and a pitfall of using form books and models to assist in the preparation of pleadings.
7. Explain what is meant by "service of process."
8. Define the term *affirmative defense*, and identify several affirmative defenses.
9. Explain the difference between a counterclaim and a cross-claim.
10. Describe the purpose of a Motion for a More Definite Statement.

8–1 Pleadings in General

When a lawsuit is begun, it is important for the court and the litigants—the competing parties—to identify the issues in dispute. If the issues are unclear, the plaintiff will be unable to prepare for trial; the defendant will be unable to prepare a defense; and the court will be unable to evaluate the competing positions. The problem is solved by the filing of pleadings. **Pleadings** are formal documents filed with the court that establish the claims and defenses of the parties to the lawsuit.

Types of Pleadings

There are several different types of pleadings. They are filed in sequence, in a manner specified by procedural rules. Some are filed by a plaintiff, some by a defendant.

The **complaint** is the first pleading filed by any party to a lawsuit. It is the filing of the complaint that actually commences the lawsuit; before the complaint reaches the court, no lawsuit is pending. The complaint tells the defendant who is suing him and why, and also identifies the nature and extent of the damages claimed.

The **answer** is filed by the defendant in response to the complaint. It generally denies the plaintiff's claim, sets forth the reasons for the denial, and identifies affirmative defenses that the defendant asserts.

A **counterclaim** or **cross-claim** may also be included in the pleadings in a particular case. A counterclaim is made by the defendant against the plaintiff—not a defense, but a new claim for damages, as if the defendant were the plaintiff in a separate suit. A cross-claim is made in a suit where there are two or more defendants, one of whom also acts like a plaintiff in a separate suit. But rather than making her claim against the plaintiff (as in the counterclaim), she makes it against another defendant.

In addition to the complaint, answer, counterclaim, and cross-claim, there are also several motions considered to be pleadings. For example, a party who believes that the claims made in the pleadings of another party are unclear can file a **Motion for More Definite Statement**. A party who believes his opponent has "failed to state a claim" for which the court can grant relief can file a **Motion to Dismiss**, which, if granted by the court, dismisses the claim. There may be available other motions with other names, or similar motions with variant names, depending on the rules of your jurisdiction; you should become familiar with the rules that apply in your area.

In this chapter we use the complaint and the answer as a backdrop for exploring the drafting of pleadings by the legal writer. We then briefly consider the other types of pleadings. Where procedural rules are mentioned, we often discuss the Federal Rules of Civil Procedure (FRCP), since they are uniform throughout the United States. Remember, however, that our purpose is to teach you how to draft a pleading, as opposed to mastering the rules. Although the two concepts are connected, teaching you to master the rules of civil procedure, whether the FRCP or state rules, is beyond the scope of this book.

We cannot, however, overemphasize the importance of learning the rules. Even when the FRCP are applicable, for example, there will be additional local rules that govern certain technical matters. Failure to follow *all* applicable rules and to file pleadings in the manner and in the order that the rules require can waive (forfeit) your clients' rights and lead to a disastrous result.

Fact Pleading and Notice Pleading Distinguished

There are two broad styles of pleading—fact pleading and notice pleading. You should always determine which style is required in the jurisdiction in which your lawsuit is pending.

Fact pleading requires that you identify all the facts necessary to allege a valid cause of action. In other words, the pleading must include, at a minimum, those facts which must be proved in order to win on the claims made.

Notice pleading, which has been incorporated into the FRCP, requires only a short, plain statement of the grounds on which a party is basing her claim, and a showing of why the party is entitled to relief. The party need not allege all the facts needed to support the claim, but only such facts as are needed to put the opposing party on notice of the claim. The text of FRCP 8(a), which sets out the requirements of notice pleading for a complaint filed in federal court, appears in Figure 8–1.

The rationale behind the less strict requirements of notice pleading is that the facts will be developed by the parties through the **discovery** process, which is the investigation aspect of pretrial procedure (which we discuss further in Chapter 9). Parties often, however, include significant detail in their pleadings anyway, for two reasons: (1) to make their claims clear from the start, and (2) because the jurors can take the pleadings into the jury room, so that the added detail helps to clarify the party's position.

Figure 8–1 Rule 8(a), Federal Rules of Civil Procedure

> **(a) Claims for Relief.** A pleading which sets forth a claim for relief, whether an original claim, counterclaim, cross-claim, or third-party claim, shall contain (1) a short and plain statement of the grounds upon which the court's jurisdiction depends, unless the court already has jurisdiction and the claim needs no new grounds of jurisdiction to support it, (2) a short and plain statement of the claim showing that the pleader is entitled to relief, and (3) a demand for judgment for the relief the pleader seeks. Relief in the alternative or of several different types may be demanded.

You should note the exceptions to notice pleading in federal court, set forth in FRCP 9. For example, when a plaintiff is alleging a fraud committed by a defendant, rule 9 requires that the facts surrounding the alleged fraud be stated with "particularity," that is, in detail. This is to protect defendants from unsubstantiated allegations of fraud, which can damage reputations.

The Caption

All pleadings filed with the court require a **caption**. The caption goes at the top of the first page of the pleading, and identifies (1) the name of the case; (2) the court in which the case is pending; (3) the docket number of the case; and

Figure 8–2 Variations of Captions

(a)   UNITED STATES DISTRICT COURT FOR THE SOUTHERN
                        DISTRICT OF CALIFORNIA

                     Civil Action, File Number _____

MICHAEL BUFFETT, et al.   §
         Plaintiffs   §
                                 §   ANSWER
vs.   §
                                 §
CARMEN BROWN, et al.   §
         Defendants   §

(b)   UNITED STATES DISTRICT COURT FOR THE EASTERN
                        DISTRICT OF NEW JERSEY

XTC CORPORATION, Plaintiff   §
              vs.   §
SMITH, INC., Defendant   §   THIRD-PARTY COMPLAINT
and Third-Party Plaintiff   §
              vs.   §   CIVIL ACTION NO. _____
FRANÇOIS BENET, Third-Party   §
Defendant

(c)   UNITED STATES DISTRICT COURT FOR THE NORTHERN
                  DISTRICT OF ILLINOIS, CHICAGO DIVISION

                     Civil Action, File Number _____

XTC CORPORATION, Plaintiff   §
              vs.   §
SMITH, INC., Defendant   §   INTERVENER'S ANSWER
FRANÇOIS BENET, Intervener   §

(d)   NO. 89-7786-J

XTC CORPORATION,   )   IN THE DISTRICT COURT OF
)
              Plaintiff   )
)
vs.   )   DALLAS COUNTY, TEXAS
)
SMITH, INC.,   )
)
Defendant   )   191st JUDICIAL DISTRICT

(4) the date on which the pleading is filed. The caption is identical for all parties in the case, whether plaintiffs or defendants. Captions vary slightly in style and format from one jurisdiction to another, as can be seen from the examples shown in Figure 8–2.

Title of the Pleading

It is necessary to identify the type of pleading with a title appearing below the caption. With multiple parties it is often helpful to include enough information in the title to clearly differentiate the pleading from other, potentially similar pleadings (for example, "Defendant Johnson's Motion to Dismiss the Second Count").

Signature

Someone must sign all pleadings, usually the attorney for the party filing the pleading. The signature constitutes a pledge by the person signing that the contents have been prepared in good faith. If it can be shown that this is not the case, a lawyer can be sanctioned (see, for example, FRCP 11).

Certificate of Service

Almost every jurisdiction requires some form of certification or guarantee by an attorney (or a party, if the party does not have an attorney) that copies of the pleading have been sent to all other parties. This certification is very important, because unless the other parties are aware that the pleading has been filed, they cannot make appropriate responses in accordance with the applicable rules and deadlines. The certification usually consists of an attesting signature of the attorney preparing the complaint to a pledge like the following:

Figure 8–3 Certificate of Service

Certification

I, Mary Attorney, hereby certify that a copy of the foregoing Motion to Dismiss was mailed to all counsel of record on this 15th day of June, 1992.

Mary Attorney

8–2 The Complaint

As noted, the complaint is the pleading that commences the lawsuit. In addition to the caption and signature block, a complaint prepared in accordance with the FRCP includes an introduction, an identification of the parties, a statement of the basis for jurisdiction, numbered paragraphs containing the allegations (including damages) and causes of action, and a prayer for relief. It does *not* include an ordinary certificate of service, because a complaint must be served according to its own special rules. Let's take a look at each of these areas.

The Caption

The caption that appears on the complaint includes the same information which appears on every other caption, with the exception of the docket number. The court clerk assigns the docket number after the filing of the complaint; subsequent pleadings will show it, but the complaint cannot until the clerk assigns it (more about the sequence of events later).

Introduction

Although the trend is to eliminate the introductory paragraph of pleadings, it is still used in many jurisdictions. The introductory paragraph identifies the party filing the pleading and the nature of the pleading. Figure 8–4 shows several examples of introductory paragraphs in a complaint.

The Body of the Complaint

The body of the complaint consists of the identification of the parties, the basis for jurisdiction, and the numbered paragraphs containing the allegations and cause of action.

The parties are identified by name and status (i.e., whether an individual, corporation, or some other status), state of citizenship, and street address. These characteristics can be important; their significance is discussed in the subsection on "service of process." Figure 8–5 shows examples of paragraphs identifying various parties.

Complaints prepared under the FRCP must also identify the basis for the alleged jurisdiction of the federal court. This usually requires identifying the substantive federal statutes that apply to the facts to form the basis of the

Figure 8–4 Introductory Paragraphs

Simple, General Clause:

Plaintiff alleges . . .

Comes Now, Plaintiff in the above-styled cause, and complains of Defendant and would show unto the Court as follows:

Single Claim Stated:

Plaintiff for his claim alleges . . .

Plaintiff for its complaint alleges . . .

Claims Made in Separate Counts:

Plaintiff for a first count alleges . . .

Alternate Forms:

The Plaintiff, for his complaint against the Defendant through Miranda Carr, his attorney, alleges . . .

The Plaintiffs bring their complaint against the Defendants and for their claims would respectfully show . . .

Figure 8–5 General Jurisdictional Allegations in the Body of Complaint

Natural Persons—Single Parties

Plaintiff is a citizen of the State of Minnesota, and resides in the City of Owatana. Defendant is a citizen of the State of Minnesota and resides in the City of Owatana. The matter in controversy, exclusive of interest and costs, exceeds fifty thousand dollars ($50,000.00).

Multiple Plaintiffs

Plaintiff, ALBERT CROSS, is a citizen of the State of Rhode Island, Plaintiff, SANDRA CROSS, is a citizen of the State of Rhode Island, and Defendant, CHRISTOPHER VAIL, is a citizen of the State of Rhode Island. The matter in controversy exceeds, exclusive of interest and costs, the sum of fifty thousand dollars ($50,000.00).

Corporations

Plaintiff is a corporation incorporated under the laws of the State of Delaware, having its principal place of business in the State of New Hampshire, and Defendant is a corporation incorporated under the laws of the State of New Hampshire, having its principal place of business in a State other than the State of New Hampshire. The matter in controversy exceeds, exclusive of interest and costs, the sum of fifty thousand dollars ($50,000.00).

jurisdiction, or, if no substantive statute is the basis for the jurisdiction, then the applicable federal jurisdictional statute (usually relating to diversity of citizenship) is cited, with a statement showing that its requirements have been satisfied. Figure 8–6 shows some examples of jurisdictional paragraphs.

Following the identifying and jurisdictional paragraphs come the allegations. The allegations set forth the claims of the party. Asserted as a group, they form the plaintiff's cause of action, which is the particular legal theory upon which plaintiff claims a right to judicial relief, or recovery of damages, against the defendant. The complaint should include all claims that plaintiff has against the defendant that arise from the same facts and circumstances. If there is more than one claim, each separate claim or cause of action is set forth in a separate **count**. Figure 8–7 on page 166 shows FRCP 8(e) regarding multiple causes of action.

The allegations are the substantive heart of the complaint. It is here that legal writing considerations come into play. The drafter cannot simply state facts and claim damages. Preliminary research must be conducted to determine what elements the law requires the plaintiff to prove. All such elements must then be pleaded, or else plaintiff has "failed to state a claim" on which relief can be granted, leaving himself open to the Motion to Dismiss discussed already. Careful drafting often requires that certain specific language be used

Figure 8–6 Statutory Jurisdictional Allegations in the Body of Complaint

General Form

The section arises under the Constitution of the United States, Article II, Section 8, and the 14th Amendment to the Constitution of the United States, U.S.C., Title 28 § 1 et seq.

Diversity of Citizenship and Federal Question

The jurisdiction of this Court is based upon diversity of citizenship and Title 15, U.S.C.A. Sections 1, et seq. The matter in controversy, exclusive of interest and costs, exceeds the sum of fifty thousand dollars ($50,000.00).

Figure 8–7 Guideline for Pleading Multiple Causes of Actions.

> **8(e) Pleading to be Concise and Direct; Consistency.**
>
> (1) Each averment of a pleading shall be simple, concise, and direct. No technical forms of pleading or motions are required.
>
> (2) A party may set forth two or more statements of a claim or defense alternately or hypothetically, either in one count or defense or in separate counts or defenses. When two or more statements are made in the alternative and one of them, if made independently, would be sufficient, the pleading is not made insufficient by the insufficiency of one or more of the alternative statements. A party may also state as many separate claims or defenses as the party has, regardless of consistency and whether based on legal, equitable, or maritime grounds. All statements shall be made subject to the obligations set forth in Rule 11.

to comply with statutory or common law requirements; the sufficiency of the complaint depends on it. The extent of detail required varies, of course, depending on whether the jurisdiction requires fact pleading or notice pleading.

Case law is never cited in the complaint, but statutes and regulations relied upon are generally identified. For example, the complaint based on the facts in the Commentary to this chapter would identify the federal age-discrimination statute on which the claim is based.

The allegations are contained in consecutively numbered paragraphs. Sometimes the identification of the parties is included in these numbered paragraphs. Each paragraph should be limited to one concise idea or statement. The language used should be accurate but adversarial—telling the plaintiff's story from the plaintiff's perspective, and sympathetic to the plaintiff for the wrong allegedly committed against her. The writer should strike a balance between mundane, unemotional language and excessively expressive language; the reader should be able to visualize events without sensing that they have been exaggerated or embellished.

Often the requirements of a later count require a restatement of allegations already set forth as paragraphs in an earlier count. If this is the case, it is not only acceptable but indeed important to eliminate redundancy by using a phrase such as the following:

Figure 8–8 Restatement of Allegations

> **Second Count**
>
> 1. Paragraphs 1–8 of the First Count are hereby set forth as paragraphs 1–8 of this, the Second Count.

By thus eliminating redundancy, the writer minimizes the risk that the reader will become bored or miss the significant points as a result of wading through repetitions.

The allegations should also identify the damages suffered by the plaintiff. The recovery of damages in the form of money is a **legal remedy**. If such legal damages are sought, you should be as specific as possible. Sometimes this is difficult, as with a personal injury situation where the nature of the damage defies precise evaluation. If the remedy sought is equitable relief (which resolves a lawsuit by directing the wrongdoer either to perform a certain act, or to refrain from performing a certain act), the specific nature of the equitable remedy sought should be identified as well.

When you begin drafting complaints, and even when you are more

Figure 8–9 Example of Body of Complaint

TO THE HONORABLE JUDGE OF SAID COURT:

1. Plaintiff Robert Andrews is an individual residing in Travis County, Texas, and is the natural parent of Francis Andrews, the minor Plaintiff. Defendant George Peters is an individual residing in Jollyville, Oklahoma, and service of process may be had at 8362 Longhorn Drive, Jollyville, Oklahoma. Defendant D.C. Computers, Inc. is a corporation duly formed and existing under the laws of the State of Texas and may be served with process by serving its agent for service, David Clark at 287 South Main, Austin, Texas 75853.

2. On the 4th day of June, 1991, Plaintiff Francis Andrews was a passenger in a vehicle driven by Plaintiff Robert Andrews, which was traveling eastbound in the 8700 block of Elm Street in Austin, Travis County, Texas.

3. Defendant Peters attempted to make a left turn in front of the Andrews' vehicle. As a result, the Andrews vehicle and the vehicle driven by Defendant Peters collided, causing injuries to Plaintiff, Francis Andrews. At the time of the collision, the vehicle driven by Defendant Peters was owned by Defendant D.C. Computers, Inc.

4. As a result of the negligent conduct of Defendant Peters, Plaintiff Francis Andrews suffered the damages and injuries set out hereinafter.

5. Plaintiffs would show that Defendant Peters was guilty of the following acts and omissions of negligence, each of which, separately or concurrently, was a proximate cause of the damages and injuries sustained by the Plaintiff, Francis Andrews:

   1) Failure to yield right of way;
   2) Failure to keep a proper lookout;
   3) Failure to take proper evasive action;
   4) Failure to apply brakes.

6. At the time of the collision described above, Defendant Peters was the agent, servant, and employee of Defendant D.C. Computers, Inc. and was acting within the scope of his authority as such agent, servant, and employee.

7. Defendant Peters was incompetent and unfit to safely operate a motor vehicle on the public streets and highways.

8. Defendant D.C. Computers, Inc. knew, or in the exercise of due care should have known, that Defendant Peters was an incompetent and unfit driver and would create an unreasonable risk of danger to persons and property on the public streets and highways of Texas.

9. Plaintiff Francis Andrews was severely injured as a proximate result of the negligent conduct of the Defendants. Plaintiff Francis Andrews has suffered physical pain and mental anguish in the past and in reasonable probability will suffer from such in the future. Plaintiff Francis Andrews has sustained physical impairment and in reasonable probability will sustain such impairment in the future.

10. Plaintiffs have sustained reasonable medical expenses in the amount of $52,000.00 as a result of the Defendants' negligence in the past and in reasonable probability will sustain additional medical expenses in the future.

11. At the time of this collision, Defendant Peters was under the influence of an alcoholic beverage. The conduct of Defendant Peters in driving the vehicle while under the influence of an alcoholic beverage constitutes gross negligence. As a result of such conduct, the Plaintiffs are entitled to recover exemplary damages.

experienced, it is often helpful to refer to form books and models. **Form books** are publications that contain complete or partial sample complaints, with sample factual situations and various alternative methods of stating the legal basis for the cause of action. **Models** are copies of actual complaints, obtained from your firm's files, that have a similar factual foundation. These sources are useful in that they give you a basic framework within which to begin drafting your complaint. In the case of a model, you have an actual complaint that has withstood scrutiny; in the case of a form book, a sample complaint that has withstood editorial scrutiny by a panel of experts. You must be careful, however, when using models and form books. There are problems which can arise. If the law has changed since the model or form book was prepared, for example, or if you fail to recognize the significance of a twist in your particular factual situation, you may make critical drafting errors. Thus, you should use models and form books to supplement your research, not in place of it.

In general, when drafting the body of the complaint you should keep in mind the many factors we've discussed in previous chapters about effective legal writing—concise sentences, a minimum of legalese, good punctuation and grammar. Figure 8–9 on page 167 shows an example of the body of a complaint.

The Prayer for Relief

The **prayer for relief** sets out the specific demands that the plaintiff has against the defendant. It requests judgment in favor of the plaintiff on the causes of action alleged, and identifies the damages (legal and/or equitable) the plaintiff asserts judgment should allow (including interest and attorneys' fees). In essence, the plaintiff is telling the court what he seeks to gain from the lawsuit.

Since the prayer for relief often begins with the phrase "Wherefore, the plaintiff claims . . . ," followed by a statement of the relief sought, it is often called the "wherefore clause." The current trend toward simplifying pleadings has streamlined the language in some jurisdictions, however, eliminating the archaic term "wherefore."

Almost all prayers for relief have a "catch-all" provision, which states that the plaintiff also seeks "such other and further relief as the court may deem proper or appropriate." By using this or a similar catch-all clause, the plaintiff gives the court discretion on the relief it may grant, even allowing it to go beyond the plaintiff's specified requests.

You should note that in some jurisdictions, the prayer for relief is also the location for a jury-trial request. You should also note that some jurisdictions require a prayer for relief at the end of every count, not just at the end of the complaint.

Examples of a prayer for relief are shown in Figure 8–10.

The Signature Block and the Verification

The attorney preparing the complaint must sign it and, as we noted earlier, Rule 11 of the FRCP states that the signature constitutes a written affirmation that she has a good-faith basis for filing it (protecting against frivolous or harassing suits). Usually the attorney's name, address, and telephone number are typed below the signature; check the rules in your jurisdiction.

Some complaints require a brief affidavit, called a **verification**, in which the plaintiff swears to the truth of the contents. By signing the verification, the plaintiff shows that he (1) has read the complaint, (2) understands the contents, and (3) pledges that, to the best of his personal knowledge, the allegations are true. The purpose of the verification is to protect further against false claims. Often the requirement applies where the allegations of the complaint are particularly

FIGURE 8-10 Prayer for Relief Section of Complaint

```
     WHEREFORE, PREMISES CONSIDERED, Plaintiffs pray that the
Defendants be cited to appear and answer herein and further
pray that upon final hearing, Plaintiff have final judgment
against each Defendant, jointly and severally, for damages
in excess of the minimum jurisdictional limits of this
Court, for exemplary damages, for prejudgment and post-
judgment interest as allowed by law, for costs of court and
for such other and further relief, both general and special,
at law and in equity, to which the Plaintiffs may show
themselves justly entitled.

OR

   WHEREFORE:

   The Plaintiffs, Robert Andrews and Francis Andrews, demand
judgment against the Defendant in the sum of Fifty-Two
Thousand Dollars ($52,000.00).

   The Plaintiff demands a trial by jury.

OR

   The Plaintiffs demand judgment . . .
```

strong, as where fraud is claimed. Signing an untruthful verification can lead to criminal prosecution, and the possible results should be explained to the plaintiff before he signs. An example of a verification appears as Figure 8–11.

Service of Process

The certificate of service is not needed in a complaint because, since the complaint is the first notice of a lawsuit that a defendant receives, the service requirements are actually much stricter than merely requiring a certificate of service. **Service of process** is the procedure by which a defendant is notified by a **process server** (a person statutorily authorized to serve legal documents such as complaints) that she is being sued. Among the papers that a defendant receives is a summons, ordering her to appear in court at a certain time or suf-

Figure 8-11 Verification

```
STATE OF NEW JERSEY              §

COUNTY OF CUMBERLAND             §

   BEFORE the undersigned Notary Public for the State of New Jersey, at large,
personally appeared, ROBERT ANDREWS, Plaintiff in the above-styled cause,
who, being by me first duly sworn, deposes and says that the averments contained
in the foregoing Complaint are true and correct.
   This the ____ day of August, 1992.


                                   _____
                                   ROBERT ANDREWS

Sworn to and subscribed before me, this _____ day of August, 1992.


                                   _____
                                   NOTARY PUBLIC IN AND FOR THE
                                     STATE OF NEW JERSEY
                                   My Commission Expires: _____
```

fer the consequences. Service of process is accomplished by delivery of the complaint and **summons**; the procedure has many technical requirements, which vary from one jurisdiction to another. The *status* of the defendants is also significant for the purpose of service of process. Rules of service differ depending on whether the defendant is an individual, a corporation, or of some other status.

In some jurisdictions the complaint is filed with the court, *then* served on the defendants, whereas in other jurisdictions it is served first, then filed. If filed before service, the procedure is as follows: (1) original is filed with the court; (2) the clerk assigns a docket number to the case; then (3) copies are returned to the plaintiff for service on the defendants. Make sure you find out and follow the proper sequence in your jurisdiction. In general, you should learn the specific rules of service for all the courts in your area, and always review questions with your supervising attorney.

Checklist

The full text of a complaint appears as Appendix A on page 177. Here, however, is a checklist for preparation of a complaint:

—— Determine the parties who will be sued.

—— Identify the court in which suit will be filed, and verify that the court has jurisdiction.

—— Research and determine the necessary elements for the causes of action you intend to allege, including the applicable statutes.

—— Identify the necessary and useful facts, and determine whether yours is a fact- or notice-pleading jurisdiction.

—— Identify the damages suffered and the relief sought.

—— Prepare the caption and the introduction.

—— Check the applicable procedural rules, form books, and models to determine the proper style of pleading.

—— Draft concise, effective statements that establish the cause of action in a light which favors your client.

—— Draft the prayer for relief.

—— Prepare the summons and determine the proper procedure to complete service of process.

—— Review and edit your draft.

8–3 The Answer

The complaint has been correctly served. Under FRCP 12(a), the defendant must file a response within 20 days of receipt of the complaint; you should always check the rules of your jurisdiction to verify such a deadline.

If the defendant believes that some aspect of the plaintiff's allegations is inadequate, he may file one of the motions described in the next section. If, however, no such motion is filed, then the defendant files his response, called an answer.

The Components of an Answer

An **answer** comprises several distinct parts. First, it contains a section responding specifically to the plaintiff's numbered paragraphs. It either admits an allegation, denies it, or pleads that the defendant "lacks sufficient knowledge or information to form a belief as to the truth or falsity" of the allegation. This last category would apply to those of the plaintiff's allegations that relate to issues of her own status or conduct, necessarily outside the knowledge of the defendant. Each and every allegation must be addressed and responded to by the defendant; failure to respond can be taken as an admission.

Figure 8–12 Answer with General and Affirmative Defenses Alleged

---

DEFENDANT'S ORIGINAL ANSWER

1. Defendant admits the allegations of Paragraph 1 of the complaint.
2. Defendant denies the allegations of Paragraph 2 of the complaint.
3. Defendant denies the allegations of Paragraph 3 of the complaint, but has no knowledge of information sufficient to form a belief regarding the ownership of the vehicle.
4. Defendant denies the allegations of Paragraph 4 of the complaint.
5. Defendant denies the allegations of Paragraph 5 of the complaint.
6. Defendant admits the allegations of Paragraph 6 of the complaint.
7. Defendant denies the allegations of Paragraph 7 of the complaint.
8. Defendant D.C. Computers, Inc. has no knowledge or information sufficient to form a belief regarding the truth of the allegations of Paragraph 8 of the complaint.
9. Defendant D.C. Computers, Inc. has no knowledge or information sufficient to form a belief regarding the truth of the allegations of Paragraph 9 of the complaint.
10. Defendant D.C. Computers, Inc. has no knowledge or information sufficient to form a belief regarding the truth of the allegations of Paragraph 10 of the complaint.
11. Defendant denies the allegations of Paragraph 11 of the complaint.

GENERAL DENIALS

12. This court lacks personal jurisdiction pursuant to Federal Rule 12(b).
13. Plaintiff has failed to state a claim upon which relief can be granted.

AFFIRMATIVE DEFENSES

14. Plaintiff was contributorally negligent in operating his automobile and is barred from recovery.
15. Plaintiff was traveling at an excessive speed and the alleged accident was unavoidable due to Plaintiff's negligence.

WHEREFORE, Defendant requests that this matter be dismissed and that Defendant be reimbursed its costs and attorneys' fees expended in the defense of this matter.

Rule 8 of the FRCP does not allow for a "general denial" disputing all of plaintiff's claims in one generalized statement; rather, each allegation must be identified and responded to. Most jurisdictions follow this rule; Texas and California are two notable exceptions.

General defenses are sometimes included in the complaint. These are items which, under the FRCP, can also be made by motion; we discuss them further in section 8–4. They cover such things as an assertion that the court lacks jurisdiction, or that the plaintiff has failed to state a claim on which relief can be granted.

The next section of the answer contains the **affirmative defenses**, which are also called **special defenses**. Affirmative defenses are those which go beyond mere denial of the plaintiff's claims; because of a separate affirmative fact, the defendant asserts that a defense exists even if plaintiff's allegations are true. Such defenses are usually waived unless specifically pleaded, which means that the defendant can only introduce evidence to prove an affirmative defense if he has included it in his answer. The affirmative or special defenses that must be included in the pleadings are often identified by statute or rule, as with Rule 8(c) of the FRCP. Examples of affirmative defenses are such issues as contributory negligence, "last clear chance" (a tort defense), assumption of risk, or statute of limitations.

Figure 8–12 on page 171 is an example of an answer with general and affirmative defenses.

Under some circumstances, the defendant includes a counterclaim after her defenses. A counterclaim may be filed with the answer or separately. It may arise out of the same facts as the complaint or be unrelated. Whatever the context, a counterclaim can be thought of as a separate lawsuit within a lawsuit, in which the defendant sues the plaintiff. The drafting considerations are similar to those for a complaint.

There are two types of counterclaims—compulsory and permissive. A **compulsory counterclaim** is one in which the facts relate to the same transaction as that set forth in the original complaint. It is *compulsory* because, if it is not included in the pending lawsuit, it is waived forever (see FRCP 13(a)). The purpose of making this sort of counterclaim compulsory is to conserve judicial resources: the court is able to adjudicate in one trial all claims arising out of the same set of facts, so that repetitive trials can be avoided. A **permissive counterclaim** (also discussed in FRCP 13) arises out of different facts. It may be filed in the pending lawsuit, but if it is not, it may be filed at a later date in a separate lawsuit. That is, no rights are waived by failing to include it. If filed as a counterclaim a plaintiff may move to sever it if its presence serves to cloud or confuse the original issues.

Figure 8–13 is an example of a counterclaim in a negligence action.

To complicate matters even more, a cross-claim, (which we discussed as a type of pleading) can be brought within the original lawsuit. A cross-claim is filed against a co-party, almost always by one defendant against another defendant, and must relate to the cause of action in the main complaint. The circumstances justifying a cross-claim often arise when a plaintiff sues two defendants who themselves have a business relationship—for example, when a person falls down in rented premises, then sues both the owner of the property and the tenant.

Although the terminology we have used applies in all federal jurisdictions, you should take great care in reviewing your state and local rules, because state and local terminology can vary dramatically. In California, for example, what we have just described as a "counterclaim" is referred to as a "cross-complaint."

Figure 8–13 Counterclaim in a Negligence Action

> The Defendant, counterclaiming against Plaintiff, says:
>
> 1.   On September 17, 1991, the Defendant was driving an automobile in a southerly direction on Highway 42 in Cumberland County, New Jersey, and entered the intersection of that highway and Atlantic County Road.
>
> 2. At the same time, Plaintiff was driving an automobile in a general easterly direction and entered said intersection after the Defendant was well within the intersection.
>
> 3. At about the same time Wesley Whittaker was driving an automobile in a general westerly direction upon the same highway.
>
> 4. The automobiles driven by Plaintiff and by Defendant came into contact within the intersection, and in the collision, the Defendant suffered damages to his property and injuries to his person.
>
> 5. At and about the time and place of the collision and just prior to it, Plaintiff negligently managed and operated the automobile he was driving. Plaintiff was negligent in the following respects: (1) In carelessly driving at an excessive rate of speed contrary to the statute; (2) In failing to use ordinary care to keep a proper lookout; (3) In failing to use ordinary care to have the automobile he was driving under proper control.
>
> 6. As a proximate result of the negligence of Plaintiff, the Defendant suffered the following damage and injuries: defendant's automobile front end was demolished; the left side of his ribs were broken; he was forced to incur expense for medical treatment and hospitalization; he suffered great pain and suffering, and was prevented from pursuing his business, thus suffering economic loss.
>
> 7. Defendant will be partially disabled for a long period and unable to attend his usual occupations, and to his damage in the sum of fifty-five thousand dollars ($55,000.00).
>
> WHEREFORE, the Defendant demands judgment as follows:
>
> (1) Dismissing Plaintiff's complaint;
>
> (2) Against Plaintiff for Defendant's damages in the sum of fifty-five thousand dollars ($55,000.00) together with costs and disbursements; and
>
> (3) For such other and further relief as Defendant is justly entitled.
>
> _____
>
> Bonnie Hiatt
> Attorney for Defendant
> 8201 South Broadway
> Charleston, MO 40387
> (304) 786-4873

Checklist

The full text of an answer appears as Appendix B on page 179. The following is a checklist that you can follow in drafting an answer:

— Check the rules to verify the deadline for filing the answer.

— Admit or deny each allegation of the complaint, or allege that you have insufficient information to respond.

— Check to be sure that every paragraph and allegation of the complaint has been responded to.

— Allege any affirmative or general defenses that apply.

— Set forth any applicable counterclaim or cross-claim.

— Review and edit your draft.

8–4 Additional Pleadings

In the previous section we mentioned general defenses, which can be raised either in the answer, or by a separate motion. Rule 12(b) of the FRCP identifies the following defenses, any one or more of which may be made by motion:

1. Lack of jurisdiction over the subject matter.
2. Lack of jurisdiction over the person.
3. Improper venue (which is an assertion that plaintiff has filed the complaint in the wrong court).
4. Insufficiency of process (which means the summons or some aspect of the papers served by the process server was not correct).
5. Insufficiency of service of process (which means that the process server did not follow the rules in delivering the lawsuit).
6. Failure to state a claim on which relief can be granted.

If a party chooses to assert these defenses in a motion, the motion is called a Motion to Dismiss. It is generally supported by a brief, to which plaintiff responds and on which the court renders a decision. Before making its decision, the court often allows oral argument. An example of a Motion to Dismiss appears as Figure 8–14.

As we noted earlier, the complexities of procedural rules are beyond the scope of this discussion. Nevertheless, as you review the six defenses listed, you should keep in mind the following points:

Figure 8–14 Rule 12(b) Motion to Dismiss

```
                     MOTION TO DISMISS

   The Defendant, RAINEY, INC., moves the court to dismiss
Plaintiff's complaint on the following grounds:

   1. That there is no actual controversy between the par-
ties under the provisions of Title 42 U.S.C. §2000(e), as
Plaintiff is not within the protected class under Title VII
of the Civil Rights Act of 1964.

   2. The court lacks jurisdiction of the subject matter of
the complaint.

   3. The complaint fails to state a claim against the
Defendant upon which relief can be granted, since Plaintiff
is male, thirty-nine (39) years of age, and not subject to
protection under 42 U.S.C. §2000(e).



                        _____
                        Katherine Haley
                        Attorney for Defendant
                        333 E. Denton Drive
                        Richardson, Texas 75221
                        (214)763-9736
```

- A defendant in a lawsuit has numerous options available to attack the claims in a complaint, in addition to admission, denial, or claim of insufficient knowledge.
- The six defenses listed constitute a sampling of these options, by no means exhaustive.
- There is great variety between and among jurisdictions as to the manner and timing of the filing of defenses, and the names of the related motions.
- It is necessary to study and master the applicable rules.
- When in doubt, discuss questions and problems with your supervising attorney.

A special kind of response, which we have referred to previously as the Motion for More Definite Statement, is authorized by FRCP 12(e) and merits brief additional mention. The filing of this motion is an assertion by the defendant that more information must be provided by the plaintiff before an intelligent response can be prepared. In some jurisdictions this pleading is called a "Request to Revise" or a "Request for More Definite Statement," or some similar name. Such a motion or request is often useful to pin down a plaintiff who has made vague allegations, and it can set the stage for the assertion of other defenses.

Strategy lies behind the filing of pleadings. Because they define the issues before the court, and because they are provided to the jury, if the matter is a jury trial, great care must be taken to ensure that the issues presented are the issues intended by the parties. The strategist/drafter should always strive to limit the issues, to the extent possible, to those most favorable to her client, and draft them in language sympathetic to her client.

8–5 Amending and Supplementing Pleadings

Although pleadings must be prepared in good faith, and hence should be prepared fully and to the best of the drafter's knowledge and ability, often information arises after filing that a party may wish to add. In addition, a party may be *required* to add information when a Motion for More Definite Statement is granted. A drafter may also have forgotten to include some information. Such additions (or analogous deletions) are made by filing amended or supplemented pleadings.

Amended Pleadings

An **amended pleading** changes, corrects, revises, or deletes information from a prior pleading. Information from the original pleading that is not changed remains in force, but information which is superseded is no longer in force. It is critically important to distinguish that which is changed from that which remains as before—your skills of writing with clarity become important in this regard. It is generally best to file an entirely new pleading, identifying it as "amended" in the title (for example, "Amended Complaint") incorporating all the old and new provisions in one place.

If an optional amended pleading (i.e., one not required by the granting of a motion) is not filed within a certain number of days of the original pleading, it generally can be filed thereafter only with the permission of the court. Check the applicable rules to verify such a deadline.

Supplemental Pleadings

A **supplemental pleading** adds to a pleading without deleting prior information. The prior pleading remains intact and is read in conjunction with the supplement. A supplemental pleading is usually filed when additional facts become known after the filing of the original pleading, perhaps after information is learned through a deposition or other discovery procedure (discussed in the next chapter). Court permission may also be required prior to the filing of a supplemental pleading.

8–6 Practical Considerations

Pleading is both a science and an art. It is a science in that specific rules must be strictly followed, or the pleading fails on technical grounds. It is an art in that the pleader must use creative skills to plot a strategic course and draft pleadings that assist in reaching the intended destination.

It is difficult to separate the science from the art, and this chapter has talked as much about rules as about writing. Mastering the rules is essential to mastering pleadings, and hence you should take the time to thoroughly review both the Federal Rules of Civil Procedure and the state and local rules applicable in your jurisdiction. We have only touched on these considerations; you should go much further.

But remember that drafting pleadings requires more than merely knowing and following rules, and more than mechanically adapting the facts of your case to the formats suggested in a form book. Pleadings define your case for yourself, the opposition, the court, and (if a jury matter) the jury. But *you* define the pleadings, by careful and effective drafting.

UNITED STATES DISTRICT COURT FOR THE SOUTHERN
DISTRICT OF CALIFORNIA

Civil Action, File Number _____

MELANIE COLEMAN,	§	
Plaintiff	§	
	§	COMPLAINT
vs.	§	
	§	
PRODUCTS OF AMERICA, INC.	§	
Defendant	§	

Plaintiff alleges:

1. Defendant is a Pennsylvania corporation, doing business in the State of Delaware. The address of its principal place of business is Philadelphia, Pennsylvania.

2. At all times relevant, Defendant was an "employer" as defined by 29 U.S.C. § 640(b) and is thus covered by and subject to the Age Discrimination in Employment Act of 1967 ("ADEA"), 29 U.S.C. § 621 et seq. This court has jurisdiction under 29 U.S.C. 640 (b).

3. As of July 15, 1991, Plaintiff was fifty-five years and two months of age and is an individual protected by the ADEA.

4. As of December 1, 1991, Plaintiff was employed by Defendant in the capacity of "project manager."

5. Plaintiff had been employed in various positions by Defendant from approximately October, 1982 until December, 1991.

6. Plaintiff was discharged by Defendant on December 2, 1991.

7. Plaintiff's discharge was because of Plaintiff's age in violation of the ADEA.

8. Defendant's violation of the ADEA was willful.

9. Plaintiff has satisfied all of the procedural and administrative requirements set forth in 29 U.S.C.§ 626.

   a. Plaintiff has filed a timely charge with the appropriate state fair employment practice office.

   b. Plaintiff has filed a timely charge with the Equal Employment Opportunity Commission.

   c. These charges were filed more than sixty (60) days prior to the filing of this action.

10. Proper venue is in this court as the unlawful action occurred within this jurisdiction where Defendant is doing business.

11. Plaintiff has suffered, is now suffering, and will continue to suffer irreparable injury as a result of Defendant's actions.

WHEREFORE, Plaintiff hereby demands a trial by jury and prays for the following legal and equitable remedies:

a. Defendant be ordered to employ and reemploy the Plaintiff to the position from which she was discharged, together with all benefits incident thereto, including but not limited to wages, benefits, training, and seniority.

b. Defendant be required to compensate Plaintiff for the full value of wages and benefits that Plaintiff would have received had it not been for Defendant's unlawful treatment of the Plaintiff, with interest thereon, until the date Plaintiff is offered reemployment into a position substantially equivalent to the one Plaintiff occupied on December 2, 1991.

c. That a final judgment in favor of Plaintiff and against Defendant be entered for liquidated damages in an amount equal to the amount of wages due and owing Plaintiff as provided by 29 U.S.C. §§ 626(b) and 216(b).

d. That defendant be enjoined from discriminating against Plaintiff in any manner that violates the Age Discrimination in Employment Act.

e. That Plaintiff be awarded against the Defendant the costs and expenses of this litigation and reasonable attorneys' fees.

f. That Plaintiff be granted such other and further legal and equitable relief as the court may deem just and proper.

KETCHUM AND WYNN

By_____
Cynthia Goodman
Attorney for Plaintiff
1801 S. Main St., Suite 104
Philadelphia, PA 40987

UNITED STATES DISTRICT COURT FOR THE EASTERN
DISTRICT OF NEW JERSEY

XTC CORPORATION, Plaintiff   §
                              §
                              §   DEFENDENT'S ORIGINAL
vs.   §   ANSWER
                              §
                              §   CIVIL ACTION NO.____
FRANÇOIS BENET, Defendant   §

1. Defendant admits the allegations contained in paragraph 1 of the complaint.

2. Defendant admits that Plaintiff seeks to bring a cause of action under Title 29 U.S.C. § 640(b), but denies that Plaintiff is entitled to relief.

3. Defendant has no knowledge of information sufficient to form a belief regarding the truth of allegations of paragraph 3 of the complaint.

4. Defendant admits the allegations contained in paragraph 4 of the complaint.

5. Defendant admits the allegations contained in paragraph 5 of the complaint.

6. Defendant admits that Plaintiff was relieved of job responsibilities but denies that Plaintiff was discharged unlawfully under Title 29 U.S.C. § 640(b).

7. Defendant denies the allegations contained in paragraph 7 of the complaint.

8. Defendant denies the allegations contained in paragraph 8 of the complaint.

9. Defendant admits that he received a charge filed by Plaintiff but denies that the charge was filed timely.

10. Defendant denies the allegations contained in paragraph 10 of the complaint.

11. Defendant denies the allegations contained in paragraph 11 of the complaint.

GENERAL DEFENSES

12. Plaintiff has failed to state a claim upon which relief can be granted.

13. Plaintiff's suit is barred by virtue of statute of limitations.

AFFIRMATIVE DEFENSES

14. Plaintiff failed to file the complaint in this court within ninety (90) days following Plaintiff's right to sue notice as required by the statute.

   WHEREFORE, Defendant requests that this matter be dismissed and that Defendant be reimbursed its costs and attorneys' fees expended in the defense of this matter.

   Respectfully submitted,

                    _____

Bonnie Hiatt
Attorney for Defendant
8201 South Broadway
Charleston, MO 40387
(304)786-4873

SUMMARY

8-1

Pleadings are formal documents filed with the court that establish the claims and defenses of the parties. The complaint is filed by the plaintiff, and commences the lawsuit. The answer is filed by the defendant in response to the complaint. There may also be counterclaims and cross-claims, and motions directed to the content of the pleadings. In filing pleadings, it is critical to know and understand the applicable procedural rules. Fact-pleading jurisdictions require more detail in their pleadings than notice-pleading jurisdictions. The caption, title, signature, and certificate of service are common components of pleadings.

8-2

The complaint begins with a caption and an introduction, followed by the body of the complaint, with a statement of the jurisdiction of the court (if in federal court), identification of the parties, and numbered paragraphs containing the allegations of the plaintiff. The language of the complaint is adversarial; the story it tells is sympathetic to the plaintiff. Each cause of action is stated in a separate count. Form books and models can be used to supplement the drafter's preliminary research, but should not be used as a substitute for such research. The prayer for relief identifies the remedy sought by the plaintiff. A complaint must be signed, and sometimes a verification is required. Rather than a certificate of service, delivery of the complaint is made by the more complicated procedure of service of process.

8-3

The answer responds to the allegations of the complaint by admitting them, denying them, or pleading insufficient information to respond. General defenses, affirmative defenses, counterclaims and cross-claims are also often included.

A general defense can be made by motion as well as in the answer; an affirmative defense must be stated in the answer, or is waived. A counterclaim is filed by a defendant against a plaintiff; a cross-claim is filed by one co-party against another, usually by a defendant against another defendant. A compulsory counterclaim must be filed or the claim is waived; a permissive counterclaim can be filed as a counterclaim, or can be filed in the future in a separate lawsuit.

8-4

A Motion to Dismiss is a means to assert certain specified defenses, including (in a federal lawsuit) an assertion that the plaintiff has failed to state a claim on which relief can be granted. A Motion for More Definite Statement seeks more information from the other party about the details of their pleading, as a means of pinning down vague allegations; it can set the stage for other defenses.

8-5

An amended pleading changes, corrects, revises, or deletes information from a prior pleading. Amendments should be carefully identified to avoid confusion; the best practice is to file an entirely new pleading, labeled as an amended pleading, that includes both the still-accurate parts of the original content and the newly drafted changes. A supplemental pleading adds to a pleading without deleting prior information. Court permission may be required for amended and supplemental pleadings.

8-6

Pleading is both a science and an art: science in that rules must be strictly followed; art in that creative skills are required for writing and strategy. Pleadings define your case, but you define the pleadings.

REVIEW

Key Terms

Before proceeding, review the key terms listed below to be sure you understand each one. If necessary, read over the corresponding section of the chapter. When you are ready to test your understanding, answer the Review Questions.

pleadings
complaint
answer
counterclaim
cross-claim
Motion for More Definite Statement
Motion to Dismiss
fact pleading
notice pleading
discovery
caption
certificate of service
count
legal remedy
form book
model
prayer for relief
verification
service of process
process server
summons
answer
general defenses
affirmative defenses
special defenses
compulsory counterclaim
permissive counterclaim
amended pleading
supplemental pleading

Questions for Review and Discussion

1. What is the difference between fact pleading and notice pleading?
2. What is a caption?
3. What is a certificate of service?
4. Why is preliminary research impor-

tant to the proper drafting of a complaint?
5. What is a count?
6. Describe a benefit and a pitfall of using form books and models to assist in the preparation of pleadings.
7. What is meant by service of process?
8. What does the term *affirmative defense* mean? List several affirmative defenses.
9. What is the difference between a counterclaim and a cross-claim?
10. What is the purpose of a Motion for More Definite Statement?

Activities

1. Draft a complaint on behalf of the Crandalls, based on the following facts:

   Mr. and Mrs. Crandall are from Maine and were traveling cross-country in their new automobile. While en route to their destination of Cheyenne, Wyoming, they traveled through Illinois. Harry Hart of New Town, Illinois was crossing through the town square in New Town and hit the Crandall's car. Mrs. Crandall was thrown against the windshield, and Mr. Crandall hit the steering wheel. Mr. Hart was barely scratched, because his car had airbags, but his car was completely destroyed. The medical and hospital expenses for the Crandalls were $78,000.00, and repairs to their car were $6,000.

2. Using the facts in Activity 1, draft the answer of Mr. Hart and allege general and affirmative defenses.
3. Go to the library and find your state's procedural requirements for complaints, answers, and defenses.

CHAPTER 9   Discovery

OUTLINE

COMMENTARY

A complaint has been prepared and served in the matter of *Ascot v. Widget Company*. Your firm represents Mr. Ascot. The attorney for Widget Company has filed an answer, denying the claim.

Your supervising attorney wants to take the deposition of Henry Widget, the president of Widget Company. Before he does so, however, he wants to do some preliminary investigation to determine the understanding of Widget Company about the chronology of events. He has asked you to prepare interrogatories, requests for admission, and requests for production of documents and things, all of which are to be answered by Widget Company.

Discovery is an important aspect of almost every lawsuit. As a paralegal, you will often be involved in preparing and responding to discovery requests.

OBJECTIVES

Involvement in the discovery process is often an important segment of a paralegal's responsibilities. After completing this chapter, you will be able to:

1. Explain why a discovery process is needed.
2. List some characteristics of a properly drafted interrogatory.
3. Explain the importance of instructions and definitions in discovery requests.
4. List appropriate areas of inquiry as to the opposition's consultation with experts.
5. Explain what is meant by the "continuing duty to respond."
6. Explain the usefulness of a request for admissions.
7. Draft requests for production that are sufficiently specific.
8. Explain who a "deponent" is.
9. Define "subpoena."
10. Explain the difference between a Motion for Protective Order and a Motion to Compel Discovery.

9–1 Discovery in General

The "surprise witness" who arrives to testify at the eleventh hour of a trial, turning certain defeat into stunning victory, is a character still seen in television or movie courtrooms, but not in reality. The days of "trial by ambush," where one side or the other held back key information until unleashing it in front of a jury, have been replaced by the era of discovery.

Discovery is the pretrial investigation process, authorized and governed by the rules of civil procedure. Discovery rules are broad, so that parties have the ability to pursue information in the hands of other parties to a lawsuit.

To be "discoverable," information must be relevant and not protected by attorney-client privilege. The party requesting the information need not show that it will be admissible at trial, however, but only that it "appears reasonably calculated to lead to the discovery of admissible evidence" (Rule 26(b) of the FRCP; see Figure 9–1). Discovery requests may be directed to other parties, but not to nonparties, except that nonparties are subject to deposition (and related production of documents) if subpoenaed (more about subpoenas later).

Figure 9–1 Rule 26(b)

> (b) Discovery Scope and Limits. Unless otherwise limited by order of the court in accordance with these rules, the scope of discovery is as follows:
>
> (1) In General. Parties may obtain discovery regarding any matter, not privileged, which is relevant to the subject matter involved in the pending action, whether it relates to the claim or defense of the party seeking discovery or to the claim or defense of any other party, including the existence, description, nature, custody, condition and location of any books, documents, or other tangible things and the identity and location of person having knowledge of any discoverable matter. It is not ground for objection that the information sought will be inadmissible at the trial if the information sought appears reasonably calculated to lead to the discovery of admissible evidence.

In Chapter 8 we discussed the Motion for More Definite Statement. You may now be wondering: If more information about a party's claim is needed, why not simply file that motion? The reason that a distinct and separate discovery process is needed, at least in part, is this: there are limits on the detail that a party can be required to place in her pleadings. Indeed, a court will often deny a Motion for More Definite Statement on the grounds that the detail requested is more appropriately sought through the discovery process, and goes beyond the requirements of even a fact-pleading jurisdiction. Pleadings are intended to be straightforward summaries, not all-inclusive tracts. Furthermore, there may be strategic reasons why one party wishes to learn information about another *without* having it placed in the pleadings. Finally, such forms of discovery as a deposition or a medical examination are of a character entirely different from mere written information—they supply not just words, but also the personal characteristics or condition of the person deposed or examined.

There are, in fact, five different types of discovery: interrogatories; requests for admission; requests for production of documents and things; requests for medical examination; and depositions. Some aspects are common to all; some unique to each. In the sections that follow, we discuss each form in turn, highlighting format, drafting, and strategy requirements.

9–2   Interrogatories

An **interrogatory** is a written question submitted by one party to another, to be answered under oath. Rule 33 of the FRCP sets out the requirements governing the use of interrogatories in the federal courts. Most states have adopted a similar rule; check the rules that apply in your jurisdiction.

By following certain preliminary procedures, you will be able to prepare more effective interrogatories. First, review the case file and pleadings to become thoroughly familiar with the facts and allegations. Identify the information you need to fill in gaps or increase your understanding. Make lists of areas of appropriate inquiry. Next, as with pleadings, you can use form books and models for assistance. Again, be wary of relying on them exclusively. Also consult the rules, and review any questions you have with your supervising attorney. Form books and models will also be helpful in drafting documents associated with the other discovery methods to be discussed.

When you draft your interrogatories, use specific and detailed language that precisely identifies the information you seek. Use short sentences in simple language. Avoid the phrase "and/or," or a large number of colons and semicolons, which can confuse the reader and lead to an unsatisfactory response. Avoid multiple subtopics and sections in the interrogatory, which can also cause confusion. Such subtopics may even be prohibited in some jurisdictions, or each subtopic may be counted as a separate interrogatory in a jurisdiction that limits the total number of interrogatories allowed.

Take care in choosing verb tenses. If an interrogatory is phrased in the present tense, the information received may be different than if worded in the past tense. Who *has* possession of the records of Widget Company, for example, may be a different party than who *had* those records.

Interrogatories should also be drafted to avoid a response of "yes" or "no." The request should require the respondent to present additional information. If all that is desired is a "yes" or "no" response, another form of discovery, such as the request for admissions, might be the better method.

Certain interrogatories are common to many different types of cases, seeking such information as identification of the person responding to the interrogatories (if the party to whom the request is directed is a corporation or other form of business); the names of witnesses and experts who will testify; and identification of documents that are relevant, such as correspondence or contracts. The format of such questions is often similar, even for different types of cases. Other interrogatories must be tailored to reflect the peculiar circumstances of the particular case at hand.

To add to the precision of individual interrogatories, the drafter often includes **instructions** and **definitions** that precede the interrogatories and define terms to avoid confusion. The drafter can often anticipate and eliminate potential problems by clarifying ambiguous terms with precise definitions. Instructions often serve to eliminate evasive answers, as, for example, an instruction that if a party objects to one subpart of a question, he should still respond to the remaining subparts.

Although you should be sure to check the rules of your jurisdiction for specific guidance in the drafting of interrogatories, the following subsections discuss elements common to all sets of interrogatories.

The Caption

Just as with pleadings, discovery requests, including interrogatories, must be identified by case name, court, docket number, and date of filing. Although jurisdictions differ on the precise documents that are filed with the court (some courts require notice of filing interrogatories, for example, but not the interrogatories themselves until answers are provided), you should always put the caption of your case at the top of the first page of your interrogatories.

Title

Also as with pleadings, discovery requests require a title. Again, the value of the title is in its capacity to differentiate documents. Thus, in a case with multiple parties and extensive discovery, it is useful to use a title that identifies the requesting party, the party from whom a response is sought, and whether the request is the first such request or a subsequent, supplemental set. For example, a proper title might be, "Plaintiff Ascot's Second Set of Interrogatories to Defendant Widget Company."

The Introductory Paragraphs

The introduction directs the interrogatories to the party from whom a response is sought, often showing that the request is made through that party's attorney of record. Figure 9–2 illustrates an acceptable introduction.

Figure 9–2 Introduction

```
TO: Irene Miller, by and through her attorney of record,
    Malcolm Anders, 1776 Declaration Drive, Boston,
    Massachusetts 20185
```

After the introduction, another introductory paragraph identifies the appropriate state or federal rule that governs the interrogatories. It also identifies the oath requirement, which mandates that the person responding attests to the truth of the responses. Figure 9–3 shows such a paragraph.

Figure 9–3 Introductory Paragraph

COMES NOW, the Defendant in the above-entitled and numbered cause pursuant to Rule 33 of the Federal Rules of Civil Procedure, and propounds the attached Interrogatories. You are advised that your answers to such Interrogatories must be answered fully in writing and under oath and served on the undersigned within thirty (30) days from the date of service thereof.

    You are further notified that these Interrogatories and your sworn Answers to them may be offered in evidence at the time of trial of the above cause.

Instructions

Following the introduction are the **instructions**, which, as mentioned, provide guidelines to the party responding. Figure 9–4 shows an example of common instructions found in interrogatories.

Definitions

Following (or sometimes combined with) the instructions is a section defining terms and abbreviations used in the interrogatories. The meanings established

Figure 9–4 Instructions Section

INSTRUCTIONS

    In answering these interrogatories, defendant is required to set out each responsive fact, circumstance, act, omission, or course of conduct, whether or not admissible in evidence at trial, known to defendant or about which he has or had information, which is or will be the basis for any contentions made by defendant with respect to this lawsuit. If you are unable to answer any Interrogatory completely, so state, and to the extent possible, set forth the reasons for your inability to answer more fully, and state whatever knowledge or information you have concerning the unanswered portion.

    These Interrogatories are deemed to have continuing effect to the extent that if, after filing your responses to these interrogatories, you obtain information upon the basis of which you know that a response was incorrect when made, or you know that a response though correct when made is no longer true, you are required to amend your response in accordance with Rule 33 of the Federal Rules of Civil Procedure. In addition, defendant is required to supplement his responses with respect to any question directly addressed to the identity and location of persons having knowledge of discoverable matters, and with respect to the identity of each person expected to be called as an expert witness at trial, the subject matter on which he or she is expected to testify, and the substance of his or her testimony.

in this section eliminate ambiguity, which in turn eliminates the justification for many potential objections. Also eliminated is the need to define terms repeatedly within the interrogatories. Figure 9–5 shows an example of a definition section.

Figure 9–5 Definition Section

```
                        DEFINITIONS

    The following terms have the meanings stated wherever used
in these interrogatories, unless otherwise indicated:

    "You" and "your" means Gilda Murray.
    "Patient" means Gilda Murray.
    "This Defendant" means Dr. Ned Radcliffe.

    "Identify" means to state the person's full name, date of
birth, marital status and spouse's name, social security
number, present or last known residence and business address-
es and telephone number, occupation, employer, and business
address at the date of the event or transaction referred to,
present or last known position and business affiliation,
present or last known employer and business address. If a
person is identified more than once, only the name need be
provided after the first identification.

    "Health care provider" means any person involved in the
examination, care, or treatment of injuries, illnesses, or
other health-related conditions, both physical and mental.
This term includes, but is not limited to, physicians, den-
tists, podiatrists, chiropractors, nurses, therapists, psy-
chologists, counselors, home care attendants, and special
education instructors.

    "Health care facility" means any organization or institu-
tion involved in the examination, care or treatment of
injuries, illnesses, or other health-related conditions, both
physical and mental. This term includes, but is not limited to,
hospitals, clinics, health maintenance organizations, outpa-
tient facilities, testing facilities, laboratories, nursing
homes, and pharmacies from which medications were obtained.

    "Person" means, in the plural as in the singular, any nat-
ural person, corporation, firm, association, partnership,
joint venture, or other form of legal or official entity, as
the case may be.
```

Interrogatories

After the definitions come the interrogatories themselves. They are numbered, and enough space is generally left between interrogatories for the party responding to type in her response. The detail in the questions should be enough to make them clear and precise, and will vary depending on the detail already set forth in the instructions and definitions. For example, if the term "identify" is defined to mean "provide the full name, residence address and phone number, business address and phone number, age, and marital status of," then a proper interrogatory designed to elicit all this information would simply state: "Identify Mr. Widget." If no such definition is provided, then the information must be requested specifically.

We next discuss interrogatories relating to five areas: background information; specific case information; information about experts consulted; content of the pleadings; and generalized conclusory information.

Figure 9–6 Interrogatory That Elicits Background Information

```
INTERROGATORY NO. 1: Please state:

a. Your full legal name and any other names by which you
   have ever been known;
b. Your date and place of birth;
c. Your social security number;
d. Your driver's license number; and
e. Each address where you have lived in the past ten years.

ANSWER

INTERROGATORY NO.2:

Please state the name, address, telephone number, and employ-
er of each and every person known to you or your attorneys
who has or may have knowledge, directly or indirectly, of any
facts relevant to this case. For each such person, state gen-
erally the subject matter of the facts which may be known to
him or her. NOTE: This interrogatory includes, but is not
limited to, any person who may be called by you as a wit-
ness at the trial of this cause.

ANSWER:
```

Background Information It is important to develop general background information about the person responding to the interrogatories. If the person is an individual defendant, it will be important to have a current address if a subpoena needs to be served in the future; other information such as past and present employers, educational background, prior medical history, marital status, age, or other general facts may become significant as well. In addition, if the person responding is an employee of a defendant corporation, it is important to know the person's job title and the scope of the person's knowledge about the events in question, as well as the person's authority to speak on behalf of the corporation. Examples of a background interrogatory appear in Figure 9–6.

Specific Case Information After requesting background information, the drafter should begin a more focused, customized inquiry. Information specific to the case should be requested about witnesses (names, addresses, and other pertinent facts should be sought), documents (volume, description of contents, and current location should be sought), and any other facts or matters that bear on the outcome. Figure 9–7 shows examples of specific interrogatories.

Figure 9–7 Examples of Case-Specific Interrogatories

```
6. Identify all employees of Widget Company with whom Henry
Widget has discussed his meeting of March 15, 1992, with John
Ascot.

7. Identify all correspondence in the possession of Widget
Company, including copies of correspondence, which in any way
references, describes, or relates to the meeting of March 15,
1992, at which Henry Widget and John Ascot were present.

8. List the dates of every in-person meeting between Henry
Widget and John Ascot between January 1, 1992 and April 30,
1992.

9. Provide the date and time of day of every phone call
between Henry Widget and John Ascot that occurred between
January 1, 1992 and April 30, 1992.
```

Figure 9–8 Interrogatories Regarding Expert Witness

<u>INTERROGATORY NO. 3</u>

Please state the following information for each person who may be called by you to testify as an expert witness at the trial of this cause:

    a. name, address, telephone number, and employer;
    b. the date on which the witness was first contacted in connection with this case;
    c. the subject matter on which the expert is expected to testify;
    d. the qualifications of the expert to give testimony on that subject;
    e. the specific opinions and conclusions of the expert regarding the matters involved in this case, and the factual basis for each;
    f. the name, address, and telephone number of each person whose work forms a basis, in whole or in part, of the opinions of the expert.

<u>ANSWER:</u>

<u>INTERROGATORY NO. 4:</u>

Identify each individual with whom you have consulted or your attorneys have consulted as an expert, indicating whether a decision has been reached about whether: (1) said individual(s) may testify in this lawsuit; and (2) written reports were made or requested, in connection with the incidents made the basis of this lawsuit. For each expert listed, please also identify the following:

    a. complete educational background of such individual, beginning with the year in which said individual graduated from high school and continuing through completion of the formal education process of such expert;
    b. his or her occupation and field of specialization, as well as qualifications to act as an expert;
    c. all published writings of the individual expert, listing the titles of any article(s) or book(s), the name(s) of the publication(s), the year(s) of publication(s), volume and page number.
    d. for what remuneration Defendant has employed said individual:
    e. whether said individual has ever been a witness in any other lawsuit, and, if so, for each lawsuit give the name of the suit, the name of the court, the date of the filing, and the name and address of the other party for whom said individual provided evidence or testimony;
    f. all mental impressions and opinions held by the expert relating to the lawsuit in question;
    g. all facts known to the expert (regardless of when the factual information was acquired) that relate to or form the basis of the mental impressions and opinions held by the expert; and
    h. the complete employment history of such expert for the preceding five (5) years, including the name and address of the employer, and the general nature of the expert's work for such employer.

Information About Experts Consulted In cases involving technical issues, expert testimony is often crucial. If such issues are present in your case, one or more interrogatories should be included that inquire into the identity and qualifications of the opposition's experts, the nature of their inquiry and intended areas of testimony, and the existence of any written reports. Figure 9–8 illustrates interrogatories drafted to gain information about experts consulted. Note that these interrogatories are submitted to the other *party*, not to the expert; interrogatories, as we noted earlier, can only be served on other parties.

Content of the Pleadings Pleadings present factual allegations and legal contentions. It is very important to explore the basis for these allegations and contentions. Interrogatories should be drafted to uncover the facts behind the pleadings.

Consider, for example, a complaint that contains the following paragraph: "The president of Widget Company, Henry Widget, forged the signature of John Ascot on the Modification of the contract between the parties." From the perspective of Henry Widget and Widget Company, this is a very strong allegation, which must be investigated. Widget Company should file an interrogatory similar to the following: "State the facts upon which you rely, in paragraph 6 of the complaint, for the allegation that Henry Widget forged the signature of John Ascot."

Similarly, if a plaintiff states a legal claim that has several prerequisites the defendant may want to inquire into the facts behind each of the prerequisite elements. However, be careful in this regard—if a plaintiff has failed to allege one or more prerequisite elements, there may be strategic reasons to avoid inquiry in discovery (it might alert the plaintiff to the deficiency) so that you can later attack the deficiency by a Motion to Dismiss.

Generalized Conclusory Information It is wise to conclude your interrogatories with generalized questions that inquire broadly into areas which may have been overlooked or omitted. An interrogatory with such a purpose is a "catch-all" designed to prevent a surprise at trial. The trick in drafting such an interrogatory is to devise language that can survive an objection that it is so broad as to constitute an unjustifiable "fishing expedition." An example of a potential concluding interrogatory appears in Figure 9–9.

Signature Block and Certificate of Service

In most jurisdictions the interrogatories are signed by the attorney preparing them, but not by the party she represents (in contrast to the *responses*, which must be signed not only by the attorney but also by the party responding; more about that later). To verify the date that the interrogatories were sent to opposing counsel, a certificate of service is required (see Figure 9–10 on page 192).

Responses to Interrogatories

Responses to interrogatories must be prepared within the time established by the applicable procedural rules. Under Rule 33 of the FRCP, the time limit is 30

Figure 9–9 Common "Catch-all" Interrogatory

```
INTERROGATORY NO. 5:

State any additional information relevant to the subject of
this action not previously set out in your answers above.
```

Figure 9–10 Signature Block and Certificate of Service

```
                              Respectfully submitted,



                              _____
                              Bonnie Hiatt
                              Attorney for Defendant
                              8201 South Broadway
                              Charleston, MO 40387
                              (304)786-4837

              CERTIFICATE OF SERVICE

     I certify that a true copy of this Plaintiff's First Set
of Written Interrogatories was served on Katherine Haley,
Attorney for Defendant, 333 E. Denton Drive, Richardson,
Texas 75221, by certified mail, return receipt requested, in
accordance with the Texas Rules of Civil Procedure on
November 29, 1992.



                              _____
                              BONNIE HIATT
```

days. Extensions can be requested by motion; at least in the early stages of the discovery process, the court will probably be lenient about granting such requests, and few opposing counsel will object to reasonable extensions.

Responses must be signed and verified by the client. The attorney preparing them signs them as well, but the client must attest to their accuracy. Figure 9–11 shows an example of a **verification**.

The response can be either a presentation of the information requested, or an

Figure 9–11 Verification Used with Interrogatories

```
THE STATE OF NEW YORK      §
                           §
COUNTY OF SUFFOLK          §


   NED RADCLIFFE, being duly sworn upon his oath deposes and
says: I am the Defendant in the above-entitled action and
have read the interrogatories served upon me by the
Plaintiff, Gilda Murray; and the foregoing answers to those
interrogatories are true according to the best of my knowl-
edge, information and belief.




                    _____
                    NED RADCLIFFE

SUBSCRIBED AND SWORN to before me this ____ day of September,
1992




                    _____
                    NOTARY PUBLIC IN AND FOR THE
                        STATE OF NEW YORK
                    My Commission Expires:_____
```

objection. Objections should be addressed to individual interrogatories; it is not proper to object to *all* the interrogatories, and it remains necessary to provide responses for all those interrogatories not objected to (which is to say that the presence of one or more objectional interrogatories does not poison the entire set of interrogatories).

As you might expect, wide-ranging requests are often met with objection. Common objections include contentions that: the instructions or definitions are overbroad, or include requirements that go beyond the scope of the rules; the information requested is privileged; the information requested is irrelevant; the request is unduly burdensome; the request is so broad as to be meaningless (an objection often raised to the generalized conclusory interrogatories); or the request is ambiguous or unintelligible.

It is important to identify and comply with time requirements in making objections. If not raised in time, objections may be waived, or dismissed.

It is also important to note that, in the federal courts and many state and local jurisdictions, there is a "continuing duty to respond" to interrogatories. This means that if new information arises *after* responses are filed that would have been included in the original responses had it been known at the time of filing, it must be forwarded to the other side as a **supplemental response**. If such supplement is not made, the court at trial can refuse to allow the presentation of evidence that includes or relates to the undisclosed materials. Such supplementation is often necessary in a case where medical treatment of an injured plaintiff is ongoing—so make sure you have provided copies of all relevant medical materials to the other side before trial.

A party is required to make reasonable good-faith efforts to locate materials and information responsive to a discovery request. Be wary of a client who has a selective memory, or who wishes to avoid the difficulty of complying with a lengthy discovery request. You may wish to file objections claiming the request is unduly burdensome; but if such objections are not sustained, your client must turn over the requested materials or information, however unpleasant and time-consuming the task may be.

In addition to filing objections, a responding party can obstruct the information-gathering efforts of the opposition by filing a Motion for Protective Order. This motion will be discussed further.

9–3 Requests for Admissions

The **request for admissions**, authorized under Rule 36 of the FRCP, provides the drafter with the opportunity to conclusively establish selected facts prior to trial. A proposition is presented to the opposing party for admission or denial; if admitted, no further evidence need be presented on the point; the trial court accepts it as fact, at least with regard to the party who admitted it. Admissions serve to limit the complexity and expense of trials.

The caption, signature of the preparing attorney, and certificate of service are the same for a request for admissions as for a set of interrogatories. The introductory paragraph and the text of the requests are discussed in the next subsections, followed by a few words about preparing responses.

The Introduction of a Request for Admission

The introductory paragraph of a request for admissions includes an identification of the party to whom the request is directed, the rule providing for the

Figure 9–12 Introductory Paragraph for Request for Admissions

```
    Plaintiffs in the above-entitled action request pursuant
to Rule 36 of the Federal Rules of Civil Procedure that
Defendant, within thirty (30) days after service of this
request, admit for the purpose of this action that the fol-
lowing facts are true:
```

request, and the time period allowed for response. Figure 9-12 shows an example of an appropriate introductory paragraph for a request for admission.

Text of a Request for Admission

The requests themselves consist of statements that are to be admitted or denied by the recipient. The statements are numbered sequentially.

An effective technique for drafting the requests is to move through the case point by point, from general points to those more specific. Alternative versions can appear as different numbered statements, and consecutive questions can feature finely drawn distinctions; the responses to such a pattern of requests can assist the drafter in reaching an understanding about the nuances of the other party's position. An example of this technique is shown in Figure 9–13.

Several different formats are acceptable for requests for admission, three of which appear in Figure 9–14. The most important consideration in drafting requests for production is that they be so straightforward that they avoid an evasive response. The more detail added to the sentence, the greater the tendency to elicit a qualified response. Although the responding party retains some freedom to explain the response (as we discuss further) your goal as a drafter should be to minimize the responder's ability to hedge, assuring a straightforward admission or denial.

A common use of requests for admission is to establish the authenticity of documents. A copy of a document can be appended to the set of requests, and the requests can ask for an admission or denial that the copy is an exact copy of the original. Figure 9–15 shows an example of a request for admission inquiring into the genuineness of a document.

Figure 9–13 Technique for Drafting Request for Admissions

Alternative requests for admission:

Admit or deny the following:

1. On June 1, 1992, defendant Jones executed the contract that is attached as Exhibit A.
2. On June 2, 1992, defendant Jones executed the contract that is attached as Exhibit A.
3. On June 3, 1992, defendant Jones executed the contract that is attached as Exhibit A.

Requests for admission with finely drawn distinctions:

1. On March 15, 1992, defendant Jones attended a meeting at which was discussed the terms of a contract with Mr. Smith.
2. On March 15, 1992, defendant Jones and plaintiff Smith attended a meeting at which was discussed the terms of a contract with Mr. Smith.
3. On March 15, 1992, defendant Jones and plaintiff Smith attended a meeting at which they executed the contract that is attached hereto as Exhibit A.

Figure 9–14 Formats for Request for Admission

```
(a)  Admit or deny that you requested a refund on March 6,
     1992 for the car repairs performed by Defendant.
(b)  Do you admit or deny that you requested a refund on March
     6, 1992 for the car repairs performed by Defendant?
(c)  Do you admit that you requested a refund on March 6, 1992
     for the car repairs performed by Defendant?
(d)  Admit or deny the following facts:
     (1)  That you requested a refund on March 6, 1992 for the
          car repairs performed by Defendant.
```

Figure 9–15 Request for Admission Regarding Genuineness of Document

```
Admit or deny that the document marked "Exhibit A" and
attached hereto is a true and genuine copy of the Lease
dated June 17, 1992.
```

Responses to Requests for Admission

Requests for admission must be answered with great care, because of the impact of an admission. If a request is impossible to respond to with a flat admission or denial, but is not otherwise objectionable, a qualified response is acceptable. A qualified response should not be used for the purpose of evading, however.

Another possible response is a motion for protective order, to be discussed. Be sure to keep in mind the deadline for a response—failure to file a timely response can, as noted, be deemed to be an admission.

9–4 Request for Production of Documents and Things

Under Rule 34 of the FRCP, a party can request the other side to produce for inspection documents or objects in its possession. The materials requested need not be specifically identified, nor need they even be known to exist; but the description in the request should be sufficiently specific so that the opposing party can reasonably determine whether a document is responsive. It would not, for example, be acceptable to ask the other side to produce "all relevant documents"; it *would*, however, be acceptable to request "all correspondence between Henry Widget and John Ascot." The request for production allows for the evaluation and assessment of the physical evidence that is available for presentation at trial.

As with other forms of discovery, the request for production has a caption, title, introductory paragraphs, the requests themselves, the signature of the attorney making the request, and a certificate of service. In preparing requests, the drafter should take care that all relevant documents have been requested; this generally requires a review of the pleadings and facts of the case. In responding, you must take care that all requests not objected to are fully complied with; failure to produce a document requested is grounds for excluding that document, even if otherwise admissible, at trial.

Figure 9–16 Introductory Paragraph for Request for Production

> Pursuant to Rule 34 of the Federal Rules of Civil Procedure, Plaintiff requests that Defendants make available for inspection and copying the documents described herein at a time and place to be arranged by counsel, but in no event later than thirty (30) days from the date of service of this request.
>
> If a document is no longer in possession of or subject to the control of Defendant, state when such document was most recently in the possession of defendant or subject to the defendant's control and what disposition was made of it. If documents have been destroyed, please identify when they were destroyed, the person who destroyed the documents, the person who directed that they be destroyed, the reason(s) for such action, and any communications or documents that relate or refer to the destruction of the documents.
>
> This request is continuing in character and requires defendant to provide any supplemental documents if, prior to trial, defendant should obtain any additional or supplemental documents that are responsive to this request.

As a practical matter, where documents are requested compliance is usually made by providing a set of copies of the requested documents. Tangible objects may not be able to be copied, requiring you to arrange a convenient time and location for them to be inspected.

An acceptable introductory paragraph for a request for production appears in Figure 9–16. An example of general requests for production of documents and things appears in Figure 9–17.

Figure 9–17 General Request for Production of Documents

> 1. All documents pertaining to or reflecting any damages for which you are seeking recovery in this suit.
>
> 2. All correspondence, notes, memoranda, recordings, or other documents evidencing or reflecting any communication, conversation, transaction, or dealing between Plaintiff and this Defendant (including Defendant's agents, employees, or representatives), or between the Plaintiff's family and Defendant (including Defendant's agents, employees, and representatives).
>
> 3. All documents and tangible things prepared by any person whose work product forms a basis, in whole or in part, of the opinions of the expert witness.
>
> 4. The expert's entire file pertaining to this case.

9–5   Request for Medical Examination

Preparing a **request for medical examination** involves issues of litigation strategy almost exclusively, with little emphasis or importance on writing other than to make the request clear and to conform to the rules that establish the right. Because an examination is a substantial invasion of the opposing party's person, it will likely be granted only in cases where the physical or mental condition is an issue, as in a personal injury case.

9–6　The Deposition

In a deposition, a party or witness is placed under oath and questioned by attorneys, and the content of the examination is recorded in a transcript prepared by a certified court reporter. The party or witness who is questioned is referred to as a **deponent**.

There are three types of deposition: the oral deposition; the deposition on written questions; and the video deposition. The nature of each varies somewhat.

The **oral deposition**, in which the witness responds to questions from an attorney, is by far the most common. Depending on the answers to the questions, the attorney generally frames **follow-up questions** that explore an area in detail.

In the **deposition on written questions**, questions are submitted in advance; only those questions are answered, with no follow-up questions allowed. Often, no attorney is even present; the court reporter swears the witness and records the responses to the prepackaged questions.

Video depositions are simply videotaped versions of the oral deposition; the videotape serves as an additional method of preserving the testimony, in addition to the transcript. If a witness is going to be unavailable for trial because he is beyond the subpoena power of the court (more about subpoenas later) or is aged or ill, a video deposition is a good means of preserving the immediacy of real testimony for trial.

There are few limitations on the areas of questioning at a deposition; objections can (and generally should) be stated by the attorneys present, but rulings on the objections are generally reserved until trial, and thus the witness answers despite the objection. A witness can be instructed not to answer by an attorney, but this is usually a dramatic step, evidence of an exceedingly bitter, contentious deposition. When a deposition grows so quarrelsome that excessive objections and instructions not to answer erode the ability of the parties to continue, the parties can file motions to the court to rule on the objections before the deposition proceeds. Courts generally frown on this, however, and costs can be imposed against the party adjudged to have caused the problem.

Depositions are useful means of learning about the demeanor of a party or witness when subjected to questioning. They are also useful as a means of immediate follow-up when answers suggest further lines of inquiry—the follow-up question can be posed on the spot. This distinguishes depositions from interrogatories, which give no opportunity for immediate follow-up. Although subsequent sets of interrogatories can be filed that follow up initial answers, they lack the immediacy of a follow-up question at a deposition. Indeed, interrogatories and requests for production are often most useful as a means of gathering information in preparation for a deposition.

Notice of Intention to Take Oral Deposition

A formal document must be drafted to notify all parties that a deposition is to be taken. This is called a Notice of Intention to Take Oral Deposition (or often simply Notice of Deposition). In addition to a caption, title, and introductory information, the notice identifies the deponent, the location of the deposition, often the rule under which the deposition is authorized, and the fact that it will be taken before a certified court reporter or official authorized to administer oaths. An example of the body of a deposition notice appears in Figure 9–18.

Figure 9–18 The Body of a Notice of Oral Deposition

```
TO:  Dr. Ned Radcliffe, by and through his attorney of
     record, Matthew Brockton, Suite 850, 3265 Montclaire
     Avenue, Waco, Texas 75683

   PLEASE TAKE NOTICE that on October 12, 1992, at ten
o'clock (10:00) a.m. at the law office of Emma M. Costello,
6301 Marley Avenue, Waco, Texas 75204, Plaintiff, GILDA
MURRAY will take the deposition of DR. NED RADCLIFFE. The
deposition will be taken on oral examination pursuant to
Rule 200 of the Texas Rules of Civil Procedure before an
officer authorized to administer oaths, and will continue
from day to day until completed.
```

Applicability of a Subpoena

If a *party* is identified as the deponent, the party is required to appear at the time and place identified, unless a Motion for Protective Order is filed (more about such a motion later). This requirement can be enforced because parties are subject to the rules of the court. Plaintiffs have submitted to them voluntarily; defendants have been brought under the control of the court by effective service of process. The deponent need not necessarily be a party, however— she may be merely a witness. A witness has not submitted to nor been brought under the control of the court; a witness might simply refuse or neglect to appear for the deposition.

The solution to this potential problem is the subpoena. A **subpoena** is a document similar to a summons, in that it is served upon an individual under authority of the court, and orders the person to appear at a certain place and certain time, or suffer the consequences. Subpoenas are often used to ensure the presence of a witness at a deposition; the subpoena and deposition notices are served simultaneously. Subpoenas can also be used to compel a witness to testify at a trial.

Production of Documents in Conjunction With a Deposition

It is possible to combine a request for production of documents with a deposition notice. In this case, the deposition notice contains an additional sentence, referring to the request for production attached to the notice. The Latin term *duces tecum* signifies a deposition notice or subpoena requiring the deponent/witness to "bring with him" specified documents or things. Figure 9–19 shows an example of a Notice of Intention to Take Oral Deposition *Duces Tecum*.

Deposition Preparation

Because a deposition is generally an oral exercise, the need for writing skills to prepare formal documents is minimal. Nevertheless, it is important to apply your organizational skills—outlining, focusing on key factual points, identifying the secondary elements of legal arguments—in order to prepare to conduct the deposition, covering all necessary areas of inquiry. For the deposition on written questions (which, as noted, is a format rarely employed), you will of course draft questions ahead of time. The key to drafting such written questions is to keep them short and precise, so as to avoid evasive answers.

Figure 9–19 Notice of Intention to Take Oral Deposition *Duces Tecum*

TO: Dr. Ned Radcliffe, by and through his attorney of record, Matthew Brockton, Suite 850, 3265 Montclaire Avenue, Waco, Texas 75683.

PLEASE TAKE NOTICE that on October 12, 1992, at ten o'clock (10:00) a.m. at the law office of Emma M. Costello, 6301 Marley Avenue, Waco, Texas 75204, Plaintiff, GILDA MURRAY will take the deposition of DR. NED RADCLIFFE. The deposition will be taken on oral examination pursuant to Rule 200 of the Texas Rules of Civil Procedure before an officer authorized to administer oaths, and will continue from day to day until completed.

Please take notice that the deponent identified above will be required to produce at the taking of his deposition all the materials described in Exhibit A attached hereto and incorporated herein. The definitions and instructions included in Exhibit A shall control the production of the materials requested in Exhibit A.

Digesting a Deposition

After a deposition is completed, the court reporter who recorded the questions and testimony prepares the **transcript**, which is a written account of the entire proceeding. The transcript of a deposition can run to many hundreds of pages or more, and a complex case can require many depositions. It is often helpful for the attorneys handling the matter to have a **digest** of the deposition, which is a summary of the testimony indexed with references to the corresponding page numbers of the deposition. (This type of digest is not to be confused with the digest we discussed in Chapter 1, which contains research topics and headnotes from reported judicial opinions.) There is no standard method of digesting a deposition; if you are given such an assignment, you should strive to be accurate, using the writing techniques we have discussed to avoid ambiguity, and you should ask your supervising attorney the appropriate format and degree of detail desired.

9–7 Discovery Motions

In previous sections we have touched upon some factors to consider in responding to discovery requests. Although these factors, coupled with the desire to protect your client, give you some flexibility in drafting responses to discovery requests, the good-faith requirement that governs discovery responses implies a duty to provide all reasonable information requested. Nevertheless, parties often try to evade in the discovery process by making indefensible requests, failing to respond to reasonable requests, or otherwise abusing the process. This may lead to the filing of motions designed to resolve disputed issues. The three principal motions seen in discovery practice are the **Motion for Protective Order**, filed by a party upon whom a discovery request has been made; the **Motion to Compel Discovery**, filed by a party seeking to force compliance with a discovery request, and the **Motion for Sanctions**, filed by any party to counter alleged violations by another. Each of these motions generally includes attachments consisting of the discovery requests objected to or sought to be enforced; check the rules for format and special requirements. Each is discussed in the subsections that follow.

Figure 9–20 Motion for Protective Order

> COMES NOW, Dr. Ned Radcliffe, Defendant in the above-entitled and numbered cause, and files this his Motion for Protective Order, and in support of this Motion would show unto the Honorable Court as follows:
>
> 1. On or about September 17, 1992, Plaintiff issued upon this Defendant Plaintiff's First Set of Written Interrogatories and Request for Production of Documents. In responding to said discovery requests, this Defendant objected to Interrogatory Nos. 4, 11, 13, and 15 and Request for Production Nos. 1, 2, and 4, as well as making general objections. Said Objections are attached hereto and incorporated herein as Exhibit A by reference for all purposes.
>
> WHEREFORE, PREMISES CONSIDERED, Defendant hereby requests that upon final hearing and trial hereof, that the Court enter an Order sustaining his objections to the discovery requests of the Plaintiff, and for such other and further relief, in law or in equity, to which this Defendant may show himself to be justly entitled.

The Motion for Protective Order

When the party upon whom a discovery request has been filed contends that the request oversteps the bounds of the rules, she can file a Motion for Protective Order. Such a motion argues that the information sought is irrelevant or privileged, or that the request is unduly burdensome or overly broad or ambiguous. It may argue that a deposition is inappropriate at the location suggested. Whatever the argument, the purpose is to obstruct the other side. Figure 9–20 shows an example of a Motion for Protective Order opposing certain interrogatories and a request for production of documents.

The Motion to Compel Discovery

The Motion to Compel Discovery is the reverse of the Motion for Protective Order—it seeks not to obstruct discovery, but to force it.

Simply because a party chooses not to disclose information, or has objected to its disclosure, does not mean it isn't discoverable. The party seeking the information must notify the court of the failure to respond, and the need to have the court rule on the dispute. This can be done through a Motion to Compel Discovery, which identifies the information sought, notes that it is relevant, unprivileged, and not otherwise subject to protection, and argues that it should be supplied. Such a motion can also be supported by a brief. A Motion to Compel Discovery is often filed in response to a Motion for Protective Order, or sometimes simply as a means of prodding a party who has allowed the deadline for discovery response to pass without having filed the response. An example of a typical Motion to Compel Discovery is found in Figure 9–21.

The Motion for Sanctions

A Motion for sanctions is filed when there have been attempts to force cooperation, but based upon alleged deliberate inaction or gross indifference of one party, discovery has been stalled. Failure to appear at a duly noticed deposition,

Figure 9–21 Motion To Compel Discovery

    Now Comes the Defendant by her attorney and moves the
Court as follows:

    1. On October 14, 1992, Defendant, after commencement of
the above-entitled action, served on the Plaintiff in this
cause ten interrogatories in writing pursuant to Rule 33 of
the Federal Rules of Civil Procedure (28 U.S.C.A.), which
interrogatories are attached hereto.

    2. Plaintiff answered Interrogatories 1, 2, 3, 4, 5, and
10, but did not answer such interrogatories under oath as
required by Rule 33 of the Federal Rules of Civil Procedure
(28 U.S.C.A.).

    3. Plaintiff failed to answer Interrogatories 6, 7, 8, and
9.

    WHEREFORE, Defendant moves that this court enter an order
directing and requiring Plaintiff to answer all of said
interrogatories under oath.

    Defendant further moves the court for an order awarding
Defendant the reasonable expenses, including attorneys'
fees incurred in this motion.

without making an objection or indicating the intention not to attend, would be an example of behavior that might justify a Motion for Sanctions, since time and resources were wasted (a court reporter had to be paid to attend) with no justification. Another example would be a failure to follow the order of the court on a Motion to Compel Discovery. The granting of a Motion for Sanctions often includes an award of attorneys' fees and expenses incurred in its preparation.

Sometimes, if the circumstances justify, a party files a Motion for Sanctions at the same time as a Motion for Protective Order or a Motion to Compel Discovery. Sanctions are an extreme remedy, however, and Motions for Sanctions should be filed only after a cautious review of the facts.

9–8 Practical Considerations

The role of paralegals in discovery is often an important one. Complex cases may involve hundreds or thousands of documents, which must be tracked, reviewed, evaluated, disclosed, requested, and catalogued. Numerous depositions may be needed; numerous areas inquired into with interrogatories; multiple medical examinations may be necessary, and lengthy medical records may require interpretation. Much time-consuming work is involved—work that can be tedious, but that requires a sharp and trained mind nevertheless. By refining your skills at organizing the discovery process, you can heighten your value as an essential member of your firm's litigation team.

The following is a checklist of items to keep in mind when formulating discovery requests and responses:

—— Review the rules of procedure to determine the applicable bounds of discovery.

—— Make a point of identifying and remaining alert to all applicable deadlines. Review your client's file and make notes about the areas of the case in which discovery is desirable or necessary.

—— Prepare discovery requests that are detailed and specific.

—— Draft requests that will survive the opposition's efforts to object.

—— Organize materials so that confusion is minimized and access maximized.

—— Coordinate with your supervising attorney at every step.

—— Analyze your client's position and determine whether objections to discovery requests are in order.

—— Evaluate discovery responses to determine whether they are in compliance with the requirements of the rules and fully responsive to the corresponding requests. Evaluate both responses that you receive from the other side and responses that you prepare.

—— If the discovery process breaks down, prepare all necessary motions.

SUMMARY

9-1

Discovery is the pretrial investigatory process authorized and governed by the rules of civil procedure. To be discoverable, information requested must be reasonably calculated to lead to the discovery of admissible evidence. Discovery requests may be directed to parties but not to nonparties, except that it is acceptable to take the deposition of a nonparty.

9-2

An interrogatory is a written question submitted by one party to another to be answered under oath. Interrogatories should be specific and precise. Definitions and instructions can be included to reduce ambiguity. Titles should be sufficiently specific as to distinguish one set of interrogatories from another, particularly in cases with multiple parties on either side. Basic background information can be sought with interrogatories, as well as specific information about the case at hand, information about experts consulted, and information about the content of the pleadings. The truth of the responses must be attested to by the signature of the party on whose behalf the responses are filed. Objections to interrogatories can be justified on several grounds, including a contention that the information sought is privileged or that the request is overbroad. There is a continuing duty to respond to interrogatories, which means that a supplemental response must be filed if new information is uncovered.

9-3

The request for admissions allows the filing party to conclusively establish contested issues prior to trial. This serves to limit the complexity and expense of the ensuing trial. A common use of requests for admission is to authenticate documents. Requests should be drafted to minimize the potential for a qualified response; responses should be made with great care due to the impact of an admission.

9-4

A request for production of documents and things enables one party to inspect the physical and documentary evidence of the other party. The responding party must be reasonably able to determine whether a given document or thing is responsive.

9-5

The request for medical examination should be drafted clearly and in conformity with the rules. The issues associated with such a request are largely issues of litigation strategy, not legal writing.

9-6

In a deposition, the deponent (who can be a party or a witness) provides testimony that is transcribed by a court reporter. The deposition can be taken in response to oral or written questions, and can also be videotaped. The opportunity for follow-up questions makes the oral deposition a useful form of discovery. A notice of intention to take deposition must be filed by the party seeking to take the deposition; if the intended deponent is a witness rather than a party, a subpoena can be served to ensure the witness's attendance. A document request can be combined with a deposition notice. Lengthy deposition transcripts can be summarized in a deposition digest.

9–7

A Motion for Protective Order can be filed by a party in opposition to a discovery request that it believes oversteps the acceptable bounds of the discovery rules. The Motion to Compel Discovery is filed by a party seeking to force compliance with a discovery request. A Motion for Sanctions can be filed by a party who believes that the opposing party's discovery conduct is particularly uncooperative or unlawful.

9–8

Complex cases often involve an extended and complex discovery process. Paralegals can heighten their value by using organizational skills to assist in the workings of that process.

REVIEW

Key Terms

Before proceeding, review the key terms listed below to be sure you understand each one. If necessary, read over the corresponding section of the chapter. When you are ready to test your understanding, answer the Review Questions.

discovery
interrogatory
instructions
definitions
verification
supplemental response
request for admissions
request for production of documents and
    things
request for medical examination
deponent
oral deposition
follow-up question
deposition on written questions
video deposition
subpoena
duces tecum
transcript
digest
Motion for Protective Order
Motion to Compel Discovery
Motion for Sanctions

Questions for Review and Discussion

1. Why is the discovery process needed?
2. What are some of the characteristics of a properly drafted interrogatory?
3. Why are instructions and definitions important to include with discovery requests?
4. What are appropriate areas of inquiry about the opposition's consultation with experts?
5. What is meant by the continuing duty to respond?
6. How is a request for admissions useful?
7. How can requests for production be made sufficiently specific to avoid objection?
8. Who is a deponent?
9. What is a subpoena?
10. What is the difference between a Motion for Protective Order and a Motion to Compel Discovery?

Activities

1. Based on the facts of Figure 8–13 in Chapter 8, draft seven interrogatories, five requests for admission, and five requests for production of documents.
2. Draft a motion for protective order, based on the fact that the information sought in the request for production of documents is overly broad and unduly burdensome.
3. Check your state rules of procedure and compare and contrast your rules for interrogatories, admissions, and production of documents. Determine the differences or similarities to the Federal Rules in your jurisdiction's discovery requirements.

CHAPTER 10   The Memorandum of Law to the Trial Court

OUTLINE

COMMENTARY

Your firm's client, Dr. Williams, has been served with a subpoena *duces tecum*, commanding her to testify at a deposition and to produce all medical records of an identified patient. Neither Dr. Williams nor her patient wishes to disclose these records.

The doctor has consulted with your supervising attorney, and a decision has been made to file a motion for protective order asserting the existence of a patient/physician privilege. Since the law on this point in your state is not entirely clear, a supporting memorandum that argues in favor of the motion must be prepared. You have been assigned the task of drafting this memorandum.

The memorandum of law to the trial court is an important document in the litigation process, commonly seen and often instrumental in defining the scope and nature of the trial and its outcome. In your role as a paralegal, you will likely be called upon to participate in the preparation of such memoranda.

OBJECTIVES

A properly prepared memorandum of law to the trial court can have substantial impact on the outcome of a lawsuit. After you have completed this chapter, you will be able to:

1. Identify the two audiences for a trial memorandum.
2. Explain how to prepare a trial memorandum so as to assist the trial judge.
3. Draft your trial memorandum so as to minimize the impact of the attack of opposing counsel.

4. Describe the characteristics of a trial memorandum in regard to a motion.
5. Identify the reasons why a judge might request a trial memorandum.
6. Explain the potential importance of an unsolicited trial memorandum that anticipates issues.
7. Understand the importance of the caption and the title of a trial memorandum.
8. Explain the perspective from which the "issues presented" section is drafted.
9. List four objectives of a statement of facts.
10. Describe the difference between the discussion section of an internal memorandum and the argument section of a trial memorandum.

10–1 The Nature and Purpose of the Memorandum of Law to the Trial Court

The **memorandum of law to the trial court** (which we will refer to as a **trial memorandum**) is an adversarial document filed with the trial court and written to persuade the trial court that one party's position on a disputed point of law is superior to the opposing party's position. It may be written in support of or in opposition to a motion; it may be written at the request of a judge to assist her in rendering a decision; or it may be an unsolicited memorandum filed at trial in order to persuade the judge on anticipated legal questions. Whatever the reason, the content should be one-sided, or *partisan*.

We have already used two names, trial memorandum and memorandum of law to the trial court, for this. There are still other names that refer to the same type of document: memorandum of points and authorities, memorandum in opposition to motion, brief in support of motion, trial brief in opposition to motion, and others. These titles all refer to the same basic document—an adversarial document setting forth legal arguments to the trial court. The title depends upon the jurisdiction, and even on individual attorneys and judges. Different courts and individuals have different styles. It is important to remember that, regardless of the name applied, the factors to take into account are essentially the same.

One potential area of confusion should, however, be cleared up at the outset. In some areas, the term *trial brief* refers to the materials that an attorney prepares, not for filing with the court, but rather to assist him with the conduct of the trial—such things as witness lists, summaries of pleadings, an outline of his opening statement, copies of important cases, possible jury instructions, and so on. In this book, such preparatory materials will be called a *trial notebook*, which we discuss in Chapter 11. Thus, we consider a trial brief to be the same as a trial memorandum.

Although some trial courts have specific requirements for the format of a trial memorandum, in general these requirements are less formal than those for an appellate brief (which we discuss in Chapter 12). You should learn your jurisdiction's requirements for a trial memorandum.

It is important to take into consideration the audience for the trial memorandum. Although your client may read your trial memorandum, and should certainly be consulted about the factual background, she is *not* part of the audience for whom the trial memorandum is written. The audience is composed of two segments—the judge, whom you must convince, and the opposing counsel, whom you must refute and whose attack your arguments must survive. Let's take a moment and consider these two audiences.

First, the judge. Unlike appellate judges, who sit in judgment only on appeals, trial judges handle varied responsibilities, from overseeing courtroom personnel, to deciding motions, to conducting trials. Often their schedules are busy, and time is short. Whereas an appellate judge may have the time and the responsibility to read and research enough to render appropriate decisions (which have broad impact), a trial judge generally only needs to know how the higher courts have dealt with the issues presented, or analogous situations. This is not to say that trial judges are not thoughtful, or do not take their responsibilities seriously; they are and they do. It is simply a warning that a trial memorandum needs to get to the point. Tell the judge what you want, why you want it, and why you are legally entitled to it, as concisely as you can. If you must make a complicated argument, by all means make it—but if it can be done more simply, it is a mistake to write a lengthy explanation. Keep your memoranda short, concise, and direct.

Opposing counsel are the second audience. Unlike judges, who will give your arguments a fair reading, opposing counsel are the enemy. They scour your arguments looking for logical holes and unjustified analytical leaps, in an effort to refute your arguments and prove that your client's position is not supported by law. You must, therefore, write *accurately*. Do not overstate your arguments, and never misstate or misrepresent the law. If you are honest in your interpretations (partisan, yes, but nevertheless honest), and if you shepardize with care, your arguments should survive the attack of opposing counsel. Indeed, by recognizing the threat posed by opposing counsel, you may well be saved from making the type of borderline argument that, if read and rejected by a judge, might tend to poison your other, more logical arguments in the eyes of the court.

10–2 Types of Trial Memoranda

All legal memoranda argue a point of law in an adversarial manner. Each of the three broad categories we identified earlier, however—a **memorandum in regard to a motion**, a **memorandum at the request of a judge**, and an **unsolicited memorandum anticipating legal issues**—presents its own unique considerations for the drafter. Let's take a look at each.

Memorandum in Regard to a Motion

Many issues arise in the course of a lawsuit—issues about the content of the pleadings, the propriety of discovery requests, the sufficiency of responses, the right of a party to file amendments, and on and on. Such issues must be resolved before the case is ready for trial. Sometimes they are resolved by mutual agreement of the parties, but often they are not. When agreement is not possible, a motion is generally made to the court in which one party requests that the court resolve the dispute in its favor, so that the case can move to trial. The motion itself generally identifies the nature of the dispute and the order or relief that the filing party seeks, but generally does *not* contain any legal analysis or arguments. These analyses and arguments are reserved for the trial memoranda filed in regard to the motion.

The trial memorandum of the party that filed the motion is drafted, of course, in support of it, whereas the opposing party files a trial memorandum in opposition. For example, in conjunction with the motion for protective order filed on behalf of Dr. Williams from our Commentary problem, a supporting trial memorandum would discuss the issues of physician/patient privilege that are posed by the motion and argue that they justify withholding the information requested; a trial memorandum in opposition, arguing for disclosure, would be filed by the party that requested the deposition. The issues discussed in the two memoranda are limited to the issues raised by the motion.

During the course of a lawsuit, there may be several motions pending and, hence, several trial memoranda in regard to these motions. Each should have a title that identifies the party filing it and the motion to which it relates. We discuss format further in the following subsections.

Memorandum at the Request of a Judge

Contested issues continually arise during the course of a lawsuit, both during the pretrial stage and during the trial itself. During oral argument on a motion, for example, the judge may raise a point that the parties had not anticipated or addressed in their trial memoranda. Or an objection to the introduction of a piece of evidence at trial may present a novel legal problem that neither the judge nor the parties have ever considered. Under such circumstances the judge, rather than ruling immediately on the issue at hand, may request that the parties submit trial memoranda setting forth their positions on the disputed issue before he makes his decision.

The response of the attorneys is the memorandum at the request of the judge. This memorandum will be adversarial, like a memorandum in regard to a motion, and will be limited to the issue that the judge raised. It is designed to provide the judge with guidance on the issue presented, in the form of legal support for the position favoring your client. Your goal is to predispose the judge to your client's position, and downplay the opponent's position. The memorandum should be direct and concise, particularly at trial, where time is short.

The judge may even request an additional memorandum on a given point *after* the trial is completed, but *before* her decision is rendered. Again, you will be emphasizing the superiority of your client's position on the issue raised.

Unsolicited Memorandum Anticipating Legal Issues

By the conclusion of a trial, the legal issues that control the trial's outcome are clear. It is often useful to prepare a trial memorandum that identifies these issues, then argues in favor of a resolution which benefits your client. By clarifying the issues and identifying your strongest arguments at the conclusion of trial and for the benefit of the judge, you can establish a foundation on which the judge can render a decision in which your client prevails.

An unsolicited trial memorandum should be straightforward, identifying the issues at the outset and presenting arguments that are clear and direct. You should highlight the issues that are most important to you, and include every issue which you believe has bearing on the result. In other words, if you are going to file an unsolicited memorandum, you should be thorough; prepare it correctly. If, for strategic reasons, you want to emphasize only a particular aspect of the contested issues, then make that absolutely clear. Otherwise, you may leave the impression that you are conceding on the points left unaddressed.

10–3 The Components of a Memorandum of Law to the Trial Court

The format of trial memoranda varies from jurisdiction to jurisdiction, and from judge to judge. The following comments are offered as a general frame of reference; you should check the rules applicable in your jurisdiction for more specific guidance.

The Caption or Heading

As with pleadings and discovery requests, trial memoranda must have captions identifying the court, parties, date, and docket number. The title of the pleading may be included as well. Figure 10–1 shows two alternative captions.

Title

If the title of the pleading is not included in the caption, it must appear below it. As mentioned earlier, the title should be specific enough to identify the party filing it and, if in regard to a motion, the title of the motion. If not in regard to a motion, it should identify the context—for example, "Plaintiff's Memorandum Regarding Admissibility of Contract X" or "Plaintiff's Trial Brief" (if an unsolicited summary of the issues after trial.)

Figure 10–1 Examples of Caption Set-Ups

```
 (a)                            No. 12344

STEPHEN GILES,          §     IN THE DISTRICT COURT OF
                        §
    Plaintiff           §
                        §
vs.                     §     DALLAS COUNTY, TEXAS
                        §
GEORGE HARRIS,          §
                        §
    Defendant           §     _____JUDICIAL DISTRICT

                       OR

 (b)         IN THE UNITED STATES DISTRICT COURT
          FOR THE NORTHERN DISTRICT OF TEXAS

STEPHEN GILES,          §
                        §
    Plaintiff           §
                        §
vs.                     §     CIVIL ACTION NO. 90-12387
                        §
GEORGE HARRIS,          §     Plaintiff's Memorandum in
                        §     Support of Motion to
    Defendant           §     Dismiss
```

Figure 10–2 Introduction to the Court

(1)

TO THE HONORABLE JUDGE OF SAID COURT:

COMES NOW STEPHEN GILES Plaintiff and files this Memorandum of Law to the Trial Court in Support of Plaintiff's Motion for Summary Judgment and would show unto the Court as follows:

or

(2)

Plaintiff STEPHEN GILES submits this Memorandum of Law in Support of this Motion for Summary Judgment in this matter:

Introduction to the Court

A formal introductory section is still required in some jurisdictions, although others, such as California, have done away with the requirement. The introduction seen in Figure 10–2 illustrates the formal tone associated with a document filed with a court. For example, the opening phrase, "To the Honorable Judge . . . ," is a means of showing respect to the court. The trend today, however, is toward the elimination of such introductions.

Issues or Questions Presented

Although similar to the analogous section of an internal memorandum, the **issues presented** section of a trial memorandum should be slanted toward your client's position. The issues should be stated accurately, but the outcome you seek should be implied in the questions.

Several styles for this section are commonly seen. The issue can be stated commencing with the word "Whether," followed by a statement of your client's position. The issue can also be drafted as a positive statement, or as an ordinary question. Figure 10–3 shows three numbered alternative formats for stating the issue presented; the (A) section of each alternative is drafted from a plaintiff's perspective, and the (B) section from the defendant's perspective.

Statement of Facts

The trial memorandum, like the internal memorandum, contains a **statement of facts** that relates the factual context of the issue posed. The critical difference between the facts as stated in an internal memorandum and those stated in a trial memorandum, however, is in the point of view of the drafter. In the internal memorandum (which is drafted to be objective) the facts are set out in straightforward fashion. In a trial memorandum, the facts should be set out accurately, but drafted so as to favor your client's position.

Facts should be presented chronologically. You seek to develop sympathy for your client's position, using descriptive words and emotional facts to predispose the court toward accepting your client's position. You have four objectives in drafting a statement of facts:

1. Introduce your client's case to the court.
2. Provide an accurate presentation of the events.

Figure 10–3 Forms of the Issues Presented Section

```
Alternative 1

(A)
Issue Presented. Whether a transaction using a blank power
of attorney is valid when agent was not authorized to act
on behalf of Plaintiff, the principal.

(B)
Issue Presented. Whether Plaintiff's acts of accepting tax
benefits ratified the transaction of an agent, where a
blank power of attorney was used.

Alternative 2

(A)
Issue Presented. A transaction using a blank power of attor-
ney is not valid when an agent was not authorized to act
on behalf of the Plaintiff, the principal.

(B)
Issue presented. A transaction using a blank power of attor-
ney is valid when the allegedly unauthorized act was rati-
fied.

Alternative 3

(A)
Issue Presented. Is a transaction using a blank power of
attorney valid when an agent was not authorized to act on
behalf of the Plaintiff, the principal?

(B)
Issue Presented. Is a transaction valid when the Plaintiff,
the principal, ratified the unauthorized acts of his agent?
```

3. Minimize those facts which favor your opponent.
4. Paint a memorable picture of your client's position.

Although you are writing from your client's perspective, do not misstate, misrepresent, or ignore key facts that are detrimental to your case. A misrepresentation of damaging facts will be pointed out to the court by the opposition; ignoring them allows the other side an unchallenged opportunity to emphasize their importance. Rather, identify them, attempt to minimize their importance in your statement of facts, then, in your argument section, show why you contend that they are unimportant.

Figure 10–4 on page 212 shows a statement of facts written from the plaintiff's perspective.

The Argument

The **argument** of a legal memorandum presents your client's position; it is the heart of the memorandum. You present the results of your research in an adversarial form intended to persuade the court of the superiority of your client's contentions. The partisan purpose and slant of the argument section differentiate it from the discussion section of an internal memorandum, where the legal analysis is objective, not adversarial. In the trial memorandum, your purpose is to have your position prevail.

Effective writing techniques are essential for this section. Outline for logical organization. Be definitive. Write to convince, not simply to inform. Use lan-

Figure 10–4 Statement of Facts

> The facts in the case are undisputed. Mr. Giles went to a holiday party on November 20, at the home of Mr. Swan, a business associate. Mr. Swan had been Mr. Giles's friend and attorney for some time. Giles was going out of town for Thanksgiving and would not be back until the first of the new year. Giles wanted to purchase a piece of real estate before the end of the year, but was going out of town. The only business discussion that evening concerned the real estate transaction.
>
> Swan suggested that Giles could execute a power of attorney, with Swan as Giles's representative. The gentlemen went into Swan's study and Giles signed a document entitled "Power of Attorney." Neither man filled in any information in the document. Swan's name did not appear anywhere on the document. Swan kept the Power of Attorney in his top desk drawer. Giles went on his trip.
>
> While Giles was on his trip, one of his partners, Mr. Harris, contacted Swan regarding a joint venture transaction completely unrelated to the real estate transaction. Giles and Harris had been discussing dissolving the joint venture, with Giles acquiring Harris's interest. Swan knew nothing about this transaction.
>
> Harris stated to Swan that Giles was supposed to assume all Harris's interest in the joint venture before January 1. Harris inquired whether Swan could help him. Swan told Harris that he had a power of attorney to close a real estate transaction, but did not know how he could help Harris out.
>
> Harris asked Swan to use the power of attorney to transfer the joint venture interest. Harris told Swan this would save his friend some money. Swan continued to tell Harris that he only had authority to close a real estate transaction. Harris however, was able to persuade Swan to execute the transfer of the joint venture interest, using the power of attorney, on December 29.
>
> When Giles came back to town, Swan informed him of the transfer from Harris and told him that he had used the power of attorney. Giles was enraged and told Swan he had no authority to transfer the interest. Giles wanted the transaction rescinded.

guage that is positive and forceful. Make the court believe that your position is correct.

Move from general points to those more specific, applying the law to the facts and using the IRAC model as your guide. Emphasize your strong points and facts; deemphasize and attack the opposition's strong points and facts. Most of all, avoid obscurity—tell the court your position clearly and effectively. An example of an argument section is provided in Figure 10–5.

Conclusion

The conclusion section is a summary of the legal position taken in the trial memorandum. It informs the court of the finding and relief sought. Although a one-sentence conclusion requesting relief is sometimes acceptable, particularly for a short trial memorandum, a better approach summarizes the entire argument, crystallizing the legal contentions. Figure 10–6 on page 214 shows a conclusion that summarizes the argument, and identifies the relief requested.

Signature Block and Certificate of Service

As with all other documents filed with a court, the trial memorandum must be signed by the responsible attorney. As we have noted before, you as a paralegal are not authorized to sign a court document on behalf of a client. The name of the attorney and firm name, address, telephone number, and sometimes a state bar identification number are among the items to be included in a signature block. Figure 10–7 on page 215 shows an example of an acceptable signature block.

Likewise, a certificate of service attesting to the fact that copies of the trial memorandum have been sent to other attorneys of record (or parties) must be included. The method of service—ordinary mail, certified mail, hand delivery, or other accepted means—is identified. A simple statement certifying delivery is adequate for the purposes of the certificate, but remember that if service ever comes into question, proof will become important. Hence the certified mail option (with a return receipt proving delivery) is better than, say, ordinary mail. Check the rules and practices of your jurisdiction to determine applicable rules and requirements. A typical certificate of service is seen in Figure 10–8 on page 215.

Figure 10–5 Argument Section

```
A power of attorney must set forth the authority and the name
of the principal and agent. The document before this court
does neither.

To determine the validity of the power of attorney and the
extent of the authority granted, certain rules of construc-
tion and interpretation must be addressed. The leading case
of Gouldy v. Metcalf, 75 Tex. 455, 12 S.W. 830 (1889) sets
out the rules of construction for a power of attorney, which
are:

    [W]hen an authority is conferred upon an agent by a
    formal instrument, as by a power of attorney, there are
    two rules of construction to be carefully adhered to:

    1. The meaning of general words in the instrument will
    be restricted by the context, and construed accordingly.

    2. The authority will be construed strictly, so as to
    exclude the exercise of any power which is not warrant-
    ed, either by the actual terms used or as a necessary
    means of executing the authority with effect.
Id. at 458.

Expanding the guidelines set forth in Gouldy, case law estab-
lishes that "all powers conferred upon an agent by a formal
instrument are to receive a strict interpretation, and the
authority is never extended by intendment or construction
beyond that which is given in terms, or is necessary for car-
rying the authority into effect, and the authority must be
strictly pursued." See Bean v. Bean, 79 S.W. 2d 652 (Tex.
Civ. App., Texarkana 1935, writ refused); Dockstader v.
Brown, 204 S.W. 2d 352 (Tex. Civ. App., Fort Worth 1947, writ
refd n.r.e.).

Giles and Swan had a specific conversation about Swan clos-
ing a real estate transaction. No mention of a joint venture
```

Figure 10–5 cont.

ever took place. Swan did not have the authority to use the power of attorney for the joint venture transfer. As stated in *Giddings, Neiman-Marcus v. Estes*, 440 S.W. 2d 90 (Tex. Civ. App., Eastland 1969, no writ), "(T)he authority will be construed strictly, so as to exclude the exercise of any power which is not warranted either by the actual terms used or as a necessary means of effecting the authority with effect." Since no authority was conferred on Swan by the document, he could not have acted on Giles's behalf. Consequently, any acts performed by Swan for Giles under the power of attorney are invalid, especially ones (like the joint venture transfer) not anticipated by the Grantor.

Swan told Harris that the power of attorney was for a specific purpose, which was to close the real estate transaction. The law is clear that a third party has a duty to inquire into the scope and fact of the agency, and the burden is on the third party to "ascertain at his peril the nature and scope of the authority of such agent." See *Lawrie v. Miller*, 2. S.W. 2d 561 (Tex. Civ. App., Texarkana 1928, no writ); *Eliot Valve Repair v. Valve*, 675 S.W. 2d 555 (Tex. App., Houston [1st Dist.] 1984, no writ); *Boucher v. City Paint & Supply*, 398 S.W. 2d 352 (Tex. Civ. App., Tyler 1966, no writ).

It was Harris's responsibility to investigate the extent of Swan's authority. Harris indeed knew the purpose of the power of attorney, but chose to coerce Swan to sign the document under the guise of "friendship." Any acts resulting from Harris's coercion and Swan's misuse of his authority cannot be imputed to Giles, and thus cannot be his responsibility.

The document that Harris is relying upon to effectuate the transfer of the joint venture interest is useless and invalid. The power of attorney does not comply with the requirements for a valid power of attorney, and Swan's actions violated Giles's instructions and interests.

Figure 10–6 Conclusion and Requested Relief

Since the purported power of attorney from Giles to Swan did not contain specific authority granted to the agent, the power of attorney is void. Based upon the strict construction doctrine, one cannot construe a grant of authority that is nonexistent. The power of attorney contained neither the name of the agent, nor the purpose of the agency, nor the authority of the agent; therefore, it could not confer any powers upon the agent. Swan's acts were therefore improper, and Giles is not legally responsible for the effects of those acts. Giles requests that the Motion for Summary Judgment be granted upon the court's finding, as a matter of law that the transfer of the joint venture interest was invalid and the power of attorney void.

Figure 10-7 Signature Block

```
                    Respectfully submitted,


                    _____
                    R.T. LANG
                    State Bar #12344567
                    1234 Main Street, #10030
                    Dallas, Texas 75202
                    (214)555-1212
                    Attorney for Plaintiff
```

Figure 10-8 Certificate of Service

```
                CERTIFICATE OF SERVICE

   I certify that a true copy of the Memorandum of Law in
Support of Plaintiff's Motion for Summary Judgment was
served on Jane Smith, Assistant District Attorney, at 111
Elm Street, Suite 123, Ft. Worth, Texas, by certified mail,
return receipt requested, in accordance with the Minnesota
Rules of Civil Procedure on May 12, 1992.


                    _____
                         R.T. LANG
```

10-4 Practical Considerations

A trial memorandum is an important document in the litigation process, because if properly drafted it can resolve issues in your favor and begin to turn the lawsuit toward your client. Furthermore, since the amount at issue in many cases will not justify the expense of an extended appeals process, prevailing at the trial level is often the guarantee of prevailing once and for all.

An example of a completed trial memorandum appears as Figure 10-9. In general, you should keep in mind the following points when preparing a trial memorandum:

- Check for local jurisdictional requirements about format or content.
- Identify your purpose.
- Always draft from your client's perspective.
- Present the law honestly and accurately, but with a partisan slant.
- Identify all significant facts, and present them in a manner that minimizes the opposition's strong points and paints a memorable picture of your client's position.
- Write convincingly, using effective and persuasive writing techniques.
- Be clear, precise, and concise.
- Tell the judge what result and relief you seek.

Figure 10–9 Memorandum of Law to the Trial Court

```
                                       No. 12344
STEPHEN GILES                  §       IN THE DISTRICT COURT OF
                               §
   Plaintiff                   §
                               §
vs.                            §       DALLAS COUNTY, TEXAS
                               §
GEORGE HARRIS                  §
                               §
   Defendant                   §       _____JUDICIAL DISTRICT
```

                 MEMORANDUM OF LAW IN SUPPORT OF
               PLAINTIFF'S MOTION FOR SUMMARY JUDGMENT

TO THE HONORABLE JUDGE OF SAID COURT:

   COMES NOW STEPHEN GILES Plaintiff and files this Memorandum
of Law to the Trial Court in Support of Plaintiff's Motion
for Summary Judgment and would show unto the Court as follows:

                          Issue Presented

Whether a transaction using a blank power of attorney is
valid when agent was not authorized to act on behalf of
Defendant, the principal.

                        Statement of Facts

The facts in the case are undisputed. Mr. Giles went to a
holiday party on November 20, at the home of Mr. Swan, a
business associate. Mr. Swan had been Mr. Giles's friend and
attorney for some time. Giles was going out of town for
Thanksgiving and would not be back until the first of the new
year. Giles wanted to purchase a piece of real estate and
wanted to do so before the end of the year, but was going
to be out of town. The only discussion that evening concerned
the real estate transaction.

Swan suggested that Giles could execute a power of attorney
with Swan as Giles's representative. The gentlemen went into
Swan's study and Giles signed a document entitled "Power of
Attorney." Neither man filled in any information in the doc-
ument. Swan's name did not appear anywhere on the document.
Swan kept the power of attorney in his top desk drawer.
Giles went on his trip.

While Giles was on his trip, one of his partners, Mr. Harris,
contacted Swan regarding a joint venture transaction completely unrelated to the real estate transaction. Giles and
Harris had been discussing dissolving the joint venture,
with Giles acquiring Harris's interest. Swan knew nothing
about this transaction.

Harris stated to Swan that Giles was supposed to assume all
Harris's interest in the joint venture before January 1.
Harris inquired whether Swan could help him. Swan told Harris
he had a power of attorney to close a real estate transaction, but did not know how he could help Harris out.

Harris asked Swan to use the power of attorney to transfer
the joint venture interest. Harris told Swan this would save
his friend some money. Swan indicated that he had no way of
contacting his friend. Swan continued to tell Harris that he
only had authority to close a real estate transaction.
Harris, however, was able to persuade Swan to execute the
transfer of the joint venture interest, using the blank
power of attorney, on December 29.

Figure 10–9 cont.

When Giles came back to town, Swan informed him of the transfer from Harris and told Giles that he had used the power of attorney. Giles was enraged and told Swan he had no authority to transfer the interest, and Giles wanted the transaction rescinded.

Argument

A power of attorney must set forth the authority and the name of the principal and agent. The document before this court does neither.

To determine the validity of the power of attorney and the extent of the authority granted, certain rules of construction and interpretation must be addressed. The leading case of *Gouldy v. Metcalf*, 75 Tex. 455, 12 S.W. 830 (1889) sets out the rules of construction for a power of attorney, which are:

> [W]hen an authority is conferred upon an agent by a formal instrument, as by a Power of Attorney, there are two rules of construction to be carefully adhered to:
>
> 1. The meaning of general words in the instrument will be restricted by the context, and construed accordingly.
>
> 2. The authority will be construed strictly, so as to exclude the exercise of any power which is not warranted, either by the actual terms used or as a necessary means of executing the authority with effect.

Id. at 458.

Expanding the guidelines set forth in *Gouldy*, case law establishes that "all powers conferred upon an agent by a formal instrument are to receive a strict interpretation, and the authority is never extended by intendment or construction beyond that which is given in terms, or is necessary for carrying the authority into effect, and the authority must be strictly pursued." See *Bean v. Bean*, 79 S.W. 2d 652 (Tex. Civ. App., Texarkana 1935, writ refused); *Dockstader v. Brown*, 204 S.W.2d 352 (Tex.Civ.App., Fort Worth 1947, writ ref'd n.r.e.).

Giles and Swan had a specific conversation about Swan closing a real estate transaction. No mention of a joint venture ever took place. Swan did not have the authority to use the power of attorney for the joint venture transfer. Since the document did not contain any specifics, it is questionable whether the power of attorney was even proper for Swan to use to execute the real estate transaction. As stated in *Giddings, Neiman-Marcus v. Estes*, 440 S.W. 90 (Tex. Civ. App., Eastland 1969, no writ), "[T]he authority will be construed strictly, so as to exclude the exercise of any power which is not warranted either by the actual terms used or as a necessary means of effecting the authority with effect." Since no authority was conferred on Swan by the document, he could not have acted on Giles's behalf. Consequently, any acts performed by Swan for Giles under the power of attorney are invalid, especially ones (like the joint venture transfer) not anticipated by the Grantor.

Swan told Harris that the power of attorney was for a specific purpose, which was to close the real estate transaction. The law is clear that a third party has a duty to inquire into the scope and fact of the agency, and the burden is on the third party to "ascertain at his peril the nature and scope of the authority of such agent." *Lawrie v. Miller*, 2. S.W. 2d 561 (Tex. Civ. App., Texarkana 1928, no writ.);

Figure 10–9 cont.

Eliot Valve Repair v. Valve, 675 S.W. 2d 555 (Tex. App., Houston [1st Dist.] 1984, no writ); *Boucher v. City Paint & Supply*, 398 S.W. 2d 352 (Tex. Civ. App., Tyler 1966, no writ).

It was Harris's responsibility to investigate the extent of Swan's authority. Harris indeed knew the purpose of the power of attorney, but chose to coerce Swan to sign the document under the guise of "friendship." Any acts resulting from Harris's coercion and Swan's misuse of his authority cannot be imputed to Giles, and thus cannot be his responsibility.

The document that Harris is relying upon to effectuate the transfer of the joint venture interest is useless and invalid. The power of attorney does not comply with the requirements for a *valid* power of attorney, and Swan's actions violated Giles's instructions and interests.

Conclusion and Requested Relief

Since the purported power of attorney from Giles to Swan did not contain any specific authority granted to the agent, the power of attorney is void. Based upon the strict construction doctrine, one cannot construe a grant of authority that is nonexistent. The power of attorney contained neither the name of the agent, nor the purpose of the agency, nor the authority of the agent, and therefore it could not confer any powers upon the agent. Swan's acts were therefore improper, and Giles is not legally responsible for the effects of those acts. Giles requests that the motion for Summary Judgment be granted upon the court's finding, as a matter of law, that the transfer of the joint venture interest was invalid and the power of attorney void.

Respectfully submitted,

R.T. LANG
State Bar #12344567
1234 Main Street, #10030
Dallas, Texas 75202
(214)555-1212
Attorney for Plaintiff

CERTIFICATE OF SERVICE

I certify that a true copy of the Memorandum of Law in Support of Plaintiff's Motion for Summary Judgment was served on Jane Smith, Assistant District Attorney, at 111 Elm Street, Suite 123, Fort Worth, Texas, by certified mail, return receipt requested, in accordance with the Minnesota Rules of Civil Procedure on May 12, 1992.

SUMMARY

10–1

The memorandum of law to the trial court is an adversarial document written to persuade a trial court on a disputed issue of law. It is also known as a trial memorandum, and other similar names, depending on the jurisdiction. The audience for a trial memorandum consists of the judge, who will read it fairly but must be convinced, and opposing counsel, who will read it looking to attack logical holes and unjustified analytical leaps. Be accurate but partisan in drafting a trial memorandum.

10–2

There are three broad categories of trial memoranda: the memorandum in regard to a motion; the memorandum prepared at the request of a judge; and the unsolicited memorandum that anticipates and addresses key legal issues. All are drafted with an adversarial purpose, designed to persuade a judge that a dis-puted question of law should be resolved in favor of a particular party.

10–3

There are several components to a trial memorandum. First come the caption, title, and introduction to the court. Next, in the "issues presented" section, the drafter presents the legal questions raised in a manner that suggests a resolution in favor of the client on whose behalf the drafter is working. Similarly, the statement of facts should state all events accurately, but with a slant toward the position of the client. The argument is the heart of the trial memorandum, presenting the results of the drafter's research in an adversarial argument designed to persuade the court of the superiority of the client's contentions. The conclusion summarizes the argument and identifies the relief sought. It is followed by a signature block and a certificate of service.

10–4

A properly drafted trial memorandum is an important part of the litigation process. Indeed, since appeals are often too expensive for clients to pursue, drafting effective trial memoranda can lead to a victory in the trial court that stands once and for all.

REVIEW

Key Terms

Before proceeding, review the key terms listed below to be sure you understand each one. If necessary, read over the corresponding section of the chapter. When you are ready to test your understanding, answer the Review Questions.

memorandum of law to the trial court
trial memorandum
memorandum in regard to a motion
memorandum at the request of a judge
unsolicited memorandum anticipating
    legal issues
issues presented
statement of facts
argument

Questions for Review and Discussion

1. Who are the two audiences for a trial memorandum?
2. How should a trial memorandum be prepared so as to assist a judge?
3. How should a trial memorandum be drafted so as to minimize the impact of the attack of opposing counsel?
4. What are the characteristics of a trial memorandum prepared in regard to a motion?
5. Why might a judge request a trial memorandum?
6. What is the potential importance of an unsolicited trial memorandum that anticipates issues?

7. What is the importance to a trial memorandum of the caption and the title?
8. From what perspective is the "issues presented" section of a trial memorandum prepared?
9. What are the four objectives of a statement of facts?
10. What is the difference between the discussion section of an internal memorandum and the argument section of a trial memorandum?

Activities

1. Assume that your attorney has been served with a request to produce tax returns in a personal injury case in your jurisdiction. Go to the library and research whether the tax returns are protected information, then prepare the argument section of the memorandum of law to the trial court, requesting an order that the documents not be produced.
2. Determine for your jurisdiction the format for a memorandum of law to the trial court. Check both the state and federal requirements.

CHAPTER 11   Settlement and Trial

OUTLINE

COMMENTARY

It has been over three years since your firm filed suit on behalf of its client, Mrs. Hudson, against her surgeon. The claim—that the operation which she underwent was not only incorrectly performed, but unnecessary in the first place—has led to extensive discovery (including several depositions of expert witnesses) and numerous bitterly contested motions. All pretrial matters were finally resolved six months ago; since that time you've been waiting for the court to schedule trial.

Finally the day has arrived. The parties, their attorneys, assisting paralegals, and witnesses are sitting at the counsel tables, awaiting the judge. Suddenly lead defense counsel motions to your supervising attorney that she would like to speak for a moment in the hallway.

It soon becomes apparent that settlement is a possibility. Counsel send word to the judge that they would like him to mediate discussions. A conference room is located; hours of negotiation ensue.

Will the case settle? Perhaps; most cases do. But negotiations may break down; the case may have to be tried. Attorneys and paralegals must be prepared for both eventualities.

OBJECTIVES

The pace of a lawsuit quickens as trial approaches—it may be the last chance for settlement discussions, and if settlement proves impossible, the parties must prepare for trial. After you have completed this chapter, you will be able to:

1. Describe what a settlement agreement is.
2. Explain what is meant by consideration.
3. Identify the importance of a release.
4. Prepare a document for execution by a corporate party.
5. Explain the difference between an order of dismissal, a withdrawal, and a stipulated judgment.

6. Identify the two assertions made by a party filing a Motion for Summary Judgment.
7. Explain the difference between a jury trial and a bench trial.
8. Explain the function of a trial notebook.
9. Identify what is meant by jury instructions.
10. Explain the difference between a judgment and a verdict.

11–1   Settlement

Trials are expensive—it's an unfortunate fact of life. Hours of lawyer and paralegal time to prepare, hours in court, preparation of exhibits, payment of experts—the costs can quickly mount up. As the litigation process comes closer to trial, then, parties tend to be more willing to negotiate, with agreements often reached "on the courthouse steps."

Agreement alone is not sufficient to bring the matter to a close, however. In addition, the lawsuit itself must be concluded in some manner. A paralegal must be prepared to assist in the drafting of documents that accomplish these objectives.

The Settlement Agreement

A **settlement** is a compromise and agreement between the parties to resolve all disputed issues. A high percentage of all lawsuits filed in the United States end by settlement. The document that contains the terms of the compromise is called the **settlement agreement**. There is no one accepted format for a settlement agreement; like any other contract, it varies with the complexities of the issues and the needs of the parties. It may even be incorporated into the documents that are filed with the court to conclude the lawsuit. Most settlement agreements, however, contain at least some of the components examined in the following subsections. As a paralegal, you will be gathering and organizing the information needed to prepare these agreements, and you may even assist in the drafting.

Introductory Paragraphs   The opening paragraphs of a settlement agreement generally identify the parties to the agreement and the basic facts of the case. If the settlement is reached before a lawsuit has been filed, no lawsuit will be referenced; if suit was started, the name of the case, the court in which it was filed, and the docket number should all be included.

Parties often include a paragraph stating that their willingness to settle should not be construed as an admission of fault or liability. This is done to minimize any precedent-setting implications; neither party wants to admit that it was wrong.

Figure 11–1 illustrates a typical introductory paragraph in a settlement agreement.

Recital of Consideration   The law of contracts generally requires that, for an agreement to be binding between the parties, there must be **consideration**. Consideration is an exchange of value—in other words, each side must receive something of value in exchange for what it relinquishes under the terms of the

Figure 11–1   Introductory Paragraphs in Settlement Agreement

```
    This Settlement Agreement (the "Agreement") is made and
entered into by and between WINWOOD LEASING, INC., here-
inafter referred to as "Plaintiff," and STEVEN ROBERTS,
Individually, hereinafter referred to as "Defendant."

1. Plaintiff filed suit against Defendant on July 14, 1992,
seeking recovery of the amount owed, such suit being styled
WINWOOD LEASING, INC. vs. STEVEN ROBERTS, Individually, Number
90-11223-Z in the 100th Judicial District Court, Harris
County, Texas (hereinafter referred to as "Litigation"), and

2. The Parties have agreed that settlement of all the dis-
putes between the Parties relating to the litigation is the
most economical, efficient, and desirable disposition for all
concerned.

3. This agreement is executed by the Parties for the sole
purpose of compromising and settling the matters involved in
this dispute, and it is expressly understood and agreed, as
a condition of the signing of this agreement, that this
agreement shall not constitute or be construed to be an
admission on the part of Defendant as to the claims assert-
ed by Plaintiff.
```

contract. In a settlement agreement, usually the value received by one party is money; the value received by the other party (which paid the money) is an enforceable promise by the first party not to pursue the claim further.

The consideration for a settlement agreement is usually explicitly identified by the terms. Nevertheless, the parties often include some language stating that the agreement has been reached based upon the exchange of "good and valuable consideration," or some similar phrase. An example of a clause reciting consideration is shown in Figure 11–2.

Figure 11–2   Recital of Consideration

```
    For good and valuable consideration, and in considera-
tion of the mutual promises, covenants, and agreements set
forth herein, Winwood and Roberts (sometimes herein referred
to collectively as the "Parties") agree as follows:
```

Terms of Settlement   A settlement agreement can be as short as one paragraph or as long as hundreds of pages, depending upon the nature of the dispute. Figure 11–3 on page 224 sets out the terms of a typical settlement agreement.

Included among the terms is usually found a release provision. A **release** is a clause by which the parties expressly abandon the right to pursue further the claims forming the basis for the dispute at hand (and, often, any other claims, known or unknown, that may exist at that time).

In other words, each party *releases* the other from further liability, thereby acting on the desire to settle the suit. Figure 11–4 shows two examples (one formal, one less formal) of a release clause.

Sometimes the release is a separate document. A separate release is commonly used where the terms of the settlement are so simple as to eliminate the need for a separate settlement agreement document (as where a release is given in exchange for a check for the agreed-upon amount, with no other terms to the settlement).

Figure 11–3   Terms of Settlement

1. Roberts shall pay to Winwood the sum of FORTY-TWO THOUSAND DOLLARS ($42,000.00) to be paid under the following terms and conditions:

   a. On or before December 1, 1992, Roberts shall pay the sum of TWENTY THOUSAND DOLLARS ($20,000.00) to Winwood in the form of certified or cashier's check, or money order; thereafter, Roberts shall make monthly payments in the amount of $2,000.00 each month thereafter until payment of the full amount is paid to Winwood by Roberts.

   b. All payments set forth in paragraph 1 are due on the first day of each month. If the required monthly payments are not received by Winwood by the 4th of the month, it shall be deemed a default entitling Winwood to pursue his available remedies.

   c. Payment of the amounts set forth in paragraph 1 above will render a total payment of $42,000.00 to Winwood from Roberts.

2. Roberts agrees to make the payments required by Paragraph 1 hereinabove to WINWOOD LEASING, INC., and to send them to the law offices of Frederick Gabriel, Attorney at Law, 1710 Oak Street, Suite 130, Houston, Texas 79222.

3. Roberts agrees that in the event of default of any or all of the obligations contained in this Agreement, Roberts also shall be responsible for all costs and attorneys' fees incurred in the collection of the remaining balance due under this Agreement.

Figure 11–4   Examples of Release Clause

Paragraph Regarding Release—Formal

7. Except for the respective covenents, promises, and agreements contained in and provided for by this Agreement, Roberts does hereby release, relinquish, remit, and discharge Winwood, its successors, legal representatives, employees, servants, agents, representatives, heirs, and assigns (collectively "Winwood"), of and from any and all liabilities, damages, debts, costs, obligations, responsibilities, covenants, agreements, expenses, and attorneys' fees, claims, demands, or causes of action, of any nature whatsoever, both known and unknown, matured or contingent, liquidated or unliquidated, direct or derivative, that now exist or that might hereafter accrue based upon any and all facts, claims, or events occuring up through the last date of signing of this Agreement, relating in any way to the Lease, the premises demised by the Lease, and the relationship between the Parties arising as a result of the Lease, including but not limited to, any and all claims that Roberts might assert against Winwood in the Litigation and/or that Roberts has asserted against Winwood to date.

Paragraph Regarding Release—Informal

Plaintiff releases the Defendant from any claims arising from the pending litigation and forever discharges Defendant from all claims, demands, damages, and causes of actions that may arise from the claims of Plaintiff.

Another paragraph commonly seen among the terms of a settlement agreement is the default provision. The default provision identifies the options of each party should the other party fail to perform its obligations under their settlement agreement. Figure 11–5 shows a typical default provision.

Figure 11–5   Default Provision

```
     Failure to pay the sums when due shall constitute
default. In the event of such default, all remaining unpaid
payments due under this agreement shall become immediately
due and payable. All such unpaid payments shall bear inter-
est, from the date of default until paid, at the maximum
rate permitted by law.
     Claimant may exercise any other rights that claimant
may have at law or in equity against the defaulting party.
```

Standard Provisions   Certain paragraphs containing background information are drafted into virtually every settlement agreement. These paragraphs generally include the addresses of the parties, the venue where suit may be filed in the event of breach of the settlement agreement's terms, definitions of words and phrases, and possibly other requirements imposed by the jurisdiction in which the agreement is made. Figure 11–6 shows some standard provisions found in a settlement agreement.

Figure 11–6   Standard Provisions for Settlement

```
     11. This Agreement states the entire agreement of the
Parties hereto with regard to the subject matter of the
Agreement. This Agreement supersedes all prior and contem-
poraneous negotiations and agreements, oral or written,
with regard to the subject matter of the Agreement, and all
prior and contemporaneous negotiations and agreements with
regard to the subject matter of the Agreement are deemed to
have been abandoned if not incorporated into this Agreement.
     12. This Agreement may be amended only by a written
agreement signed by all the Parties to this Agreement, and
a breach of this Agreement may be waived only a written
waiver signed by the party granting the waiver. The waiv-
er of any breach of this Agreement shall not operate or be
construed as a waiver of any other similar or prior or
subsequent breach of this Agreement.
     13. This Agreement shall be governed by the laws of the
State of Texas and venue for its enforcement shall be exclu-
sively in Harris County, Texas.
     14. This Agreement shall bind and inure to the benefit
of the respective successors and assigns of the Parties.
     15. The persons signing this Agreement represent and
warrant that they are authorized to do so.
```

Date and Signatures   The date that appears on a settlement agreement is significant, particularly where the terms include a release that relinquishes any and all claims which the parties have against each other "from the beginning of the world to the date of this document" (a colorful phrase often seen in release clauses). Make sure the date reflects the understanding of the parties about the effective date of the settlement.

Problems can arise when a settlement agreement is revised prior to execution (putting into effect). The drafter may neglect to change dates in the text of the document, or dates identified in the text may conflict with the date of final execution. A similar problem can occur when parties execute the document on different dates (as where originals have to be mailed to geographically distant parties). Take care to choose language that ensures that after execution is complete there will be no confusion about the operative and effective date of the agreement.

Figure 11–7 Examples of Jurats

(a) Form of Jurat—Corporate

EXECUTED effective this _____day of November, 1992.

WINWOOD LEASING, INC.

By:_____
Deborah Patterson, President

THE STATE OF TEXAS   )
)
COUNTY OF HARRIS   )

    BEFORE ME,the undersigned authority, on this day person-
ally appeared DEBORAH PATTERSON, known to me to be the person and officer whose name is subscribed to the foregoing
instrument and acknowledged to me that the same was the act
of the said WINWOOD LEASING, INC., a Texas Corporation, and
that she executed the same as the act of such corporation for
the purposes and consideration therein expressed and in the
capacity therein stated.
    GIVEN under my hand and seal of office this _____day of
November, 1992.

_____
NOTARY PUBLIC IN AND FOR THE STATE OF TEXAS

    My Commission Expires:_____

(b) Form of Jurat—Partnership

EXECUTED effective this _____day of November, 1992.

PETERSON & SWAN

By:_____
Daon Peterson, Partner

THE STATE OF TEXAS   )
)
COUNTY OF HARRIS   )

    BEFORE ME, the undersigned authority, on this day per-
sonally appeared DAON PETERSON, known to me to be the person and partner whose name is subscribed to the foregoing
instrument and acknowledged to me that the same was the act
of the said PETERSON & SWAN, a Texas Partnership, and that
he executed the same as the act of such partnership for the
purposes and consideration therein expressed and in the
capacity therein stated.
    GIVEN under my hand and seal of office this _____ day of
November, 1992.

_____
NOTARY PUBLIC IN AND FOR THE STATE OF TEXAS

    My Commission Expires:_____

Figure 11–7 Cont.

```
              (c) Form of Jurat—Individual
EXECUTED effective this _____ day of November, 1992.


              _____
              STEVEN ROBERTS, Individually

DATED:November _____, 1992
THE STATE OF TEXAS   )
                     )
COUNTY OF HARRIS     )

   BEFORE ME, the undersigned authority, on this day per-
sonally appeared STEVEN ROBERTS, Individually, known to me
to be the person whose name is subscribed to the foregoing
instrument and acknowledged to me that he executed the same
for the purposes and consideration therein expressed.
   GIVEN under my hand and seal of office this _____day of
November, 1992.


      _____
      NOTARY PUBLIC IN AND FOR THE STATE OF TEXAS

        My Commission Expires:_____
```

Signatures are, of course, a critically important aspect of the settlement agreement. The only parties bound by the settlement agreement are the parties who sign. If a corporation is a party, for example, and an individual officer is signing on behalf of the corporation, it is absolutely essential to make it clear that he is signing on behalf of the corporation, and not as an individual. This can be done by crafting a signature block identifying the corporation and indicating that the corporation is signifying its agreement by the signature of its president of other officer (see Figure 11–7).

It is often appropriate to have the signature to the agreement notarized or acknowledged. If this is necessary, the drafter must be sure to include the proper **jurats** at the end of the document. A jurat is a clause following the signature that identifies when, where, and before whom the signature was sworn or affirmed (Figure 11–7 also shows examples of jurats).

Concluding the Lawsuit

If the suit had already been filed at the time agreement was reached, the parties must conclude the lawsuit in a manner acceptable to all concerned. There are generally three methods of concluding a lawsuit after settlement—by dismissal, by withdrawal, or by stipulated judgment.

Conclusion by Dismissal A dismissal occurs when the court concludes the case by entering an **order of dismissal**. This occurs in one of two ways. The parties can *jointly* draft it, making reference to their settlement agreement and the fact that neither objects to entry of the order. The order is then signed by the parties (or their attorneys), signed by the judge, and placed in the court file. This abruptly ends the lawsuit at whatever stage it has reached. In the alternative method, one party can file a Motion to Dismiss, which also references the settlement agreement and indicates to the court that neither party objects to the dismissal. The court then orders the motion granted, which also terminates the lawsuit.

The most important point in drafting an order of dismissal or a Motion to Dismiss is to indicate whether the dismissal is "with prejudice" or "without prejudice." A case dismissed *with* prejudice is a final resolution of the claims raised by the complaint; those same claims can never be brought before a court again. If dismissal is *without* prejudice, the same claims can be refiled in another lawsuit, as long as the claim is still within the statute of limitations (the time limit within which a claim must be filed, or else expire). In most cases that are settled, the dismissal entered is with prejudice; the same claims can never be refiled, although if the settlement agreement is breached, a contract claim can be brought alleging breach of the agreement.

Figure 11–8 shows the body of a Motion to Dismiss, prepared with an accompanying order for the court to enter.

Conclusion by Withdrawal   The parties can also conclude the matter by **withdrawal**. A withdrawal is a document filed by the party who originally filed a claim against another, by which the claim is abandoned. The party filing would be either a plaintiff who is giving up one or more of the claims in the complaint, or a defendant who is abandoning a counterclaim or cross-claim. For a lawsuit to be effectively concluded, all claims by the plaintiff, or counterclaims and cross-claims by the defendant, must be concluded. It is possible for one party to file a

Figure 11–8   Body of Motion to Dismiss

Motion to Dismiss

    PLAINTIFF, WINWOOD LEASING, INC. files this Motion to
Dismiss Defendant STEVEN ROBERTS, Individually, with prejudice as follows:
    Plaintiff and Defendant have reached an agreement to com-
promise and settle this litigation. Therefore, Plaintiff
does not desire to prosecute its cause of action against
Defendant STEVEN ROBERTS, Individually.
    WHEREFORE, Plaintiff, WINWOOD LEASING, INC., requests
that its cause of action against Defendant STEVEN ROBERTS,
Individually, be dismissed with prejudice.

                                    Respectfully submitted,

                                    _____
                                    FREDERICK GABRIEL
                                    State Bar #2209900
                                    1710 Oak Street, Suite 130
                                    Houston, Texas 79222
                                    (713)455-1234

Order of Dismissal

    On this day, the Court considered Plaintiff's Motion to
Dismiss all causes of action against STEVEN ROBERTS,
Individually, and concluded that the Motion should be grant-
ed. It is therefore,
    ORDERED, ADJUDGED AND DECREED that all causes of action
asserted herein against Defendant STEVEN ROBERTS,
Individually, are hereby dismissed with prejudice.
    SIGNED this _____ day of November, 1992.

                     _____
                     JUDGE PRESIDING

Figure 11–9   Stipulated Judgment

> On November 24, 1992, came on to be heard the announce-
> ment of counsel for Plaintiff, WINWOOD LEASING, INC. and
> counsel for Defendant STEVEN ROBERTS, Individually, to the
> effect that the parties have agreed and desire to have entered
> in this cause a judgment in favor of WINWOOD LEASING, INC.
> against STEVEN ROBERTS, Individually, as indicated by the
> approval of the parties below. The Court is of the opinion
> that the judgment should be granted. It is, therefore,
> ORDERED, ADJUDGED AND DECREED that WINWOOD LEASING, INC.
> have and recover judgment of and from STEVEN ROBERTS,
> Individually, for the principal sum of FIFTY-THREE THOUSAND
> DOLLARS ($53,000.00); for postjudgment interest at the rate
> of ten percent (10%) per annum on all amounts awarded here-
> in until paid; and for all costs and attorneys' fees in col-
> lection of the judgment.
>
> Signed this _____ day of _____, 1992.
>
> _____
> JUDGE PRESIDING
>
> AGREED AS TO FORM AND CONTENT:

withdrawal of one claim in a lawsuit, with other claims proceeding; but a settlement generally involves resolution of *all* outstanding claims (although when there are multiple parties in a lawsuit, it is more common to see piecemeal settlements).

As with the Motion to Dismiss, an important point in a withdrawal is whether it is with or without prejudice. If not expressly stated in the withdrawal, the effect can vary, depending on the jurisdiction and the nature of the matter. Be sure that the documents you file are drafted with language that carries out the intent of the parties.

Conclusion by Stipulated Judgment   A third alternative is to conclude the matter by **stipulated judgment**. This is the equivalent of a decision of the court on the merits, except that the parties indicate to the court that they have agreed to the terms of the stipulated judgment by signing, along with the judge, at the bottom. A stipulated judgment constitutes a conclusion with prejudice, in that it is a final decision that precludes the parties from ever again making the same claims. An example of a stipulated judgment appears in Figure 11–9. You will learn more about judgments in the sections that follow.

11–2   Summary Judgment

Another pretrial resolution of a lawsuit flows out of the **summary judgment** motion, which, if granted, ends the lawsuit by the entry of a judgment in favor of one side. The granting of a summary judgment motion differs from settlement in that it is not the result of an agreement between the opposing parties; rather, it involves a decision of the court on a contested motion in which one party asserts (1) that there is "no genuine issue of material fact," and (2) that it is entitled to judgment in its favor "as a matter of law" (see Rule 56 of the FRCP). To explain these concepts fully, a brief discussion is in order.

There are two aspects to every legal controversy—the *facts* and the controlling *law*. When a lawsuit is filed, the parties involved are in essence saying to the court, "We will each present our version of the facts and our interpretation of the law; you decide who is right." The presentation of evidence in the form of documents, exhibits, and witness testimony is designed to enable the trier-of-fact (the jury or the judge; more about this later) to weigh the competing positions and determine whose version of the facts is accurate. Once the facts have been established by the trier-of-fact, the judge applies the controlling law and renders a decision.

Sometimes there is no dispute as to the facts, or at least one party *asserts* that there is no significant and genuine controversy over important facts. If the court finds this assertion to be true, no trial is necessary. The only matter left for the court is to apply the controlling law to these facts. When one party files a Motion for Summary Judgment, the other party can contest it by asserting (1) that there *is* a genuine factual dispute that needs to be decided by the court, or (2) that, although there is no factual dispute, the court should nevertheless find against the moving party based on the controlling law. Sometimes both parties file Motions for Summary Judgment simultaneously, agreeing to stipulate as to the facts. Then the only things necessary to resolve the lawsuit are for the parties to file trial memoranda stating their competing legal arguments, and for the court to decide the contested legal issues.

Motions for Summary Judgment are not readily granted by courts. Where the nonfiling party contends that there *are* contested issues and can show even a slight amount of evidence (physical evidence or deposition testimony) that supports its version of the facts, a court will not grant the motion but will, rather, allow the factual issues to be decided after the full presentation of evidence at trial.

The Motion for Summary Judgment should include a brief statement of the basis for the motion, and you should attach all documentary evidence and deposition passages that support your position. A brief in support of the motion, arguing that there is no contested factual issue and developing the filing party's legal position, is generally filed as well (and sometimes the attachments are appended to this brief rather than to the motion).

Rule 56 of the FRCP, quoted previously, governs the procedure for Motions for Summary Judgment filed in federal court. You should check your local jurisdiction for its requirements. The body of a Motion for Summary Judgment in a case involving a lease agreement, and the ensuing order granting the motion, are shown in Figure 11–10.

11–3   The Scope and Nature of a Trial

The level of disagreement in some matters is so great that nothing short of trial will resolve the dispute. The parties then proceed in one of the two basic types of trial, which differ with regard to the identity of the trier-of-fact mentioned in the last section. The two types are the **jury trial**, and the **trial before the court**, or **bench trial**.

In a jury trial, selected citizens act as jurors. These jurors hear all the evidence, then, after receiving instructions from the judge, go to the jury room, where they deliberate until they have decided all contested issues of *fact*. Issues of *law* are always decided by the judge, who also makes rulings during the trial on the admissibility of evidence and other procedural disputes that arise. Usually all issues of law have been settled by the point at which the jury begins its deliberations—indeed, the instructions provided to the jury by the judge usually incorporate the decisions she has made with regard to contested legal issues.

Figure 11–10   Summary Judgment: Body of Motion and Order

Body of Motion for Summary Judgment

1. Plaintiff's Complaint has been filed and served on Defendant VICTRONIC, INC. Defendant has appeared and answered herein. Plaintiff's action is based upon a lease agreement.

2. The pleadings on file herein, together with all the pretrial discovery documents on file herein, the official records of the Court, and the Affadavits of Victor Brennan and Amelia Johnson, attached hereto, all show that there is no genuine issue to any material fact and that the Defendant, as moving party herein, is entitled to judgment in its favor as a matter of law.

3. Defendant asks the Court that, on hearing of this Motion, judgment be entered against Plaintiff.

4. If the Court grants this Motion for Summary Judgment, Defendant requests that immediately after hearing of the Motion, the Court shall award Defendant its attorney fees and costs of suit.

Order Granting Summary Judgment

The motion of the Defendant for summary judgment pursuant to Rule 56(c) of the Federal Rules of Civil Procedure, having been presented, and the court being fully advised,

The court finds that the Defendant is entitled to a summary judgment as a matter of law.

IT IS THEREFORE ORDERED, ADJUDGED AND DECREED that the Defendant's motion for summary judgment be, and the same hereby is granted, that Plaintiffs have and recover nothing by their suit, that the Defendant, VICTRONIC, INC., be dismissed, and that Defendant recover its costs and charges in this behalf expended and have execution therefor.

In a bench trial, there is no jury. The judge decides not only issues of law, but issues of fact as well. The presentation of evidence is conducted in a manner identical to that in a jury trial (except that attorneys may slightly alter their style or technique for strategic reasons), and at the conclusion the judge renders a decision that incorporates both his findings of fact and his conclusions of law.

Whether before a jury or before the bench, a trial requires a great deal of preparation and work. Let's turn to some of the legal writing assignments you may face in connection with a trial.

The Trial Notebook and the Course of Trial

There are many practical and technical matters that need to be addressed by attorneys and paralegals prior to trial. In the **trial notebook**, each party gathers together in one central location as much useful information as is reasonable and efficient. Although the layout and content of the trial notebook vary from one attorney to the next, the following elements are generally addressed or included in one form or another:

- copies of all pleadings, with summaries;
- list of the elements to be proven;
- copies of relevant cases, statutes, and regulations;
- pretrial motions and decisions thereon;
- internal memoranda and other research on legal issues;

- questions to ask potential jurors in *voir dire*;
- outline of the opening argument;
- list of witnesses with addresses and phone numbers;
- key passages from deposition transcripts;
- digests of all depositions;
- list of exhibits and copies of key documents;
- outlines of questions for witnesses;
- outline of closing argument;
- proposed jury instructions; and
- drafts of potential posttrial motions.

As can be seen from this list, the trial notebook provides a blueprint for the trial to come. The lawyer can follow through the sections, step by step, when in the courtroom trying the case. Unanticipated situations almost always arise during trial, but by preparing the trial notebook with care, counsel can minimize surprises. You should study the list, and use it when preparing a trial notebook according to your firm's accepted format. Legal writing considerations for the preparation of the trial notebook include proper indexing for ease of reference and drafting subsections (for example, the internal memoranda) using the guidelines we have discussed in previous chapters.

Some of the references in the list refer to items we have yet to discuss, for example, the questions to witnesses or the outline of opening argument. These items should be drafted in a clear manner with an adversarial tone. Their content, however, delves into areas of trial strategy that go beyond the scope of this book. In any event, as a paralegal, if you have occasion to assist in the preparation of these items, you will be acting under the direction and guidance of your supervising attorney, and should be closely following her preferences.

The last two items in the list, jury instructions and posttrial motions, refer to trial documents that may be needed at the conclusion of the evidence. For example, a **Motion for Directed Verdict** can be prepared ahead of time.

Such a motion can be made in a jury trial; it requests that the judge enter an order finding that the other side failed to offer sufficient evidence to make its case, hence the jury should be directed to find in favor of the moving party. An example of the body of a Motion for Directed Verdict is seen in Figure 11–11.

Jury instructions are another item that can and should be prepared ahead of time. At the end of a jury trial, the judge must instruct the jury on the legal principles or rules that it must follow in reaching its conclusions. Such instructions take into account the manner in which the judge has interpreted the law. Prior to the submission of instructions to the jury, each side presents to the judge its version of proposed jury instructions, prepared in an adversarial manner to influence the jury in its favor. The judge weighs the competing proposals in light of the controlling law, and submits what he determines to be the appropriate instructions (either one party's version, or the judge's own original draft) to the jury.

Some jury instructions are in the form of questions that must be answered "yes" or "no" depending on the jury's conclusions. Some are direct statements. To prepare jury instruction proposals, the parties may have to conduct legal research on the status of the law in the relevant area. Most jurisdictions have relatively standardized instructions for questions that commonly arise (such as in an ordinary negligence claim), which must be tailored to the facts of the specific case. Figure 11–12 shows some typical jury questions.

We discuss some other posttrial motions in a later subsection.

Figure 11–11   Body of Motion for Directed Verdict

```
     Now comes the Defendant, CHAPMAN, INC., at the close of
Plaintiff's case, and moves the court to withdraw the evi-
dence from the consideration of the jury and to instruct the
jury to find the Defendant not liable, instruction to that
effect being attached hereto.
     As grounds for the allowance of this motion and the giv-
ing of the attached instruction, the Defendant avers that:
     (1) no evidence has been offered or received upon the
trial of the above entitled cause to sustain the allegations
of negligence contained in Plaintiff's complaint;
     (2) no evidence has been offered or received upon the
trial proving or tending to prove that the Defendant was
guilty of any negligence whether alleged or not;
     (3) the proximate cause of the occurrence in question
was not the negligence of the defendant;
     (4) by the uncontroverted evidence, the decedent was
guilty of contributory negligence, which was the sole cause
of her death; and
     (5) no evidence was offered or received on the trial
proving or tending to prove that the decedent was engaged
in interstate transportation immediately before and at the
time of her death.
```

Figure 11–12   Sample Jury Questions

```
Question No. 1
"Do you find from a preponderance of the evidence that the
Defendant CHAPMAN, INC., was guilty of negligence in per-
forming any one or more of the specific acts of negligence
alleged by the Plaintiff?"

ANSWER: Yes __ or No __

Question No. 2
"Do you find from a preponderance of the evidence that the
negligence of the Defendant CHAPMAN, INC., was either the
sole proximate cause or a contributing proximate cause of
the injuries and death of Roslyn Shearson?"

Answer: Yes__ or No __

Question No. 3
"Do you find from a preponderance of the evidence that
Roslyn Shearson, deceased, was guilty of negligence in per-
forming any one or more of the specific acts of negligence
alleged by the Defendants?"

Answer: Yes__ or No __
```

Judgment

The decision rendered in a bench trial is called a **judgment**. The decision rendered by a jury is called a **verdict**; however, it must also be incorporated into a subsequent judgment. For both jury and bench trials, then, the judgment is the official, written decision of the court reciting the relief, if any, that is granted and the damages, if any, allowed.

Upon the signing of the judgment, the time for appeal or posttrial motions begins to run. The judgment, which may be prepared by the prevailing party for the court to execute, or by the court itself, contains a caption, title, introductory paragraphs, an identification of the findings of fact, an identification of the rulings of law, often a discussion of the legal principles and analysis

Figure 11-13 Completed Judgment

> On May 10, 1992, came on to be heard the above-entitled cause. All parties appeared both in person and by and through their counsels and announced ready for trial. A jury was thereupon selected, composed of twelve qualified persons, and such jury was impaneled and sworn. After hearing the pleadings, evidence, and argument of counsel, the jury did receive the charge of the court, and return into open court on May 12, 1992, its verdict resolving all issues in favor of the Plaintiff's contentions, and awarding the sum of TWENTY THOUSAND DOLLARS ($20,000.00) to Plaintiff as compensation for his injuries, the sum of TEN THOUSAND FIVE HUNDRED TWENTY-NINE DOLLARS AND SEVENTEEN CENTS ($10,529.17) as compensation for hospital and medical expenses incurred by reason of treatment of Plaintiff, together with the sum of FIVE THOUSAND DOLLARS ($5,000.00), being the difference between the reasonable cash market value of his 1990 Chrysler automobile immediately before and immediately after such collision.
>
> The verdict of the jury was received and filed by the court, and in consonance therewith,
>
> IT IS ORDERED, ADJUDGED, AND DECREED by the Court that the Plaintiff have and recover from Defendant the sum of TWENTY THOUSAND DOLLARS ($20,000.00) for his personal injuries, the sum of TEN THOUSAND FIVE HUNDRED TWENTY-NINE DOLLARS AND SEVENTEEN CENTS ($10,529.17) for hospital and medical bills, together with the sum of FIVE THOUSAND DOLLARS ($5,000.00) for damage to his vehicle, making in all the sum of THIRTY-FIVE THOUSAND FIVE HUNDRED TWENTY-NINE DOLLARS AND SEVENTEEN CENTS ($35,529.17).
>
> IT IS FURTHER ORDERED, ADJUDGED, AND DECREED that this judgment bear interest at the rate of ten percent (10%) per annum from date hereof until paid, and that Plaintiff recover his costs of suit.

involved, the specification of relief, including damages allowed, and generally ends with a concise statement of the judgment, such as "judgment for plaintiff." An example of a judgment appears in Figure 11–13.

When a defendant fails to respond to a complaint within the time allowed for a response, or if one party fails to comply properly with procedural deadlines or requirements, a **default** may occur and be followed, ultimately, by a **default judgment**. The default judgment is entered without a trial or hearing against the party who failed to respond or follow proper procedures. An example of a default judgment is shown in Figure 11–14.

Posttrial Practice

The issuance of the judgment does not end the lawsuit. The parties can still exercise one or more of several options at this point.

If new evidence is found, or if errors on evidentiary or other procedural matters prejudiced one or the other of the parties, a **Motion for a New Trial** (governed by Rule 59 of the FRCP) can be filed that, if granted, negates the result of the first trial and allows a second to proceed. The grounds for a new trial, as they are stated in Rule 59 of the FRCP, are set forth in Figure 11–15; an example of the body of a Motion for New Trial appears in Figure 11–16.

Figure 11-14　Default Judgment

    CAME ON to be heard this day the above-entitled and num-
bered cause wherein FRAME CONSTRUCTION, INC. is Plaintiff and
BERNIE'S DRYWALL, INC., is Defendant; and
    It appearing to the Court that Defendant BERNIE'S DRYWALL,
INC., having been duly and legally cited to appear and
answer, and wholly made default; and Plaintiff having
announced ready for trial, and no jury being demanded and it
further appearing that this is a suit upon a credit purchase
offered in evidence, and the Court having read the pleadings
and heard the evidence and argument of counsel, is of the
following opinion;
    The wrong done by Defendant was aggravated by that kind
of willfulness, wantonness, and malice for which the law
allows the imposition of exemplary damages. The Defendant
acted with an evil and deliberate intent to harm Plaintiff.
Its conduct was intentional, willful, and wanton, and without justification or excuse, and it acted with gross indifference to the rights of the Plaintiff. Plaintiff therefore
seeks exemplary damages in the amount of $8,547.00, three
times the actual amount of damages the Plaintiff incurred.
The Court is further of the opinion that Plaintiff should
have the relief for which it prays, it is therefore,
    ORDERED, ADJUDGED AND DECREED, that Plaintiff, FRAME CON-
STRUCTION, INC., do have and recover from the Defendant
BERNIE'S DRYWALL, INC. the sum of TWO THOUSAND EIGHT HUNDRED
FORTY-NINE DOLLARS ($2,849.00), together with interest at the
rate of six percent per annum on the outstanding balance from
September 1, 1992, until judgment, plus EIGHT THOUSAND FIVE
HUNDRED FORTY-SEVEN DOLLARS ($8,547.00) in exemplary damages,
plus reasonable attorneys' fees in the amount of $2,000.00,
plus interest at ten percent (10%) per annum from the date
of judgment until paid, plus all costs of Court expended.

    SIGNED THIS _____DAY OF _____, 19___.

    _____
    JUDGE PRESIDING

Figure 11-15　Federal Rules of Civil Procedure—Rule 59

New Trials; Amendments of Judgments

(a) Grounds. A new trial may be granted to all or any of the
parties and on all or part of the issues (1) in an action
in which there has been a trial by jury, for any of the reasons for which new trials have heretofore been granted in
actions at law in the courts of the United States; and (2)
in an action tried without a jury, for any of the reasons
for which rehearings have heretofore been granted in suits
in equity in the courts of the United States. On a motion
for a new trial in an action tried without a jury, the court
may open the judgment if one has been entered, take additional testimony, amend findings of fact and conclusions of
law or make new findings and conclusions, and direct the
entry of a new judgment . . .

Figure 11-16   Body of Motion for New Trial with Statement of Grounds

```
     The defendant, CHAPMAN, INC., moves that the verdict of
the jury in the above-entitled cause be set aside and that
the judgment entered on the verdict be vacated and set aside
and that a new trial be granted to the defendant for one or
more of the following reasons:
     1. The verdict is contrary to law.
     2. The verdict is contrary to the evidence.
     3. The verdict is contrary to the law and the evidence.
     4. The verdict is contrary to the weight of the evidence.
     5. There is no substantial evidence that the Defendant
        is guilty of negligence.
     6. The evidence shows that the sole proximate cause of the
        decedent's death was his own contributory negligence.
     7. The court erred in denying Defendant's motion to direct
        a verdict in his favor at the close of Plaintiff's case.
     8. The court erred in denying Defendant's motion to
        direct a verdict in his favor at the close of all the
        evidence.
     9. There is no sufficient or substantial evidence tend-
        ing to support the amount of the jury's verdict.
    10. The verdict is excessive and appears to have been
        given under the influence of passion and prejudice.
```

Figure 11-17   Motion for Judgment Notwithstandng the Verdict

```
     Plaintiff, by his attorney, moves the court for judgment
in favor of Plaintiff and against Defendant for SIXTY THOU-
SAND DOLLARS ($60,000.00) principal, interest thereon at ten
percent (10%) per year from June 4, 1991, and Plaintiff's
costs, notwithstanding the general verdict of the jury in
favor of the Defendant returned herein on February 4, 1992,
on the grounds and for the reasons that:
     1. the general verdict is wholly contrary to and cannot
        be reconciled with the findings of the jury on all
        the special issues submitted to the jury; and
     2. the findings on the special issues are all consistent
        with each other and fully support judgment as prayed for
        in Plaintiff's complaint, and as herein requested, and
        negate and deny the defense asserted by the Defendant.
This motion is based on all the records, papers, pleadings,
and files of this action, including the full record of the trial.
```

Another type of posttrial motion is the Motion for Judgment Notwithstanding the Verdict (also known as a judgment n.o.v., or *non obstante veredicto*) pursuant to Rule 50 of the FRCP. This motion is filed when the losing party in a jury trial contends that the evidence presented is not sufficient to support the verdict that the jury rendered (an example of the body of such a motion, in which it is alleged that the specific findings of fact made by the jury are not consistent with its general verdict, is shown in Figure 11–17.) It often follows on the heels of a Motion for Directed Verdict that was denied. The following sequence is not unusual: (1) at the close of evidence, Party A concludes the evidence is insufficient to allow a verdict for Party B, and makes a Motion for Directed Verdict; (2) Judge denies Motion for Directed Verdict; (3) jury returns verdict in favor of Party B; (4) Party A files motion for Judgment Notwithstanding the Verdict. Since the judge denied the Motion for Directed Verdict, she will probably deny the Motion for Judgment Notwithstanding the Verdict as well; this brings us to the appeal, a common posttrial practice.

Figure 11–18   Express Findings of Fact and Conclusions of Law

> The above-styled and numbered cause came for trial before the court without a jury on June 20, 1992. All parties and their attorneys were present. After considering the pleadings, the evidence, the argument, and briefs of counsel, the Court in response to a request from DENTAL CLINICS OF THE WORLD, INC. ("Dental Clinics"), Plaintiff, makes its findings of fact and conclusions of law as follows:
>
> FINDINGS OF FACT
>
> 1. On or about November 17, 1991, Defendant voluntarily resigned his employment with Plaintiff.
> 2. Defendant became a Vice President of DENTAL CLINICS on or about February, 1986.
> 3. Defendant had access to the books and records of DENTAL CLINICS.
> 4. Defendant was an employee and Vice President of DENTAL CLINICS.
>
> CONCLUSIONS OF LAW
>
> 1. Plaintiff had the burden of proving a probable right and a probable injury in gaining a temporary injunction.
> 2. Defendant was a fiduciary of Plaintiff.
> 3. Defendant was in a confidential relationship with Plaintiff.
> 4. Even in the absence of an employment contract, a former employee may not breach a confidential relationship.
> 5. Even in the absence of an employment contract, a former employee may not disclose trade secrets to use his competitive advantage to the Plaintiff's detriment.

An **appeal** is a demand by the losing party that a higher court review the decision of the trial court. The party that loses on a Motion for Judgment Notwithstanding the Verdict can appeal; indeed, the losing party almost always has some recourse to appeal, regardless of whether any posttrial motions are filed (although the decisions in certain matters, such as small claims actions, may not be appealable; check the statutes in your jurisdiction). The most important consideration in filing an appeal is to do so within the time limitations allowed by the rules. It is also sometimes necessary to request express findings of fact and conclusions of law from the court, if the judgment is vague. An example of express findings of fact and conclusions of law appears in Figure 11–18. Check the rules of your local jurisdiction, and consult with your supervising attorney if this situation arises.

11–4   Practical Considerations

The surest way to settle a case is to convince the other side that you are fully prepared to go to trial. And the surest way to win a case that can't be settled is, likewise, to be fully prepared.

The key, then, to both settlement and trial is preparation. The attorney and paralegal who have done their homework—who have digested the depositions, researched the law, painstakingly prepared the trial notebook, prepped the witnesses, organized the exhibits, anticipated potential problems and made contingency plans, drafted jury instructions and posttrial motions ahead of time—make a team that will be able to negotiate from strength and, if necessary, engage the opposition with focused precision. Ask any experienced trial attorney, any successful litigation firm, any seasoned trial judge, and they will tell you that preparation is the most important factor for success in the courts.

As a paralegal, you will likely have a central role in trial preparation. By honing your writing skills and organizational abilities, you will contribute to each client's prospects for a successful resolution of her matter.

SUMMARY

11–1

A settlement is a compromise and agreement between the parties to resolve all disputed issues. A settlement agreement is a document that incorporates the terms of a settlement. The settlement agreement recites the consideration, and generally contains a release and default provisions. A lawsuit that is settled is terminated by a dismissal, a withdrawal, or a stipulated judgment.

11–2

A summary judgment motion is granted where the court finds that (1) there is no genuine issue as to any material fact and (2) the moving party is entitled to judgment as a matter of law. Motions for summary judgment are usually supported by a brief; the opposing brief can argue either that (1) there is a genuine dispute as to a material fact, of (2) even if there is no such dispute, the court should find against the moving party based on the controlling law.

11–3

In a jury trial, the jury is the trier-of-fact. In a bench trial, the judge is the trier-of-fact. A trial notebook includes a great deal of basic information, such as an exhibit list, proposed witness questions, copies of pleadings, and an outline of opening and closing arguments, which helps the attorney who is trying the case. A Motion for Directed Verdict is filed when the moving party asserts, at the end of the evidence, that the other party has offered insufficient evidence to support a verdict in its favor. Jury instructions are provided by the judge to the jury to inform the jurors of the legal principles and rules that they must follow in reaching their conclusions. A verdict is the decision reached by a jury; a judgment is the official, written decision of the court (which, in a jury trial, incorporates the verdict). After the trial, a losing party can file a Motion for a New Trial or a Motion for Judgment Notwithstanding the Verdict. The losing party can also appeal.

REVIEW

Key Terms

Before proceeding, review the key terms listed below to be sure you understand each one. If necessary, read over the corresponding section of the chapter. When you are ready to test your understanding, answer the Review Questions.

settlement
settlement agreement
consideration
release
default provision
jurat
order of dismissal
withdrawal
stipulated judgment
summary judgment
jury trial
trial before the court
bench trial
trial notebook
Motion for Directed Verdict
jury instructions
judgment
verdict
default
default judgment
Motion for a New Trial
Motion for Judgment Notwithstanding
    the Verdict
appeal

Questions for Review and Discussion

1. What is a settlement agreement?
2. What is meant by consideration?
3. What is the importance of a release?
4. How does a corporation execute a document?
5. Explain the difference between an order of dismissal, a withdrawal, and a stipulated judgment.

6. What are the two basic assertions that are made by a party filing a Motion for Summary Judgment?
7. What is the difference between a jury trial and a bench trial?
8. What is the function of a trial notebook?
9. What are jury instructions?
10. What is the difference between a judgment and a verdict?

Activities

1. Review the facts in the Internal Memorandum of Law from Chapter 6 and draft a Motion for Summary Judgment as submitted by the Client.
2. Negotiate a settlement based on the facts in the Appellate Brief in Chapter 12 and draft the settlement agreement that is the result of your negotiation.

CHAPTER 12 The Appellate Brief

OUTLINE

COMMENTARY

Closing arguments have concluded a court trial in which you have been the assisting paralegal, and the judge informs counsel that a decision will be rendered after trial briefs are submitted. Briefs are then filed and both sides nervously await the result.

Within a week the decision arrives in your office mail. The judge has denied the permanent injunction sought by your supervising attorney—in short, your client has lost. The supervising attorney reviews the opinion, determines that there are valid reasons to question the judge's reasoning, consults with the client, and decides that she will file an appeal.

The next morning there is a memorandum on your desk. You have been assigned to assist in the legal research and preparation of the appellate brief.

OBJECTIVES

In Chapter 10 you learned how to prepare a brief (or memorandum of law) to the trial court. In this chapter we consider the briefs that are filed with the appellate court if the decision of the trial court is appealed. After completing this chapter, you will be able to:

1. Explain the importance of following the appellate rules.
2. Explain the function of the appellate brief.
3. Identify the components of the record on appeal.
4. Differentiate errors of fact from errors of law.
5. Describe the jurisdictional statement section of an appellate brief.
6. Explain the "road map" function of the table of contents.
7. Identify two key points to remember in drafting the statement of facts section.
8. Use point headings to divide the body of your brief into distinct segments.
9. Make a public policy argument.
10. Distinguish between an appellant's brief, an appellee's brief, a reply brief, and an *amicus curiae* brief.

12–1 A Preliminary Note About Procedural Rules

Although this chapter addresses the preparation of the appellate brief, a proper examination of that subject requires that we consider two preliminary steps essential to *all* phases of an appeal, from its initiation through the briefing phase, and even beyond. These preliminary steps relate to the content of the rules of your specific jurisdiction.

Appealing the decision of a trial court is a complicated process. It involves extensive technical requirements. Before the appellate court will review your client's arguments, it must be satisfied that posttrial motions, briefs, and other filings comply with specific, detailed criteria. This is true in every appellate court, state or federal.

Fortunately, these criteria are spelled out in the **appellate rules** of each jurisdiction. Although there are many broad similarities among the rules of various appellate courts, a word of caution is in order. There are often significant differences on specific formats, filing deadlines, and other particulars. Furthermore, the rules can be strict in their requirements (see Figure 12–1, which reproduces sections of Rule 32 of the Federal Rules of Appellate Procedure and Rule 33 of the U.S. Supreme Court Rules). Failure to follow with precision the rules that apply to your jurisdiction can be fatal to your appeal. Never assume anything; check to make sure.

The *first step* in pursuing an appeal, then, is to obtain a copy of the applicable rules of your jurisdiction, and to verify that they are current.

The *second step*, having obtained the current rules, is obvious but commonly disregarded. Simply stated, you must read the rules, and make sure you understand them.

The importance of the two steps cannot be overemphasized for the preparation of the appellate brief as well as every other aspect of an appeal. They are critical. Although the attorney for whom you work is ultimately responsible for compliance with the rules, your value as an assisting paralegal is directly related to your ability to follow the detailed requirements that govern the appeal process.

Figure 12–1 Appellate Brief Requirements

Federal Rules

Rule 32. Form of Briefs, the Appendix, and Other Papers

(a) Form of Briefs and the Appendix. Briefs and appendices may be produced by standard typographic printing or by any duplicating or copying process which produces a clear black image on white paper. Carbon copies of briefs and appendices may not be submitted without permission of the court, except in behalf of parties allowed to proceed in forma pauperis. All printed matter must appear in at least 11 point type on opaque, unglazed paper. Briefs and appendices produced by the standard typographic process shall be bound in volumes having pages 6 1/8 by 9 1/4 inches and type matter 4 1/6 by 7 1/6 inches. Those produced by any other process shall be bound in volumes having pages not exceeding 8 1/2 by 11 inches and type matter not exceeding 6 1/2 by 9 1/2 inches, with double spacing between each line of text. In patent cases the pages of briefs and appendices may be of such size as is necessary to utilize copies of patent documents. Copies of the reporter's transcript and other papers reproduced in a manner authorized by this rule may be inserted in the appendix; such pages may be informally renumbered if necessary.

If briefs are produced by commercial printing or duplicating firms, or, if produced otherwise and the covers to be described are available, the cover of the brief of the appellant should be blue; that of the appellee, red; that of an intervenor or *amicus curiae*, green; that of any reply brief, gray. The cover of the appendix, if separately printed, should be white. The front covers of the briefs and of appendices, if separately printed, shall contain: (1) the name of the court and the number of the case; (2) the title of the case (see Rule 12(a)); (3) the nature of the proceeding in the court (e.g., Appeal; Petition for Review) and the name of the court, agency, or board below; (4) the title of the document (e.g., Brief for Appellant, Appendix); and (5) the names and addresses of counsel representing the party on whose behalf the document is filed.

Rules of the Supreme Court

Rule 33 Printing Requirements

1. (a) Except for papers permitted by Rules 21, 22, and 39 to be submitted in typewritten form (see Rule 34), every document filed with the Court must be printed by a standard typographic printing process or be typed and reproduced by offset printing, photocopying, computer printing, or similar process. The process used must produce a clear, black image on white paper. In an original action under Rule 17, 60 copies of every document printed under this Rule must be filed; in all other cases 40 copies must be filed.

(b) The text of every document, including any appendix thereto, produced by standard typographic printing must appear in print as 11-point or larger type with 2-point or more leading between lines. The print size and typeface of the United States Reports from Volume 453 to date are acceptable. Similar print size and typeface should be standard throughout. No attempt should be made to reduce or condense the typeface in a manner that would increase the content of a document. Footnotes must appear in print as 9-point or larger type with 2-point or more leading between lines. A document must be printed on both sides of the page.

(c) The text of every document, including any appendix thereto, printed or duplicated by any process other than standard typographic printing shall be done in pica type at no more than 10 characters per inch. The lines must be double spaced. The right-hand margin need not be justified, but there must be a margin of at least three-fourths of an inch. In footnotes, elite type at no more than 12 characters per inch may be used. The document should be printed on both sides of the page, if practicable. It shall not be reduced in duplication. A document which is photographically reduced so that the print size is smaller than pica type will not be received by the Clerk.

What follows is a discussion of those elements of an appellate brief that are in large measure uniform across all jurisdictions. This discussion is intended to provide you with the background and insight necessary to follow your own local rules. Mastering the elements described will prepare you to assist in preparation of an appellate brief. But remember: there is no substitute for a thorough understanding of the precise requirements of the specific appellate court in which your brief will be filed.

Know the rules!

12–2 The Appellate Brief Defined

In order to understand the purpose of an appellate brief, and thus properly prepare it to achieve your objective, it is necessary to consider the context in which the brief is drafted and the role it plays in the appellate process.

An **appellate brief** is a legal document filed with an appellate court and drafted so as to persuade that court to decide contested issues in favor of the filing party. The appellate court uses the appellate briefs filed by the parties to gain familiarity with the facts and controlling law of the case. The appellate brief that you and your supervising attorney prepare will not present this information objectively, however, but will argue from your client's viewpoint, with the goal of convincing the court of the validity of your client's position. An example of an appellate brief appears as the Appendix to this chapter.

After reviewing the arguments set forth in the briefs, the appellate court often allows the parties to elaborate on their positions in oral argument. The attorneys appear before the court and verbally present their competing positions, emphasizing the strong points and clarifying any complex or confusing points. The oral argument stage also enables the appellate judges to directly question the attorneys on specific points that require further explanation.

The appellate court will not always allow oral argument, however. Thus, you must prepare the appellate brief as if it is your only opportunity to present your client's position. Use skill and care; each word must count.

There are two key elements of the context in which the appellate brief is filed: (1) the records; and (2) the standard of review.

The Record

At trial, having defined the disputed issues in the pleadings, the parties began the presentation of evidence with a blank slate. They could bring to the attention of the court any and all facts that were relevant and material, and were free to cite to any and all legal authorities deemed applicable. With a few technical exceptions, such as failure to disclose information during the discovery stage (which need not concern us here), there were generally no prior restraints on the introduction of evidence, nor was there any limitation on the right to formulate legal arguments.

The situation is quite different on appeal. The parties do not start with a blank slate in an appellate court. *No* new evidence is presented on appeal. The appellate court considers only whether, based upon the evidence and legal arguments already offered in the trial court, the trial court in fact reached the correct conclusion. If a particular piece of evidence or legal argument was not at least offered in the trial court, as a rule it will not be considered by the appellate court.

This brings us to consideration of the **record**. The record is the documentation of the trial, including pleadings; briefs; physical evidence introduced; a transcript of the proceedings, including all witness testimony and judge's rulings on admissibility of evidence and testimony; and the decision of the trial court.

It is the record on which the appellate court will rely in evaluating the appeal. A consideration of the individual components of the record is worthwhile.

Pleadings The **pleadings** appearing in the record include the complaint, which defines the underlying claim; the answer and special defenses, which define the response to the complaint; and all cross-claims and responses thereto. The pleadings establish the bounds of the lawsuit.

Briefs The briefs filed by the parties in the lower court are often part of the record as well, and can set the stage for the legal arguments addressed in the appellate court.

Physical Evidence All exhibits admitted into evidence by the trial court, as well as those exhibits offered into evidence but denied admission by the trial court, are part of the record. The issues on appeal often result from the trial court's rulings on admissibility of the **physical evidence**.

Transcript The **transcript** is a written account of all proceedings in the trial court, including questions and comments of the attorneys; witness testimony; and the judge's rulings and comments. The transcript is usually a stenographic record created by a **court reporter** (who is a court employee certified to record and transcribe court proceedings).

Decision of the Trial Court The decision of the trial court, and any written opinion of the judge explaining her reasoning, is always a part of the record.

The Standard of Review

As stated, the issue on appeal is whether, based on the evidence and legal arguments presented at trial, the trial court decided the case correctly. You and your supervising attorney will be scouring the record to determine whether the lower court made any errors in reaching its conclusion. If errors are found and an appeal taken, the appellate court must then evaluate these alleged errors and determine whether reversal of the lower court is justified or, rather, that the lower court be upheld. The guideline that the court applies in evaluating the alleged errors is called the **standard of review**.

There are two types of error to which a standard of review must be applied: errors of fact and errors of law.

Errors of Fact The parties at trial often present competing versions of the facts. The trial court must sift through the evidence and decide which version of the facts is correct. The party whose version was not accepted by the trial court has the right to appeal the decision, on the ground that the facts as found by the trial court are not supported by the evidence that was admitted—in other words, that there was an **error of fact**. The standard of review by which the appellate court evaluates such an appeal, however, is extremely difficult to satisfy. In general, an appellate court shows great deference to the trial court's judgment with regard to fact finding. Only if the facts found by the court are wholly unsupported by the record can a decision be overturned based on errors of fact. For example, a trial court's factual findings with regard to an injunction application (as in our Commentary problem) will be overturned in most jurisdictions only if the appellate court finds that the trial court's interpretation of the facts constituted an **abuse of discretion**, meaning that it was completely unreasonable and not logically based upon the facts.

Errors of Law The more common basis of appeal is an **error of law**. Errors of law include procedural errors, in which the trial court allowed the lawsuit to proceed in a manner not authorized by the rules; evidentiary errors, where the court admitted evidence that should have been excluded, or excluded evidence which should have been admitted; and substantive errors, where the court incorrectly interpreted the specific rules of law applicable to the facts of the case. Procedural or evidentiary errors must be shown to have caused harm to the appellant's position for a reversal to be granted (another term for this is that the appellant was "prejudiced" by the error). Otherwise it is considered to be **harmless error**, and the original decision is allowed to stand. Where errors are substantive, the appellate court will generally reverse if its interpretation of the law differs from that of the trial court.

12–3 The Sections of an Appellate Brief

There are several basic sections to an appellate brief required by the rules of virtually all appellate courts. Though the precise title of each section, as well as its order of appearance in the finished brief, may differ between jurisdictions, the substantive content is universal. Keeping in mind, then, that you should refer to your own local rules for specific guidance, what follows is a general discussion of the sections:

- Title or Cover Page
- Certificate of Interested Parties
- Table of Contents
- Table of Authorities
- Jurisdictional Statement
- Statement of the Case
- Questions Presented
- Statement of Facts
- Argument
- Conclusion
- Signature Block
- Certificate of Service
- Appendix

Title or Cover Page

The first page of an appellate brief is called the **title page** or the cover page. The title page identifies:

- the *court* in which the appeal is pending;
- the *lower court* in which the case originated;
- the *names of the parties* involved in the appeal;
- the *docket number* of the case;
- the name of the *party on whose behalf* the brief is being filed;
- the name of the *attorney* or *law firm* filing the brief; and
- the *date* of filing.

Some courts also require that, if oral argument is desired, it be requested on the title page. If your appeal is pending in such a court, failure to include this request may waive your client's right to demand oral argument at a later stage. This can damage the outcome of the appeal. Part of your responsibility as a paralegal, then, is to know your jurisdiction's rule for requesting oral argument.

When the list of parties involved in an appeal is long, some jurisdictions allow the use of the abbreviation *et al.*, which means "and others," to substitute for a full listing. Again, check your local rules.

A question always arises as to the order in which parties are listed in the appellate caption. In the past, the party making the appeal was generally listed first. This could lead to confusion when a defendant was making the appeal, however, since a case known as *Smith v. Jones* in the trial court (with Smith being the plaintiff and Jones the defendant) would become *Jones v. Smith* in the appellate court. The modern practice is to retain the caption order as it appeared in the lower court and simply identify the parties as appellant or appellee. Of course, you must check your own local rules on this point.

Some courts require that the color of the title page correspond to the status of the filing party. Thus, an appellant might have a light blue title page, an appellee a red title page, and an *amicus curiae* (literally, "friend of the court," discussed further in section 12–4) a green title page. Jurisdictions are not consistent on this practice, so again you must check.

A title page appears in Figure 12–2, (see page 248) with various components identified.

The Certificate of Interested Parties

The **certificate of interested parties** identifies all those parties to the case who have an interest in the outcome. It appears immediately after the title page (see chapter Appendix) and is intended to provide the appellate judge with an opportunity to determine the existence of a conflict between her own financial and personal interests and those of a party to the appeal.

If the judge determines that a conflict exists, she will exercise the **recusal** option. A recusal occurs when the judge voluntarily disqualifies herself from further participation in the disposition of the case.

Some jurisdictions do not require the certificate of interested parties. Check your local rules.

Table of Contents

Although the **table of contents** exists primarily to identify section headings with corresponding page numbers, it is far more than just an index. It is, rather,

Figure 12–2 Format of Title Page

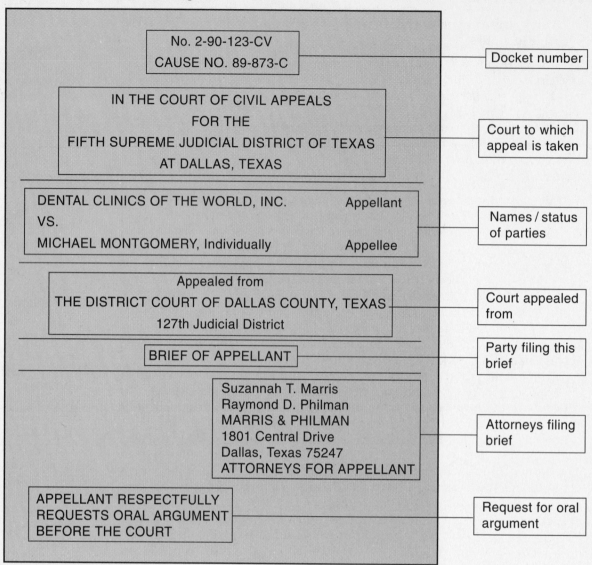

a concise outline of your client's contentions, the road map by which the court will follow the path of your argument.

The "road map" objective is achieved through expanded reference to the "argument" section. As will be discussed further, point headings and subpoint headings in the argument section identify, in an orderly and logical fashion, the rationale behind your client's position on appeal. In the table of contents, the complete text of each of these headings is set forth. Thus, simply by referring to the table of contents the court will be able to learn the broad parameters of your argument before exploring the details. Review the table of contents that appears in Figure 12–3.

Although the table of contents is one of the first sections to appear in your brief, it is one of the last sections you will draft. This is because page numbers, and perhaps even the text of the point headings, will not be finalized until you approach completion of the project.

Figure 12–3

Table of Authorities

The term **table of authorities** refers to the cases, statutes, constitutional provisions, and all other primary and secondary sources that are cited in your brief. Since both the court and opposing parties will be examining these sources in detail, is is useful to have an easily referenced list. Although the requirements for the table of authorities may vary in different jurisdictions, Table 12–1 on page 250 provides a common format. References appearing in the table of authorities should be drafted in conformity with the rules of *A Uniform System of Citation* (discussed in Chapter 1 and commonly known as the bluebook) unless your appellate court has its own special requirements. The table should also reference every page on which each authority appears in the brief. (See chapter Appendix.)

As with the table of contents, the table of authorities is one of the last sections prepared. Accuracy in both is important. If inaccurate and sloppy, they will undermine the court's confidence in the credibility of your arguments.

Preparing these tables is a task often left to paralegals. Great care should be taken.

Jurisdictional Statement

The **jurisdictional statement** identifies the legal authority that grants to the appellate court jurisdiction over the appeal. It usually makes reference to the statute establishing the right of appeal. The jurisdiction conferred by such a statute is a prerequisite to the appeal. (See chapter Appendix.)

Table 12–1 Table of Authorities

Case Opinions	Judicial decisions are listed first and *alphabetically* (some states require cases ranked by court: The U.S. Supreme Court, the U.S. Courts of Appeal, etc.). List each page number where case appears.
Constitutional Provisions	Federal constitutional provisions are listed first, with state constitutional provisions to follow. List the provisions in descending numerical order.
Statutory Provisions	Federal statutory provisions are listed after constitutional provisions; state statutes follow. As with the constitutional provisions, list in descending numerical order.
Secondary Authority	Secondary authorities are listed last, alphabetically by author. Secondary authorities range from legal periodicals to treatises, and include all other sources that are neither case decisions, constitutional provisions, nor statutes.

Statement of the Case

The **statement of the case** sets forth the procedural history of the case. It identifies the lower court or courts in which the case has been heard and the decision of each. It is analogous to the "prior proceedings" section of a case brief. (See chapter Appendix.)

There are several different titles in use for this section besides "statement of the case." Others include "preliminary statement," "nature of the action," or "nature of the case." The case history information is also frequently incorporated into the statement of facts.

Your statement of the case should include the following items:

- a concise statement of the nature of the cause of action (one or two sentences), not to be confused with the detailed statement of facts;
- whether the appeal is from a court trial, a jury trial, or a hearing;
- the name of the court whose decision is being appealed;
- the name of other courts that have had jurisdiction over the case, and the nature of their disposition; and
- the party bringing the appeal.

Questions Presented

In the **questions presented** section of the brief, you provide the appellate court with a convenient, concise statement of the grounds upon which the decision of the trial court is being questioned. For each ground, there should be a separately numbered question.

Although at first glance it might appear that drafting these questions is an objective task, in fact, you should be applying your persuasive skills. The questions should be framed so as to suggest an answer that favors your client. Useful techniques include:

- identifying the erroneous ruling of the lower court and suggesting, in question form, the result you seek;
- keeping the questions short, clear, and succinct;
- presenting separate issues in separate questions; and
- identifying the applicable standard of review.

Figure 12–4 Examples of Contrasting Versions of a "Question Presented"

> **From the appellant's perspective:**
>
> Did the District Court err and abuse its discretion by denying appellant's application for a temporary injunction, since appellant proved a probable right and probable injury and thereby established sufficient grounds to impose an injunction and preserve the status quo?
>
> **From the appellee's perspective:**
>
> Was the District Court correct in denying plaintiff's request for an injunction?

The "questions presented" section is sometimes referred to as "points of error," "issues presented," or "assignments of error." As always, check your local rules.

In Figure 12–4, two questions are set forth that were drafted by opposing sides on the same appeal. Note the manner in which the appellant and appellee have stated the same basic issue in a contrasting, and partisan, fashion.

Statement of Facts

The **statement of facts** is the first of the two major sections of the appellate brief, the other being the argument. In it you set forth the background information and significant facts of your client's case, so that the appellate court has a clear factual framework within which to consider the legal questions presented. (See chapter Appendix.)

The statement of facts is not based upon your memory of events in the case, nor is it based upon those facts which you believe you can prove, since there is no opportunity to "prove" facts on appeal. It is based, rather, on the record of the case. If a fact is not contained in the record of the case, then, for the purposes of the appellate court, that fact simply doesn't exist.

There are two key points to remember in drafting your statement of facts:

- every fact set forth should be followed by a reference in parentheses to that portion of the record in which the fact appears; and
- the statement of facts should be drafted in a persuasive fashion, setting forth the facts in a light most favorable to your client, while at the same time remaining accurate, straightforward, and faithful to the record.

The first of these points, making reference to the record, is easy to understand but often difficult to accomplish. The record of a trial court can be bulky. Many trials are lengthy, and the transcript can run to hundreds of pages or more, with a large number of exhibits. Sometimes the exhibits themselves are lengthy and complicated documents, the meaning of which is disputed by the parties.

There is no magic solution to mastering the record. Simply stated, you must study the transcript and exhibits until you develop a full understanding of their content. It is likely that, in your role as a paralegal, you will be responsible for having a good working knowledge of the record. You will be expected to locate references quickly. Your supervising attorney may draft a statement of facts without parenthetical references, and then expect you to provide the missing information.

One method that is useful for mastering the record is the **indexing method**. By preparing an index to the transcript—for example, identifying (1) the party testifying, (2) the attorney conducting the examination, (3) the content of the testimony, and (4) the transcript page on which the testimony appears, you will have a useful shorthand reference enabling you to locate specific items quickly. An index can also be used to summarize documentary exhibits.

Indexes are sometimes also called "digests." Although some might say that a "digest" suggests a summary more detailed than an index, the difference is largely semantic, and the purpose of each is identical—namely, to summarize a lengthier document.

Different appellate courts have different rules with regard to referencing the record. For example, references to the transcript might be identified by "(T-78)," meaning "page 78 of the transcript," or a variation such as "(R-78)," meaning "page 78 of the record." You should check your local rules for the appropriate style in your jurisdiction.

Though a tedious task, providing comprehensive parenthetical references is very important to the success of your brief. By identifying all those portions of the record that support your factual claims, you not only provide a useful summary of the record but also establish credibility in the eyes of the court. A thorough and well-referenced statement of facts provides the foundation on which you build your arguments and persuade the appellate court.

The second point requires that your statement of facts be not only honest and accurate but also partisan. Although on the face of it this might seem to be inconsistent, in fact it goes to the essence of persuasive legal writing. In order to set the stage for your legal arguments, you want the court to interpret the facts in a light most favorable to your client. At the same time, you do not want the court to think that you are distorting the record. In order to accomplish these objectives, you should employ several techniques:

- set forth the facts in chronological order, which is the easiest and most logical to follow;
- emphasize those facts which support your client's position; and
- when negative facts are essential to an accurate presentation, resist the temptation to omit them, since this will erode your credibility in the eyes of the court (you can be sure that the other side will draw such facts to the court's attention anyway). You should address these negative facts in such a way that their impact is minimized.

Argument

The most important section of the appellate brief is known as the **argument**. In this section you analyze the legal issues raised by the "questions presented" section and interpret the applicable cases and statutes to demonstrate that your client's position should prevail on appeal.

The argument section of an appellate brief is the highest point of persuasive legal writing. Its preparation represents the climax of all your training in written advocacy. The success or failure of your appeal will turn in large measure on your ability to state logically and forcefully, in writing, your client's position. Every stylistic decision has an impact; every substantive choice a consequence; every word an effect.

The argument section comprises two components, the point headings and the body. (See chapter Appendix.)

Point Headings **Point headings** are brief synopses of the argument to follow, set apart from the body of the brief by underlines or type style. (See chapter Appendix.) They perform both a stylistic function, in that they divide the brief into distinct sections for easier reading, and a substantive function, in that they separate the argument into logical components. They provide concise answers to the questions posed in the "questions presented" section, thus giving the court a preview of the detailed argument, and in general, introduce the complex reasoning to follow.

The level of complexity of the brief determines the number of point headings. Isolate the distinct legal issues presented, and begin the discussion of each separate issue with a new point heading.

If the discussion of a given legal issue is complex, you may need subpoint headings as well. In deciding whether subpoint headings are needed, you must keep in mind that too many subpoint headings may actually confuse the reader. If you decide that subpoint headings are justified, choose a format or type style that clearly distinguishes subpoint headings from point headings, so as to maintain clarity.

The brief in the Appendix shows both point headings and subpoint headings. In reviewing this brief, note both the substantive content of the headings and the manner in which capitalization, indenting, spacing, and underlining are used to differentiate headings from the body, and point headings from subpoint headings.

Body The **body** of the argument is the section in which the main text is set forth. (See the chapter Appendix.) It is here that you inform the court of the detailed arguments that support your client's position.

The sole purpose of the body of the brief is to present the law so as to persuade the court. Although this purpose may appear obvious, many attorneys and paralegals lose sight of this consideration when drafting a brief. The problem arises as a result of the interpretation that the drafter attaches to the term "detailed argument." Appellate courts often see briefs that exhaustively document the issue presented, but fail to persuade. You must keep in mind that your job is not to draft a treatise on the issues raised, but rather to persuade the court to resolve the issues in favor of your client. This requires that you cite essential sources and discuss relevant concepts, hence the word "detailed." It does not require that you cite every source, nor discuss every concept, that might arguably be deemed relevant to your brief.

If the issue presented is not complex (or even in many cases where it *is* complex), it is possible that one or two controlling cases and one or two applicable statutes may adequately define and support your argument. If you address such a context in an excessively complicated manner, you dilute the impact of these essential authorities.

Remember that deciding upon the final content of a brief is often a balancing act between simplifying the issues for ease of understanding on the one hand, and accurately reflecting the state of the law on the other. Your goal is a brief that is easy to understand, thorough, and an accurate and defensible representation of the law—in a word, *persuasive*. In achieving this goal, you should follow the basic rules and techniques of writing that we addressed in previous chapters, including clarity and brevity. In addition, keep in mind the following points:

- Place your strongest point first.
- The court will be relying on precedent, not your personal theories. When the law is on your side, *tell* the court. When it is not, distinguish the precedents by pointing out factual or other differences between their context and that of your appeal. It is almost always advisable to avoid the temptation to improvise theory.
- Where the case law is against you, argue that "justice and fair play"

compel the court to find for your client and reverse the precedents. This is the so-called **equitable argument**.

- *Never* misrepresent facts or case law to the court.
- A court is often persuaded by **public policy arguments**. Whether your case is supported by precedent or not, it is always useful to show the court how a decision in your favor will benefit the public interest.
- **String citations** (long lists of cases that you claim support your point) may actually undercut your argument, if the significance of the most important precedent is diluted. The trend is to cite the one best and/or most recent case for your point.

Conclusion

The **conclusion** is a brief statement appearing after the "argument" section. It does not summarize your argument, but rather "respectfully submits" that, based upon the logic of your argument, the court must grant the relief you desire. In other words, the appellant concludes that the trial court should be reversed, whereas the appellee concludes that it should be upheld.

The key here is to be specific. Do not leave the court to guess at the relief you seek—*tell* the court. (See chapter Appendix.)

Signature Block

The **signature block** provides a line for the signature of the attorney who is ultimately responsible for the brief. His name, address, and telephone number are typed below the signature. The client on whose behalf the brief is filed is also identified, and sometimes other information as well. (See chapter Appendix.) Check your local rules for the specific requirements in your jurisdiction.

Certificate of Service

The **certificate of service** is an acknowledgment at the end of any court-filed document, including an appellate brief, that verifies delivery of the document to all persons entitled to a copy, and identifies the date and type of service. (See chapter Appendix.) Mail delivery is usually sufficient.

Those entitled to service generally include the attorneys in the case, as well as parties who represent themselves without the assistance of an attorney. Sometimes the certification must also verify that a copy was served upon the court.

The certificate of service is attested to by the attorney filing the brief. Your local rules will provide specific guidance.

Appendix

Appellate briefs often contain an **appendix**, which is a supplementary collection of primary source materials. Most of these materials are taken from the record. In many jurisdictions it is mandatory to include certain portions of the record in the appendix, for example, those pages from the transcript that are referenced in the text of the appellate brief.

The appendix appears as the last section in the brief. In addition to transcript pages, it often contains relevant passages from pleadings, evidentiary exhibits introduced at trial, and the lower court's judgment and opinion.

12–4 The Four Categories of Appellate Briefs

All appellate briefs share the same basic characteristics outlined. The approach to drafting a specific appellate brief, however, varies somewhat with the procedural status of your client. An appellant, for example, takes a different approach than an appellee, whereas the brief filed by an *amicus curiae* has its own unique emphasis. The stage at which a brief is filed also affects its content, a reply brief being a different creature altogether from an opening brief. It is worthwhile to take a moment and review the differences in emphasis among the four categories of appellate brief: appellant's; appellee's; the reply brief, and that of the *amicus curiae*.

Appellant's Brief

The appellant, as you recall, is the party making the appeal. It is the appellant who asserts that the decision of the trial court must be overturned. Almost without exception, the **appellant's brief** will be filed first. Thus the appellant has the opportunity to set the tone of the appeal and define the issues that will be brought before the appellate court. Although this might appear to be an advantage, any edge inferred is offset by the fact that the appellant is seeking to overturn the judgment of a trial court that has carefully considered the issues and found for the other side. The burden of proving the trial court wrong is on the appellant.

Appellee's Brief

The **appellee's brief** is filed in response to the appellant's brief. Thus the appellee has the appellant's brief in hand as the response is prepared. This enables the appellee to review and attack the specific arguments made by the appellant. In addition to attacking the arguments of the appellant, the appellee should also set forth independent reasons that demonstrate why the lower court should be upheld.

Reply Brief

The term *reply brief* could be attached to any brief filed by a party in response to an earlier brief filed by an opposing party. The appellee's opening brief is thus technically a reply brief, since it is filed after, and in response to, the appellant's brief. In general, however, the term **reply brief** refers to a brief filed by the appellant in response to the appellee's opening brief.

The justification for allowing such a reply brief is simple. It would be unfair to deny the appellant an opportunity to respond to the arguments of the appellee, since the appellee had the opportunity to review and attack the arguments set forth in the appellant's first brief. Hence the appellant is authorized to file a reply brief.

When preparing a reply brief, the appellant should resist the temptation to restate arguments already set forth in the first brief. The court will not forget these earlier arguments. Rather, the appellant should concentrate on addressing issues raised for the first time in the appellee's brief. It is similarly inappropriate (although probably prudent) for the appellant to raise points in the reply brief that it failed, through negligence or oversight, to address in the opening brief. If such points are raised in the reply brief, the court may allow the appellee another chance to respond, or disregard the new points entirely.

Amicus Curiae Brief

An *amicus curiae* is a person or organization that was not directly involved in the lawsuit between the parties, but which has an interest in the outcome of the appeal and has succeeded in petitioning the court for the right to file a brief on the issues presented. An *amicus* **brief** (as it is often called) may correspond to any of the other three categories of brief, depending on whose interest the *amicus* brief mirrors and what stage the appeal has reached. One difference between the *amicus* brief and others is that the *amicus* brief argues from a public policy viewpoint.

12–5 Practical Considerations

An appellate brief is not prepared in a day. Unlike briefing schedules in the trial court, often characterized by tight deadlines imposed by the trial judge, an appellate briefing schedule is generally established by specific rules that set reasonable minimum time periods.

Thus the most important practical consideration in preparing an appellate brief is twofold: first, you have ample time to polish your brief; second, because of this appellate judges *expect* a polished product. You must schedule sufficient time to perform the tasks that go into every appellate brief—reviewing the record; researching the issues; writing a draft; editing; finalizing your draft; preparing the tables of contents and authorities, as well as all other supplements; and reviewing the final version to ensure that it is as polished as you can make it. It's easy to delude yourself into thinking, "The brief's not due for four weeks—I'll do other things first." If you fall into this trap, you'll end up with a major headache—a brief due in a week or less, and insufficient time to prepare it correctly.

There is one other important practical consideration. Remember that this chapter is only an *introduction* to writing the appellate brief, and is not the final word. There are as many opinions on appellate advocacy, briefing strategies, and brief writing as there are on trial advocacy. But all good briefs have a few common characteristics—they are thorough, yet concise; accurate, yet partisan; and most of all, they are *persuasive*.

No. 2-90-123-CV
CAUSE NO. 89-873-C
IN THE COURT OF CIVIL APPEALS
FOR THE
FIFTH SUPREME JUDICIAL DISTRICT OF TEXAS
AT DALLAS, TEXAS

DENTAL CLINICS OF THE WORLD, INC.   Appellant

vs.

MICHAEL MONTGOMERY, Individually   Appellee

Appealed from
THE DISTRICT COURT OF DALLAS COUNTY, TEXAS
127th Judicial District

BRIEF OF APPELLANT

Suzannah T. Marris
Raymond D. Philman
MARRIS & PHILMAN
1801 Central Drive
Dallas, Texas 75247

ATTORNEYS FOR APPELLANT

APPELLANT   RESPECTFULLY
REQUESTS ORAL ARGUMENT
BEFORE THE COURT

Refer to the corresponding key numbers to identify each element of
this Brief.

❶ — Title or Cover Page   ❽ — Statement of Facts
❷ — Certificate of Interested Parties   ❾ — Argument
❸ — Table of Contents   ❿ — Point Heading
❹ — Table of Authorities   ⑪ — Body
❺ — Jurisdictional Statement   ⑫ — Conclusion
❻ — Statement of the Case   ⑬ — Signature Block
❼ — Questions Presented   ⑭ — Certificate of Service

CERTIFICATE OF INTERESTED PARTIES

The following are all the interested parties in this Appeal:
1. Dental Clinics of the World, Inc.
2. Michael Montgomery
3. Joseph Dean

(i)

Table of Contents

Table of Authorities

UNITED STATES SUPREME COURT

E.I. DuPont De Nemours Power Co. v. Masland, 244 U.S. 100 (1917)

TEXAS SUPREME COURT

City of Spring v. Southwestern Bell Telephone Company, 484 S.W. 2d, 579 (Tex. 1974)

Hyde Corp. v. Huffines, 158 Tex. 566, 314 S.W. 2d 763 (1958)

International Bankers Life Ins. Co. v Holloway, 368 S.W. 2d 567 (Tex. 1963)

K & G Oil Tool & Service Co. v. G & G Fishing Tool Service, 158 Tex. 594, 314 S.W. 2d 782 (1958)

Southland Life Insurance Co. v. Egan, 126 Tex. 160, 86 S.W. 2d 722 (1935)

Texas Foundries, Inc. v. International Moulding & Foundry Workers Union, 151 Tex. 239, 248 S.W. 2d 460 (1952)

Transport Co. of Texas v. Robertson Transports, 152 Tex. 551, 261 S.W. 2d 549 (1953)

TEXAS COURT OF APPEALS

Green v. Stratoflex, Inc., 596 S.W. 2d 305 (Tex. Civ. App., Ft. Worth 1980, no writ)

Jeter v. Associated Rack Corp. 607 S.W. 2d 272 (Tex. Civ. App., Texarkana 1980, writ ref'd n.r.e.) cert. denied, 454 U.S. 965 (1980)

Lamons Metal Gasket Co. v. Traylor, 361 S.W. 2d 211, (Tex. Civ. App., Houston, 1962, writ ref'd n.r.e.)

Morgan v. City of Humble, 598 S.W. 2d 364, (Tex. Civ. App., Houston [14th Dist.] 1980, no writ)

Plagge v. Gambino, 570 S.W. 2d 106 (Tex. Civ. App., Houston [1st Dist.] 1978, no writ)

Texas Shop Towel, Inc. v. Haine, 246 S.W. 2d 482 (Tex. Civ. App., San Antonio 1952, no writ)

Weed Eater v. Dowling, 562 S.W. 2d 898 (Tex. Civ. App., Houston [1st Dist.] 1978, writ ref'd n.r.e.)

JURISDICTIONAL STATEMENT

This court has jurisdiction of this appeal pursuant to the Texas Constitution Art. 5 § 6 and Tex. Civ. Prac. & Rem. Code Ann. § 51.014 (Vernon 1986).

5

STATEMENT OF THE CASE

This case is an appeal from the denial of a temporary injunction. DENTAL CLINICS OF THE WORLD, INC. ("DENTAL CLINIC" or "Appellant") filed suit against MICHAEL MONTGOMERY ("MONTGOMERY" or "Appellee") alleging that Appellee used Appellant's confidential and proprietary information and trade secrets. MONTGOMERY used information that he gained through his employment with DENTAL CLINIC to bid on a servicing dental clinic's contract with Health Care, Inc., Dallas, Texas. The information was DENTAL CLINIC's proprietary, confidential information and trade secrets, which MONTGOMERY acquired and used in violation of his obligations to DENTAL CLINIC. MONTGOMERY also contacted other persons to attempt to establish a business that would compete with Appellant, using DENTAL CLINIC'S information. A temporary injunction hearing was held by the 127th Judicial District Court, Dallas, Texas. On June 20, 1992, the Court entered an Order denying the temporary injunction.

6

Question Presented

Did the District Court err and abuse its discretion by denying appellant's application for a temporary injunction, since appellant proved a probable right and probable injury and thereby established sufficient grounds to impose an injunction and preserve the status quo?

7

Fact Statement

DENTAL CLINIC is a Texas corporation specializing in dental clinic services. DENTAL CLINIC offers personnel and equipment (for example, drills, x-ray machines, and other equipment; Tr. 47) to dental clinics in Texas.

In 1980, DENTAL CLINIC employed MICHAEL MONTGOMERY as a salesperson. MONTGOMERY became Vice President of the company in 1986. (Tr. 36) While Vice President, MONTGOMERY had many responsibilities, including hiring employees, purchasing equipment, compiling marketing data, selling the company's services, and dealing with customers. (Tr. 38) Throughout his tenure with DENTAL CLINIC, MICHAEL MONTGOMERY gained confidential knowledge and information.

DENTAL CLINIC's business is service-oriented. Through contracts with its customers, DENTAL CLINIC provides equipment and personnel. The customers are normally small clinics or health centers. (Tr. 45) DENTAL CLINIC installs the equipment and provides the technicians. Only three other companies provided a similar service in Texas. (Tr 31)

8

To determine whether an area is appropriate for a dental clinic, a sizable amount of research and development takes place. This research and development takes years. (Tr. 51) If competitors obtained this information, thousands of research dollars could be saved, as well as the time spent researching. Having this information would allow a competitor to set up a clinic in an area or forego an area based on DENTAL CLINIC's research.

DENTALCLINIC treated this information as confidential, proprietary data and trade secrets. This information was kept from employees unless needed in their job functions. (Tr. 55) MONTGOMERY was one of the few employees

1

of DENTAL CLINIC who had access to <u>all</u> Company information. (Tr. 55) This information included, but was not limited to, customer lists, supplier lists, pricing lists, clinics, and manufacturers. As an employee and fiduciary of the Company, MONTGOMERY knew this information was confidential and proprietary. (Tr. 56)

MONTGOMERY worked directly with DENTAL CLINIC's customers. In fact, MONTGOMERY worked with clinic administrators and found out that one of DENTAL CLINIC's customers had received a bid from another company. MONTGOMERY was asked to revise DENTAL CLINIC's prior contract and gave the information to the President of DENTAL CLINIC. (Tr. 71) The new bid was resubmitted to the clinic with MONTGOMERY's new prices. (Tr. 72) MONTGOMERY gained all this information while employed with the Company.

On November 17, 1991, MONTGOMERY resigned and terminated his employment with DENTAL CLINIC. (Tr. 95) Not more than one month after he left DENTAL CLINIC, MONTGOMERY formed his own company, DENTAL HEALTH CARE. This company offered the same services as DENTAL CLINIC. (Tr. 98)

MONTGOMERY contacted one of DENTAL CLINIC's customers regarding a dental services contract. (Tr. 101) The clinic turned out to be the same clinic MONTGOMERY had revised the pricing for while employed with DENTAL CLINIC. MONTGOMERY did not contact anyone for pricing information. In fact, MONTGOMERY knew his bid would be lower than DENTAL CLINIC's since he had access to the information while employed with DENTAL CLINIC. (Tr. 107) Months later, in January 1992, DENTAL CLINIC was notified that its contract with the clinic would be cancelled and that MONTGOMERY's company would receive the contract. (Tr. 158) MONTGOMERY also contacted other customers of DENTAL CLINIC and attempted to gain their contracts. Clearly, MONTGOMERY knew all DENTAL CLINIC customers, the services performed for them, and the prices charged. This information could only be gained from MONTGOMERY's employment. DENTAL CLINIC sued MONTGOMERY for misappropriation of trade secrets and confidential proprietary information and requested a temporary injunction. This injunction was denied, and the denial has been appealed.

ARGUMENT AND AUTHORITIES

I. THE TRIAL COURT ABUSED ITS DISCRETION BY NOT GRANTING THE TEMPORARY INJUNCTION.

The standard of review for an appeal in a temporary injunction hearing is whether the trial court abused its discretion in granting or denying the temporary injunction. <u>Texas Foundries, Inc. v. International Moulding & Foundry Workers Union</u>, 151 Tex. 239, 248 S.W. 2d 460 (1952); <u>City of Spring v. Southwestern Bell Telephone Company</u>, 484 S.W. 2d 579 (Tex. 1974). In determining whether the granting or denial of a temporary injunction is proper, this Court must look to the record in the trial court and determine whether the party requesting relief is entitled to preservation of status quo of the subject matter pending trial on the merits. <u>Green v. Stratoflex, Inc.</u>, 596 S.W. 2d 305 (Tex. Civ. App., Ft. Worth 1980, no writ). In evaluating whether or not the trial court abused its discretion in granting or denying a temporary injunction, this Court must consider whether the trial court erroneously applied the law to undisputed facts, where pleadings and evidence presented a probable right and probable injury. <u>Southland Life Insurance Co. v. Egan</u>, 126 Tex. 160, 86 S.W. 2d 722 (1935); <u>Plagge v. Gambino</u>, 570 S.W. 2d 106 (Tex. Civ. App., Houston [1st Dist.] 1978, no writ); <u>Morgan v. City of Humble</u>, 598 S.W. 2d 364 (Tex. Civ. App., Houston [14th Dist.] 1980, no writ).

2

The purpose of the temporary injunction is to preserve the status quo of a matter in controversy until final hearing on the merits of the case. For a temporary injunction to be issued by a trial court, a party need show only a <u>probable right</u> and a <u>probable injury</u>, and is not required to establish that he will finally prevail in the litigation. Therefore, the burden in a temporary injunction hearing is substantially different than it is in a trial on the merits. The movant has to prove there is a probable right to recovery at a trial on merits, but does not have the burden to prove that he would ultimately prevail at a final hearing. <u>Transport Co. of Texas v. Robertson Transports</u>, 152 Tex. 551, 261 S.W. 2d 549 (1953). At the temporary injunction hearing, DENTAL CLINIC proved that a probable injury was suffered and that DENTAL CLINIC had a probable right to recovery. MONTGOMERY took information from his employer, DENTAL CLINIC, and used the information to injure DENTAL CLINIC. The misappropriation of this information was wrongful, for which DENTAL CLINIC was entitled to relief in the form of a temporary injunction. The trial court abused its discretion by failing to properly apply the law to the facts. DENTAL CLINIC made a proper showing to meet the standards necessary for issuance of an injunction.

II. TEXAS PROHIBITS THE USE OF TRADE SECRETS AND CONFIDENTIAL PROPRIETARY INFORMATION WHEN MISAPPROPRIATED BY A CORPORATE OFFICER.

MONTGOMERY was a Vice President of DENTAL CLINIC. The Supreme Court of Texas has held that corporate officers are fiduciaries of the corporation. <u>International Bankers Life Ins. Co. v. Holloway</u>, 368 S.W. 2d 567 (Tex. 1963). Not only do the courts impose a general fiduciary obligation on officers, but additionally, the courts have articulated a specific rule that an employee has a duty not to disclose the confidential matters of its employer. <u>Lamons Metal Gasket Co. v. Traylor</u>, 361 S.W. 2d 211 (Tex. Civ. App., Houston 1962, writ ref'd n.r.e.); <u>Jeter v. Associated Rack Corp.</u>, 607 S.W. 2d 272 (Tex. Civ. App., Texarkana 1980, writ ref'd n.r.e.), cert. denied, 454 U.S. 965 (1980). Certain information was considered confidential by DENTAL CLINIC. The undisputed testimony of the President shows that DENTAL CLINIC considered customer lists, renewal dates, and pricing as confidential. (Tr. 57–59)

MONTGOMERY disregarded his fiduciary responsibilities to further his own personal endeavors. But for MONTGOMERY's relationship to DENTAL CLINIC, he would not have known the trade secrets and confidential and proprietary information. The law is clear that Texas prohibits the use of confidential information by a former corporate officer. <u>Weed Eater v. Dowling</u>, 562 S.W. 2d 898 (Tex. Civ. App., Houston [1st Dist.] 1978, writ ref'd n.r.e.)

A. A trade secret by definition may be a compilation of information, including a customer list.

In defining a trade secret, the Texas Supreme Court has adopted the <u>Restatement of Torts</u>, 2nd § 757, which defines a trade secret as follows:

> A trade secret may consist of any formula, pattern, device, or <u>compilation of information which is used in one's business and which gives him an opportunity to obtain an advantage over competitors who do not know or use it.</u> It may be a formula for a chemical compound, a process of manufacturing, treating or preserving materials, a pattern for a machine, or other device, or a <u>list of customers</u>.* * * Trade secret is a process or device

for continuous use in the operation of the business. <u>Hyde Corp.</u> <u>v. Huffines</u>, 158 Tex. 566, 314 S.W. 2d 763 (1958) (emphasis supplied).

The <u>Restatement of Torts</u> § 757 further states that:

One who discloses or uses another's trade secrets, without a privilege to do so, is liable to the other if (a) he discloses the secret by improper means, or (b) his disclosure or <u>use</u> constitutes a breach of confidence reposed in him by the other in disclosing the secret to him. <u>Hyde Corp. v. Huffines, supra</u> (emphasis supplied).

DENTAL CLINIC had developed confidential and proprietary information that it used in its business. This information gave it an advantage over competitors. For years DENTAL CLINIC compiled information. The information included but was not limited to customer lists, contact persons at clinics, pricing information, financial information, and market planning strategies. (Tr. 57) Information had been exclusively developed through DENTAL CLINIC's financial investment and research and was not readily accessible to outsiders of DENTAL CLINIC without substantial monetary and time investment. This compilation of information is DENTAL CLINIC's trade secrets and proprietary and confidential information, which it uses in the development of its business activities.

MONTGOMERY had access to trade secrets and confidential and proprietary information of DENTAL CLINIC by virtue of his position of confidence and trust with the President, Joseph Dean. As the testimony showed, Joseph Dean and MONTGOMERY worked together in the development of DENTAL CLINIC. MONTGOMERY had access to all the information regarding DENTAL CLINIC. The information that MONTGOMERY acquired is a valuable asset of DENTAL CLINIC. A temporary injunction is the only remedy that will protect DENTAL CLINIC's investment. A temporary injunction will preserve the status quo pending a trial on the merits. Without the injunction, DENTAL CLINIC will continue to suffer harm and injury. MONTGOMERY admitted he took information that he gained while employed with DENTAL CLINIC to contact other dental clinics. He made offers and submitted proposals to the clinics. (Tr. 88) Specifically, MONTGOMERY contacted Dental Resources of the Southwest, with whom DENTAL CLINIC had been negotiating a renewal of its contract. MONTGOMERY breached his fiduciary relationship with DENTAL CLINIC by using its proprietary and confidential information and trade secrets. When a vice president breaches his fiduciary duty, it is proper under Texas law to grant a temporary injunction. <u>Weed Easter v.</u> <u>Dowling</u>, 562 S.W. 2d 898 (Tex. Civ. App., Houston [1st Dist.] 1978, writ ref'd n.r.e.).

In any analysis of trade secrets and confidential and proprietary information, the Court must evaluate how the information was acquired. Although it may be argued by MONTGOMERY the information was generally available for someone with time and money to accumulate the information, the fact is clear that the data which MONTGOMERY utilized to compete with his former employer came from DENTAL CLINIC's investment of hundreds of hours and substantial sums of money to accumulate and develop the data. Even if MONTGOMERY could acquire the information, that does not mean that he is entitled, through a breach of confidence, to gain the "information in usable form and escape the efforts of inspection and analysis." <u>K & G</u>

4

<u>Oil Tool & Service Co. v. G & G Fishing Tool</u> [...]
S.W. 2d 782 (1958). The law in Texas imposed [...]
an individual who has breached a fiduciary re[...]
porary injunction. As the court in its dicta [...]
<u>Dowling</u>, <u>supra</u>, recognized,

> [W]here an employee will acquire trade secrets [...]
> employment, the law permits greater restrictio[...]
> on the employee than in other contracts of emp[...]
>
> <u>Confidential business information</u> is not given pr[...]
> ly as a reward to its accumulator. The courts co[...]
> ment of improper means to procure trade secrets. <u>T</u>[...]
> <u>a trade secret is of such a nature that it can be</u> [...]
> <u>by experimentation or other fair and lawful means</u> [...] <u>ot</u>
> <u>deprive its owner of the right to protection from</u> [...] <u>se who</u>
> <u>would secure possession by unfair means</u> (emphasis supplied).

Texas law clearly imposes a responsibility on a corporate officer such as MONTGOMERY not to disclose information gained during employment. The responsibility of the corporate fiduciary is implied and is part of a contract of employment.

Although the appellee would suggest that liability can be imposed only if a written contract existed, this is not the law. In confidential and proprietary information actions, a contract of employment is not necessary to create the right. As <u>Texas Shop Towel, Inc. v. Haine</u> points out:

> [A]n owner may protect a trade secret even in the total absence of any contract with his employees, and the agents and employees who learn of the trade secret or secret formula are prohibited from its use. <u>In the case of a trade secret, a contract does not</u> <u>create the right, for the right exists by reason of the confi-</u> <u>dence.</u> It will exist in the total absence of a contract. A contract may be additional evidence of the existence of the trade secret but an owner's rights in his secrets do not depend upon a contract (emphasis supplied). <u>Texas Shop Towel, Inc. v. Haine</u>, 246 S.W. 2d 482 (Tex. Civ. App., San Antonio 1952, no writ).

No employment contract is necessary to hold MONTGOMERY legally responsible for his actions.

The testimony and the evidence before this Court are undisputed. MONTGOMERY received DENTAL CLINIC's confidential, proprietary, and trade secret information in confidence as DENTAL CLINIC's employee, and MONTGOMERY was an officer of DENTAL CLINIC and as such was a fiduciary of the corporation. In <u>E.I. DuPont De Nemours Power Co. v. Masland</u>, 244 U.S. 100 (1917), the Supreme Court of the United States recognized the importance of a fiduciary duty and the consequence of a breach of that duty. The Supreme Court in dicta made the following observation:

> [W]hether the Plaintiffs have any valuable secret or not, the Defendant knows the facts, whatever they are, through a special confidence that he accepted. The property may be denied, but the confidence cannot be. Therefore, the starting point for the present matter is not property or due process of law, but that

5

stood in confidential relations with the
, or one of them. These have given place to hostili-
the first thing to be made sure of is that the Defendant
ll not fraudulently abuse the trust reposed in him. It is
the usual incident of confidential relations. If there is any
disadvantage in the fact that he knew the Plaintiff's secrets,
he must take the burden with the good. Id., at 102.

The U.S. Supreme Court recognized the rights of an employer over
fifty years ago. It is a right that continues today. The only remedy
DENTAL CLINIC has is a temporary injunction.

B.   An injunction is an appropriate remedy for misappropriation of trade
     secrets and for the breach of a fiduciary relationship.

The evidence is clear that MONTGOMERY acquired trade secrets and confidential and proprietary information from DENTAL CLINIC while an employee. After his resignation, MONTGOMERY used the trade secrets and confidential and proprietary information of DENTAL CLINIC to his own benefit.
Though the information may have been available to a competitor, that
availability did not give MONTGOMERY the right to violate his confidential relationship with DENTAL CLINIC. Texas Shop Towel, Inc. v. Haine,
supra.

⑪ By not issuing a temporary injunction and preserving the status quo,
the trial judge abused his discretion. The facts in this case are undisputed by the evidence and the testimony.

By applying the undisputed facts to the law, DENTAL CLINIC was entitled to a temporary injunction to preserve the status quo. DENTAL CLINIC
proved through the testimony and evidence that it had a probable injury,
which would result from (1) MONTGOMERY's utilizing information to undercut DENTAL CLINIC's contract bid, and (2) MONTGOMERY's contacting users
of DENTAL CLINIC services. DENTAL CLINIC also showed that there was a
probable right to recovery since the information was admittedly gained
from MONTGOMERY's employment with DENTAL CLINIC. MONTGOMERY admitted
that he learned the information that he utilized to prepare that clinic's contract from his employment with DENTAL CLINIC. The trial court
abused its discretion by not granting the temporary injunction as the
court did not properly apply the law to the undisputed facts. In Weed
Eater v. Dowling, supra, the Houston Court of Appeals recognized that a
temporary injunction is a proper remedy when there is a breach of confidence and a misuse of proprietary information and trade secrets. The
facts in this case support such a conclusion of probable injury and probable right and the law dictates the issuance of an injunction.

CONCLUSION

In a temporary injunction hearing, DENTAL CLINIC had to show only a
probable right to recovery and a probable injury and that there was not
an adequate remedy at law. In applying the law to the facts, DENTAL CLINIC
showed an injury, MONTGOMERY's interference with a business contract, and
a right to recovery arising from MONTGOMERY's use of information gained
while employed with DENTAL CLINIC. As a matter of law, this information
⑫ was confidential and proprietary and trade secrets of DENTAL CLINIC. By
not granting the temporary injunction, the trial court erred and abused
its discretion by misapplying the law to the facts. DENTAL CLINIC requests
that this court instruct the trial court to issue and enter a temporary
injunction to preserve the status quo in this case until a final trial on
the merits can be heard.   6

DENTAL CLINIC requests that this Honorable Court instruct the trial court to issue and enter a temporary injunction against MONTGOMERY to preserve the status quo until a final trial on the merits by ordering MONTGOMERY not to contact any customers or dentists who are customers of DENTAL CLINIC during the pendency of the litigation.

Respectfully submitted,

_____
SUZANNAH T. MARRIS
State Bar #18769283

RAYMOND D. PHILMAN
State Bar #27619317

13

MARRIS & PHILMAN
1801 Central Drive
Dallas, Texas 75247
(214)512-0927

ATTORNEYS FOR APPELLANT

CERTIFICATE OF SERVICE

I certify that a true and correct copy of the foregoing Brief of Appellant has been forwarded to Appellee, by and through their attorney of record, C. J. Coldaway at 617 Renewal Tower, Dallas, Texas, 76202, by certified mail, return receipt requested, on this_____day of_____, 1992.

14

_____
Suzannah T. Marris.

7

SUMMARY

12–1

The first step in pursuing an appeal is to obtain a copy of the current appellate rules applicable in your jurisdiction. The second step is to read and understand them.

12–2

An appellate brief is a legal document filed with an appellate court and drafted so as to persuade that court to decide contested issues in favor of the filing litigant. An appeal is based on the record, which is the written documentation of the trial. The guideline that the court applies in evaluating an appeal is called the standard of review. There are two types of errors to which a standard of review is applied: errors of fact and errors of law.

12–3

There are several basic sections to an appellate brief, which may vary slightly in designation or content from one jurisdiction to the next, but are otherwise always required. The title page identifies the parties and court, and usually also contains the request for oral argument. The certificate of interested parties identifies those parties with a direct interest in the outcome of the case. The table of contents provides section headings with corresponding page numbers, and performs a "road map" function. The table of authorities identifies references cited. The jurisdictional statement identifies the legal authority that grants the appel-

late court authority over the appeal. The statement of the case sets forth the procedural history of the case. The questions presented section provides a convenient and concise statement of the grounds of the appeal. The statement of facts is based upon the record, and should be both accurate and partisan. The argument is the most important section of an appellate brief, comprised of point headings and the main text or body, and containing the legal and factual positions of the party preparing it. The conclusion identifies the relief sought. A signature block and certificate of service are also included, as well as an appendix containing source materials from the record.

12–4

An appellant's brief is filed first, and sets the tone and defines the issues. The appellee's brief is filed in response to the appellant's brief, and both attacks the appellant's arguments and makes its own arguments. The reply brief is filed by the appellant in response to the appellee's brief. An *amicus curiae* brief is filed by a nonparty presenting public policy arguments.

12–5

Because of the nature of appellate briefing schedules, you have ample time to prepare an appellate brief. However, this means that judges expect a polished product, so make sure that you leave yourself adequate time to do your best work.

REVIEW

Key Terms

Before proceeding, review the key terms listed below to be sure you understand each one. If necessary, read over the corresponding section of the chapter. When you are ready to test your understanding, answer the Review Questions.

appellate rules
appellate brief
record
pleadings
physical evidence
transcript
court reporter

standard of review
errors of fact
abuse of discretion
errors of law
harmless error
title page
amicus curiae
certificate of interested parties
recusal
table of contents
table of authorities
jurisdictional statement
statement of the case
questions presented
statement of facts
indexing method
argument
point headings
body
equitable argument
public policy argument
string citation
conclusion
signature block
certificate of service
appendix
appellant's brief
appellee's brief
reply brief
amicus brief

Questions for Review and Discussion

1. Why is it important to follow the applicable appellate rules?
2. What is the function of the appellate brief?
3. What are the components of the record on appeal?
4. Explain the difference between errors of fact and errors of law.
5. What is a jurisdictional statement?
6. What is the "road map" function of the table of contents?
7. What are two key points to remember when drafting the statement of facts?
8. What are point headings?
9. What is a public policy argument?
10. Describe the different characteristics of the appellant's brief, the appellee's brief, the reply brief, and the *amicus curiae* brief.

Activities

1. Check the federal, state, and local appellate court rules for your jurisdiction and answer the following questions:
   a) When must an appeal be filed?
   b) When must the record be filed? The transcript?
   c) How much time does the appellant have to prepare and file the appellant's brief? The appellee?
   d) List the page length, the paper size, color of cover page, and binding requirements.
2. Compare your state rules of appellate procedure and the Federal Rules of Appellate Procedure, and list the differences in the rules.

CHAPTER 13   Drafting Operative Documents

OUTLINE

COMMENTARY

Your client, Mr. Hardrive, has spent months in his basement developing a computer program that will forecast stock market trends. His program must really work, because a major software manufacturer has expressed an interest in buying and marketing the program.

Mr. Hardrive recently contacted your supervising attorney. He needs help in negotiating a contract with the software company. After a lengthy conference with Mr. Hardrive, your supervising attorney provides you with a list of preliminary terms that Hardrive would like to see in the ultimate contract, copies of two contract forms from a form book, and a letter and proposed contract that Hardrive received from the software manufacturer. She asks you to draft a contract proposal that reflects Hardrive's position, rather than the manufacturer's.

Preparing contracts and other operative documents is a task for which a paralegal must be able to lend his training and assistance.

OBJECTIVES

Legal writing is not limited to correspondence, research memoranda, and litigation documents. After completing this chapter, you will be able to:

1. Explain what is meant by operative documents.
2. Identify the importance of determining client intent.
3. Explain how an operative document becomes a fifth source of law.
4. Explain the usefulness of a form.
5. Identify a possible pitfall when using a model.

6. Explain what a contract is.
7. List several important considerations in a lease.
8. Explain the importance of an accurate property description.
9. Identify who a testator is.
10. Explain the importance of a residuary clause in a will.

13–1 Operative Documents in General

In Chapter 3 we identified a category of documents called **operative documents**. We defined operative documents as those documents which, as a result of their language and content, serve to define property rights and performance obligations. They are drafted to express the intent of the parties who execute them—be they multiple parties with competing interests, as with a contract; or a single party with individual interests, as with a will.

In this section we discuss some characteristics and considerations that apply across the spectrum of operative documents. In the succeeding sections we address specific considerations for contracts, leases and deeds, and wills, then conclude with a few practical considerations.

Client Intent and Approval

The first step in drafting any operative document is to determine the intent of the client. The purpose for, and importance of, determining client intent is quite simple—it is the *client's* rights that will be affected by the operative document. Determining the client's intent is often not as easy as it might sound, however. The client may not be quite sure about what she wants, or the controlling law may prevent the client from obtaining the precise result desired in the manner envisioned.

Two possible situations illustrate the dilemma. First, consider the client who comes to you with a fully negotiated agreement, a transaction complete except for documentation. This client simply wants you to commit to paper, in proper and binding legal form, details already worked out. Be wary in this situation—the client may not fully understand the implications of his agreement; it is for you and your supervising attorney to unravel the mysteries of the substantive law as it applies to the proposed transaction, and determine whether the language of proposed operative documents best reflects the intent and interests of your client.

Second, consider the client who comes to your firm with a wholly different problem—she is seeking representation in negotiating a contract. This client has certain goals in mind, but understands that, in the ebb and flow of negotiation, compromise and flexibility may be necessary. Once again, the substantive law must be sorted and explained; this time legal consideration may vary as the negotiation proceeds into new areas, and the client must be made aware of shifting options and possibilities. Only after receiving full explanation of all alternatives can the client determine and transmit her true intent.

In explaining the meaning of a draft operative document, an attorney or paralegal should explain the need to balance technical legal requirements with practical client needs. The possibility of changed future circumstances, and the effect such changes may impose on the usefulness of a given draft, should be explored as well. Potential risks should be explored and explained, both as they exist on the face of the draft and as they might exist under these changed circumstances.

After determining the client's purpose, informing him of options, and explaining the meaning of a proposed draft, the attorney and paralegal must obtain the client's approval for the finished product. It is often wise to explain the draft in some permanent written form, such as an extended cover letter with an enclosed copy of the draft, both to assist the client in understanding the draft and to protect the law firm if the client later claims to have been misinformed.

The Importance of Clarity

An operative document, as we have noted, creates rights and obligations. It is, in some sense, a law unto itself—for although a court, in considering whether to enforce an operative document, will follow general rules in construing its content, if the format is acceptable and the content within the bounds of the law, then the court will also follow the specific guidelines established by the parties.

For this reason, it is extremely important that an operative document reflect the intent of the parties. Clarity in drafting is essential; the words used must accomplish the purpose sought.

The need for clarity doesn't mean that there isn't sometimes a place for ambiguous language, however odd it may seem. There are situations where the parties to a contract, for example, struggle to reach agreement on certain issues but simply can't. In the manner of the maxim "agreeing to disagree," the parties may intentionally leave the contract ambiguous as to one or more terms, hoping the need to resolve the ambiguity never arises but, in any event, leaving such resolution for another day. They have sacrificed clarity for the sake of commerce—they have made a deal that would otherwise have been impossible. If you are faced with such a situation, there are two factors to keep in mind: first, be sure to explain carefully the implication of the ambiguity to the client; second, be sure that the ambiguous expression accurately reflects the intent of the parties (in other words, state the ambiguity *clearly*!). An example of an intentionally ambiguous clause is shown in Figure 13–1.

Boilerplate and Form Books

We spoke briefly about **boilerplate** and **forms** in Chapter 3. Many operative documents have common language that must always be used to achieve a desired intent. Hence forms, boilerplate and **form books** (which we touched on briefly, in the context of pleadings, in Chapter 8) can be very helpful in the

Figure 13–1 Example of an Intentionally Ambiguous Clause in a Contract

"The widgets shall be guaranteed against failure for a commercially reasonable period of time, under all the circumstances present herein."

Explanation: The parties to this contract were unable to reach agreement as to the period during which the widgets (which were being sold under the terms of the contract) were to be guaranteed. The seller did not anticipate that his widgets would fail, but was hesitant to commit a specific period to writing; the buyer insisted on a guarantee against failure. The parties compromised on the above clause, which left open and ambiguous the issue of what was a "commercially reasonable period of time."

preparation of operative documents. But there are also pitfalls that need to be avoided.

Forms, as you recall, are printed documents incorporating standardized language and leaving blank spaces for specific information. Boilerplate is a term applied to the standard language in operative documents; to some extent, a form can be thought of as entirely boilerplate, with specific information to be filled in when available. Form books are collections of forms, often from many jurisdictions or covering many areas of the law. Form books can be multivolume collections with an enormous variety of sample provisions.

The usefulness of forms, form books, and boilerplate is apparent. By providing standardized language that reflects the controlling law, they represent a valuable means of shortcutting what could be time-consuming and repetitive research. For example, a simple lease of residential property will likely require virtually the identical boilerplate (and general format) as prior residential leases.

The problem with forms and boilerplate, however, lies in a phrase lurking in the previous paragraph—"reflecting the controlling law." Forms and boilerplate are only valuable as long as they do reflect the controlling law. If the controlling law changes, and the drafter uses an outdated form, the result could be disastrous.

The bottom line: never rely on a form over knowledge of the substantive area addressed. What does this imply in practical terms? Basically, two things: first, understand *why* the form or boilerplate uses the language it does (in other words, research the statutes, regulations, and case law that dictate the requirements in the subject area at issue). Second, keep up with developments in the subject area to assure yourself that the form or boilerplate remains reflective of the controlling law. An example of a problem that might occur when using a form is shown in Figure 13–2.

Figure 13–2 Example of Potential Problem When the Drafter Relies on a Model

> **Circumstance:** Formerly the mechanic's lien statute required that a mechanic's lien had to be filed within 90 days after a job for which services had been performed or materials supplied was completed. If not filed within 90 days, the claim was lost forever. The legislature recently amended the time limit to 60 days.
>
> **Clause from preexisting form:** "The above-referenced party who is filing this mechanic's lien hereby affirms that the services and/or materials for which payment has not been made were performed and/or supplied for a job that was completed within the 90 days immediately preceding the date of filing of this mechanic's lien."
>
> **Explanation:** If the drafter relies on the form she may be led to believe that she can wait up to 90 days from the date the work was completed to file the mechanic's lien. Research would have revealed the amendment to a 60-day time limit; the form should have been modified and the lien filed within 60 days.

A special kind of form is a **model**, which we also touched on briefly in Chapter 8. A model is a copy of a completed document taken from one of your firm's files, and which was formerly used to accomplish the same purpose you wish to accomplish with the document you are drafting. By using the model as a guide, you can copy the boilerplate and insert your own specific information where needed. Three factors need to be considered when using a model: first, is it attempting to accomplish the same objective you are seeking to accomplish now? A slight difference in objective can lead to significant differences in content. This is a factor to consider with regard to forms as well; see Figure 13–3.

Figure 13–3 Example of Difference in Objective Requiring Different Model

Drafter's intent: The drafter wants to initiate a lawsuit by filing a complaint that includes a request for attachment.

Basic law: A plaintiff who shows "probable cause" of success is entitled to file an attachment on real estate owned by the defendant. The attachment can be made either at the beginning of the suit or after suit is commenced. The petition that demonstrates probable cause must include a copy of the complaint and an affidavit attesting to its truth.

Problem: The drafter used as his model a set of papers that were used to obtain an attachment *after* suit had earlier been initiated. The model contained a copy of the complaint, as the law required, but did not contain a summons to court, since the lawsuit had already started. The drafter's papers, based on this model, failed to contain a summons and, when served on the defendant, were defective; hence the suit was not commenced and no attachment was granted.

If the drafter had recognized that his objective, namely commencing suit and obtaining an attachment, was different from the objective of the model (namely, obtaining an attachment *after* suit was started), he would either have used another model, or modified his draft to account for the difference in objective.

Second, did it succeed in accomplishing that objective? Third, has the law changed since the model was used?

Substantive Law

In the following sections on contracts, leases and deeds, and wills, we touch upon some aspects of substantive law in these areas. You should be aware, however, that these subjects, and others that may be the subject of operative documents, are far more complex than represented herein. In drafting operative documents (or for that matter, legal documents of any kind) legal writing skills are never sufficient to overcome lack of understanding of the substantive law.

13–2 Contracts

What is a contract? The question is not easy to answer, but we will try. A **contract** is an enforceable agreement. There you have it—a nice, tidy definition, the implications and complexities of which have filled volumes and require an entire course, and more, in law school.

The law of contracts is filled with words like "consideration" (which we addressed briefly in our discussion of settlement agreements in Chapter 11), "offer and acceptance," "third-party beneficiary," "performance," "breach," and so on. The meaning of most of these terms is readily apparent, at least in a general sense; their specific and detailed quirks in the context of contract law are beyond the scope of this book. But in your role as a paralegal it is almost certain that you will have, from time to time, either the opportunity to draft a contract, or the need to interpret a contract already drafted. In either event, the following comments should be useful.

The meaning of a contract must be clear. To say this is, perhaps, repetitious of comments already made, but in the repetition you may gain a sense of its importance. Since a contract defines the rights and obligations of the parties, its intent should be unambiguous (or ambiguous only as expressly intended by the parties). Furthermore, it must be clear not only to the parties to the agreement, but also to the court that may someday search its provisions to determine that intent.

Beware of using models for drafting contracts. Provisions and laws vary from state to state; circumstances vary from matter to matter. You must be very careful to perform adequate research to assure that a model or form is adequate.

Be sure your document is internally consistent. Particularly when ongoing negotiation changes provisions from draft to draft, it is critical that all provisions affected by a change are altered to reflect the new basis for agreement. Dates, terms of payment, character of performance, and other key terms must be checked and rechecked for consistency.

Terms should be defined. Even if you believe a definition to be widely accepted, it is better to be safe than sorry. Redundancy is less of an evil in contract drafting than in other forms of legal writing; your concern is not that the reader might get bored, but only that the contract represent without doubt the intentions of your client. If you believe it is necessary to state the same basic proposition twice to make the point clear, by all means do so, but make sure that the redundant statement doesn't lead to confusion (as when the person interpreting the contract presumes that every word has an independent meaning, and searches for a new meaning from a phrase you intended as mere restatement).

Another point to ponder is the value of submitting your draft for review by others. It can be very useful to have another person, either another paralegal or another attorney, read your draft at various stages of preparation. Their differing interpretations can assist you in determining where ambiguities lie.

13–3 Leases and Deeds

A **lease**, which relates to the rental of property, is really just a special kind of contract. A **deed** is also, in a sense, a contract—it documents the exchange of land for money (or some other form of consideration). Let's turn to an analysis of these two areas.

Leases

Leases involve two parties: the owner of property, and a party desiring to use that property in some way. By entering into a lease, the parties are able to pursue mutually beneficial interests. The owner receives a payment while retaining ownership of the property, and the other party is able to use the property. The owner is typically referred to as a **landlord** or **lessor**; the user of the property is typically referred to as a **tenant** or **lessee**. Leases can involve material items, such as a car, or **real property**, which is defined to mean *land*.

There are several considerations that are important to the drafter of a lease of real property. In general, the following items should be addressed:

- the agreed-upon rent;
- the manner in which rent payments will be made (for example, mailed or hand-delivered to the landlord's residence);
- the term of the lease (i.e., how long it is for);
- a description of the property (we discuss the legal description of a parcel of real estate further in the next subsection on deeds);
- who is responsible for repairs, maintenance, and damage to the premises;
- whether either party may assign its rights under the lease, and whether the tenant may sublet;

- the right of the landlord to inspect or enter the premises; and
- the rights of the parties should the other party default on the agreement.

Deeds

A deed is a document by which an interest in land is passed. There are several different kinds of deeds: a **quitclaim deed**, which makes no warranty as to title but only passes such interest as the seller is ultimately shown to have (in other words, the buyer is accepting the risk of a defective title); a **general warranty deed**, in which the seller pledges that the title is good; or a **special warranty deed**, in which a seller warrants the title against defects arising during her period of ownership, but not those that may exist from an earlier time.

Figure 13–4 Sample of General Warranty Deed

General Warranty Deed

KNOW ALL MEN BY THESE PRESENTS, that John Q. Public, of the Town of Anytown, State of North Anywhere, in consideration of eighty-five thousand dollars ($85,000.00) to me paid by Henry Doe, the receipt of which is hereby acknowledged, do hereby give, grant, convey, sell, and transfer unto the said Henry Doe a certain parcel of land situated at 123 Main Street in Anytown and more particularly described as follows:

> Beginning at a brass plate known as "Plate 171" at the corner of Main Street and Jones Street, proceeding north exactly 101.2 feet; east along land now or formerly owned by Elmer Johnson, 96.3 feet; south along land now or formerly owned by Agnes Miller, 101.2 feet; and west along Main Street 96.3 feet back to the same brass plate; and being the same premises and parcel conveyed in a deed from Eleanor Public to John Q. Public dated April 1, 1960 and recorded at page 65 of volume 1501 of the land records of the Town of Anytown.

To have and to hold the said premises, with all the privileges and appurtenances thereto, by the said Henry Doe, his heirs and assigns, from this day forward and forevermore.

And I hereby, for myself and my heirs, executors, and administrators, do hereby covenant and warrant with the said Henry Doe and his heirs and assigns that I am the lawfully seised owner of a fee simple interest in said premises, that they are free from any and all encumbrances except as set forth in the deed of Eleanor Public to John Q. Public hereinbefore referenced, that I have the full right and power to transfer title to said premises, and that I, my heirs, executors, and administrators shall warrant and defend the said Henry Doe, his heirs and assigns against the claims of any person at any time, forever.

In witness whereof we set our hands and signature this ____day of _____, 1992.

_____
Witness

_____
Witness
                                                          _____
                                                          John Q. Public

Sworn and acknowledged before me, the undersigned_____, Notary Public in and for the town of Anytown, North Anywhere, on this _____ day of _____1992.

_____
Notary Public

An example of a general warranty deed, the most common form seen, is shown in Figure 13–4. Note the property description (which is contained in the indented section). It is very important to make sure that this property description accurately reflects the description on an earlier deed. In other words, in Figure 13–4, the description should be identical to the description that appeared on the earlier deed referenced therein (identified as being "from Eleanor Public to John Q. Public dated April 1, 1960 . . . "). Accuracy as to the property description is important because if the description is inaccurate, there may be confusion over precisely what parcel of property was, in fact, transferred by the deed.

The language appearing in Figure 13–4 is fairly standard. However, when preparing a deed for your jurisdiction, you must make sure that the format used conforms to the applicable requirements. This will require research, as well as consultation with your supervising attorney.

13–4   Wills

When a person dies, he may leave behind property; a system generally referred to as the **probate system** has developed to regulate the distribution of this property. If the deceased person, called a **decedent**, left no instructions for the distribution, she is said to have died **intestate**, and the property passes according to the intestate laws. In addition to distribution under the intestate laws, the probate system offers another means of distribution by which an individual can avoid the automatic distribution of the intestate laws—by specifically identifying, in a formal document, the parties to whom distribution should be made at death. The formal document is called, of course, a **will**. The person who makes the will is called the **testator**.

A will is yet another type of operative document. The law of wills is significantly intertwined with substantive tax law, trust law, and the law of future interest (which regulate, in general, how long after the decedent's death his testamentary wishes can continue to encumber his property). Legal writing considerations, however, play an important role as well.

The first step in drafting a will is to obtain as complete a background as possible on the client's property, family structure, potential beneficiaries, and **testamentary intent** (which means, simply, her intentions about disposition of her property after death). An example of a checklist for information about preparation of a will appears in Figure 13–5 on page 278. Once all information is obtained, a will can be prepared. It must be prepared according to the requirements of your jurisdiction; this can get tricky, particularly where an individual retires to another jurisdiction, or lives in a jurisdiction different from the one in which his will is being prepared. Be sure to do adequate research to ensure that your format is proper.

Forms and models are often useful in preparing wills, particularly simple wills. By using the format and boilerplate of previous wills that have succeeded in their purpose, and by researching for any subsequent changes in the law, you will be able to prepare a document that is both time-tested and in compliance with current law.

An extremely simple will appears in Figure 13–6. It contains a title and introductory clause; an appointment of executor and instructions; bequests and devises; a residuary clause; and signature, witness, and acknowledgment blocks. These provisions, or similar ones, are commonly seen, but you must

Figure 13–5   Sample Checklist of Information for Will Preparation

—— Name
—— Other names by which known
—— Address
—— Name of spouse
—— Name of children
—— Employer's name and address
—— Employer-provided insurance
—— Employer pension plan or profit-sharing plan
—— Medical insurance
—— Life insurance
—— Property insurance
—— Automobiles and boats owned
—— Other personal property
—— Real estate, with reference to specific deeds (and with original cost and present value)
—— Bank accounts (including name and address of bank, contact person, and account numbers)
—— Stocks; stock certificates with numbers; stock options held
—— Jewelry and art (original cost and present value)
—— Leases held
—— Mineral rights
—— Debts and liabilities, including mortgages

verify that the format you use is adequate to satisfy the requirements of your jurisdiction. The format shown in Figure 13–6 is simply to illustrate. With that cautionary note in mind, let's briefly consider each of these segments of a will.

Title and Introductory Clause

The title identifies the document as the "Last Will and Testament of John Q. Public." The introductory paragraph following the title (below the double bar in Figure 13–6) is important for the purpose of specifically identifying the testator. Enough information should be provided to make it clear who is making the will. If a father and son share the same name, for example, or if the name is a common one, such information as address, date of birth, or other facts needed to distinguish the testator from other individuals with the same or similar names should be included.

In addition, some effort should be made to indicate any other names by which the testator was known (particularly if he owns property in those names that he seeks to transfer through this will). For example, depending on the law of your jurisdiction, the name "John Q. Public" may be problematically different from "John Public." This becomes more an issue of substantive estate law than legal writing; the point for our purpose is simply to be sure to adequately identify the testator.

It is also important , again, to specifically identify this document as the Last Will and Testament of the testator, and to specifically revoke all wills and codicils previously made (a **codicil** is an amendment to a will).

Figure 13–6   Last Will and Testament

Last Will and Testament
of
John Q. Public

I, the undersigned John Q. Public, of 123 Main Street, Anytown, North Anywhere, U.S.A., being of sound mind, do hereby make and execute this document as my Last Will and Testament, revoking and superceding any and all wills and codicils previous executed.

Article I.   I hereby appoint the First National Bank of Anytown as my Executor, to pay all debts justly owed at my death, and to perform all the duties of an Executor as specified in the laws of the State of North Anywhere, U.S.A.

Article II.   At my death, I wish to be buried in the Town Cemetery of Anytown. It is my wish that funeral expenses not exceed the sum of $4000.00 (Four Thousand Dollars and no cents).

Article III.   To my son, John Q. Public, Jr., I leave the sum of $10,000.00 (Ten Thousand Dollars and no cents).

Article IV.   To my daughter, Mary Public Doe, I leave the sum of $10,000.00 (Ten Thousand Dollars and no cents).

Article V. If either or both my son or daughter predecease me, their shares under Articles III and IV shall pass to their children, *per stirpes.*

Article VI. To my wife, Mary Public, I give, devise, and bequeath all my interest in the real property located at 123 Main Street and identified in a certain deed from Eleanor Public to John Q. Public dated April 1, 1960.

Article VII.   All the rest, residue, and remainder of my estate, in whatsoever form and wheresoever situate, I leave to my wife, Mary Public. If the specific provisions of Articles III, IV, and V of this Last Will and Testament shall fail, then it is my wish and intent that the bequests identified in those Articles pass under this residuary clause to my wife, Mary Public.

The undersigned acknowledged this to be his Last Will and Testament by signing by his own hand in our presence on this _____ day of _____, 1992.

_____
Witness

_____
Witness

I hereby set my hand and signature to this my Last Will and Testament on the _____ day of _____, 1992.

_____
John Q. Public
Anytown, North Anywhere, U.S.A.

Sworn and acknowledged before
me, the undersigned _____,
Notary Public in and for the town
of Anytown, North Anywhere, on this
_____ day of _____, 1992.

_____
Notary Public

Appointment of Executor and Instructions

In Articles I and II of Figure 13–6, the testator has appointed a bank as his executor, has called for the payment of all debts justly owed, and has established a spending limit for his funeral. Sometimes these items all appear in one article, sometimes they are combined with the bequests, sometimes they all appear in different articles—again, it depends upon the jurisdiction. The requirement to "pay all justly owed debts" is probably superfluous, since it would be required anyway, but it is a holdover still frequently seen in wills. From a drafting standpoint, the key is to accurately reflect the testator's wishes in a manner consistent with the controlling law.

Bequests and Devises

A gift under a will is called a **bequest**; if the gift is real estate, it is called a **devise**. The important thing to remember when drafting sections that make bequests and devises is, once again, to accurately reflect the testator's wishes. Clarity and precision are essential; a slight error in drafting may invalidate or confuse the ultimate effect of the will. For example, does a bequest "to my children" made in 1985 apply to children born after the will was executed? You must understand the substantive law in order to reflect, in your draft, the client-testator's intent.

Property that is bequeathed should be accurately identified. Account numbers of bank accounts, serial numbers of stock certificates, and references to deeds all assist in clarifying the intent of the will.

The phrase *per stirpes* appears in Article V. This term indicates an intention that, should a person identified as a beneficiary die, then her descendants should divide the share that she would have received had she lived.

Residuary Clause

Most deeds contain a **residuary clause** by which that portion of the deceased's estate which is not specifically identified in the will is bequeathed. Often the party identified in the residuary clause is the principal beneficiary under the will—a few specific items are bequeathed to others, with the "rest, residue, and remainder" going to that party. Make sure the testator understands the impact of the residuary clause.

Witness, Signature, and Acknowledgment Blocks

Once again, the primary consideration as to signature format, witnesses, and acknowledgments is not a legal writing consideration, but rather a formal, substantive one. Be sure your will is witnessed and signed as required by the applicable jurisdiction; the format shown in Figure 13–6 is simply by way of example.

13–5 Practical Considerations

You've seen a message repeated over and over in this chapter—to reflect the client's intent. There is no more important advice to give with regard to the drafting of operative documents.

But the client's intent is not the only consideration. You must make sure the client understands what he is doing, and you must make sure that what you have done meets all the requirements of the controlling law.

Drafting operative documents is an art form different from the drafting of correspondence or litigation documents. If two competing parties are involved, as with a contract or a lease, the adversarial aspect has been concluded through negotiation. If a will, where there is only one party's intent to consider, there is no adversarial purpose at all. The sole purpose of drafting operative documents, then, is, after determining the intent of the parties, to *accurately reflect* that intent in the language of the operative document. To the extent that you are able to do this, you will succeed as a draftsperson.

SUMMARY

13–1

Operative documents define property rights and performance obligations in and of themselves, as a result of their content and language. It is important to determine the client's intent for an operative document, and obtain his approval for the finished product. Clarity is critical. Forms and models may be of assistance in drafting operative documents. Writing technique cannot substitute for knowledge of the substantive area of law to which an operative document relates.

13–2

A contract is an enforceable agreement. A contract's meaning must be clear from the language used. Since circumstances vary from matter to matter, be wary of using models for contracts. Keep the contract internally consistent; be particularly careful where ongoing negotiation leads to frequent revised drafts. Define terms clearly. Be redundant if necessary, and have others review your draft for clarity.

13–3

By entering into a lease, one party (the owner) allows another to use her property. The owner of the property is referred to as the lessor or landlord; the person using the property is referred to as the lessee or tenant. Among the items

addressed by a lease of real property are the rent, the term of the lease, and the rights of the parties upon a default. A deed transfers ownership of real property. There are three basic types of deed: a quitclaim deed; a general warranty deed; and a special warranty deed. The property description is an important element of a deed. It must be accurate in order to avoid confusion over the parcel of property transferred.

13–4

The probate system governs the disposition of a person's property after death. If an individual dies without a will, he is said to have died intestate. A will is a formal document by which an individual can avoid the automatic distribution of the intestate laws. It often has an introductory clause that precisely identifies the testator, who is the person making the will. The testator can appoint an executor in his will, leave instructions as to his funeral, and make bequests and devises. Property not specifically mentioned in the will often passes through a residuary clause.

13–5

If you can accurately reflect the interest of the parties when you draft operative documents, you will be a successful drafter.

REVIEW

Key Terms

Before proceeding, review the key terms listed below to be sure you understand each one. If necessary, read over the corresponding section of the chapter. When you are ready to test your understanding, answer the Review Questions.

operative documents
boilerplate
forms
form books

model
contract
lease
deed
landlord
lessor
tenant
lessee
real property
quitclaim deed
general warranty deed
special warranty deed

probate system
decedent
intestate
will
testator
testamentary intent
codicil
bequest
devise
residuary clause

Questions for Review and Discussion

1. What is meant by operative documents?
2. What is the importance of determining client intent when drafting an operative document?
3. How can a form be used to assist in drafting an operative document?
4. Identify one possible pitfall of relying too heavily on a model.
5. What is a contract?
6. What are some important items that should be addressed by the text of a lease?
7. Why is an accurate property description important in a deed?
8. To whom does the term *testator* refer?
9. What is the importance of the residuary clause in a will?

Activities

1. Find the case *Frigaliment Importing Co. v. B.N.S. International Sales Corp.*, 190 F. Supp. 116 (S.D.N.Y., 1960), and read Judge Henry Friendly's fine decision, which indicates the confusion that can result from contract language.
2. Go to your local land records and try to find a quitclaim deed; a general warranty deed; and a special warranty deed (you may have trouble finding the latter).
3. Review the probate statutes that apply to your jurisdiction.

INDEX

Lessee, 275
Lessor, 275
Letterhead, 137
Letters, 68–69
   advisory, 134–135
   authorization, 156
   components of, 136–140
   confirmation, 135
   cover, 136
   demand, 140–149
   informative, 134
   in medical malpractice case, 148–149
   opinion, 150–153
   requests for information, 155
   retainer, 156
   transmittal, 154
LEXIS, 36–37
Looseleaf services, 35, 36
   format and publishers of, 21–23
   Supreme Court decisions, 18, 19

Majority opinion, 51
Mandatory authority, 3–4
Mann, Thomas, 112
Marbury v. Madison, 5
Material facts, 54
Medical examination, request for, 196
Memorandum
   internal memorandum of law, 69, 119–130
   postinterview, 118
Memorandum of law to the trial court. *See*
   Trial memorandum
Metaphors, 101, 103–104
Microfilm and microfiche, 37
Models, 168, 185, 273–274
Modifiers, 85
Motion for a New Trial, 234–236
Motion for Directed Verdict, 232, 233
Motion for Judgment Notwithstanding the
   Verdict, 236
Motion for More Definite Statement, 161,
   175
Motion for Protective Order, 200–201
Motion for Sanctions, 200–201
Motion to Compel Discovery, 200, 201
Motion to Dismiss, 161, 174–175
Motions, 70
   discovery, 199–201
   dismissal, 227–228
   disposition of, 51
   as pleadings, 161
   posttrial, 234
   summary judgment, 229–230, 231
Municipal administrative regulations, 32
Municipal ordinances, 29

National Reporter System
   abbreviations, 7, 8
   advance sheets, 8
   digests
      defendant/plaintiff table, 16

      descriptive word index, 13–14
      importance to research, 8–9
      pocket parts, 16–17
      table of cases, 16
      words and phrases, 14–15
   federal court decisions, 19–20
   headnotes, 8–9
   key number system, 8–16
   states covered, 7–8
New York Supplement, 8
Northeastern Reporter, 7
Northwestern Reporter, 7
Notice pleading, 161–162
Nutshell series, 34

Object ambiguity, 102–103
Objective documents, 65
Official reporters, 6–7
Old English terms, 62
Operative documents
   clarity in, 272
   contracts, 69, 274–275
   deeds, 69, 276–277
   defined, 69, 271
   form books for, 272–273
   leases, 69, 275–276
   wills, 69, 277–280
Opinion letter, 150–153
Oral deposition, 197
Order of dismissal, 227–228
Outlines, 67–68, 112

Pacific Reporter, 7
Paragraphs
   allegations in, 166
   body of, 89–90
   drafting, 107
   introductory
      in complaint, 164
      in interrogatories, 186–187
      in opinion letter, 150
      in request for admissions, 193–197
      in settlement agreement, 222, 223
      of wills, 278–279
   structured enumeration of, 109
   topic sentence in, 88–89, 90, 107
   transitional language, 90–91, 107
Parallel citations, 6, 45
Parallel construction, 91, 100
Parentheses, 82
Parenthetical phrases, commas in, 76–77
Parties to the case, 52–53
Passive voice, 108–109
Per curiam decision, 51
Periodic sentences, 107–108
Periodicals, 35
Permissive counterclaim, 172
Persuasive authority, 4
Phrases
   parenthetical, 76–77
   restrictive, 77